GRAND
STRATEGY

GRAND STRATEGY

Principles and Practices

John M. Collins

Naval Institute Press
Annapolis, Maryland

Library of Congress Catalogue Card No. 73–76606
ISBN 0–87021–683–X

Printed in the United States of America

To
SWIFT
my ever-loving wife,

whose innate understanding of strategy
has enabled her to outmaneuver me at
every turn for almost twenty-three years

Contents

FIGURES

TABLES

MAPS

Preface

A dependable defense posture at an acceptable cost is the cornerstone of every independent state that cherishes freedom of action. No national program, foreign or domestic, can flourish for long in a competitive global environment unless it has a credible shield.

Successful national defense measures, in turn, hinge on sound strategies. Bloated defense budgets and oppressively large armed forces can be borne needlessly unless they relate to a master plan that closely correlates political objects with military aims in manners that best serve national interests.

As chance would have it, U.S. decision-makers, their advisors, critics, and observers search library shelves in vain for a consolidated guide to strategy. Consequently, they must shuffle through countless publications, many of which yield minimum rewards in return for maximum time expended.

The primary purposes of this treatise therefore are fourfold:

1. To stimulate broad interest in strategy.

2. To produce a concise compendium of strategic principles, considerations, and techniques for use by aspiring strategists.

3. To outline ways of generating and sustaining strategic thought.

4. To give concerned citizens in all walks of life a firm grasp of strategic interactions, thereby affording them a better understanding of defense issues, and the nation a better-informed electorate.

A brief survey of strategic thought through the ages substitutes for an introduction. Part I correlates the whole field of grand strategy with national security interests, objectives, policies, and elements of national power, taking cognizance of the threat. Concurrently, it reviews fundamental concepts and principles. Part II concentrates on the contemporary strategic environment, which generates a spectrum of strategic problems. Part III outlines past and present U.S. responses. Part IV concerns special considerations and constraints, other than political interactions, which are interwoven throughout the whole book. Part V addresses the characteristics of successful strategic innovators, and recommends ways to detect, mobilize, motivate, and direct talented individuals, both in and out of uniform. Part VI completes the package by evaluating opposing strategies for the Vietnam War, using analytical tools provided in previous chapters.

Many paragraphs in this text could be expanded into chapters. Every chapter could be expanded into a book. Instead, facts, propositions, problems, issues, trends, and conflicting schools of thought have been capsulized, so that readers have immediate access to key ideas. An annotated list of suggested reading provides a degree of depth. Except for the Vietnam case study, there is no attempt by the author to champion any position. Each reader must weigh the pros and cons for himself and arrive at independent conclusions. He is then prepared to project tentative feelers into the strategic unknown.

Nobody knows better than I that this labor of love is a collective enterprise. The text is a patchwork of my own thoughts meshed with other people's opinion, published and unpublished. Quotations are generously interspersed to give readers the flavor of authoritative works and to emphasize controversy. Wherever practical, credits are reflected in the body of the book, but innumerable bits and pieces are too fragmentary.

In addition, I owe a debt of lasting gratitude to numerous associates, both military and civilian. Lieutenant General John E. Kelly, U.S. Army (Retired), a former commandant of the National War College, sowed the original seeds when he appointed me as his Director of Military Strategy Studies. In so doing, he opened up a whole new field of interest for me and reshaped my goals in life. Lieutenant General John B. McPherson, U.S. Air Force (Retired), the succeeding commandant, triggered my decision to write this book, through his ceaseless search for better ways and means of getting high-caliber recruits interested in strategy. Mr. George J. Stansfield, the National War College Librarian, together with Carol Hillier, Joe Simcoe, and many other cooperative members of his staff, greatly simplifed research by ferreting out source materials and compiling bibliographic references. Selected students and faculty at the National War College, plus a dozen or more officials, reviewed the original manuscript. In addition, anonymous individuals in the Department of State, the Department of Defense (International Security Affairs), the Joint Staff (J-3 and J-5), and service staffs (plans and operations) checked the first draft for accuracy and policy implications. They contributed numerous substantive and editorial comments that have been incorporated to good advantage. A platoon of secretaries, particularly Gloria Eakin, Clare Pierce, and Carol McLain, gratuitously saved me endless hours of one-finger, hunt-and-peck typing by converting my scrawl into an administratively acceptable missive. My long-suffering wife, God bless her, lived with this project morning, noon, and night for the better part of four years. She acted as a sounding board, provided essential encouragement, and helped type, proof successive drafts, and index the final product. I am forever grateful to the world's number one salesman, Rear Admiral Donald T. Poe, U.S. Navy, who found me a publisher. And last, but not least, I salute Mary Veronica Amoss, an unexcelled critic, who translated gibberish into English, expunged purple prose, challenged premises, and curbed the Collins ego because she was always right.

The result is an introduction to grand strategy. If it fires the imagination of just one creative thinker and inspires one really original idea, it will serve its purpose well.

John M. Collins

Alexandria, Virginia
31 March 1973

The Evolution of Strategic Thought

The objective value of a broad survey
of war is not limited to the research for
new and true doctrine. If a broad
survey is an essential foundation for
any theory of war, it is equally necessary for the ordinary . . . student who
seeks to develop his own outlook and
judgment. Otherwise, his knowledge of
war will be like an inverted pyramid
balanced precariously on a slender
apex.

B. H. LIDDELL HART

Strategy

Millions of men have fought wars since the dawn of time, but over the
millenia, creative thinkers in the realm of strategy have been mystifyingly few. Many
supposedly original contributors, both pedagogues and practitioners, merely mimicked
their predecessors, applying new twists to old ideas. Few innovators committed their
theories or precepts to paper until the nineteenth century. Most left that task to
historians, who wrote long after the fact, concealing a few scraps of strategic lore in
endless discourses on organization, weapons, campaigns, battles, and tactics.

PECULIARITIES OF THE EARLY ENVIRONMENT

Authorities generally agree that grand strategy as we know it today—the
application of national power to satisfy national security objectives under all conceivable circumstances—was an unusual commodity in olden times. There was good reason.
The strategic environment was the soul of simplicity in ancient China, Greece, Persia,
Carthage, and Rome.

National interests, objectives, and policies were nonexistent, since there were no nation states. The political matrix was uncomplicated. Only a few countries posed more than a local threat.

Trade was important, but most states were reasonably self-sufficient. Industry as we understand it today was unknown. There were no foreign investment or international monetary systems. Sophisticated foreign-aid programs were things of the future. Finances were based on ready money, not a national debt. Economic warfare was still elementary.

Military power, then as now, dominated most strategic equations, but armed forces were still primitive. Most of them were essentially land-oriented organizations. Even the Greek navy that turned the trick for Themistocles at Salamis was a coastal force, designed to support ground combat at home or abroad. So was the Roman fleet.

Manpower and mass predominated. Command and control posed no great problem. Forces were constantly concentrated—primitive communications and poor maps made loose formations unwise. Leaders were closely guarded, for, in many cases, if they fell, all would be lost.

Mass-destruction weapons had not been invented. Firepower depended mainly on muscle. Only siegecraft, such as catapults, were mechanical, and their effective range was severely limited. Most armies were similarly armed and equipped. Grave disparities analogous to those of today, when some countries have nuclear weapons and others do not, never perplexed strategists. Relationships between power and personnel strength thus were fairly direct.

Strategic and tactical mobility were virtually synonymous. Time-distance factors were enormous. This had a decisive bearing on logistics. The troops carried little baggage and were wont to live off the land. The inability to maneuver rapidly and at will frequently fostered "battle by mutual consent." Either party generally could refuse combat if conditions seemed unfavorable.

Legal-moral-ethical codes were elemental. There was no counterpart of the Hague or Geneva conventions. Arms control was nonexistent. Total war was a way of life. The concept of limited war, typified by voluntary restraints, had not been invented. Mao-style revolutions would not be seen for centuries (although subversion was widespread and there were some guerrilla actions). Cold war was not yet an art—Machiavelli set the stage in the sixteenth century.

Nevertheless, the pillars of present-day strategy were all present in the Ancient World. Collective security, flexible response, massive retaliation, and negotiation were variously in vogue. The world's first deterrent strategy emerged as the Pax Romana.

STRATEGIC INNOVATORS IDENTIFIED

The first great mind to shape strategic thought in that setting belonged to Sun Tzu, who produced the earliest known treatise on *The Art of War* sometime between 400 and 320 B.C. His thirteen little essays rank with the best of all time, including those of Clausewitz, who wrote twenty-two centuries later. No one today has a firmer feel for strategic interrelationships, considerations, and constraints. Most of his ideas make just as much sense in *our* environment as they did in his.

Another paragon among the ancients was the peerless Alexander (356–323 B.C.), the prototype of western grand strategists. His dream of a universal world empire permeated the minds of many successors, but few of them originated equally effective concepts. Alexander obviously recognized that war always operates on two planes: one physical, the other psychological. The former deals with material matters, the latter with ideas. His campaigns can be used to demonstrate perfectly every Principle of War, which he applied like a master, not just militarily, but in other ways as well.

Those two trailblazers had some spectacular successors. One was Hannibal (249–183 B.C.), whose Alps and elephants odyssey triggered the Second Punic War between Carthage and Rome. His prime opponent was Scipio Africanus (236–184 B.C.). Both Hannibal and Scipio were masters of the indirect approach, in the military sense. Both were consummate strategists. So was Julius Caesar (100–44 B.C.).

There was a hiatus in the development of strategic thought during the Dark Ages. The lamp of learning flickered feebly in other fields, but for all practical purposes it died in the field of strategy, and stayed dead for 1,000-plus years. The sole shining exceptions were found in Byzantium, where the likes of Belisarius, Narses, and Leo the Wise held sway. Errant excursions by barbarians, the early Moslem and Mongol conquests, and most warfare in the Middle Ages (particularly the Crusades) produced no consciously contrived strategic patterns.

Finally, in the sixteenth century, sages began to differentiate formally between strategy and tactics, interrelating military action with political policy on a grand scale. Two strategic giants stood out during the Renaissance and the era immediately thereafter: Niccolo Machiavelli (1469–1519), a politico-military theorist, whose discourses on the sources, applications, and limitations of power served particularly as inspiration for latter-day dictators; and Frederick the Great (1712–1786), who is perhaps best remembered for his "strategy of interior lines."

Paradoxically, Napoleon Bonaparte (1769–1821), acclaimed as one of history's great strategists, was not an intellectual pioneer in the purest sense. His forte was to develop existing theories and apply them with perfection, taking advantage of a huge manpower pool fired with enthusiasm by the French Revolution, but he left no written record of his concepts and philosophies, save 115 maxims, which are military clichés. In consequence, the world reviews his strategic contributions through the eyes of others. By far the most important interpreters are Antoine Henri Jomini (1779–1869) and Karl von Clausewitz (1780–1831).

As pointed out so aptly in Edward Mead Earle's *Makers of Modern Strategy,*

> In his attempt to explain Napoleon's career, General Jomini made his own contribution to the innovations of the age. He began, not indeed the study of war, but the characteristically modern, systematic study of the subject in the form it has retained ever since. With Clausewitz, whom he antedates a bit, Jomini may be said to have done for the study of war something akin to that which Adam Smith did for the study of economics. . . . The work Jomini did was in effect scientific pioneering—not the first daring penetrations of an unknown country, but the first really good map making.[1]

Clausewitz approached strategy from an entirely different angle. Where Jomini sought to devise a theoretical system for winning battles, Clausewitz was concerned with the basic nature of war. In his own words, he wished "to avoid everything common, everything that is self-evident, that has been said a hundred times, and is commonly accepted; for my ambition was to write a book that would not be forgotten in two or three years, and which anyone interested in the subject would be sure to read more than once."

He succeeded beyond his dreams, leaving his imprint on generations of strategists to follow. Even today, those who read his monumental treatise *Vom Kriege* (On War) for the first time are impressed with its breadth and diversity. This abstract work still is acclaimed as the most controversial and influential dissertation on strategy ever published. Much of it can be applied successfully to present problems, although some aspects have been discredited and adjustments must be made for the altered strategic context.

In contrast with earlier eras, strategic evolution since Clausewitz's death in 1831 has been dominated not so much by individuals as by events. Even before the Napoleonic period drew to a close, the Industrial Revolution already was unleashing forces which ultimately would permit total war on a global scale. New systems of propulsion encouraged fluid strategic mobility. Innovations in communications concurrently extended means of control. Great dispersion of forces, combined with effective, centralized direction, became a practical reality for the first time in history. Hand-in-glove came the Managerial Revolution, a practical necessity for any nation which aspired to organize, train, equip, and maneuver the military might needed to defend its homeland under the new conditions or to project its power abroad. A thoroughgoing revision of educational systems in particular had to predate the creation of professional officer corps. The attendant Social Revolution transformed the attitudes and aptitudes of people and the ways to manipulate mankind. Karl Marx sowed philosophical seeds of monstrous importance in the realm of modern strategy.

The U.S. Civil War and Franco-Prussian War were the first major conflicts to test embryonic concepts which emphasized the growing importance of politico-economic factors and the implications of telescoping time-distance relationships. Refinements in strategic theory and practice were recorded on the battlefield by Lee, Grant, Sherman, and Moltke, and by masters like du Picq and Delbrück on the printed page.

At this juncture, Alfred Thayer Mahan (1840–1914), perhaps America's first legitimate luminary in the field of theoretical strategy, took the center of the stage. As Louis Hacker indicates, Mahan left an indelible impression:

> Mahan's *The Influence of Sea Power Upon History, 1660–1793* at once circled the globe, for it was translated into all the important modern languages; it was read eagerly and studied closely by every great chancellory and admiralty; it shaped the imperial policies of Germany and Japan; it supported the position of Britain that its greatness lay in far-flung empire; and it once more turned America toward those seas where it had been a power up to 1860, but which it had abandoned to seek its destiny in the conquest of its own continent.[2]

No other book has exerted greater weight with regard to naval strategy.

World War I, whose beginnings coincided with Mahan's death, ushered in several great coalition conflicts in the twentieth century. It exploded in response to childish provocations, developed without realistic objectives on either side, soon deteriorated into a pointless, static war of attrition at great expense in life and national treasure, and defied satisfactory termination. Perhaps no other war in history demonstrated so clearly the classic lag of strategic thought in relation to technology. Military and political leaders alike underestimated the impact that increased firepower would have on accepted concepts. Georges Clemenceau bitterly declared that "generals cannot be entrusted with anything—not even war" (often translated as "war is much too important to be left to the generals"), and there seems to have been ample justification for his distrust.

The tragedy of 1914–1918 had a profound influence on strategic thought during the 20-year armistice that followed World War I. Reactionaries everywhere equated strategy with defense. In France, the Maginot Line mentality began to take shape. Britain and the United States drew into isolationist shells. However, as always, a few forward-thinkers surfaced.

Civilians made some very clever contributions. Churchill, Hitler, Lenin, and Stalin all dealt with strategy on a grand scale. Military oracles included Guilio Douhet, whose best-known treatise, *The Command of the Air,* published in 1921, laid the foundation for modern strategic bombing concepts. Charles de Gaulle, Heinz Guderian, and J. F. C. Fuller pioneered mechanized warfare. Billy Mitchell confirmed that land-based aircraft could challenge navies in their maritime habitat. B. H. Liddell Hart, a Britisher, initially was more widely read in Germany than he was at home, but he later influenced Allied strategy to a considerable degree.

The proving ground of these imaginative men was World War II, the first truly global combat, wherein concepts of total war melded diplomacy, economic and psychological warfare, subversion, geopolitics, science, and military action into a unified whole that recognized no sharp distinction between war and peace. Collective security came into its own as an ingredient of strategy.

Since 1945, the strategist's world has been wracked by cataclysmic change brought on by the emergence of mass-destruction weapons and exotic forms of propulsion, plus immensely improved means of command, control, and communications. The new matrix demands wholly new strategic solutions. Radically different approaches have been exhibited by the latest pride of strategists, whose ranks have included Mao, Giap, and Sokolovsky, Robert McNamara, and Douglas MacArthur, among others.

The names sprinkled throughout this brief summary, of course, are merely representative, but one fact does stand out. Until the advent of nuclear warfare, which has produced a few U.S. pathfinders, Alfred Thayer Mahan, in his ivory tower at the Naval War College, was regarded as the only American to attain international stature as a strategic theorist and source of original thought. The accuracy of that judgment is a matter for speculation, but the list of U.S. innovators certainly is not long.

LESSONS OF HISTORY

This nation is unsurpassed at devising tactics. It excels at military technology, having introduced the world to the rifle with interchangeable parts, the machine gun, the parachute, submarines, and aircraft. It adapted mass-production techniques to the needs of war. But the allegation persists that, over the years, U.S. military professionals and their civilian colleagues have failed to do their homework in the field of grand strategy. They are charged with "winning" battles but "losing" wars, and with "winning" wars but failing to attain national security objectives by disregarding the lessons of history and thus duplicating past mistakes.

Such accusations are neither new nor indigenous to the United States, and they are just as difficult to document today as they were in King Tut's time. Nothing is black or white. There are only shades of gray. Which ancient precepts are applicable in the Nuclear Age and which are obsolete is mainly a matter of judgment. Some dictums, such as Bülow's stereotyped recipes for combat, Foch's immutable belief in the offensive, and Painlevé's static doctrine, have been widely discredited. Others still seem sound. As a result, it is possible to "prove" that present U.S. national security objectives and supporting strategies are good, bad, or indifferent by judiciously selecting quotations from some bygone spokesman.

Responsible U.S. citizens rarely quarrel with the broad national security interests couched in our Constitution: to "insure domestic tranquillity [and] provide for the common defense," thereby securing "the blessings of liberty to ourselves and our posterity." Except for a lunatic fringe, nearly everyone agrees that we must preserve the United States as a free and independent nation, safeguarding its fundamental institutions and values, while concurrently retaining reasonable freedom of action to chart our destiny.

Specific objectives, policies, and supporting strategies cause most of the disputes. For years, for example, the United States has been a leading maritime power. We now are allowing our surface navy to be overtaken by that of the U.S.S.R., despite Themistocles' sage statement 2,500 years ago that "he who commands the sea has command of everything," and the subsequent admonition of John Paul Jones: "Without a respectable Navy—alas, America!" However, strong opponents of those beliefs support Billy Mitchell, that flamboyant proponent of air power, who prophesied the ascendance of aircraft over "sitting ducks" on the water. His strategic descendants firmly believe that missiles tipped with nuclear warheads make surface fleets obsolete.

Consider a second illustration. Sir Francis Drake would have vetoed a second-strike strategy for general nuclear war, declaring, "I hold it lawful and Christian policy to prevent a mischief betimes, as to revenge it too late." Colmar von der Goltz, excusing Boer tactics in forcing war with Britain, had even stronger views: "The statesman who knowing his instrument to be ready, and seeing war inevitable, hesitates to strike first is guilty of a crime against his country." On the other hand, Bismarck, speaking to Wilhelm I, remonstrated: "I would never advise Your Majesty to declare war forthwith, simply because it appeared that our opponent would begin hostilities in the near future. One can never anticipate the ways of divine providence securely enough for that." His words seem to suit U.S. ethics.

Serious students of grand strategy find it difficult to identify which of Clausewitz's teachings apply best to U.S. concepts for limited war. To be sure, he recognized that "war is a mere continuation of policy by other means," and thus must match costs carefully with gains, but he also cautioned,

> Woe to the Cabinet which, with a policy of half measures and a fettered military system, comes upon an adversary who . . . knows no other law than that of his intrinsic strength. Every deficiency in activity and effort then is a weight in the scales in favor

of the enemy. . . . [In consequence, he continued,] if bloody slaughter is a horrible spectacle, then it should only be a reason for treating war with more respect, but not for making the sword we bear blunter and blunter by degrees from feelings of humanity, until once again someone steps in with a sword that is sharp, and hews away the arms from our body.[3]

The applicability of those words to U.S. problems in Southeast Asia may well be argued for the next century.

In the final analysis, few lessons to be learned from the plethora of historical strategic advice are clean-cut. The mission is to understand what transpired before and to appreciate the context, so that experience can be applied to the future with perspicacity. As Santayana said, "Those who cannot remember the past are condemned to repeat it."

PART I

THE
FRAMEWORK
OF
GRAND STRATEGY

1   Ends Versus Means

"Cheshire puss," she began rather timidly, ..."
would you tell me, please, which way I ought to
go from here?"

"That depends a good deal on where you want
to get to," said the cat.

LEWIS CARROLL
Alice in Wonderland

The Cheshire Cat made its point perfectly. A clear sense of purpose must underlie all meaningful plans, programs, and actions. That is an elemental idea, but it is often unappreciated or ignored.

NATIONAL SECURITY INTERESTS

At the highest levels, national interests comprise the underpinnings for sound strategy. Interests are highly generalized abstractions that reflect each state's basic wants and needs. They sometimes are difficult to identify, since they rarely are clean-cut. Instead, they interlock and overlap. Nearly every interest, for example, bears on national security to one degree or another, but if you were to ask an employee at the Department of Health, Education, and Welfare if defense is his principal concern, the answer would be "no." Grand strategists need to sort out those interests that relate specifically to national security.

The only *vital* national security interest is survival — survival of the State, with an "acceptable" degree of independence, territorial integrity, traditional life styles, fundamental institutions, values, and honor intact. Nothing else matters if the country is exterminated as a sovereign entity. No other end is worth risking national extinction to attain. Further, there are grades of survival, conditioned by future prospects. At the upper end of the scale is Germany, whose national way of life, fundamental institutions, and values were destroyed during World War II, and whose territory was divided. The important thing, however, is that the nation survived, and West Germany today is the preeminent power in Free Europe. By way of contrast, some satellites behind the Iron Curtain survived as political, economic, and social zombies. Most

1

Americans, discounting those who would "rather be Red than dead," find that form of survival "unacceptable."

FIGURE 1
The Strategic Matrix

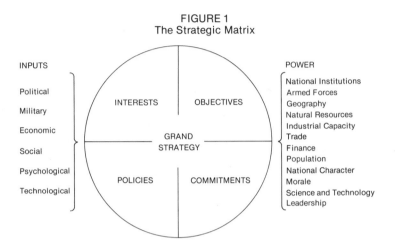

Tributary interests, positive and negative, regional and worldwide, supplement the most elemental drive. These are mainly specific. All are ranked in order of priority. Responsible men everywhere are willing to die for the most compelling, which are related to survival. John F. Kennedy put this country's life on the line during the Cuban Missile Crisis in the interest of a Soviet-free Caribbean. We were less decisive during the Korean War. The cause was not worth it. At the bottom of the priority list are attractive, but deferrable, interests that no rational leader would spill blood or spend billions to satisfy. Such interests might merit indirect pressures, but not a shooting war.

Which interest fits in which of the above categories is a controversial matter of judgment. Solutions are reasonably simple in totalitarian states, where parties in power can disregard public opinion to a considerable degree, but even there crises occur when the ruling cliques fail to reach a consensus. Agreement is more difficult to reach in open societies. Differences in opinion there are ultimately resolved by national leaders (in our own case, the President), whose decrees are conditioned by their own personalities and experience, the views of their advisors, and the temper of their countrymen.

National security interests rarely exist in a vacuum. People the world over are either for them or against them. Hardly anyone is really neutral. Every successful international security coalition is founded on mutual interests. Cooperation continues as long as those interests coincide; when cooperation ceases, the coalitions collapse. Nearly all of the world's foreign policy problems can be traced to conflicts of interest that produce philosophical collisions, and sometimes physical combat.

Interests are particularly destabilizing when they demand changes to the status quo. The Nazis' longing for *Lebensraum* threw Europe into a turmoil in the 1930s. Arab aspirations for a Hebrewless Holy Land helped create chaos in the Levant after Israel came into being. However, even innocuous interests, such as the U.S. penchant for world peace, can cause trouble. Our current desire for stability in the Middle East, which stems from that interest, puts us in direct competition with the Kremlin.

2

An old adage says, "there are no such things as permanent friends or permanent enemies — only permanent interests," but even that is untrue. National survival is the only abiding interest. In 1947, we helped frame a constitution that caused Japan to "forever renounce war as a sovereign right of the nation and the threat or use of force as means of settling international disputes. . . . Land, sea, and air forces, as well as other war potential, will never be maintained." Today, a good many critics in the United States are upset because Japan will not contribute what they perceive to be her fair share to the defense of East Asia. Similarly, some express concern over allegedly insufficient military participation in NATO by the Federal Republic of Germany. Our interests obviously have changed in the past thirty years. Unfortunately, all kinds of problems can arise before decision-makers consciously recognize that change has occurred.

NATIONAL SECURITY OBJECTIVES

However difficult it may be to articulate them, national security interests are the wellspring of valid objectives that spell out *what a country is trying to do*. These objectives, sometimes called goals, aims, or purposes, may be short-, mid-, or long-range, lasting from a few weeks or months to a decade or more. As Figure 1 illustrates, national security objectives, like interests, have political, military, economic, and other subdivisions.

Liddell Hart quite properly believed the term *objective* often is misleading when related to national security:

> The term "objective," although common usage, is not really a good one. It has a physical and geographical sense — and thus tends to confuse thought. It would be better to speak of "the object" when dealing with the purpose of policy, and of "the military aim" when dealing with the way that forces are directed in the service of policy.
>
> The object in war is a better state of peace — even if only from your own point of view. . . .
>
> History shows that gaining military victory is not in itself equivalent to gaining the object of policy. But . . . there has been a very natural tendency to lose sight of the basic national object, and identify it with the military aim. In consequence, whenever war has broken out, policy has too often been governed by the military aim — and this has been regarded as an end in itself, instead of as merely a means to the end.[1]

Those pertinent points were demonstrated conclusively during World War II, when the persistent U.S. preoccupation with military victory largely ignored future political implications. Shortsighted concessions by this country at Teheran, Yalta, and (to a lesser extent) Potsdam helped boost the Soviet Union to superpower status, helped settle Stalin in Eastern Europe, and ushered in the Cold War on the Kremlin's terms. Political objects and military aims diverged during other wars in other ways, to our detriment.

Technically, we have a built-in advantage in being able to ascertain the *enemy's* long-term goals, since political dreamers, demagogues, and dictators are prone to propagandize. Marx laid the ground work for communism in 1848 with his *Manifesto*.

3

Lenin followed up. Hitler outlined his objectives precisely when he produced *Mein Kampf* in 1925. Most of Mao's serious works were written in the 1930s. However, warning signs such as those are truly advantageous only if national decision-makers read them, take them seriously, and interpret them correctly.

By way of contrast, Free World goals are subject to many mutations. Democratic regimes rotate frequently, and the "new brooms" sweep clean. Equally pertinent, Free World politicians are perennially feeling the public pulse to see if they are winning personality contests. What they say and what they do often are at variance. The resultant vacillation may not be all bad. Unanticipated alterations in friendly objectives must complicate communist estimates considerably.

There is a direct correlation between solid objectives and what Clausewitz called the "strategic center of gravity."[2] That is the point of decision. National War College students recently applied that principle to Vietnam. The group generally agreed that the strategic center of gravity for South Vietnam always was the people. Not body counts on the battlefield, but the *minds of the people.* It took U.S. leaders a long time to figure that out. The primary pressure point for the United States was national will. The enemy found *that* out early, and continually turned the screws. No one determined the strategic center of gravity for North Vietnam. It may even have been in some other country. That is one reason why it was so hard for us to define decisive objectives. Contrast the overriding U.S. objective during the Civil War, which was to preserve the Union, with our amorphous goals in Vietnam during the formative stages of that fiasco, and you will see that the platforms for strategic planning were vastly different.

NATIONAL SECURITY POLICIES

National security policy is nothing more than a set of ground rules. By all standards, political policy is predominant.

Policy, like interests and objectives, has wheels within wheels. In the late 1940s and 1950s, when the communist policy was "expansion," we countered with "containment." Not rollback. Containment. There were tributary policies on both sides. We made up our minds to meet the Reds head-on everywhere, not on a selective basis. We chose to throw in our lot with allies, not to go it alone. And during that same period, we elected not to strike first, no matter what the provocation, when we could have eradicated the enemy. We were the only ones who had nuclear weapons.

Since then, the situation has changed. It is important to understand that policies, like objectives, can shift overnight, *without any alteration in interests.*, National prestige became an indelible U.S. interest in Vietnam in the mid–1960s. Presidents Johnson and Nixon *both* predicted that if this country failed to honor its commitments, it would lose credibility around the world. But, given that selfsame interest, those two men produced diametrically different policies — one predicated on massive U.S. military involvement, the other on Vietnamization.

NATIONAL SECURITY COMMITMENTS

Policy is very broad. Commitments, whether formal or informal, pledge the parties concerned to take specific actions at specific times and places. U.S. collective

4

security policy simply sets forth a philosophy that links us loosely with a community of other nations that have common interests and common needs. However, eight mutual defense pacts with forty-two partners, plus less specific agreements with more than thirty others, *obligate* the United States.[3]

Obviously, our defense commitments differ widely. We are heavily committed in NATO, but that is not so in SEATO. The United States has no obligation to shore up the Israelis, either economically or militarily, in event that country is invaded. We support their political independence and territorial integrity as a matter of policy, but that is *not* a commitment to take particular actions in particular circumstances.

THE POSITION OF NATIONAL POWER

National security interests, objectives, policies, and commitments constitute "ends," or guidance for achieving them. In broad terms, "means" are the elements of national power, including assets available to allies: political power over the minds and actions of men at home and abroad; geographic strengths and weaknesses; the economy, particularly natural resources, industrial capacity, and finances; the people, including their numbers, location, temperament, morale, and education; the scientific and technological base; the military establishment, active and reserve; and, as the integrating factor, leadership. If they are present in the proper proportions, these ingredients enable their possessors to exert influence at times and places of their choosing.

Paradoxically, *military* power may be the primary means of satisfying *economic* purposes. Japan poured on military pressure to prop up her economic imperialism during World War II. By the same token, psychological power can be used to gain military goals. Many countries have been conned into quitting when they still had a chance to win. When political, economic, or psychological power can satisfy objectives, military requirements usually can be reduced. If the United States could get the Kremlin even more preoccupied in Asia, our troop strength in Europe might be sliced significantly without any serious repercussions. However, the tradeoffs are not always obvious. When time is a critical factor, firepower may furnish the *only* answer.

MATING ENDS WITH MEANS

Discrepancies between ends, which we have identified as interests and objectives, and means — available resources — create risks, which rarely can be quantified. One consideration prevails: the probability of success versus the stakes. A sixty percent chance of making a killing might tempt a poker player to take the plunge, but not a nuclear strategist. The stakes are much too high.

Degrees of risk are mainly a matter of judgment. While the U.S.S.R. continues its buildup, the United States is cutting back. What is the risk involved? Even if all estimators had access to the same sources of information, they still would draw different conclusions, because they have different personalities, temperaments, inclinations, backgrounds, experiences, and intuitions.

Risks can result from miscalculation. Overrating the capabilities of friends, underrating the opposition, or placing great store in shaky assumptions are common errors. *Calculated* risks are incurred deliberately. Either way creates problems.

Général d'Armée André Beaufre, in his provocative *An Introduction to Strategy,* outlined five distinctive approaches to the business of mating ends and means. These are summarized below:

1. *Ends Limited, Means Abundant*　When resources are abundant, the mere threat of force may be sufficient to satisfy objectives, if vital enemy interests are not imperiled. This combination correlates with U.S. deterrent strategy for general nuclear war. None of our national objectives jeopardize Soviet or Chinese Communist survival; our goal is simply to inhibit aggression.

2. *Ends and Means Both Limited*　When available resources are inadequate to create a credible threat or the enemy deterrent is discouraging, political, economic, or psychological pressures may supplant force successfully, provided the goals are modest, or appear to be. This ploy is most suitable when military freedom of action is cramped. The Soviets wield these tools with considerable skill.

3. *Ends Critical, Means Limited*　When objectives are critical, but resources are restricted and freedom of action is abridged, piecemeal actions that combine direct and indirect pressures with controlled military force may be effective. This approach favors nations that are in a strong defensive position and are content to proceed slowly. It was used to perfection by Hitler before World War II.

4. *Ends of Variable Consequence, Means Minimal*　When freedom of action is great but the means are insufficient to secure a decision, protracted struggle at a low level of military intensity may suffice. This gambit demands strong motivation, great moral endurance, and highly developed national solidarity. It has been displayed to advantage in revolutionary wars, where the issues at stake were of far greater import to one side than to the other.

5. *Ends Critical, Means Decisive*　When objectives are vital and military resources are strong, complete victory on the battlefield is feasible. Destroying enemy armed forces may suffice, even if enemy interests are vital, although hostile territory sometimes must be occupied. Unfortunately, if victory is not rapid, costly stalemates may produce decisions "only after a prolonged period of mutual attrition out of all proportion to the issue at stake."[4]

An infinite number of other approaches supplement the five exemplary patterns above, each with unique advantages and disadvantages. Regardless of the choice, if probable risks exceed potential gains, decision-makers must accommodate. Seven alternatives are available:

They can eliminate waste, whatever the cause — institutional, organizational, procedural, cultural, or what have you.

They can compress objectives, as the United Nations did in Korea when Red China intervened.

They can adjust their strategy, as the Soviets did when we blocked their armed aggression in the 1960s.

They can augment available assets, as the United States did at Hiroshima and Nagasaki, when it unveiled the first atom bombs.

They can whittle the ends and increase the means, a compromise we tried with indifferent success in Indochina.

They can bluff, as Hitler did in 1936 when he marched into the Rhineland with his shadow army, flouting the Treaty of Versailles.

Or, they can decide that the goal is not worth it, swallow hard, and get out, as the French did in Algeria.

Colonel Charles F. Bunnell, U.S. Marine Corps, formerly of the National War College Strategic Research Group, addressed several considerations, which bear recapitulation:

Take care when you trim military fat. It is possible to sacrifice force structure, readiness, and modernization in various combinations, but for every gain, there is a loss in current combat capabilities or in future options.

Tinkering with strategies can be very tempting. After all, new strategies cost less than new weapons systems, and they are less likely to stir up political storms than changes in national objectives. This tack seems to work best after diplomatic or technological breakthroughs, but its effectiveness usually is temporary.

Compressing objectives can backfire if care is not taken. Remember what happened in 1950 after the United States left South Korea outside its defense perimeter. Interests rarely go away just because decision-makers adjust their goals.

Finally, overoptimizing military forces for any particular strategy is risky business. Nations can eliminate *all* elements that do not contribute directly to the chosen concept, as the United States nearly did during the days of Massive Retaliation, but that stifles flexibility. Tyrannosaurus Rex, the most menacing monster the world has ever seen, was a victim of overspecialization. His only survivors are in museums.[5]

STRATEGIC INTERRELATIONSHIPS

To tie these diverse ingredients together:

Interests and objectives establish strategic requirements.
Policies provide the rules for satisfying them.
Available assets provide the means.

In combination, those elements form the framework within which sensible strategies fit like the pieces in a jigsaw puzzle. Given proper consideration, they help strategists to match realistic ends with measured means, minimizing risks in the process.

However, strategy, unlike solitaire, is not a game that states can play by themselves, without outside interference. Enemy actions and reactions must always be acknowledged. Threat-assessment problems, and their impact on strategy formulation, therefore, are outlined in the following chapter.

2 Threat-Assessment Problems

To lack intelligence is to be in the ring
blindfolded.

GENERAL DAVID M. SHOUP
Former Commandant of the U.S. Marine Corps

National security interests, objectives, and policies are meaningful only when viewed in context with threats, both external and domestic. The nature of the opposition as often as not dictates what *should* be done, what *can* be done, and *how* to go about it.

THREAT IDENTIFICATION

The basic threat is military. It is the easiest to identify and, in many ways, the easiest to counter, since it is direct, overt, and places all parties on fairly familiar ground. However, indirect forms of connivance and coercion are equally effective and much more difficult to cope with. Deception dates back well before the Trojan Horse. The Old Testament is riddled with records of subversion reminiscent of fascist infiltration and communist conspiracies in the twentieth century. National interests and influence can be jeopardized just as unerringly by political, economic, and psychological warfare as by force of arms.

Merely identifying the immediate *bête noire* can bedevil the best intelligence services, as Stalin discovered in June 1941, when his erstwhile Nazi allies suddenly began to overrun western Russia. Spanish Republicans girded their loins to meet a military threat, when in fact the greatest danger was subversion, in the form of the famed "Fifth Column." Further, the roles of the players change. Twenty-five years ago, the United States and Germany were at each other's throats; today they are good friends. Moreover, it is a fortunate country that has only one foe, real or imagined. When the threat is hydraheaded, strategists must establish priorities, then concentrate on the greatest hazards.

8

CAPABILITIES, INTENTIONS, AND VULNERABILITIES

Three basic considerations dominate the threat-evaluation process:

1. Capabilities   What *can* the enemy do?
2. Intentions   What *will* the enemy do?
3. Vulnerabilities   What *are* the enemy's salient weaknesses?

Strategic capabilities, as opposed to intentions, constitute the *ability* of any given state to satisfy its purposes or to thwart the aims of others at particular times and places, in peace as well as war. They enable the nation to carry out desired courses of action without unduly damaging its socioeconomic structure or jeopardizing its vital interests. Capabilities are the sum total of national power — political, military, economic, social, scientific, technological, psychological, moral, and geographic — combined with the means of applying power effectively.

Capabilities are relatively stable and are rarely subject to rapid change. They can be quantified, compared, and analyzed objectively. Consequently, they afford a fairly solid platform for planning. One word of caution, however. Traumatic defeats, like the French disaster at Dien Bien Phu, political upheavals (including coups), and so on, can cause sudden shifts in capabilities by altering available leadership, morale, or other elements in the equation.

Intentions deal with a state's *determination* to execute certain designs. They are generally less palpable than capabilities, being subjective states of mind, easily concealed and sensible to mercurial shifts. Intentions are shaped by interests, objectives, policies, principles, and commitments, some of which never have been or will be articulated. As a result, they are very tricky to deal with. Military men in particular prefer to leave them alone.

Nevertheless, some feel for the enemy's probable courses of action is essential to the formulation of meaningful strategy. Sole reliance on estimates of enemy capabilities *or* intentions is very risky business. Smart strategists take *both* considerations into account, recognizing that the best indication of intentions often is not what people *say,* but what they *do.*

Vulnerability is the susceptibility of a nation or military force to any action by any means through which its war potential or combat effectiveness may be reduced or its will to fight diminished. From the strategist's standpoint, vulnerabilities must be specific, and preferably should be vital. Countries with concentrated strategic areas, for example, risk instant extermination by mass-destruction weapons. States such as Israel, with small populations, normally could not afford protracted conventional wars with populous opponents; attrition would quickly be deadly. Vulnerabilities arising from internal unrest invite subversion.

One thing is certain: the margin for error is great at every stage in the threat-evaluation process. Strategists never have access to all the right answers concerning enemy capabilities, intentions, and vulnerabilities, or even to answers that they *believe* are right. Some pieces to the puzzle invariably fit only approximately. Some are always missing. The mission is to do the best one can with the tools available, understanding their limitations.

THE INTELLIGENCE CYCLE

The point of departure for relevant estimates must be the situation, as it is perceived or rationally constructed. This is not nearly as simple as it seems, because assumptions concerning adversaries, times, places, means, and other variables often cloud the issue. Moreover, since enemy views of the situation may differ substantially from friendly appraisals, it is entirely possible for both sides to start off with wholly erroneous impressions.

Requirements

Gaps in available information, whether identified by decision-makers or deduced by the intelligence community, must be scrutinized to ascertain what line of inquiry would be most likely to fill them. That involves asking the right questions, an art that few have mastered. Sherman Kent, whose *Strategic Intelligence for American World Policy* is something of a classic in the field, emphasizes the importance of good guidance:

> Unless the intelligence organization knows why it is at work, what use its end product is to be designed to serve, and what sorts of actions are contemplated with what sorts of implements, the analysis and proper formulation of the substantive problem suffer in proportion.[1]

Collection

Problems in turn generate requirements for data, from basic background material to topical subject matter.

A huge compilation of raw information and finished intelligence normally is on file. In fact, its very volume can be a disadvantage. Maintaining current and responsive data banks of great diversity is increasingly difficult for the major powers, even with the aid of computers. Moreover, it is impossible to anticipate all contingencies.

Overt, covert, and clandestine collection agencies therefore must continually respond to current requests for additional coverage. Accumulating information about intentions is particularly bothersome. Even the glamorous cloak-and-dagger profession, personified by James Bond's 007, has serious limitations in that regard, as Sherman Kent pointed out, using Korea in 1950 as an illustration:

> Suppose the Soviets had had the run of our most sensitive files, would they have come across the document that told them . . . that we would fight? This clearly would have been a document of very highest importance. But they never would have found it. It did not exist. The decision to fight was Mr. Truman's, and he made it on the spot after the Soviet-supported attack was on. Thus, if knowledge of the other man's intentions is to be divined through the reading of his intimate papers and one's own policy is to be set on the basis of what one discovers, here is a case where policy was on the rocks almost by definition.[2]

Processing

Once acquired, information must be evaluated as to its pertinence, accuracy, and validity, as well as the fidelity of its source, which may range from completely reliable to untrustworthy or unknown. When a proven agency contributes input that correlates closely with data from other sources, planners normally can proceed more confidently than they would had they received uncorroborated fragments supplied by dubious contacts, but not necessarily so. Intelligence analysts constantly must be alert for "shell games." Even publications straight from the opposition's closely guarded, limited-distribution files are suspect, as the following suggests:

> There is no question that General [Alexander] Orlov's successors in the Soviet secret intelligence organization have directed the lifting of a great many secret documents. But when they had them in hand, what then? Did every document proclaim on its face: "I am *not* the offbeat thoughts and recommendations of a highly placed but erratic advisor; I am *not* a draft from high quarters intended solely as a basis for discussion; I am *not* one of those records of decision which will be rescinded orally next day, or pushed under the rug and forgotten, or nibbled to death by disapproving implementers. *I am the McCoy; I am authoritative and firm; I represent an approved intention and I am in effect.* "[3]

The most important question of all, of course, is: what does the raw information mean? Answers are derived from interpretation, a crucial step in the intelligence cycle, which combines analysis, postulation, and deductive reasoning.

Interpreting evaluated information amounts to sifting and sorting the pieces with regard to the over-all situation, friendly objectives, and knowledge of the enemy, including his doctrine and past practices. Brigadier General Washington Platt, U.S. Army (Retired), a student of strategic intelligence, likens this process to a basic principle of integral calculus, which asserts that "if you take enough nothings, their sum is something." He goes on to observe that apparently unrelated jumbles of facts, each meaningless by itself, can produce meaningful mosaics if juggled appropriately:

> A few words even when written in the simplest substitution cipher are impossible to decipher; but a whole page in such a simple cipher can be read very speedily. . . .

> The application to counterintelligence of the piecing together of facts is evident. Security restrictions are always unpopular and often onerous. In regard to any given restriction we often say: "How can this bit of information possibly help the enemy?" The answer is, "It can't, when confined to that one bit of information." But, as we have shown, this bit of almost completely harmless information, if put together with many other bits of almost completely harmless information can often help the enemy a great deal.[4]

Combining scraps to form logical patterns leads to the development of hypotheses, a task that demands great native intellect, a high order of training, imagination, and an open mind. This is an intensely speculative pursuit, even when the postulator is dealing with such prosaic problems as, "What are Soviet objectives in the Indian Ocean?" or "What would trigger Chinese Communist intervention in Indochina?" The process can be infinitely more frustrating if available information leads into the frightening unknown, where nothing in the analyst's schooling or experience seems to assist in reaching sensible conclusions. Hitler's secret weapons project at Peenemünde, involving V–1 and V–2 rockets, produced just such a situation in the early 1940s. British aerial-photo interpreters were puzzled for months by the peculiar launch pads that showed on their stereoscopes before the puzzle was finally solved. Replicate riddles will continue to crop up in the future.

Deductive reasoning applied to hypotheses is the final step in interpretation. Given professionalism (and a bit of luck), the full significance of statistics and events should emerge. If not, strategists who rely on the findings may be in deep trouble.

INTELLIGENCE ESTIMATES

From the mass of raw information converted to intelligence through evaluation and interpretation come short-, mid-, and long-range estimates that purport to predict probable enemy courses of action. Some threats menace national survival of the fatherland or of allies. Others merely infringe on low-priority interests.

Forecasting intentions — and that is the prime purpose of estimates — offers strategic intelligence specialists a greater chance for success than it does their combat intelligence counterparts, since there generally is more time to study the situation and reach conclusions concerning enemy capabilities, limitations, specific vulnerabilities, habit patterns, and needs. Nevertheless, estimating is a hazardous occupation. Prerequisites are a broad knowledge of natural and social sciences, derived mainly from education; knowledge of intelligence procedures; insight into the intellectual habits and idiosyncracies of enemy personalities in power; and the wisdom and mature judgment that derive from experience. Efforts at objectivity notwithstanding, every estimator is a captive, to one degree or another, of his background and biases.

Equally to the point, estimators, being only human, sometimes become emotionally involved. Some tend to champion their products long after prudence and common sense should have sent them back to the drawing board. For example, trying to sell a "greater-than-expected threat" when all evidence indicates that no such possibility is any longer valid can cause both the intelligence community and gullible consumers to lose credibility. To guard against such behavior, which may be hard to detect and even harder to document, it is common practice for several competing individuals or agencies to analyze the same basic data, despite the duplication of effort and extra expense. *Even so, strategists should recognize that the best of estimators are fallible, and should fashion solutions that will still work if the prognostications prove wrong.*

Regardless of the processes employed or the competence of the compilers, the whole agonizing endeavor can be completely inconsequential if it fails to deliver the goods to the right users in time to be of value. As a result, studies of the greatest importance sometimes must be produced under extreme pressure, sacrificing scholarship for speed. Fortunately, this sort of undesirable tradeoff can be kept to a minimum if requesting parties exercise a bit of foresight and if intelligence analysts have done their basic homework.

COUNTERINTELLIGENCE

Counterintelligence, as well as positive intelligence, conditions the threat-assessment process.

First, a definition. Counterintelligence, commonly called "CI," degrades the effectiveness of inimical foreign intelligence activities by protecting friendly information against espionage. By diluting the enemy's ability to apply his power effectively, CI reduces risks and guards against surprise. It also deals with domestic threats in the form of subversion and sabotage.

Counterintelligence activities generally seek to satisfy two requirements: to maintain physical security and to safeguard state secrets. The kit bag includes a wide variety of active and passive programs: cover and deception planning; electronic countermeasures; foreign travel limitations; civil movement control; political surveillance; special handling for certain types of classified information; and industrial plant protection. Closed societies excel at counterintelligence, since their apparatus permeates all aspects of national life. The Chinese Communists, in particular, are past masters. Very little hard information is ferreted from their borders by whatever means. Conversely, this country is obsessed with debating national security matters in public, is intolerant of communications security restrictions, and sponsors a national life style that simplifies operations for enemy agents. The penalty the United States pays for such luxuries is that its CI screen is more pervious than that of any other first-rate power. The two environments are hugely different for strategy-formulation purposes.

CAPSTONE

In sum, every step in the threat-evaluation process is strewn with stumbling blocks. The quantity, quality, and timeliness of strategic intelligence is a constant and critical constraint on decision-makers who, at best, are forced to work with a factual fabric full of holes. At worst, they work with holes around which a little fabric has been woven. It is not always easy to tell the difference.

3 The Essence of Strategy

[Strategy is] a plan of action designed. . . . to
achieve some end; a purpose together with a
system of measures for its accomplishment.

REAR ADMIRAL J. C. WYLIE, U.S. NAVY
Military Strategy

Definitions of *strategy* abound. Laymen find it the loosest sort of word, subject
to wide interpretation. Even the professional opinion expressed above has shortcomings, since it implies that strategy is essentially an operational matter. In fact, strategy
occupies two distinctive but interrelated planes, one abstract, the other concrete. The
former is peopled with strategic philosophers and theoreticians, the latter with practical
planners.

NATIONAL, GRAND, AND MILITARY STRATEGIES DIFFERENTIATED

The term *strategy* originally meant "the art of generalship," but it encompasses much more today. Strategy no longer is the exclusive preserve of the military,
nor does it deal merely with armed combat. Men in mufti, as well as those in uniform,
now pursue strategic matters at the national level.

National strategy fuses all the powers of a nation, during peace as well as war, to
attain national interests and objectives. Within that context, there is an over-all political
strategy, which addresses both international and internal issues; an economic strategy,
both foreign and domestic; a national military strategy; and so on. Each component
influences national security immediately or tangentially.

This text is devoted primarily to "national security" strategies which have a direct
bearing. In compilation, they constitute "grand strategy," the art and science of employing national power under all circumstances to exert desired degrees and types of
control over the opposition through threats, force, indirect pressures, diplomacy, subterfuge, and other imaginative means, thereby satisfying national security interests and
objectives.

"Military strategy" and "grand strategy" are interrelated, but are by no means

FIGURE 2
Strategic Approaches

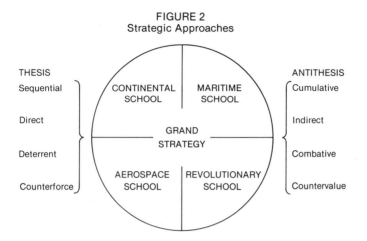

synonymous. Military strategy is predicated on physical violence or the threat of violence. It seeks victory through force of arms. Grand strategy, if successful, alleviates any need for violence. Equally important, it looks beyond victory toward a lasting peace. Military strategy is mainly the province of generals. Grand strategy is mainly the purview of statesmen. Grand strategy *controls* military strategy, which is only one of its elements.

Grand strategy, which embraces such niceties as bluff, negotiation, economic skulduggery, and psychological warfare, debunks the belief—widely held since Clausewitz's day—that strategy simply is "the use of engagements to attain the object of war."[1] On the contrary, it cleaves closely to Liddell Hart's conclusion that "the true aim *is not so much to seek battle as to seek a strategic situation so advantageous that if it does not of itself produce the decision, its continuation by a battle is sure to achieve this.*"[2] Not exactly a new idea, one might add. Sun Tzu recognized that "to subdue the enemy without fighting is the acme of skill."[3]

BASIC APPROACHES TO STRATEGY

Within the parameters established by imperative ends, available means, and the intervening threat, strategists can attack philosophical and practical problems from many different angles.

Sequential and Cumulative Strategies

In his little book *Military Strategy,* Rear Admiral J. C. Wylie identified two elemental, perhaps irreducible strategies, which he entitled "sequential" and "cumulative."[4]

Sequential strategies, as he describes them, comprise successive steps, each contingent on the one preceding, that lead to the final objective. Efforts to undermine the enemy's morale, isolate him from allies, deny him external supply, and destroy his internal lines of communication before invading his homeland would be a typical sequential strategy.

15

Cumulative strategies conversely constitute a collection of individual, random actions that eventually create crushing results. Strategic bombardment and naval campaigns against enemy shipping are prime examples. The Soviets used cumulative techniques in a different vein in the 1940s when, one by one, they incarcerated nine countries behind the Iron Curtain. No single loss seemed shattering to the Free World, but suddenly (it seemed) the Kremlin dominated all of Eastern Europe.

Sequential and cumulative strategies are by no means incompatible — they are usually reinforcing. To illustrate the interaction, Wylie submits that the United States simultaneously prosecuted two separate schemes against Japan during World War II:

> We conducted the sequential strategy campaigns, our drives across the Pacific to the coast of Asia and up to the shores of Empire. And apparently quite apart from them we conducted a cumulative strategy aimed primarily at Japan's economy [by means of air and sea interdiction]. These two went along together in time but were essentially independent in the day-to-day activity.[5]

Direct and Indirect Strategies

General Beaufre surveys strategy from a somewhat different vantage point, alerting readers to the alternatives afforded by direct and indirect approaches in various combinations:

> The game of strategy can, like music, be played in two "keys." The major key is direct strategy in which force is the essential factor. The minor key is indirect strategy, in which force recedes into the background and its place is taken by psychology and planning. Naturally, any strategy may make use of both these keys in varying degree and the result is a large number of "patterns.". . .[6]

He then amplified his remarks with the thought that direct and indirect strategies, different though they may be, have the same objective — to bend or break the enemy's will:

> They use the same methods, the basis of which is the struggle for freedom of action.
> . . . Each is a [special] amalgam of procedures selected because they are best suited either to the resources available or to the enemy's vulnerable points which it is desired to strike. This choice of the best procedure is perhaps the most important function of strategy; the choice is very wide, ranging from suggestion to physical destruction. It is strategy which makes it possible to deal with different situations and it is strategy which often enables the weaker side to emerge as the victor.[7]

The raw application of physical power, direct and devastating, has dominated strategic thought since Cain killed Abel. Only a handful of strategic pioneers, like Alexander, Machiavelli, Lenin, Liddell Hart, and Mao, have devised innovative ways to substitute subtleties for brute force.

Deterrent and Combative Strategies

A third set of basic approaches match deterrence with combative (war-fighting) strategies. The former are designed to *prevent* or limit the scope of wars, the latter to *prosecute* them if they start.

Since 1945, some of the world's best brains have dealt with problems of deterring general nuclear war. The fruits of those labors are reviewed in Chapters 6, 11, 12, and 13. Far fewer great minds have been concerned with deterring low-intensity conflicts. Some authorities are convinced that revolutionary wars may be impossible to prevent — the insurgents know they are outnumbered and outgunned from the start, and are prepared to accept the consequences. Others are less pessimistic. They believe that oncoming generations of strategists eventually will cope effectively with that problem. Meanwhile, until genuine "zero war" strategies can be promulgated (not an easy task without cooperation from the opposition), war-fighting strategies will have to remain in vogue.

Counterforce and Countervalue Strategies

Sharp splits in opinion have produced two specialized strategies that apply mainly to general nuclear war: counterforce and countervalue.

One faction favors countervalue (sometimes called *counter city*) targeting, which poses what it presumes to be an unacceptable threat to the enemy's civilian population and production base. The purpose is to establish a stable "balance of terror," and thereby obviate any need to fight a nuclear war.

Skeptics suggest that, all efforts to the contrary, deterrence in fact may fail. Therefore, they promote counterforce strategies designed to disarm the enemy. Preventive and preemptive operations to seize the initiative are possible options. So are damage-limitation measures.

Pure counterforce and countervalue strategies probably would prove impractical, although dogmatic proponents of each deny that. In consequence, several compromise concepts have been advanced. Among them are counterforce variations that avoid collateral injury to countervalue targets, and others that welcome collateral damage as a bonus. American and Soviet strategies capitalize on counterforce *and* countervalue approaches, but in different proportions.

ELEMENTAL SCHOOLS OF STRATEGIC THOUGHT

Within the broad precincts of sequential and cumulative strategies, direct and indirect, slanted toward deterrence, armed combat, or other types of conflict, three "conventional" schools of military thought collide: continental, maritime, and aerospace. Considerable overlap occurs. All three, for example, ultimately depend on land bases, but even so, the adherents of each customarily think in terms of geographically different environments, and consequently they assail strategic problems in sharply different ways. The following summaries are deliberately oversimplified in order to highlight dissimilarities.

The Continental School

Land-power proponents, the direct strategic descendents of Clausewitz, tend to compartmentalize the globe into separate theaters. They are committed to the conviction that the destruction of enemy armies is the ultimate object of war. Navies and air forces exist primarily to transport troops to the scene of action and support them after they get there. Land power will force a decision leading to lasting control, by physical occupation of enemy territory, if necessary.

The Maritime School

Those theories are fairly foreign to the maritime school, whose members have a global reach channelized only by the continents. They favor the teachings of Mahan and Corbett, who preached that control of the seven seas determines decisions ashore. The goal is to dominate critical sea lanes and choke points that influence forces afloat. Land masses then can be mastered by indirect pressures, including blockades, or by the selective projection of power inland.

The Aerospace School

The aerospace school of strategy was founded by Douhet, whose disciples now are legion.* Their basic beliefs are, first, that air power unaided can be decisive; second, that given a free hand air power could make protracted wars obsolete; and third, that control of the air and destruction of the enemy's war-making potential, mainly his population centers and his industrial base, are the principal missions. Air support for ground forces is strictly secondary.

The Revolutionary School

A fourth school of thought, "unconventional" in character, has cropped up in the recent past and been expounded by the likes of Marx, Lenin, Mao, Ho Chi Minh, Ché Guevara, and Giap. Whereas land, sea, and aerospace schools are mainly military, revolutionary war is primarily political, social, and psychological. It exploits the indirect approach and cumulative, rather than sequential, strategies. Revolutions rarely produce any such thing as a Clausewitzian grand battle. Dien Bien Phu, Giap's 1968 Tet offensive, and Hanoi's invasion of South Vietnam in 1972 were exceptions that prove the rule. Territory is not terribly important. The main battleground is in men's minds.

The Need for a Comprehensive School

Admiral Wylie postulates that all four contemporary schools of strategic thought are deficient, and he is right.[8] None of the military variations, continental, maritime, or aerospace, addresses grand strategy. The revolutionary school comes closer, but in a very specialized context. The need is for a unifying grasp that could enable masters to apply national power in all its manifold forms, to manipulate strategic centers of

---

* Ballistic-missile submariners are at least as closely related to the aerospace school as to the maritime.

gravity, and thus influence national security matters to their best advantage. It behooves this country to reach that intellectual pinnacle before the opposition does.

STRATEGIC OPTIONS

Within the matrix of interests, objectives, theories, concepts, and schools of thought, countless strategic combinations are conceivable. A few sample strategic options, paired to emphasize contrasts, are listed below:

Offensive War or Defensive War
Preemptive War or Second Strike
Massive Retaliation or Flexible Response
Forces in Being or Rapid Mobilization
Regional War or Global War
Blitzkrieg or Attrition
Armed Strife or Subversion
Passive Resistance or Active Response
Isolationism or Collective Security
Counterforce or Countervalue
Controlled Escalation or Insensate Attack
Spheres of Influence or Universal Confrontation

The United States, being a leading contender for world power, juggles global and regional strategies simultaneously. We have a strategy for Europe, another for the Middle East, a third for East Asia and the Western Pacific, and a fourth for worldwide nuclear war, each custom-blended to match specific conditions. Other countries adapt to meet their peculiar needs and situations. Secluded Sweden gambled on neutrality during both World Wars, and succeeded because no one required her territory. Embattled Belgium, a passage state, was not so lucky. Israel banked on a first-strike strategy in 1956 and 1967, featuring rapid mobilization and quick termination of hostilities. That amalgam worked well for a nation that could afford neither large standing armed forces nor lengthy wars of attrition, but it would not seem so attractive if the Arabs were more alert and better organized.

Every strategy must be tailored to meet specialized needs. The French failed to take that into account in 1940, when they tried to refight the last war. Strategies cannot be transferred intact from one period to another without very precise appreciation for changes that transpire in the interim. Neither can strategies be transplanted from place to place unless the situation in one locale is pertinent in the other. Most of the things the United States has done right in Vietnam, for instance, would not work in Europe.

In sum, strategy is the art and science of options. What reactions are right for one leader or nation may be wholly inappropriate for others. It is just as hard to imagine pepperpots like Harry Truman or Teddy Roosevelt adopting devious, subtle, or passive strategies as it is to see Stalin as straightforward. Americans, being impetuous, abhor the strategy of protracted war which seems to suit stoic orientals. Sir Robert Thompson, a disinterested observer, put that matter in proper perspective with a few well-chosen remarks related to Vietnam:

Weaknesses in the American character were to play their part. Of these, the greatest was and still is impatience. . . . More than any other factor, coupled with the frustration which automatically follows, it has led to a desire for quick results which, in a war concerned with people and immune to the application of power, are just not obtainable.[9]

STRATEGIC CONSTRAINTS

Regardless of their philosophical convictions, all strategists are fettered by a cornucopia of constraints — political, military, economic, cultural, geographic, and technological. Some are intangible, like national will and world opinion. The precepts of humanity and chivalry play a role, along with ethics and legal limitations. Customary law prescribes well-defined, firmly established rules of war, but those sometimes are counterbalanced or countermanded by other influences. The so-called Principle of Military Necessity, for example, invokes the right to apply whatever pressure is necessary to bend or break the enemy's will with the least possible expenditure of time, lives, and money.

Most grand strategists also must contend with national myths and tradition. In the United States, these are intensely inhibitive, as the following samples suggest:

Never strike the first blow.
Fight "fairly," in accord with "the rules."
Champion the underdog.
Avoid secret alliances or agreements.
Submit all major strategic decisions for popular approval.
Support minimum forces in peacetime; mobilize for war.

All of the above have been violated at one time or another, but each instance was almost invariably accompanied by national fits of conscience.

The spectrum of war conditions strategies by creating a spectrum of problems. There is general nuclear war, limited war — with or without nuclear weapons — and a smorgasbord of low-intensity hostilities, including insurgencies and cold war. The causes, conduct peculiarities, and termination problems associated with each category are in many ways unique. National leaders of world powers, primarily the United States and the Soviet Union, must understand the lot and proceed accordingly, since strategies that work well in one environment do not necessarily work well in the others.

THE ROLE OF ASSUMPTIONS

This brings us to a quick survey of assumptions which, for better or worse, underlie nearly every strategic decision, and which in themselves can sow the seeds of success or failure.

Some "wishful thinkers" are tempted to assume away problems when the going gets difficult. Pessimistic strategists cause costs to skyrocket unnecessarily by assuming the worst. Those polarized approaches produce dramatically different strategies. The following fifteen conflicting assumptions illustrate the diversity of opinion that underlies contemporary strategic debates in the United States:

1. Force is (not) outmoded as a foreign-policy tool.
2. The United States does (not) need to be "Number One."
3. Domestic needs should (not) take priority over defense.
4. Detente does (not) reflect benign Soviet intentions.
5. The Sino-Soviet split is (not) permanent.
6. U.S. nuclear superiority is (not) essential.
7. Controlled nuclear war is (not) feasible.
8. Alliances are (not) preferable to unilateral defense.
9. The United States should (not) be the world's "policeman."
10. Asia should (not) dominate U.S. regional strategy.
11. U.S. support should (not) be limited to democratic regimes.
12. Time is (not) on our side in any ideological struggle.
13. Budgetary concerns should (not) dictate strategy.
14. Reserve component forces are (not) imperative.
15. Surface fleets are (not) obsolete.

Many other assumptions, some sound, some suspect, could embellish that list. Each influences strategy in its own special way. All should be subject to constant surveillance, so that conjecture will correspond as closely as possible with fact when the real world and real threats replace planning assumptions.

THE STRATEGIC CHALLENGE

Clausewitz summarized the essence of strategy nicely when he wrote:

A prince or general, who knows how to organize his war exactly according to his object and means, who does neither too much nor too little, furnishes thereby the greatest proof of his genius. . . .

But let us admit that there is no question at all here of scientific formulas and problems. The relations of material things are all very simple. The comprehension of the moral forces which come into play is more difficult. . . . [At the highest levels,] strategy borders on politics and statesmanship, or rather it becomes both itself, and, as we have observed before, these have more influence on how much or how little is to be done than on how it is executed [which is tactics].

Thus, then, in strategy everything is very simple, but not on that account very easy.[10]

4   The Principles of War

If men make war in slavish obedience to rules,
they will fail.

ULYSSES S. GRANT
Personal Memoirs

Strategists and tacticians alike, who traffic in intangibles and imponderables, are guided — consciously or unconsciously — by the Principles of War, a collection of basic considerations accumulated over the centuries.[1]

ORIGINS OF THE PRINCIPLES

The Principles of War, according to Napoleon, are those which

> have regulated the great captains whose deeds have been handed down to us by history: Alexander, Hannibal, Caesar, Gustavus Adolphus, Turenne, Prince Eugene and Frederick the Great. The history of [their] campaigns, carefully written, would be a complete treatise on the art of war; the principles which ought to be followed in offensive and defensive war, would flow from it spontaneously.[2]

Unfortunately, those early strategists paid homage to the principles, but did not jot them down in any orderly form. The extent of their individual contributions therefore is subject to broad interpretations, which vary with the biases of biographers.

Specific principles seem to date from Clausewitz, who enunciated five in a memorandum written for the Prussian crown prince in 1812. They were first published as an appendix to his collected works *On War*. At least three others appeared as "elements" in Book III of that text. Mackinder, Mahan, Foch, Douhet, and Lenin are among the subsequent donors. J. F. C. Fuller apparently fathered the forerunner of current U.S. adaptations, which originally appeared in War Department Training Regulation 10–5 in 1921.

The Principles of War differ from list to list. The British, for example, subscribe to ten, the Russians to half that many (*see* table opposite for a representative sampling). Furthermore, the lists keep changing. One recent schism occurred in 1947, when the U.S. Air Force became a separate service: our Army switched from the Principle of Coordination to Unity of Command, while the aviators, who treasure independence,

PRINCIPLES OF WAR

Principles Including Alternative Titles	United States	United Kingdom	Soviet Union	Sun Tzu	Clausewitz	Fuller
Purpose Aim Objective Direction	X	X		X	X	X
Initiative Offensive	X	X		X	X	X
Concentration Mass	X	X		X	X	X
Economy of Force	X	X			X	
Maneuver Mobility Movement	X			X	X	X
Unity of Command	X*					
Cooperation Coordination	X			X		
Security	X	X				X
Surprise	X	X		X	x**	X
Simplicity	X					
Flexibility Freedom of Action		X				
Administration		X				
Morale		X	X		x*	
Exploitation Pursuit					x**	
Quantity/Quality of Divisions			X			
Armament			X			
Ability of Commanders			X			
Stability of the Rear			X			

*   U.S. Army only.
** Listed as an "element," rather than a principle.

retained the original. Nevertheless, a good many principles remain reasonably constant. Only a few are strikingly discordant — to wit, Red China advocates Annihilation, which is missing from most other versions.

EFFICACY OF THE PRINCIPLES

The efficacy of *any* principles has long been in dispute. Some authorities, among them Liddell Hart, doubt their value (although he himself identifies several):

> The modern tendency has been to search for principles which can each be expressed in a single word — and then need several thousand words to explain them. Even so, these "principles" are so abstract that they mean different things to different men, and, for any value, depend on the individual's own understanding of war. The longer one continues the search for such omnipotent abstractions, the more do they appear a mirage, neither attainable or useful — except as an intellectual exercise.[3]

It is true that none of the principles are immutable, like some laws of physics, economics, and the natural sciences, which deal with certain conditions that create certain results. Nor are they hard-and-fast rules that inflict fines for minor infractions. Not every principle is appropriate for every occasion, and some seem antithetical.

Nevertheless, the Principles of War *can* be used as a practical checklist to assist sound judgment by the architects and appraisers of strategic theories, concepts, and plans, provided they are administered sensibly. Users simply should recognize that no two situations are quite alike, and apply the principles accordingly.

Over the years, the Principles of War have been interpreted mainly by military tacticians. Grand strategists need a special rendition that interrelates ends and means at the national level, taking cognizance of many considerations besides armed force. The handpicked dozen principles discussed below draw from and modify several common lists, both foreign and domestic. The tabulation is in no particular order, except perhaps for the first four:

1. Purpose	5. Economy	9. Security
2. Initiative	6. Maneuver	10. Simplicity
3. Flexibility	7. Surprise	11. Unity
4. Concentration	8. Exploitation	12. Morale

INDIVIDUAL PRINCIPLES DISCUSSED

1. Purpose

Most lists open with the Principle of the Objective. Since the term *objective* is subject to some confusion, as noted in Chapter 1, it is helpful to substitute the Principle of Purpose, which connotes political objects, *plus* military aims.

Decisive and attainable purposes establish the mission, for which strategy is the concept of operation. To be effective, every plan and action must contribute to realistic ends. Subsidiary goals never should contradict the central theme.

The ultimate purpose most often is some degree of control over the opposition, by physical, economic, psychological, or other means. The type, duration, and intensity of control may range from relatively inconsequential concessions to unconditional surrender or oblivion. Purposes professed in peacetime are subject to change in war, when rationality gives way to emotion. Strategists should be prepared to adjust.

2. Initiative

Offensive operations are the most effective way to gain and retain the initiative, and with it freedom of action to pursue prescribed purposes. They enable the wielder to engage the opposition at times and places of his choosing in manners he desires. Defensive strategies should be adopted deliberately only as temporary expedients while awaiting opportunities to assume or resume the initiative.

Grand strategy places a premium on intellectual offensives as well as physical action. Active striving for innovative ideas, diplomatic assaults, incessant searches for technological breakthroughs, and concerted efforts to capture men's minds are just a few alternative avenues that may obviate the need for pitched battles. All manner of seemingly contradictory combinations apply. It is possible to advance by retreating and vice versa, or to display a posture that is aggressively defensive one moment and defensively aggressive another.

No matter what the strategic sphere, whether concrete or metaphysical, the side with the initiative forces the foe to react rather than act. As General Henry Halleck advised more than 100 years ago, offensive warfare

> is waged on a foreign soil [literally or figuratively] and therefore spares the country of the attacking force; it augments its own resources at the same time it diminishes those of the enemy; it adds to the moral courage of its own [people], while it disheartens its opponents.[4]

3. Flexibility

The Principle of Flexibility recognizes the inevitability of change in purposes, policies, plans, and procedures. This leads to a basic premise enunciated by Admiral Wylie: no one can predict with certainty the pattern war will take.[5]

The need is for alternate solutions to potential problems, which must be addressed according to their character, imminency, importance, and probability of occurrence:

> The player who plans for only one strategy runs a great risk simply because his opponent soon detects the [deficiency] — and counters it. The requirement is for a spectrum of strategies that are flexible and noncommittal, a theory that by intent and design can be applied in unforeseen situations. Planning for uncertainty is not as dangerous as it might seem; there is, after all, some order in military as well as other human affairs. But planning for certitude is the greatest of all . . . mistakes.[6]

Physical capabilities unfortunately afford less margin for flexibility than intellectual plans. Deciding where to place the material emphasis is a matter of considerable consequence, determined by assigning priorities. Whatever the verdict, it should be imaginative. Triteness in the field of strategy is the eighth deadly sin.

4. Concentration

Concentrating sufficient efforts, moral or material, at the proper time and place to accomplish decisive purposes is indispensable to the successful prosecution of national security affairs in peace as well as war. Over-all quantitative, or even qualitative, superiority is not a prerequisite. Proper concentration may permit inferior assets to prevail.

Primary stress must be devoted to top-priority projects and the most serious threats, external or internal, so that friendly strength is concentrated against enemy weakness. The side with the initiative enjoys a huge advantage, since it can focus its energy on known objectives, while the opposition must dissipate its power in preparing for contingencies.

5. Economy

Available assets, whether spiritual or substantive, never are unlimited. Concentration at points of decision, therefore, implies the need for economy elsewhere.

Measured application of power in the main may be accomplished in two ways: by allotting minimum essential efforts and resources to those endeavors that require the least emphasis; or by temporarily diverting strength from selected high-priority areas, recognizing that this involves calculated risks. The former method is most frequently used, but both call for canny judgment.

In imposing their will on the enemy, promulgators of purposes and supporting policies must select degrees of control that guarantee the attainment of goals without resort to extremes which would be wasteful or ineffective. Frequently, it is possible to "win" merely by not "losing."

6. Maneuver

Maneuver gives form and shape to concentration. It is the antithesis of mental stagnation or static physical positions. It further implies a faculty for rapidly shifting strategic emphasis from one mode to another, which is just as important as redeploying tangible assets in time and space.

Sun Tzu, many centuries ago, discerned that "in battle, there are not more than two methods of attack: direct and indirect; yet these two in combination give rise to an endless series of maneuvers." Mobility may be political, economic, and psychological, as well as military, responding to plans, pressures, or unexpected opportunities. In any event, clever strategists avoid costly frontal assaults by relying on imaginative approaches whenever possible, striving to apportion crushing power at decisive times and places in manners that expeditiously fulfill vital purposes. Movement, soundly conceived and executed, contributes directly to freedom of action, capitalizes on successes, abridges failures, and reduces vulnerability.

7. Surprise

Surprise, aided and abetted by various combinations of secrecy, speed, deception, originality, and audacity, can shift the balance of power decisively, paving the way for victories far out of proportion to the efforts expended. The enemy need not be wholly unaware of impending actions; it is only necessary that he grasp their full significance too late to react effectively.

Strategic surprise can assume many shapes, of which conventional military surprise, involving recognizable forces and well-understood procedures, may worry defenders the least. Other approaches can have even greater strategic consequence if conditions are ripe. The ouster of Sihanouk, which dramatically changed the course of the war in Indochina, was political surprise par excellence. Economic surprise resulting from the unexpected U.S. embargo on iron and steel scrap staggered Japan before Pearl Harbor. The psychological surprise of Hanoi's 1968 Tet offensive unseated President Johnson and precipitated widespread pacifism in the United States. Technological surprise can be equally devastating. The strategic implications of Sputnik I, for example, were unsurpassed.

Surprise admittedly does not vouchsafe success, but it vastly increases the odds in its favor.

8. Exploitation

The Principle of Exploitation encourages momentum. It makes it possible for friendly elements to expand and consolidate gains, keeping the enemy off balance and on the defensive. Sage strategists follow lines of least resistance that lead to vital objectives, pour on the pressure when opponents falter, reinforce successes, and abandon failures.

Strategic exploitation involves far more than capitalizing on military advantage. It profits equally from political, economic, or psychological primacy and augments technological leads.

9. Security

Security preserves power and reduces the probability that enemy activity, direct or indirect, might interfere unduly with vital friendly interests, assets, plans, or operations. By reducing vulnerabilities, security increases freedom of action.

Physical security protects key elements of the national entity — the civilian population, institutions, installations, resources, and armed forces — from all violence, both foreign and domestic. Counterintelligence contributes to that goal by pinpointing possible sabotage and subversion and diluting enemy espionage efforts. Positive intelligence programs provide critical information concerning enemy capabilities and intentions, thereby guarding against surprise.

The Principle of Security by no means implies undue caution or the avoidance of risks. A good offense often is an outstanding defense. Seizing and retaining the initiative can interrupt inimical activity.

10. Simplicity

Simple concepts and clear, concise orders reduce misinterpretation and resultant confusion. The most complex theories and undertakings usually can be reduced to understandable terms. Whatever the requirements, the simplest solutions are almost always preferable.

11. Unity

Power improperly focused can prohibit the fulfillment of fundamental goals. The Principle of Unity embraces solidarity of purpose, effort, and command. It directs all energies, assets, and activities, physical and mental, toward desired ends. An acceptable degree of coordination can be achieved through cooperation if all participants, civil and military, function willingly as a team. However, since human nature is often opportunist and individualistic, proper orchestration can better be assured if requisite responsibilities and authority are vested in command.

12. Morale

Last, but not least, is the Principle of Morale. In the final analysis, war, whether hot or cold, resolves itself into a test of wills, not just of armed forces, but of entire peoples. When the urge to compete expires, all is lost.

General George C. Marshall, speaking at Trinity College in Hartford, Connecticut, on 15 June 1941, described morale as

> a state of mind. It is steadfastness, courage and hope. It is confidence and zeal and loyalty. It is elan, esprit de corps and determination. It is staying power, the spirit which endures to the end — the will to win. With it, all things are possible, without it everything else, planning, preparation, production, count for naught.

Leadership, discipline, comradeship, self-respect, and unflagging belief in a cause all help build morale. Paradoxically, pain and privation may do the same thing. Psychological offensives pave the way for force, rather than vice versa. Napoleon's conviction that "in war, the moral is to the material as three to one" may be slightly overdrawn, but spirit is often decisive.

IMPLICATIONS OF THE PRINCIPLES

This brief survey highlights a lesson: successful strategists never knowingly violate the Principles of War unless they first evaluate the risks and estimate expenses. Readers who apply this yardstick to any conflict or period of international tension in history must conclude that — critics notwithstanding — the Principles of War *are* utilitarian and they *do* make sense. The record shows that winners, by and large, took heed of the Principles. The losers, discounting those who were overcome by sheer weight of manpower and materiel, by and large did not.

PART II

THE STRATEGIC ENVIRONMENT

5 The Nature of General War

You ask what is our aim? I can answer in one
word: victory — victory at all costs; victory in spite
of all terror, victory however long and hard the
road may be, for without victory, there is no
survival.

WINSTON CHURCHILL

*Speaking to the House of Commons upon
becoming Prime Minister, 13 May 1940*

Sir Winston's brave words in some respects are the echo of a bygone age. Even those idealists who still believe "there is no substitute for victory" grudgingly concede that Webster's dictionary definition of the vague term *victory* is subject to specialized interpretation when viewed in context with general war.

General war is identified by the U.S. Joint Chiefs of Staff as "armed conflict between major powers in which the total resources of the belligerents are employed, and the national survival of a major belligerent is in jeopardy." That definition is inaccurate on two counts. First, war between regional powers like France and Germany would by no means be "general." And second, a spasmic encounter between superpowers conceivably could be over before total resources were brought to bear. In practice, therefore, the term *general war* commonly is reserved for a genocidal showdown between this country and the Soviet Union, during which an epidemic of mass destruction weapons might endanger the entire planet. That restricted interpretation will continue to apply until other countries acquire comparable capabilities.

THE UTILITY OF GENERAL WAR

General war poses strategic problems unparalleled in the past. The potential for global devastation is prodigious. Risks are grossly magnified in relation to most gains. Technological competition is unprecedented. There is little margin for strategic error. Consequently, men for the first time in history now devote more mental energy to the prevention of war (at this level of the spectrum) than to its prosecution.

31

Indeed, some say with utter conviction that force is no longer an appropriate means to attain political ends. They echo opinions expressed by fifty-two Nobel laureates who signed the Mainau Declaration in 1955: "*All* nations must come to the decision to renounce force as a final resort of policy. If they are not prepared to do this they will *cease to exist.*"

Persuasive arguments can be expounded in support of that thesis, but not everyone is convinced. Annihilation may *not* be automatic in event of general war in their estimation. Professor William R. Kintner of the Foreign Policy Research Institute, University of Pennsylvania, forwarded thoughts on this matter to the Department of Defense early in 1970:

> It is not true that the advent of nuclear weapons has brought an end to the history of five millenia and has opened a "new" historical epoch. The struggle for power has entered another phase; but it is still the same struggle for power. . . . The very fact that the risks have grown larger confers strategic advantage upon those who know how to exploit and manipulate the opponent's perceptions of these risks. The so-called nuclear stalemate has neither inhibited the use of force nor invalidated the axioms of classical strategy. To the contrary, judicious escalation of force now serves to attain political objectives, just as it has always served this purpose.[1]

Nevertheless, the cause for caution is undeniable. Herman Kahn provided the following perspective:*

> A thermonuclear war is quite likely to be an *unprecedented catastrophe* for the defender. Depending on the military course of events, it may or may not be an unprecedented catastrophe for the attacker, and for some neutrals as well. But an "unprecedented" catastrophe can be a far cry from an "unlimited" one. Most important of all, sober study shows that the *limits on the magnitude of the catastrophe seem to be closely dependent on what kinds of preparations have been made, and on how the war is started and fought.*[2]

POTENTIAL CAUSES OF GENERAL WAR

No strategist has much chance of coping with the problems of general war unless he has a sound working knowledge of potential causes. Six categories stand out:

Deliberate initiation
Accidental initiation
Miscalculation
Misunderstanding
Catalysis
Irrational acts

Each of these warrants a brief survey.

---

* Chapters 6, 11, 12, and 13 draw heavily on the published and unpublished works of Herman Kahn. Numerous other authors have addressed the subject of thermonuclear war, but no one has so succinctly articulated as many aspects from as many angles.

Deliberate Initiation

Probably no sane individual who appreciated the implications ever would deliberately trigger a general war unless one of two preconditions existed: desperation or solid self-confidence. If, for example, a potential protagonist believed that his country was about to be eradicated by an inevitable attack, he might think he had nothing to lose by preempting. Should that same party achieve a spectacular technological breakthrough, such as the birth of an airtight antiaircraft and antiballistic-missile defense that precluded effective retaliation, he might consider that probable risks would be more than outweighed by prospective gains. It is possible even to postulate scenarios that combine transitory self-confidence with impending desperation.

Regardless of the reasoning, however, any premeditated instigation of general war would involve soul-searching of the first order, as Kahn explained in his treatise *On Thermonuclear War*. To survive a conflict of this kind (let alone profit from it), national decision-makers would have to be completely convinced that their country could successfully solve a series of political, military, economic, social, psychological, and technological problems: wartime performance; the effects of acute fallout; survival and patchup; the maintenance of economic momentum; long-term recuperation; postwar medical care; and genetic aberrations. Failure to cope effectively with any of those areas would cancel accomplishments in the others.[3]

The likelihood of deliberate initiation therefore seems low, as long as prospective victims maintain a credible deterrent posture.

Accidental Initiation

Accidental general war between the United States and the U.S.S.R. is even less plausible, lurid tales like *Failsafe* and *Dr. Strangelove* notwithstanding. The safeguards against mechanical and human error and unauthorized tampering with nuclear delivery systems are virtually foolproof, although such may not be the case if nuclear weapons proliferate among careless or less responsible countries.

Miscalculation

Miscalculation is more to be feared than either of the causes above. The most innocuous annoyances could escalate to general war, either through poor judgment or through loss of control by any antagonist. Sophisticated games of politico-military "chicken," in which one country or coalition seeks to blackmail or out-bluff another, are also in that category. None of the parties involved in those practices would *want* a head-on collision, but if no one yielded it would be unavoidable. The United States and the Soviet Union had a brief flirtation with "brinkmanship" in the 1950s and early 1960s, but since then have sought to attain desired ends in manners that minimize the likelihood of direct military confrontation.

Misunderstanding

Misunderstandings, which can lead to preemption in response to false alarms, are a constant hazard. To help forestall communications failures that prevent the timely transmission of precise, coherent messages, the two superpowers exploit multiple means of contact that include common-user electronic circuits, personalized facilities like the Washington-to-Moscow "hot line," routine diplomatic relations, and conferences between chiefs of state. In addition, nations often supplement written and oral exchanges with strategic signals that clarify intentions: for example, when President Kennedy dispatched Strategic Air Command bombers to holding patterns along the Soviet periphery in October 1962, he gave clear evidence of U.S. resolve during the Cuban missile crisis.

Catalysis

Catalytic conflicts, touched off intentionally by a third country or coalition, have occurred in the past and probably will in the future. Potential motives are many — ambition, desperation, and revenge are among them. Collective security systems, such as those maintained by the United States and the U.S.S.R., offer opportunities for catalysis, and the U.S.–Soviet–Chinese Communist triangle opens temptations for any one of the three to play the others off to its benefit.

Irrational Acts

Finally, the possibility that normally responsible men might commit irrational acts can never be discounted. Anticipating abnormality, however, is very difficult, since "rationality" varies remarkably from culture to culture. Courses of action that appear wholly unrealistic to Americans, who place a high premium on human life, might be completely compatible with the coveted goals of "impetuous," "immoral," or "less civilized" combatants. Moreover, illogicality inspires divers causes and effects, as Max Lerner notes:

> When people say that "irrationality" spoils deterrence they mean — or ought to mean — only particular brands of it. Leaders can be irrationally impetuous or irrationally lethargic, intolerable of suspense or incapable of decision. A Hitler may be hard to deter because he is "irrational," but a Chamberlain is equally irrational and especially easy to deter. . . . This is no consolation when we confront the wrong kinds of madness; still, we may as well get the theory straight.[4]

STRATEGIC OPTIONS

The range of strategic options for general war reflects mankind's reactions, which run the gamut from despair to optimism. At one end of the scale is pacifism. At the other is preventive war.

Attitudes Toward Deterrence

Deterrence aims at obviating war. It is a compound of *threats,* the *capability* to carry them out, and the *will* to execute, if necessary. Successful combinations preclude unwanted aggression by imposing on deterees the prospect of exorbitant costs in relation to anticipated gains. The end product is stability.

Credibility is the key. Y. Harkabi, in his *Nuclear War and Nuclear Peace,* abstracts the following "rules": for a threat to deter it must be credible, but not every credible threat deters. It must be of sufficient magnitude. As the threat of punishment mounts, deterrent value grows, but only to some undefinable point. At that juncture, the probability that the threat will be implemented begins to decline, and so does credibility.[5]

The quest for credible deterrence is pursued by two schools of thought whose strategic concepts and supporting force postures are in diametric opposition. One is unequivocally convinced that the horrors of a holocaust are sufficient in themselves to guarantee absolute deterrence and automatic stability. The other is not.

Members of the "mutual homicide" school anticipate no need ever to fight a nuclear war. They place total store in countervalue weaponry, which poses a direct threat to civilian populations and industry, with the expressed purpose of establishing a "balance of terror." Comparatively small atomic arsenals are adequate to accomplish that mission. Any move to mitigate the promised calamity reputedly would dilute the deterrent. Damage limiting features that might degrade the enemy's destructive power, such as antiaircraft, antiballistic missile, or civil defenses, thus are alien to the theory.

Agnostics are less confident that deterrence is infallible. In their opinion, all efforts to the contrary, preventive measures could collapse. Instead of threatening the foe with annihilation, they adopt an approach that takes advantage of several inhibitors, only one of which is fear, and concurrently affords capabilities to handle contingencies should deterrence founder. Counterforce weapons, designed to disarm the enemy rather than punish his population, play a prominent role. Force requirements and attendant budgetary costs are high, whether the aim is to gain quick ascendancy or to wage a war of attrition, since superior technology and large numbers of deliverable nuclear weapons are essential.

Pure counterforce and countervalue strategies, of course, represent extremes. Numerous alternatives intervene. Champions of both positions outlined above claim that compromises are ineffective, but many students of the subject now believe that a continuum of capabilities between the two poles must be maintained by countries that hope to deter general war.

Approaches to War-Fighting

If deterrence were abandoned or failed, a variety of war-fighting options would be available. The sampling below, arranged without regard for matching pairs, demonstrates the diversity. The two columns illustrate differences between offense and defense, but considerable overlap occurs.

OFFENSE	DEFENSE
Malicious First Strike	Preemptive Surrender
Preemptive Attack	Accommodation
Surprise Attack	Launch-on-Warning
Attack After Ultimatum	Calculated Second Strike

OFFENSE	DEFENSE
Insensate (Spasm) Attack	Massive Retaliation
Controlled Attack	Flexible Response
Exemplary Attack	Tit-for-Tat Response
Intrawar Blackmail	Intrawar Deterrence

The situations facing attacker and defender would be sharply dissimilar. The instigator could almost always count on having the edge. War would begin at the time, place, and under circumstances of his choosing. Should he elect to capitalize on surprise, his ability to alert, augment, and redeploy assault forces, or even to evacuate cities, would be significantly greater than that of the opposition. The defender, having absorbed a first strike, would have to retaliate with truncated elements whose coordination and control were disrupted. He would have to function in a chaotic atmosphere, where nuclear effects — blast, heat and radiation — might drastically decrease anticipated capabilities. Herman Kahn speculates that operating in a post-attack, general war environment might be analogous to training at the equator, then moving incomplete units to the arctic. The likelihood is low that their performance would immediately equal expectations.[6]

GENERAL-WAR OBJECTIVES

As in all other types of strife between states, national security objectives shape general-war strategies. Representative goals might be to eliminate intolerable threats, to restore the balance of power, to acquire territory, gain material wealth, or propagate an ideology. Possony and Pournelle point up the relationship between ends and means:

> The political objectives are the factors that determine what price a government is willing to pay; and these objectives are not set in absolute terms. If world domination is the objective, then no price is too high provided that the rulers of the aggressor nation will survive and remain in control and all other countries will be reduced to impotence. Conversely, if the probable result of the war will be the overthrow of the ruling structure, no victory, no matter how cheap in lives and property, is worth the winning.[7]

Prime peacetime objectives, such as the prevention of general war, would have to be replaced if deterrence failed. Damage limitation doubtless would be high on the list. Distinctions between goals adopted by aggressors and those espoused by defenders could be clear-cut or coalesce, depending on the cause of the conflict and the war-fighting philosophies.

Whether war was started deliberately or resulted from misunderstanding, for example, would have great bearing on subsequent events. Further, counterforce and countervalue schools would fancy different ends. The former would strive to "win" the war in the classic sense, to "prevail" at some level below outright military victory, or simply to terminate the war on favorable terms. The latter school, lacking extensive war-fighting capabilities, could only hope to restore stability by punishing the enemy population until enemy leaders called it quits.

Counterforce-Countervalue Considerations

Counterforce strategies are popularly coupled with offensive operations, countervalue with defense, but those stereotypes are misleading. A first strike, for example, might be directed against cities to break the enemy's spirit and pave the way for bargaining. Further, the two approaches can be applied unadulterated or in combinations. General Curtis E. LeMay, a former SAC commander, laid out a few possibilities:

> "Pure" counterforce implies the destruction of all enemy strategic forces, regardless of the collateral damage to industry or population caused by attacking co-located targets. In other words, if an enemy airfield is located in a city, we would destroy it regardless of what incidental damage might be done to the city. . . .
>
> [Pure countervalue would be antithetical.]
>
> Counterforce-plus-avoidance . . . is an attempt to signal the enemy that we have no wish to harm his population, in hopes that he will avoid such targets in our country. Here, although the destruction of the enemy's nuclear forces remains primary, it is tempered . . . by not attacking a co-located target at all, by accepting a lower probability of destruction and attacking with fewer or smaller weapons, or by placing the aiming point of the weapons on the side of the target away from the population complex. . . . Counterforce-plus-bonus is the opposite of counterforce-plus-avoidance, in that population destruction incidental to counterforce attacks would be considered desirable for intrawar deterrence or retaliation.[8]

FORCE REQUIREMENTS

What kind of forces would be needed to fight a general war? Some experts foresee a decision in hours or days. They would stake everything on a specialized active military establishment tailored for nuclear combat. Others, who admit the possibility of protracted war, would stress greater versatility, including conventional land, air, and naval elements to consolidate gains or repel invaders.

In one respect, however, there is no argument. Effective command and control systems that could survive a nuclear war would be essential, beginning at the national level and filtering down through every politico-military echelon. This requirement generates a need for elaborate, interlocking webs of alternate headquarters in secure locations and for redundant communications. Standard procedures designate individuals or organizations to assume command automatically should higher echelons cease either to exist or to function in prescribed manners.

Quantitative force requirements are perennially open to question. One faction presses for numerical superiority. Another believes that parity would suffice. A third would settle for "sufficiency." In fact, the number necessary to create a credible deterrence or fight a nuclear war is obscure. Statistical supremacy in gross delivery systems, warheads, or megatonnage might be militarily mandatory under certain circumstances, parity would be satisfactory under others, and inferiority might sometimes suffice.

One caveat is essential. Anything less than superiority (or even apparent superiority) could destroy the credibility of a deterrent if either the aggressor or defender *believed* that preeminence was vital. By the same token, total numbers influence the confidence of allies and the uncommitted. Ultimately therefore, political and psychological considerations may be at least as important as material requirements in ascertaining numerical needs for general war.

GENERAL-WAR PLANNING

General-war planning, for deterrence or for combat, must be comprehensive, both in depth and scope, to a degree unprecedented in history. Once again, Herman Kahn speaks:

> In previous times, it was not essential for the war plans staff to think through the many steps of the war *before* the event, for campaigns moved slowly enough so that they could improvise as problems arose. Today, this is no longer possible. One of the reasons why modern war is likely to be excessively destructive is that, with events moving so fast, unless preattack preparations for evaluation, negotiation, and operational flexibility have been made there is no way for knowledge of the actual military course of events to improve the conduct of operations. . . . Today these possibilities must be thought about in advance. To some extent we must try to think a war right through to its termination.[9]

TERMINATION PROBLEMS

A general nuclear war *could* erupt abruptly and subside spontaneously. However, Tom Schelling suggests that starting a general war may be much easier than stopping it:

> Some kind of cease-fire or pause would have to be reached and phased into an armistice, by a bargaining process that might at the outset have to be largely tacit, based on demonstration more than on words, but that sooner or later would have to become explicit. . . . the closing stage, furthermore, might have to begin quickly, possibly before the first volley had reached its targets.[10]

Certainly, the Number One prerequisite would be to maintain communications with enemy representatives who have the authority, ability, and inclination to take appropriate actions. This need instills a good incentive for sparing capital cities and alternate seats of government, so that persons in authority not only live, but retain access to operational communications that are indispensable to war-termination dialogues. It might also justify avoiding the devastation of other population centers to prevent vindictive reprisals resulting from overheated emotions.

Schelling sees half a dozen issues as subjects for bargaining: the conduct of the war; the cease-fire or truce; who to negotiate with among the enemy authorities; matters concerning "sideshows," or regional conflicts within the general war frame; long-term disarmament agreements; and the final political settlement.[11]

In negotiating a settlement to end a general war, two serious dangers appear:

> One is that the enemy may cheat and get away with it; the other is that he may not cheat but appear to, so that the arrangement falls apart for lack of adequate inspection.

38

Suppose the armistice is barely one hour old and several nuclear weapons go off in our own country. Has the enemy resumed the war? We may know within another few minutes. Is he testing us to see how willing we are to resume hostilities, or is he sneaking in a few revenge weapons or perhaps trying to whittle down our postwar military capability? Or was this a submarine or a few bombers that never got the word about the armistice, or confused their instructions? . . . Was this an ally or a satellite of the main enemy, who has not been brought into the armistice? Would the enemy know it if some of his weapons had hit us since the armistice; if we fire a few in reprisal to keep him honest, would he have to assume that we were taking a new initiative, possibly resuming the war? . . .

If questions like these are to be answerable, it will be because they were posed and thought through in advance, recognized at the time the pause or agreement was reached, and even appreciated as pertinent when the weapons themselves were designed and the war plans drawn up.[12]

THE TREND

The nature of general war is constantly changing as new concepts evolve. The prospect of an all-out nuclear exchange is withering away, but as it does the situation grows increasingly complex. The proliferation of nuclear weapons may prove irrepressible. If so, additional complications will be created. Stability will no longer be a two-party game, and the survivability of retaliatory forces and the population will become an even more awesome issue, particularly for the United States which is wedded to a second-strike strategy.

Endless weapons-testing, war games, exercises, philosophizing, and analysis by military and governmental officials, civilian contract agencies, and scientific and academic communities on both sides of the Iron Curtain provide some means of estimating the validity of theories, but broad areas of uncertainty remain. Combat experience, after all, is still restricted to the almost clinical use of two atom bombs under conditions that precluded reciprocation. Chapters 11, 12, and 13 highlight the derivative issues and help to sharpen the debate.

6 The Nature of Limited War

I was left with one single conclusion: General
MacArthur was ready to risk general war. I was
not.

HARRY S TRUMAN

LIMITED WAR DEFINED

Between general war at one extreme and cold war at the other lies a wide
range of conventional hostilities loosely described as *limited war.* That scope is a bit
too comprehensive for strategy formulation purposes, because it lumps conflicts that
are of little consequence even locally with serious confrontations that verge on global
catastrophe. This chapter therefore concentrates on armed encounters, excluding incidents, in which one or more major powers or their proxies *voluntarily* exercise various
types and degrees of restraint in order to prevent unmanageable flare-ups.

Limited war thus is markedly different than it was in ages past, when conscious
conflict management to avoid unacceptable escalation was almost unknown. Wars then,
Brodie notes, were mainly

> limited by the small margin of the national economic resources available for mobiliza-
> tion and by the small capability for destruction that could be purchased with that
> narrow margin. Today . . . we speak of limited war in a sense that connotes a deliberate
> hobbling of a tremendous power that is already mobilized and that must in any case
> be maintained at a very high pitch of effectiveness for the sake only of inducing the
> enemy to hobble himself to a like degree.[1]

WAYS TO LIMIT WARS

The scope of war can be limited with regard to political objects and military
aims, the choice of weapons (especially chemical, biological, and nuclear), target selection, the nature of participating forces, and geographic areas. Restrictions rarely are
imposed by formal agreements. They usually result from "understandings." The room

40

for interpreting "rules of the game" thus is fairly large, but since the dawn of the Nuclear Age strategists on both sides of the Iron and Bamboo Curtains have striven to reconcile incompatible international objectives without creating conditions that cause the unlucky living to envy the insensible dead.

Limited Objectives

Limited war commonly is linked with limited objectives, but that need not be the case. Restraints most often relate primarily to means, not ends. The crucial U.S. national security objective in Korea, which was to contain communism, never was compromised, even though the subsidiary goal of reunifying Korea had to be abandoned. When the Kremlin refused to reinforce its Arab clients during the Six Day War with Israel in 1967, it accepted a humiliating setback, but that temporary adjustment of immediate aims in no way suggested that Soviet long-range objectives in the Middle East had been scaled down.

Choosing goals calls for caution if the foe possesses mass-destruction weapons. The trick is to avoid directly endangering, or appearing to endanger, the enemy's vital or compelling interests. With those criteria in mind, it is easy to understand why so many modern chiefs of state persist in playing platoon leader, although there is by no means any universal agreement that the advantages of such action outweigh the liabilities. Robert McClintock addressed that matter in *The Meaning of Limited War:*

> In the pax ballistica there has emerged a new dimension of risk — of what one authority has called the danger of "irreversibly becoming irremediable"; and thus we find an extraordinary new limitation on limited war — that the President himself or the Chairman of the Soviet [Presidium] may make the smallest tactical decisions. The process commenced with President Truman in Korea and continued with the "eyeball-to-eyeball" confrontation of Kennedy and Khrushchev over Cuba, to the personal interventions of President Johnson as Task Force Commander in the Gulf of Tonkin and at the American landing in Santo Domingo. Where in past wars the military commander was given military objectives to achieve and told to go on with the task, in present limited war the military objectives must be so carefully evaluated by the Chief of Government to prevent escalation into general war, and the political objective must be kept so clearly in mind, that the military commander is now an executive agent at one or two removes from the real source of decision and power.[2]

Arms Limitations

The role of nuclear weapons in limited war has always been controversial. Nearly everyone agrees that strategic nuclear bombardment of an enemy's homeland, particularly population centers, must be avoided, but there is no consensus concerning other uses.

One sizeable group, for example, predicts that the first blast, regardless of yield, would *automatically* lead to Armageddon. The Soviets implicitly espoused that view at one time, according to the 1962 edition of Marshal Sokolovsky's book *Military Strategy,* although they since have changed their minds.[3]

41

A second faction rejects the idea of limited nuclear war, but for different reasons. In the opinion of its advocates, any use of nuclear weapons would encourage escalation. This time Thornton Read speaks:

> It is hardly consistent to argue that nuclear weapons will inevitably be introduced because they are more efficient than conventional weapons and then assume that, once nuclear combat begins, both sides will be content to employ only the least efficient nuclear weapons. Nor is it convincing to argue that nuclear war will be limited merely because neither side wants the disaster of all-out war. The most appalling disaster can occur if there is a step-by-step mechanism that leads to it with strong pressures at each stage to take the next small step.[4]

A third school of thought endorses Alain Enthoven's "Firebreak Theory," which holds that "because nuclear war is so destructive, the use of nuclear weapons must be reserved only for the most desperate circumstances. . . . The side with strong conventional forces is likely to be able to have its way on all issues less than vital."[5]

Despite its widespread appeal, Enthoven's intriguing notion has detractors, including some in the U.S.S.R. Skeptics, typified by Bernard Brodie, note that the Soviets' reluctance to subscribe has

> worked markedly to the advantage of the United States. It would otherwise be difficult to explain why the Russians yielded so quickly and completely in the Cuban crisis of October 1962. They obviously feared to let a situation develop where one of our destroyers might so much as fire a shot over the bows of one of their transport ships. They clearly wanted no fighting at all, apparently because they felt that any fighting was extremely dangerous. . . .
>
> It would similarly be hard to understand why the development of the Cuban crisis resulted in an immediate amelioration in the tension over Berlin. . . . Clearly the Russians enjoyed local conventional superiority in and around the Berlin area, but they seemed not at all ready to test their local ascendancy on that basis. Raymond Aron, the distinguished French writer on political affairs, has several times pointed out that the United States and the Soviet Union each seems to favor strategic ideas more appropriate to the forces of the other, and that it is a great advantage to the West that the Russians seem unready to accept those special strategic ideas that are so popular in the United States [see, for example, Aron's The Great Debate, pp. 152–4].[6]

At the opposite end of the spectrum from the total abstainers is a band of "hawks," who believe that nuclear weapons could and should be brandished in the conduct of limited wars. General Nathan F. Twining, during his tenure as Chairman of the Joint Chiefs of Staff, was an avid spokesman for that group:

> I inevitably came to the conclusion that the use of tactical nuclear weapons in certain limited war situations and employed selectively and with discretion could truly be in the overall best interests of humanity and civilization. These weapons, if employed, once or twice on the right targets, at the right time, would, in my judgment, stop current aggression, and stop future . . . limited wars before they start.[7]

The efficacy of any given option probably would depend largely on the contestants' states of mind. If the United States and the Soviet Union both steadfastly *believed* that detonating one low-yield nuclear warhead would inevitably trigger a general war, then no doubt it would. If world leaders *really* classified the first blast since 1945 as a symbolic event, then its significance would far exceed the radius of damage and casualties. Otherwise, it would not.

One thing, however, seems certain. If the genie were unleashed, whether casually to shore up a single shaky position or after grave consideration to secure otherwise unattainable ends, the problems of controlling nuclear weapons in limited war would increase severalfold. A whole new set of ground rules would have to supplant total abstinence. Should nuclear weapons be used offensively, defensively, or both? Should there be some restriction on yields and delivery means? Should surface bursts be outlawed? How could any of these restrictions be effectively policed? Agreements would be difficult to obtain and more difficult still to keep.

Chemical and biological warfare create similar problems for strategists who wrestle with concepts for limited war.

Target Limitations

Target selection, as well as choices of ordnance, can be an important factor in limiting the scope and intensity of war. Assorted alternatives are evident, including the following couplets, in endless combination:

Vital — Nonvital
Tactical — Strategic
Animate — Inanimate
Military — Civilian
Combatant — Noncombatant
Mobile — Stationary
Immediate Effect — Delayed Effect

The Vietnam War affords splendid examples.

The United States' air-interdiction operations over North Vietnam were shackled from the very beginning, as Major General Gilbert L. Meyers, former Deputy Commander of the Seventh Air Force, testified before Congress:

> When I arrived on the Vietnam scene in April of 1965, we were receiving our [fixed] targets from CINCPAC one or two a week, on a weekly scheduled basis. . . . These targets at that stage were located in the Panhandle just north of the DMZ. . . . [They] gradually went north over the period of time that I was there, and finally, of course, we were receiving targets in the Hanoi area.[8]

Previous witnesses had noted that armed reconnaissance missions predominated in 1966, against targets of opportunity such as trucks, trains, troops, and waterborne transport. Fewer than one percent of all sorties flown during that year were directed against the JCS list of ninety-seven high-priority, fixed targets — ports, bridges, ferries, rail yards, and other important facilities.[9] Hanoi, together with a buffer zone along the Chicom border (including much of the northeast rail line), dikes, and selected airfields in the Red River Delta, were placed off-limits. Surface-to-air missile (SAM) sites could be struck only after the presence of missiles had been confirmed. Most frustrating of all to U.S. military men was the proscription against attacks on Haiphong Harbor. Failure to close that port placed our air power in the impossible position of "mopping up water on the ground floor, instead of turning off the tap upstairs." All that in the name of limited war, to avoid situations that could result in a direct confrontation between the United States and Red China or the U.S.S.R.

Tactical nuclear weapons probably could have been employed effectively in Indochina, despite widespread beliefs that there were no appropriate targets. In fact, attractive aiming points existed in many isolated locales, miles from population centers. Nuclear detonations might have been used to seal off mountain passes on the Ho Chi Minh Trail, to destroy underground installations in or near the Demilitarized Zone, or to eliminate subterranean Viet Cong base areas. Political, not military, prohibitions prevailed, in an effort to limit the war.

Force Limitations

Limiting the type, number, roles, and origins of participating military forces also can circumscribe the scale and severity of war. Defensive, support, and advisory troops are less provocative than front-line combat units. Confrontations between proxies are apt to be less incendiary than direct clashes between superpowers. Forces from world organizations are less subject to condemnation than those from separate states. The application of conventional air or naval power normally is less risky than are ground invasions.

Three recent conflicts help illustrate those points.

More than twenty Free World nations participated with the United States in Korea under the U.N. banner. Their presence blurred the edges of what actually developed into a struggle between this country and Red China. The Chinese, in turn, clung steadfastly to the fiction that their troops south of the Yalu were exclusively "volunteers." The U.S.S.R., for all practical purposes, furnished no regular forces of any kind, but funneled supplies and technical assistance to its communist cohorts, while exerting a dominant politico-military influence behind the scenes.

Twenty years later, the Indochina War produced analogous situations. Neither Ho Chi Minh nor his successors ever admitted that *any* of their forces infiltrated south of the 17th parallel, much less in multidivision strength. For several years, the United States limited its participation to logistic support and advisors. With one exception — the shallow incursion into Cambodia in 1970, which was rigidly restricted in time — U.S. ground combat troops were never committed outside South Vietnam. By 1972, all Army and Marine maneuver units had been withdrawn from the theater, leaving air and naval power as the only U.S. military means of influencing future actions.

The Soviet Union, as well as the United States, has labored to limit wars. Brezhnev has been very circumspect in backing his U.A.R. partner in the Arab-Israeli dispute. Soviet training teams, service troops, surface-to-air missile crews, and interceptor pilots, all noncombatant or defensive in nature, once flooded the Nile Delta to help protect Russia's massive investment in military aid, but offensive forces in Egypt have always been exclusively Arab.

Geographic Limitations

Geographic restrictions have been stringent in every limited war. The Korean conflict was confined to a small peninsula. Military maneuvering during the Cuban missile crisis (other than general war alerts in the United States and the U.S.S.R.) centered on the Caribbean. Military aspects of the Vietnam War were regional. The U.S. Navy's concepts for "war at sea," far from populated places, are specialized geographic limitations.

Areal prohibitions might be more difficult to honor in Western Europe, as Robert E. Osgood indicates in his book *Limited War:*

> We must recognize that in some highly industrialized and economically integrated areas — certainly the core of the NATO area — even limited military incursions would constitute such a serious threat to our security interests (and would be so difficult to check on a purely local basis) that we could not afford to confine our resistance to the immediate combat area. This might even be true if the topography, the industrial and transport linkages, and other physical features made restriction theoretically feasible.[10]

The concept of sanctuaries in limited war, born during the Korean embranglement and reinforced in Indochina, received a sharp setback when President Nixon elected to clean out communist safehavens in North Vietnam, Laos, and Cambodia. A rule of thumb might be that sanctuaries from which serious threats derive can survive only if the probable penalties for disturbing them surpass the potential benefits.

ESCALATION PROBLEMS

The conduct of limited war, which involves restrictions such as those outlined above, is an exercise in risk-taking, resolve, and the matching of local resources. Usually, either side could "win" by increasing the pressure in some way, provided the opposition declined to raise the ante. Herman Kahn's views follow:

> There are at least three ways in which a would-be escalator can increase, or threaten to increase, his efforts: by increasing intensity, widening the area, or compounding escalation. . . . [The last] could consist of an attack on an ally or client of the principal opponent — though it could also be an attack on troops or colonies of the principal, but geographically outside the central sanctuary [homeland]. . . .

> Thus, in any escalation, two sets of basic elements are in constant interplay: the political, diplomatic, and military issues surrounding the particular conflict, and the level of violence and provocation at which it is fought. . . . There are [also] two basic classes of strategies that each side can use. One class of strategies makes use of features of the particular "agreed battle" that is being waged in order to gain an advantage. The other class uses the risks or threat of escalation and eruption from this agreed battle. . . .

> Escalations are thus relatively complex phenomena. They are not to be ordered in a simple fashion, yet for some purposes we wish to do exactly this, even if it does some violence to reality. Very roughly, at any particular instant in a crisis or war, the degree of escalation might be measured by such things as:

1. Apparent closeness to all-out war
2. Likelihood of eruption
3. Provocation
4. Precedents broken
5. Committal (resolve and/or recklessness) demonstrated
6. Damage done or being done
7. Effort (scale, scope, or intensity of violence)
8. Threat intended or perceived.[11]

A CAUTION FOR STRATEGISTS

Paradoxically, limitations adopted to avoid general war may actually increase risks if they destroy too many strategic options. Dr. Kissinger delineated that danger a decade ago in *The Necessity for Choice:*

> Since limited war by definition does not involve *all* the resources of the opponents, it is easy to "prove" how a war *could* expand. No one can know whether either side would accept defeat. But we must be clear about what is involved in pressing the argument about escalation too far. A country prepared to risk mutual destruction rather than forego the possibility of gaining its objectives can be deterred only by surrender. . . . An aggressor convinced that its intended victim is unwilling to run *any* risk may be positively encouraged to resort to the direst threat. A country not willing to risk limited war because it fears that resistance to aggression on *any* scale may lead to all-out war will have no choice in a showdown but to surrender.

> The purpose of a strategy of limited war, then, is first to strengthen deterrence and, second, if deterrence should fail, to provide an opportunity for settlement. . . . The *worst* that could happen if we resisted aggression by means of limited war is what is *certain* to happen if we [capitulate or participate in a general war].[12]

7 The Nature of Revolutionary War

All mass movements generate in their adherents
a readiness to die and a proclivity for united
action; all of them, irrespective of the doctrine
they preach and the program they project, breed
fanaticism, enthusiasm, fervent hope, hatred and
intolerance; all of them are capable of releasing
a powerful flow of activity in certain departments
of life; all of them demand blind faith and
singlehearted allegiance.

ERIC HOFER
The True Believer

Revolutionary war occupies a separate and distinct niche in the conflict spectrum. The term connotes conscious efforts to seize political power by illegitimate and coercive means, destroying existing systems of government and social structures in the process. From the standpoint of their perpetrators, revolutions are "total war." Any and all means are justified to attain desired ends without, as Mao Tse-tung said, regard for "stupid scruples about benevolence, righteousness, and morality."

REVOLUTIONARY WARS DIFFERENTIATED

Revolutionary wars assume assorted shapes. In his book *Revolution and the Social System,* Chalmers Johnson identified several separate categories, distinguished from each other on the basis of origins, sponsors, goals, and targets.[1] However, most variations are merely matters of academic interest to strategists, because they are over and done with almost instantaneously or enjoy such popular support at the onset that effective counteraction is impossible. Conspiratorial coups, for example, may entail prolonged preparations by elitist cliques, but their implementation is precipitate and never involves many people. The Russian Revolution of 1917 was an explosive upheaval, sudden, brief, and unplanned. The masses moved spontaneously while Lenin was in Switzerland.

47

This treatise deals exclusively with the brand of revolution which is variously called "mass military insurrection" or "insurgency." Revolutionary wars of that sort are nationalistic in nature. They are protracted struggles that demand great patience. If unabated, they move methodically, step-by-step, through intermediate objectives until they culminate in calamity for the existing order. Nothing is left to chance. Leadership emerges first, then manipulates the masses.

PRINCIPAL THEORISTS

Modern revolutionary war is commonly, though by no means always, communist-inspired and -led. It is typified by the so-called "wars of national liberation" and "people's wars" that have flourished in the emerging nations of Africa and Asia for the past twenty-five to thirty years. A wide variety of visionaries have contributed doctrine, but as Sir Robert Thompson notes:

> putting aside for the moment the extent of communist involvement in any particular revolutionary war, it is . . . to avowed communists that we must look for the main characteristics of this new form of war: to Marx for the original concept of struggle, to Lenin for the party organisation, to Mao Tse-Tung for its application to a peasant society, to his heir-apparent Marshal Lin Piao for its application to world revolution, to Truong Chinh and General Vo Nguyen Giap for the refinement of its techniques in Vietnam and to Ché Guevara for its spiritual appeal to the intellectual youth of the west. These were its inventors, its exponents, its prophets and its chief practitioners.[2]

REVOLUTIONARY AND CONVENTIONAL WARS COMPARED

Revolutionary and conventional wars differ in several respects. David Galula, who exhibited rare insight in the field of insurgency, highlighted the gross asymmetry that characterizes opposing camps at the onset of revolutions:

> An appraisal of the contending forces at the start of a revolutionary war shows an overwhelming superiority in tangible assets in favor of the counterinsurgent. Endowed with the normal foreign and domestic perquisites of an established government, he has virtually everything — diplomatic recognition; legitimate power in the executive, legislative, and judicial branches; control of the administration and police; financial resources; industrial and agricultural resources at home or ready access to them abroad; transport and communications facilities; use and control of the information and propaganda media; command of the armed forces and the possibility of increasing their size. He is *in* while the insurgent, being *out,* has none or few of these assets.
>
> The situation is reversed in the field of intangibles. The insurgent has a formidable asset — the ideological power of a cause on which to base his action. The counterinsurgent has a heavy liability — he is responsible for maintaining order throughout the country. The insurgent's strategy will naturally aim at converting his intangible assets into concrete ones, the counterinsurgent's strategy at preventing his intangible liability from dissipating his concrete assets.

The insurgent thus has to grow in the course of the war from small to large, from weakness to strength, or else he fails. The counterinsurgent will decline from large to small, from strength to weakness, in direct relation to the insurgent's success.

The peculiarities that mark the revolutionary war as so different from the conventional one derive from this initial asymmetry.[3]

Whereas conventional conflicts normally erupt abruptly because the instigator wants to capitalize on surprise, the transition from peace to war in insurgencies is almost imperceptible. Revolutionaries project very little political or military power during the early stages, and thus must inch their way onto the scene.

Conventional wars are comparatively stylized and rigid. In revolutionary war, there are no front lines or rear areas. Spectacular, conclusive campaigns are rare.

Perhaps most important of all, revolutionary wars, as opposed to their conventional counterparts, are primarily political and social processes, rather than military operations. Unfortunately, dramatic, newsworthy ambushes and actions at barricades get most of the publicity, while unobtrusive but climacteric inner workings go unnoticed.

In conventional wars, the antagonists are separate and distinct. In revolutionary wars, insurgents and the incumbent government both seek to create and preserve power by controlling the same population. Society at large, therefore, is the medium in which a revolution operates and, at the same time, control over society is the objective. Everything else, however flamboyant, is secondary and supporting. Force is simply one tool in the total kit.

Revolutionary wars of this ilk are protracted by their very nature. Conventional wars are not, although prolonged stalemates are common. Insurgents are prepared to accept the penalty of time, because the strength ultimately generated by their strategy can be crushing.[4]

THE PREREQUISITES FOR REVOLUTION

The Environment

Revolutions originate and prosper under so many different conditions involving man's dissatisfaction with his lot that it is difficult to generalize. Some are predominantly urban, others are rural. Some are "bad," as seen from the U.S. standpoint. Others can be "good." Most often they occur in underdeveloped countries, but they also crop up in some very sophisticated environments.

The conditions that spawn insurgency are remarkably similar. Revolution rarely rears its head in the midst of abject poverty and despair. Zealots most often surface in societies where rising expectations breed impatience. Intolerable frictions are commonly compounded by communications gaps, between parties in power and the people; rich and poor; young and old; peasants and proletariat; ethnic groups and religious factions. The resultant antagonisms can be deftly exploited by demagogues. The breakdown of tradition, which almost inevitably occurs in modern societies, frequently is a factor. Influential intellectuals who shift their allegiance to revolutionary ideals contribute inadvertently or deliberately. If such circumstances combine with flagrant economic or social injustices, real or imagined, the situation is ripe for revolution.

The Cause

The second prerequisite for any revolution is an emotional cause, one worth dying for. It must have broad appeal and be vague enough so that each man can supply his own interpretation. There is no need for it to be realistic or attainable. Abstract themes like freedom, human rights, colonial oppression, equal opportunity, and self-determination, are causes that fire men's imaginations. The strongest appeals since World War II have been patriotic and nationalistic.

Organization

Dreams without direction, of course, are useless. The cause, whatever it is, must be promoted by clever leaders who are skilled in mobilizing and manipulating people, and can focus the endemic energies of the mass to generate power. The initial objective is to establish a system of "dual power," wherein a subversive shadow government vies with duly constituted authority for control. Its operatives concurrently undermine the incumbent regime and root out internal opposition within the revolutionary body. The key is sound organization. Sir Robert Thompson, an authority on this subject and sometime advisor to President Nixon, rates infrastructure as "quite the most vital feature of revolutionary war":

> [The infrastructure] is established in two parts. The first, and by far the most important, is the political underground organisation within the population in which cells are created, by a process described as "bead stringing," throughout the country in all villages and towns. . . . The main function of the underground organisation as a whole is to provide a support base for the second part . . . the military guerrilla units. No army can be raised and maintained unless it has a home base on which it can rely for its supplies and recruits. . . .
>
> It is essential at this point to understand the relationship between the organisation [and] the cause. . . . [As the war progresses] the original cause will become less and less relevant because the immediate concern of most people will be survival for themselves and their families and there will be an inclination to support the side which looks like winning. It is at this point that the [revolutionary] party, as one means of hastening the collapse of government and the existing structure, will be better able to exploit all the contradictions which exist within any society. . . .
>
> In studying any revolutionary war, therefore . . . it is necessary to assess whether its organisation or its ostensible cause (often no more than a pretext) is the vital factor because this will dictate the emphasis of the response. If the organisation is the vital factor, then the revolutionary movement will not be defeated by reforms designed to eliminate the cause. It will only be defeated by establishing a superior organisation and applying measures designed to break the revolutionary organization. . . .
>
> Generally it can be said that, where both the cause and the organisation are good, the revolutionary movement will win, probably at an early stage. The long-drawn out struggle occurs when the organisation is good and the cause is weak.[5]

An ailing body politic with low resistance to infection usually presages a successful insurgency. Regimes that lack national consensus, that are irresolute and indecisive, that are ignorant of counterrevolutionary strategy and tactics, and lack the machinery for effective control — political, administrative, or military — are asking to be replaced.

PHASES OF REVOLUTIONARY WAR

The classic three-phase strategy for revolutionary war, expounded by Mao in 1938 during China's war with Japan, outlines a practical framework that has been adopted by most insurgent groups around the world, modified to suit their particular circumstances.[6]

Phase I (Organization, Consolidation and Preservation)*

Phase I is devoted to organizing, consolidating, and preserving the incipient insurgent mechanism. It lays the political and psychological groundwork for expansion to be achieved later.

The first steps are to investigate social class structure, identify grievances, and compile the intelligence base needed to formulate campaign plans and supporting propaganda objectives/themes aimed at enlisting enthusiastic, voluntary support. Dedicated revolutionary cadres must be recruited and trained and an apparatus must be developed.

Skilled revolutionaries capitalize on a prominent quirk in human nature: man is a social animal, conformist rather than individualistic. He clings to small primary groups, like the family, friends, classmates, and business associates, which set and support standards, sustain their members in time of stress, and approve or disapprove performance. The clusters may be as rigidly regimented as a rifle squad or as loosely structured as a car pool. Controlling these primary groups inevitably is a high-priority project. Those that resist are destroyed. New cliques are created where no effective ones exist, all presumably representing the people's will. The task is monumental, since it entails realigning entire societies, but the end product is well worth the effort. Using techniques just described, revolutionaries can infiltrate the policy machinery of mass organizations — the news media, unions, schools, cooperatives, associations, armed forces, police, and the government itself. No activity or institution is too ostentatious or too obscure if it grants close contact with the people.

Success results in near monopoly of access to the rank and file. This is particularly true in developing countries where rudimentary road, rail, and telecommunications nets inhibit correspondence between the central government and the provinces, and where ruling elites frequently lack psychological rapport with either urban workers or peasants.

Finally, the overt struggle commences, including sporadic low-intensity military

---

* Titles of revolutionary war phases vary. Those used in this text are most descriptive. Another popular version is: Phase I. Strategic Defense: Phase II. Preparation for Offense; Phase III. Strategic Offense.

operations. Revolution flourishes in an atmosphere of social and administrative disorder that seriously disrupts the daily lives of the population. Strikes, riots, sabotage, black markets, insidious rumor campaigns, and agitation among minorities are typical of the discord fomented by subversive parties. Such activities are cheap to produce and costly to prevent. Governmental expenditures in money, manpower, and materiel may exceed those of the insurgents by 20 : 1 or more. If these tactics proceed unchecked, social disruption eventually becomes so severe that the revolutionists' political program is the only perceived alternative to chaos. The entire arrangement is completely flexible. Incentives are applied along with coercion. Operations habitually are recycled, even in areas solidly under revolutionary control.

Phase II (Progressive Expansion)

Phase II involves progressive expansion with two basic motives in mind: to solidify mass support and bring pressure to bear on the enemy. This is a period of terror, sabotage, and active guerrilla war. The insurgents begin to depend heavily on raids and ambushes as primary sources of arms, ammunition, medical supplies, and radios. They seek food, clothing, shelter, information, and security from the civilian populace. Home guard or militia units are formed to handle local security and to act as reserves.

Favorable terrain, which can cover revolutionaries and inhibit the opposition, is crucial during Phase II. Jungles, swamps, mountains, and urban areas seem to be best suited for guerrilla operations. Open country with few places to hide is a distinct disadvantage.

Geographic contiguity with a friendly foreign power becomes increasingly important during this second stage, when the growing revolutionary movement displays an avid appetite for the accoutrements of armed combat. Outside military and economic aid often plays a critical role, as it does today in Palestine and Southeast Asia; it occasionally is decisive. Isolated insurgents frequently run into trouble, as demonstrated during the past two decades in Angola, the Philippines, and Malaya. However, that need not be the case. Cuba is a striking exception. Moral support, including diplomatic gestures, may prove even more effective than logistical contributions by outsiders. In addition, sponsors sometimes furnish leaders, organizers, cadremen, advisors, funds, and training facilities.

As the insurgent movement gains momentum and major elements break cover, survival and success hinge heavily on a steady stream of timely, accurate intelligence concerning the government's capabilities, intentions, activities, and plans. The positive intelligence apparatus must be complemented by an effective counterintelligence screen. Failure to satisfy either requirement during Phase II can be disastrous.

Stepped-up propaganda campaigns, directed primarily at the local populace *and* revolutionary forces, solicit support and security from the community. Written and oral attacks degrade the government, discourage the people from tendering it comfort of any kind, and suggest that the rebels eventually will prevail, regardless of temporary setbacks or sacrifice. Scare tactics supplement suasion on demand — threats, intimidation, coercion, mental and emotional stress all help to create converts when logic and inducements fail. Revolutionary propaganda holds a heavy advantage, since the rebels are judged by *promises,* not what they produce. Incumbents, who are tied to responsibilities, must run on their records.

Phase III (Decision)

During Phase III, insurgents step up the scale of armed combat to defeat the enemy with orthodox forces on the field of battle. Vigorous negotiations may be featured at this time to buttress political, military, economic, or social positions, to wear down and frustrate opponents, and to influence world public opinion. Concessions are rare, and are made only to further the insurgents' strategic design. Phase III confrontations almost never revert to strictly conventional war. Even during the culminating stages, territory is of little moment to the revolutionaries. Their main interest is in *people.*

No hard-and-fast rules fix the over-all sequence. It is characteristic for different phases to be in progress concurrently in different parts of an afflicted country. Phase III conceivably could stem directly from Phase I if the strategic climate were conducive. When revolutionaries run into unexpectedly effective resistance, they can always face reality and retrench, retrograding from Phase III to Phase II, or even Phase I, if the situation dictates, with the expectation of rejuvenation later.

THE STRATEGIC CHALLENGE

However it is conducted, revolutionary war poses some very sticky problems for established regimes. The first, and by far the most important, requirement is to *prevent* revolutions from flowering. That task can best be accomplished by attacking insurgent causes at the grass roots level *before* revolutionary signs appear. A substantial body of serious scholars maintains that insurgencies cannot be deterred effectively after they start — the rebels know their initial position is weak, but take heart from future possibilities, and are determined to pursue their course. Consequently, counterthreats are seldom credible.

Concepts for coping with active insurgencies are outlined in Chapter 19. The challenge is considerable. Revolutions lack the potential to literally atomize this planet, as a general nuclear war could do, but a coordinated communist strategy of cumulative encroachment using insurgent techniques nevertheless could endanger the entire Free World just as surely and just as effectively.

8   The Nature of Cold War

In times of war, talking is action.

ADOLF HITLER
Mein Kampf

COLD WAR DEFINED

Cold war is an active state of international tension at the lower end of the conflict spectrum, wherein political, economic, technological, sociological, psychological, paramilitary, and military measures short of sustained, armed combat are orchestrated to attain national objectives. Finesse and fraud replace brute force. Pressures range from decorous diplomacy during times of temporary detente to donnybrooks with no holds barred, save shooting wars. Nevertheless, most cold-war machinations have one thing in common: they epitomize the indirect approach.

Man's efforts to gain his ends through threat or persuasion predate Sun Tzu. Machiavelli laid many of the ground rules nearly half a millenium ago. Hitler transposed theory into practice with great verve in the 1930s. The Soviets under Stalin pirated Nazi techniques and began to perfect them in the years after World War II. For the past two decades, communist scholars in particular have taken some of the guesswork out of a process which until quite recently was generally a fortuitous admixture of wisdom, instinct, and luck. As the subject is explored and new methods emerge, the game is bound to get still tougher. It therefore behooves straightforward Free World strategists, who on the whole score poor marks, to concentrate on the capabilities, limitations, and applications of circuitous cold-war pursuits, so they can better learn to cope.

In the interest of brevity, the following discourse skirts underground activities, such as subversion, blackmail, sabotage, and espionage, which are touched on in other chapters, and homes in on legitimate practices that — while they sometimes have unsavory overtones — are largely within the law.

COLD-WAR OBJECTIVES

Robert Byfield, in his pamphlet *The Fifth Weapon,* identified two basic Soviet cold-war objectives which for our purposes can be generalized since, appropriately modified, they could be applied by other parties, including ourselves.

54

The first of these, which he calls "amputation," seeks to enfeeble the foe on a global basis. Six subordinate goals, not necessarily in priority, are to:

1. Separate the enemy from raw materials abroad.
2. Destroy the opponent's foreign markets for manufactured goods.
3. Diminish or eliminate the opposition's overseas assets through nationalization, socialization, confiscatory taxation, burdensome regulations, and so on.
4. Stop the flow of enemy capital abroad.
5. Disaffect the enemy's friends and allies.
6. Induce the opponent to weaken himself financially by scattering random largesse without relating the Law of Diminishing Returns to power politics and psychology.

The second basic objective is "self-paralysis." It strives to create disintegrating domestic problems in the enemy homeland. Steps which add to the national debt, depreciate currency, hobble industry, induce high taxes, shake confidence in national institutions, inhibit innovation, and create internal conflicts fit in this category. The desired effect is confusion, lethargy, and fear in the enemy camp.[1]

Readers no doubt could add a dozen items to each list, but these broad objectives are good enough for starters.

COLD-WAR TECHNIQUES

Multiple methods can be applied to attain cold-war ends. Nine alternatives, identified by catchy code words, have been used politically, economically, socially, and psychologically in endless combinations. Most are adaptable to hot war and cold war alike.

Salami   Such tactics seek success slice-by-slice, each sliver small enough to avoid arousing grievous animosities.

Trojan Horse   The classic "Fifth Column" corrupts from within. Infiltration, permeation, and actions to control politico-economic operations are high on the agenda. Paramilitary putsches often provide the climax.

Talkaton   Obstructionism, procrastination, the legal monkey wrench, Roberts Rules of Order as a weapon system, endless propensity for debate and disruption at conferences combine to wreck international discussions, law-making, and parliamentary institutions.

Zig-Zag   Alternation between tension and relaxation, which raises hopes and then dashes them, creates alarm, frustration, and despondency in the opposition. Sharp, unexpected switches in the party line can exert similar pressures.

Quicksand   This approach accentuates "the big lie." It is calculated to exhaust the victim, who must consume exorbitant energies struggling with and trying to refute damaging allegations.

Halo and Horns   Perpetrators of this technique paint themselves as saints, the opposition as sinners. "We are progressive, they are reactionary" is a popular theme.

55

Baited Hook Unjustified self-praise can be used to delude the gullible, causing them to promote programs that they might otherwise fear. The Soviet Constitution, which erroneously promises its adherents freedom of speech, press, worship, and assembly is a Baited Hook hoax.

Wedge This ploy creates or aggravates "class conflicts" between rich and poor, blacks and whites, consumers and producers, labor and management, town and country, "hawks" and "doves," and so on. Such techniques work equally well against international alliances.

Logocide Political power can be enhanced insidiously by manipulating meanings, language, and symbols. Logocide strives to control opponents' minds by replacing disagreeable images with dulcet ones, or vice versa, even though the substance remains the same.[2]

PSYCHOLOGICAL WARFARE

The most versatile tool for carrying out cold-war aims is psychological warfare (psywar), which can be applied in a bewildering variety of ways.

In essence, psywar is the planned use of propaganda, supplemented by other means as required, to influence the opinions, emotions, attitudes, and behavior of amicable, hostile, or neutral audiences in support of stated objectives. That simple definition, however, means different things to different people, as Paul Linebarger pointed out in philosophizing about World War II:

> In the American use of the term, psychological warfare was the supplementing of normal military operations by the use of mass communications; in the Nazi sense of the term, it was the calculation and execution of both political and military strategy on studied psychological grounds. For the American uses, it was modification of traditional warfare by the effective, generous use of a new weapon; for the Germans it involved a transformation of the process of war itself. This is an important enough distinction to warrant separate consideration.[3]

Propaganda Categorized

Propaganda, the principal component of psywar, comprises any communication deliberately calculated to form, control, or alter mass viewpoints to the advantage, direct or indirect, of the sponsor. Cold-war propaganda generally is designed for home consumption; for enemy or potential enemy consumption, including domestic dissidents; and for consumption by neutrals or waverers.

Strategic propaganda can be promulgated in three ways, each of which displays salient advantages and disadvantages.

White Propaganda

White propaganda, emanating from official, acknowledged sources, is ideal for airing government policies, plans, intentions, activities, and other matters of interest, but must be used with caution. Truth is indispensable, even if it hurts; otherwise credibility soon suffers. Effectiveness is substantially reduced if the target audience is hostile or unfavorably biased against the source. And since anyone can monitor, statements that soothe one segment of the population might well irritate another.

Gray Propaganda

Gray propaganda solves some of those difficulties because its source is concealed. Sensational themes that otherwise would be impolitic at home, among allies, or in neutral nations are admissable when the originator is masked. Gray propaganda also is ideal for floating trial balloons. Unfortunately, it is difficult to cover the source while keeping it authoritative, since third-party assistance often is essential.

Black Propaganda

Black propaganda deliberately misrepresents the source. There is no obligation to be reputable. Contradictions can be cranked in where none exist. Countermeasures are generally ineffective as long as the source stays clandestine. The black mode is particularly appropriate when the originator must operate in hostile or neutral territories, but as might be expected, there are serious drawbacks. Preparations demand long lead times and extreme care to avoid compromise. Further, black propaganda is difficult to control. Its executing agencies must be decentralized, and once they are discovered the themes they dispense can be easily discredited. Most important of all, the application of black propaganda by members of open societies is strictly limited.[4]

Propaganda can be categorized in several other ways. It may be direct or indirect, offensive or defensive, slanted to convert, consolidate, or divide. The purpose of direct propaganda is obvious — "cleave to communism and condemn capitalism" is a common example. The intent of indirect propaganda, including subliminal variations, is secret. Other variations are self-explanatory.

The means by which propaganda is disseminated may be as stylized as stage shows or as shapeless as rumors. Communications that capitalize on mass media (radio, television, newspapers, periodicals, and the like) reach huge audiences more or less instantaneously, but word-of-mouth transmission can be equally devastating under given circumstances. Symbolic acts frequently play specialized roles — the fruitless U.S. raid to retrieve prisoners of war from Son Tay stockade, outside Hanoi, in December 1970 was an operational disappointment, but its psychological message to the North Vietnamese was dramatic: their heartland was vulnerable to invasion.

Psywar Tactics

Holt and van de Velde frame the tactics of psychological warfare in two dichotomies. The first of these they designate "deception-enlightenment," which

> are best explained in relationship to the distinction between the material and apparent worlds. Tactics of deception attempt to make the audience build up a psychological environment which differs from the material environment. In the terms of perceptual psychology, tactics of deception try to provoke non-veridical percepts, and tactics of enlightenment are attempts to bring a skewed perception in line with reality.[4]

Three criteria normally must be satisfied: deceptive propaganda must be reasonable;

it must be disguised so that the duped find it difficult to ascertain the true facts; and it must not discredit a potentially valuable future source. The list of rhetorical booby-traps used to implement the logocide technique is repeated here as one illustration of the gamut that themes can run:

False Label
This form of misrepresentation distorts the meaning of words. In communist jargon, for example, the term *people's democracy* is substituted for *totalitarianism.*

Dwarf and Giant
Juggling the significance of facts and figures through contrived comparisons can confuse highly sophisticated audiences. (Average men seem small standing next to giants, but they tower over dwarves.)

Siamese Twins
Dissimilar subjects can be made to appear identical through association, as "imperialism" and "capitalism" are equated by communists.

Bandwagon
Charlatans can capitalize on the human proclivity for jumping on bandwagons by falsely insinuating that "everyone is doing it."

Albatross
Hanging a dirty adjective around the neck of an innocent noun is a handy way to discredit persons, thoughts, or actions. "Dirty dollars" and "puppet politicians" are typical appositions.

Lone Tree
Emphasizing a single subject in the statistical forest can create factual aberrations. Half-truths and quotations out of context are particularly popular.

Court Room
Smear tactics can be successfully employed, even by guilty parties who tar the judge, jury, and judicial system while demanding a change of venue.

Time Machine
Scrambling the sequence of past events can confuse cause and effect. Clever propagandists sometimes also suggest that grievances long since corrected are still prevalent.

ABC
Oversimplified solutions to complex problems lend themselves well to slogans. "Ban the bomb," "power to the people," and "get out of Vietnam" are characteristically corrosive.[5]

The other half of the deception-enlightenment dichotomy is usually referred to as "the strategy of truth." Its potency "derives from the fact that dire consequences may result for an individual if his world of meaning differs very greatly from the material world," which increasingly has been so since the technological revolution began. Using truth to enlighten entails "a thorough analysis of how the listener, given his beliefs and attitudes and his situation, will interpret the truth and translate it into action . . . [since] the behavioral consequences of broadcasting the truth in certain situations would be exactly opposite to those that may seem logical, if not inevitable."[6]

The second dichotomy in psychological warfare tactics was labeled "terror-reassurance" by Holt and van de Velde. They observed that sheer terror is a prime component of most deterrent strategies. The policy of massive retaliation adopted by peace-loving President Eisenhower, for example, was heavily predicated on Soviet fears. Reassurance, by contrast, lulls suspicions.[7]

Psywar Limitations

Psywar operations in the Free World confront restrictions that are unknown to totalitarian states, whose standards are somewhat different:

> Let him who will advocate American use of the war of nerves! He will not get far with commentators publishing his TOP SECRET schedule of timing, with legislators very properly catechizing him on international morality, with members of his own organization publishing their memoirs or airing their squabbles right in the middle of the operation. He would end up by amusing the enemy whom he started out to scare. Psychological warfare has its place in our military and political system, but its place is a modest one. . . .[8]

The United States in particular, as ethical standard bearer for the non-communist world, is subject to several sharp limitations. It cannot impose any purpose on mankind or establish a party line that is binding on allies. Any U.S. attempt to conduct covert activities routinely is ferreted out and broadcast by our mass media. Budget allocations are subject to caprice. Tradition is a tremendous inhibitor. Nevertheless, the psywar field — while not wide open — offers opportunities for imaginative strategists.

ECONOMIC WARFARE

Economic warfare which, like political warfare, may have strong psychological overtones, somehow seems more ethical to most Americans than psywar. Freely defined, it comprises any and all means used to maintain or expand the economies of the user and his allies at the expense of the enemy, and to neutralize or diminish the opposition's economic capacity and potential. Success can satisfy many important national security objectives.

General objectives cited at the beginning of this chapter as "amputation" and "self-paralysis" apply to economic warfare, amended and amplified as the situation demands. Penetrating foreign powers to gain influence or control, encouraging neutrals to cooperate or choose sides, and exploiting regional dissatisfactions are subsidiary goals.

Economic Warfare Tactics

Yuan-li Wu, whose *Economic Warfare* is a standard reference, identifies several cogent factors that influence the choice of tactics: conflicts between long- and short-term objectives; the relative economic development of the user and targeted countries (there is not much probability of making an economic satellite out of an equal); the nature of international political alignments; the qualitative and quantitative importance of foreign trade and investment to the respective parties; the economic organization of the opponents (capitalist, socialist, and so on); the recent economic experience and environment of each antagonist, including such matters as monetary inflation, large-scale land reform, and credit status; and the expertise of competitors in the realm of economic warfare. "Success is more probable if action is based upon an accurate assessment of one's own limitations as well as those of the enemy."[9]

Numerous ingenious techniques have been brought into play during the current era of competitive coexistence, some bilateral in character, some multilateral, and nearly all controversial as to desirability or effectiveness.

Sanctions

Sanctions to deprive the foe of strategic materials generate endless arguments. To begin with, it is next to impossible to obtain any agreement on the definition of "strategic materials." One school of thought would include only items of evident military value — petroleum and derivative products, arms, ammunition, certain minerals, (every country has deficiencies which could scarcely be replaced by synthetics or substitutes), and the like. Counterclaimants contend that *everything* is consequential, since enemy resources and labor would have to produce the goods denied. Several compromise positions lie between. Wu finds only two justifications for trading with the enemy, whether "strategic materials" are involved or not: first (and most important), if the goods or other means of payment exacted were "of even greater value to him *from a military point of view* than the imports," and second, if the strategic advantage to one's own country were greater than that accruing to the opposition.[10]

Sanctions obviously are subject to other shortcomings. Widespread cooperation by both allies and neutrals is necessary, unless the principal has a near monopoly on the banned products. Unfortunately, "cheating" is common, owing to the proclivity of disinterested parties, the ill-informed, and rapscallions for trafficking with the enemy for their own personal gain. Nonetheless, embargoes have a considerable nuisance value, and pose potentially serious threats.

Foreign Aid

Foreign aid can be a powerful economic-warfare weapon. Unsuspecting recipients, lured by low-interest rates and apparently attractive incentives, are easy prey. Long-term loans, rather than grants, assure continuing connections. Military and/or technical assistance programs guarantee maximum political penetration. Generating a persistent state of overdependence is a key objective. The U.S.S.R. has used these techniques particularly well in the Middle East, despite periodic setbacks.

Monetary Manipulation

Fiscal and financial pressures designed to shake confidence in the enemy's currency and to destroy his credit are fertile fields for economic warfare. One off-beat example serves to illustrate.

Thomas W. M. Smith, a U.S. Foreign Service Officer with extensive experience in economics and a stint as a Senior Fellow with the National War College Strategic Research Group, has reviewed the interrelationships between international monetary systems and grand strategy. In his view, "a viable international monetary system is both a determinant and an objective of national strategy . . . [Indeed] it should be possible to influence . . . the system to gain, or retain, some strategic advantages, or to minimize the loss of some others." Specific goals might be to degrade an enemy's ability to:

act unilaterally on short notice.
maintain an effective alliance apparatus.
implement effective foreign investment and aid programs.[11]

In short, strategic possibilities in the realm of international finance, still largely untapped, bear study for cold-war purposes.

Big Business
Market manipulations, quota systems, blacklisting, preemptive purchases, the freezing and liquidation of enemy assets, and control over technological advances — particularly the acquisition of patent rights — characterize economic warfare pressures in the business world.

Colonel Richard A. Bowen, U.S. Air Force, also a former Senior Fellow with the National War College Strategic Research Group, explored potential applications of such techniques in context with the growth of multinational enterprise, "a distinct trend with major implications for intersocietal competition in the world." U.S. multinational corporate operations account for nearly three-fourths of the world's total. Their aggregate corporate sales equal the world's third largest gross national product. The resultant power potential is enormous. The communist camp has nothing comparable. The question is: can this power be turned to strategic advantage?

Bowen believes it can, but only if handled adroitly. A heavy-handed direct approach could accrue short-term advantages, "but at a high cost in political tension among our allies and those adversaries we wish to penetrate and engage in competition. This would clearly be . . . counterproductive," unless it were to occur during a period of grave crisis and it served the interests of collective security. However, he suggests that "in the longer range, our pervasive corporate operations could become the primary element of an indirect strategy aimed at perpetuating and projecting our principles and values."[12]

The Economic-Warfare Balance Sheet

It is important to understand that for every strategic gain there is a cost, political as well as economic. For one thing, cutting an antagonist off from the world economic community *forces* him to become independent. And there is always the danger of boomerangs. Wu laid the choices out well when he said: "In considering the efficacy of economic warfare . . . and in coordinating economic measures with other methods of warfare, a comparison of cost with the expected result is rational and indispensable. *For no nation, not even the richest, can afford to act blindly, in a struggle for survival.*"[13]

61

THE FUTURE

In sum, *The* Cold War that followed World War II will eventually disappear, if it has not already, but cold war as an element of the conflict spectrum is likely to be eternal. As such, it presents unique strategic challenges for extraordinarily high stakes. To be successful in meeting those challenges, strategic innovators must find new ways to intermesh political, economic, and psychological warfare with military pressures to attain national security objectives without risking cataclysmic consequences.

PART III

CONTEMPORARY U.S. SCHOOLS OF THOUGHT

9 External Threats to U.S. Security

How can any man say what he should do himself
if he is ignorant of what his adversary is about?

JOMINI
Précis de l'Art de la Guerre

HISTORICAL SURVEY

The threat to U.S. security seemed distinct during the first decade or so after World War II. There was little question in the minds of our leaders, or among the mass of the American people, that international communism, organized, equipped, and directed by malefactors in Moscow, was the Number One menace.

Enemy aims and aspirations all appeared unambiguous:

The interest: universal communism.
The objective: world domination.
The policy: progressive expansion.
The strategy: world revolution.

The evidence seemed solid. Communist goals had been laid down by Lenin. Stalin was carrying them out. In short order, he swallowed most of Eastern Europe, then rang down the Iron Curtain. Mao, with Soviet backing, absorbed Chiang Kai-shek's China. Communist-instigated insurgence flared from Greece to the Philippines. Red armies ravaged Korea. Duplicity and disruption were rampant. Most indications implied a massive master plan.

That simplistic view of the threat disappeared in the 1960s, after Khrushchev and Mao split. Hardly anyone still believes in a monolithic communist conspiracy, calculating, and coordinated by the Kremlin. The sole serious menace to U.S. security today is posed by the Soviet Union, the only country in the world that has the capability, military or otherwise, to vie with us internationally or to harm our home base. However, there is no consensus concerning the imminence or intensity of potential perils.

65

THE SOVIET THREAT

Broad Strategic Guidelines

The United States and Soviet Union share several national security interests: survival; the perpetuation of their particular institutions and values; prosperity; and probably "peace," a term which each defines in its own way. Other interests obviously conflict, although the degrees of divergence and their ramifications are subjects of speculation. So are specific Soviet objectives. In one respect, however, there has been no ambiguity. Since 1962, neither nation has wanted to risk a general nuclear war.

Precisely how the U.S.S.R. will go about satisfying its national security interests and objectives in the 1970s is problematical. William S. Kintner and Robert L. Pfaltzgraff, Jr., spelled out three possible policies in a pamphlet entitled *Soviet Military Trends: Implications for U.S. Security.*[1]

The Policy of Condominium, engendered by Soviet hesitance to confront the United States directly, has prevailed for ten full years. Considerable compromise and accommodation have been evident. That approach has been paralleled in some areas by a Policy of Caution. It too is predicated on Soviet reluctance to accept serious risks, but it reflects greater willingness to stimulate rivalry that scrupulously avoids vital or compelling U.S. interests. The third option, a Policy of Opportunity, could come into play, should diminishing U.S. capabilities bolster Moscow's confidence. The temptation to increase pressures in arenas which involve central U.S. interests, such as the Middle East, then might be irresistible. As Kintner and Pfaltzgraff see it:

> The Soviet Union need have no intention of carrying confrontation to the point of actual military action. In fact, it would be likely that its intention would be to avoid superpower hostilities under all circumstances. But confrontation . . . is a process the length and the number of whose stages depend on how cleverly it is directed. The longer a confrontation lasts, the more likely that a democratic political system will gravitate toward concessions rather than provoke war against a power perceived as being strategically superior.[2]

Those three hypothetical policies, of course, are far from clean-cut. In borderline cases, Soviet leaders generally could be expected to prefer prudent policies, unless the issues at stake were of immediate and immense importance — experience indicates that members of the ruling hierarchy are essentially conservative, despite their revolutionary tradition. National character, communist doctrine, and unshakable convictions that time is on their side all repress impulses to take unwarranted risks.

Since the Cuban missile crisis, Soviet grand strategy has hinged on an indirect approach. Political, economic, psychological, and technological competitions have superseded naked force as the principal tools, but military might constitutes an indispensable and constant backdrop.

Soviet Military Capabilities

Historical Precedent

Certainly, Moscow's power potential is impressive. For more than fifty years, the

Kremlin has been straining to improve its position economically and militarily, at great expense to its people, whose personal comforts are still largely disregarded. Neither the death of Stalin nor the subsequent internal upheavals altered that aim, whose continued primacy is reflected in a preference for heavy industry, in the consistent promotion of production needed to project national power, and in the geographic dispersion of industry to enhance security in time of war. Further, the U.S.S.R. has created the scientific-technological base required to challenge the United States in any field of military research, development, testing, or engineering, should her leaders choose to allocate the necessary resources.[3]

Until quite recently, Soviet armed forces were dominated by a mammoth army, organized, trained, and equipped to defend Mother Russia, and to support overtures along the Soviet border. When the U.S.S.R. began to break out of its continental shell and exert increasing influence on the global scene, adjustments were in order. A diversified, modern military establishment has consequently emerged. Every facet is being cumulatively expanded and/or upgraded.[4] (*See* the table below for a comparison of selected U.S. and Soviet combatant forces.)[5]

Strategic Forces

The assets needed to prevent and, if necessary, prosecute a general nuclear war have been assigned top priority.

Until about 1965, the United States enjoyed distinct quantitative and qualitative superiority over the Soviet Union in strategic offensive weaponry. Our commanding lead has since been quashed. We retain reasonable parity in numbers of nuclear delivery systems (counting our tactical aircraft aboard carriers or based overseas), but the U.S.S.R. has many more intercontinental ballistic missiles (ICBM), soon will outstrip us in submarine-launched ballistic missiles (SLBM), and has attained a 3:1 advantage in gross megatonnage. Only in total bombs and warheads have we retained the edge, which U.S. leaders anticipate will increase to 3:1 in our favor over the next five years, owing largely to our Multiple Independently Targeted Reentry Vehicle (MIRV) program.[6]

Moscow's present posture represents a potent deterrent, since Soviet general-war strike forces are numerous enough, and are sufficiently invulnerable, to survive a preemptive attack by any world power and still inflict unacceptable damage in return. However, the presence of considerable counterforce capabilities in the Soviet arsenal, including multimegaton SS-9 ICBMs (for which no country has a counterpart), suggests that Soviet strategy embraces war-fighting options in addition to deterrence based on "assured destruction." A comprehensive air defense system, plus limited missile defenses, complete the strategic nuclear package.

General-Purpose Forces

Strategic offensive and defensive forces retain undisputed primacy, but the Soviets' improved general-war posture now permits them to pay greater attention to general-purpose forces. Several factors probably contribute to that renewed emphasis: the U.S. military structure, NATO's tactical nuclear capabilities, and tensions with China.

Massive ground elements are supported by up-to-date tactical air forces, medium-range and intermediate-range ballistic missiles (MRBM, IRBM), long-range transport

SELECTED COMBATANT FORCE STRENGTHS[a] U.S. Versus U.S.S.R. As of Spring, 1973		
	United States	**Soviet Union**
STRATEGIC FORCES		
ICBM Launchers	1,054	1,618[b]
SLBM Launchers	656	560
Heavy Bombers	460[c]	140[d]
Bombs/Warheads[e]	5,700	2,500
Fighter-Interceptors	619	3,100
SAM Launchers	840	10,000
ABM Launchers	0	64
GENERAL-PURPOSE FORCES		
Active Divisions	16[f]	160
IRBM/MRBM	0	700
Medium Bombers	0	1,200
Tactical Aircraft	5,000+[g]	4,000+
Aircraft Carriers	16	0[h]
Other Major Surface Combat Vessels	244	230
Ballistic-Missile Submarines	41	25[i]
Nuclear Attack Submarines	60	60
Diesel Attack Submarines	46	235

a   Figures for U.S.S.R. are estimates, rather than precise intelligence.
b   Includes ICBMs at test and training sites.
c   Reflects number of B-52s and FB-111s in operational squadrons. There are about 515 in total inventory.
d   Excludes about 50 tankers and several reconnaissance aircraft.
e   Weapons that could be loaded simultaneously on available delivery systems. Does not include reserve weapons in storage.
f   Includes three USMC divisions.
g   Includes Navy and Marine fighter aircraft.
h   One Soviet aircraft carrier is believed to be under construction.
i   U.S.S.R. is believed to have 16-18 Y-Class ballistic-missile submarines under construction. Table does not reflect more than 30 G- and H-Class vessels, which are approaching obsolescence.

aircraft, an increasing inventory of giant helicopters, and a modest amphibious fleet. The bulk of these forces still are deployed in the west, opposing the North Atlantic Treaty Organization (NATO), but a substantial air-ground buildup has concentrated along the Sino-Soviet border.[7]

The Warsaw Pact reinforces Muskovy's military machine in Eastern Europe.[8] Its armies and air forces are important factors in maintaining security within satellite states, and have been used in suppressive roles outside their own borders: the invasion of Czechoslovakia in August 1968 is exemplary. However, the military effectiveness of individual satellites varies considerably, as does their political reliability. How well they would perform offensively against NATO is open to speculation.

The Soviet Union now is escaping its centuries-old continental confinement by promoting balanced and integrated naval forces, merchant fleets, professional oceanic education, and research. Remarkable differences between U.S. and Soviet naval missions have evolved, as Admiral Elmo R. Zumwalt, Jr., Chief of Naval Operations, explains:

> Both navies are designed in part for nuclear deterrence. To that extent, our tasks are similar. Beyond that point, however, U.S. Naval forces are designed to support distant U.S. forces overseas, and, under the Nixon Doctrine, when required, the indigenous armies of our allies, necessitating forward defense, sea control, and the ability to project power ashore. . . . We have, in addition, a logistic defense requirement of vast proportions.

> The Soviet Navy, by contrast, . . . is designed largely to prevent the U.S. Navy from carrying out its missions. At the same time we see increasing evidence of the growing use of the Soviet Navy to further the political designs of the USSR. The Soviet Naval units have been optimized in design for strong initial striking power, with relatively limited reload and endurance and hence less tonnage per unit and little need for nuclear propulsion. Except for their submarine force, the Soviets' Naval forces are expected to operate closer to home. . . .

> They have built cruise missile armed submarines and surface ships designed to combat our fleet. We have built carriers in order to be able to control the sea lines of communication as well as to project tactical air power overseas from flexible, mobile, air bases. . . .[9]

The Soviet Navy thus described is already the world's second largest. Despite its lack of combat experience, it represents a serious challenge to the United States. If the present course continues, and considerable evidence suggests that it will,[10] the U.S.S.R. could compel this country to either augment its sea power significantly, or drastically revise its naval strategy. However, the implications of the evidence are in dispute,[11] and the ultimate outcome is still in doubt.

An Evaluation

Soviet leaders seem satisfied that their military establishment is progressing satisfactorily as a policy instrument which not only affords basic security, but constitutes the psychological underpinning for their conduct of world affairs. It facilitates political dealings which often are undertaken in difficult circumstances with reluctant partners and suspicious neighbors. No doubt, they desire to maintain their momentum. Indeed, their decision to participate with the United States in Strategic Arms Limitation Talks (SALT) (see Chapter 22) may have reflected growing apprehension that they might otherwise have to undertake expensive new defensive programs merely to retain — let alone improve — their present strategic position, which has been achieved at great cost and effort.

Conflicting Views of the Soviet Threat

What does this all mean? Is the Soviet posture menacing or is it reassuring?

A substantial segment of U.S. opinion perceives no serious threat, embraces each apparent shift in Soviet policy that seemingly portends a detente, and is undismayed by disappointments. Put yourself in the Kremlin's position, its adherents say. The United States has ringed Russian rimlands with military bases and fosters the most fearsome missile strike forces in history. We are at least half responsible for the continued tensions. If this country creates an atmosphere of confidence and trust, the difficulties will disappear.

Conservatives disagree. They contend that the Soviets have in no way abandoned their ultimate goal of world domination. In their eyes, the Kremlin still strives to extend Soviet influence abroad, isolate the United States, nullify our deterrent power, and undermine our international position.

The strategic implications of those two threat assessments are dramatically different. Neither view is in complete ascendancy. Compromise solutions thus are common, as succeeding chapters will bear out.

THE CHINESE COMMUNIST THREAT

Chicom Military Posture Reviewed

By way of contrast, there is nearly universal concurrence among informed individuals, in the official establishment and in academia, that Red China, despite her awesome size, is a "paper tiger" that currently poses no critical threat to the national security of the United States.[12] The danger lies largely in the future. Only within its own borders or along its immediate periphery does the Chinese behemoth exert real strength today.

In fact, the fiercely militant policy and strategy which Communist China proclaims from time to time has generally been in sharp contrast to actual practice. Saber-rattling regarding the resurrection of ancient ambitions to reestablish hegemony over all territories regarded as being historically Chinese — most notably Taiwan, Outer Mongolia, bits along the Indian border, parts of Soviet Central Asia and southeastern Siberia — rarely is buttressed by serious overt action. Short of accident or preemptive Soviet attacks, no substantial change in this situation seems likely, at least until the Chicoms pass through the present period of internal adjustment and consolidation, which inhibits major international forays.

Chicom Strategic Concepts

Meanwhile, Red China pursues a two-pronged strategy, one tine being offensive, the other geared to national defense: the doctrine of revolutionary war and the preservation of mainland China.[13] Both demonstrate Mao's almost mystical belief in mobilized and indoctrinated masses, his emphasis on the political objectives of war, and his unshakable conviction that man ultimately will triumph over machine in a protracted war of attrition and annihilation, where human will and perseverance prevail. Peking has not yet produced a full-fledged strategy for nuclear combat, and may not do so until Mao passes from the scene, although China detonated her first nuclear device on 16 October 1964, and followed up with the first of several multimegaton thermonuclear blasts in the spring of 1967.

What the ruling Chinese hierarchy currently seems to fear most is aggression by the U.S.S.R.

Chicom resistance reputedly would be predicated on defense in depth, capitalizing on China's vast territory, prodigious population, renowned resilience, and recuperative powers to trade space for time. According to Mao, the Peoples' Liberation Army (PLA) must "dare to lure the enemy in deep," where he will bog down in endless battle and "drown in a hostile human sea." As early as 1961, when the United States was still the prime prospective enemy, Chicom plans called for improved air defenses and communications, extensive defensive works, and the dispersal, camouflage, and hardening of military sites. According to Mao's dogma, "modern long-range weapons, including atomic bombs, will be helpless and ineffective" in protracted war when opposed by aroused masses and politically motivated military robots who are not afraid to die.[14]

That whole strategy, of course, is predicated on the dubious assumption that *any* antagonistic superpower would have to follow up nuclear bombardment with battle on the ground. Nevertheless, since China has no credible nuclear deterrent as yet, Peking has few options. The resultant predicament may well have prompted Chinese leaders to relax their xenophobic policies and respond to overtures by the United States, beginning with Henry Kissinger's secret conference in Peking in July 1971.

Mao's doctrine for "peoples' wars" is outlined in Chapter 7, but one or two points bear elaboration here.

To begin with, there are significant differences between Chinese and Soviet thought in this regard.[15] Marx prescribed a revolution of the proletariat. Mao calls for communist-inspired-and-led peasant insurrections.

The concept of using rural revolutionary bases to encircle and finally capture cities has been projected on a global scale. Lin Piao's writings view Africa, Asia, and Latin America as springboards from which to overcome urban Europe and the United States.[16] The scheme thus envisaged establishes a final goal, with no time limit, but with short- and mid-range ramifications. One obvious object is the progressive creation of pro-Peking regimes around the globe. Another is to weaken and overextend the Free World by confronting it with multiple, concurrent, subversive insurrections. The Chicoms have had precious few successes in this regard, but the intent is important.

It is significant that Peking refuses to intervene directly in support of "peoples' wars," like the one in Vietnam. Revolutionaries of the world are promised advice, support, and "spiritual atom bombs," but no reinforcements. Revolutions, Mao says, must be fought and won by indigenous elements — a philosophy that parallels the Nixon Doctrine in multiple ways, but predates it by many years.

Chicom Capabilities

Despite her ambitions, Communist China has published almost nothing regarding conventional military operations beyond her frontiers. This is not surprising. Whereas the story of Soviet military might is mainly one of capabilities, the Chinese

Communist story is still largely one of limitations, despite recent progress.[17]

China has an insignificant Navy and an obsolescent Air Force. Her ability to project military power internationally is still limited. Offensive missile strikes against European Russia or Western Europe currently are out of the question, although the Chicoms have recently deployed a few medium- and intermediate-range ballistic missiles. However, a limited-reach ICBM, now nearly ready for deployment, *could* strike Alaska or deep into the Soviet Union. An ICBM system, now under development, will be able to engage any strategic target in this country, but the best estimates indicate it will not be in service before 1975 or 1976.[18] At that time, our strategic picture will change. Even a few ICBMs might give China an assured-destruction capability against the United States. New U.S. concepts then will be in order.

When China's nuclear weapons program matures, including the development of effective delivery means, major political and military changes in her strategy also may ensue. These could range from increased political maneuvering on the international scene to nuclear blackmail, particularly among neighboring small powers in Asia. Which tack the Chicoms will take is uncertain.[19]

Excessive political control of the PLA by the Communist Party smothers military competence. Apart from, and in advance of, normal national defense responsibilities, PLA energies are siphoned off by internal-security missions, participation in agriculture and industry, and by responsibilities for nationwide indoctrination and education.[20]

In sum, Red China has numerous debilitating military deficiencies that will take a long time to eliminate. Alignment with North Korea and North Vietnam would strengthen her position somewhat along the periphery of East Asia, but for the present there is no suggestion that the three are likely to form a coalition analogous to the Warsaw Pact. Nevertheless, U.S. operations in Indochina were conducted with great circumspection to avoid any direct confrontation with the Chinese, and similar ground rules doubtless would go into effect if the situation heated up again in Korea.

THE TREND

The dissolution of what once was portrayed as a monolithic Sino-Soviet bloc produced an entirely new set of strategic problems for U.S. planners in the 1960s, and these persist today. From our standpoint, numerous advantages accrued from the communist schism, which sapped the combined strength of our two most formidable foes and diverted part of the attention they formerly focused on undermining the Free World. However, the situation has become vastly more complex. Strategic problems that once were relatively simple and uncompromising now are laced with nuances that spark continuing controversy among U.S. leaders.

This oversimplified appraisal has stressed Soviet and Chinese Communist *military* concepts and capabilities, but less spectacular political, economic, and psychological perils may be even more potent, as succeeding discussion will bring out. We must always be aware that it is possible to "win" or "lose" without a shot being fired, depending on how power is applied. Ideas can be just as lethal as bullets.

10 An Overview of U.S. Grand Strategy

> Strategy cannot be a single defined doctrine; it is a
> method of thought, the object of which is to codify
> events, set them in order of priority and then choose
> the most effective course of action. There will be a
> special strategy to fit each situation, any given
> strategy may be the best possible in certain
> situations and the worst conceivable in others.
>
> GÉNÉRAL d' ARMÉE ANDRÉ BEAUFRE
> *Introduction to Strategy*

U.S. NATIONAL SECURITY INTERESTS AND OBJECTIVES

Sound national security interests and objectives are the keys to effective strategies.

For most of the past decade, this posed some awkward problems in the United States, since no interests or objectives were formally recorded by the Executive Branch during either the Kennedy or Johnson administrations. As a result, strategists in the Departments of State and Defense, and in the Joint Chiefs of Staff, were compelled to identify, interpret, and contrive their own lists from National Security Action Memorandums, private and public pronouncements of the President, and from speeches, presentations to Congress, and individual statements by other influential officials in the U.S. government. That "do-it-yourself" system was seldom satisfactory, since it depended on too many conflicting or ambiguous utterances which were subject to irreconcilable interpretations, and thus were rendered almost meaningless by compromise.

President Nixon is alleviating, if not eliminating, that deficiency. Critical U.S. national security interests and objectives still are not identified as such in unclassified print, but the revived and revitalized National Security Council (NSC)* routinely

---

* Statutory members of the NSC are the President, Vice President, Secretaries of State and Defense, and the Director of the Office of Emergency Preparedness. The President's Assistant for National Security Affairs attends all meetings and directs the NSC staff. The Chairman, Joint Chiefs of Staff, and the Director of Central Intelligence are present as observers and consultants. Other senior officials, such as the Secretary of the Treasury and the U.S. Ambassador to the United Nations, are invited to attend when matters under their purview are considered.

ventilates such matters in closed session, and many of its conclusions can be deduced rather easily from official proclamations available to the general public.

U.S. National Security Interests

This country's national interests, which underlie the idealistic American way of life and all associated activity, conform closely to the six sketched by our founding fathers almost 200 years ago in the Preamble to the Constitution: the yearning for a more perfect union, justice, domestic tranquility, adequate defense, economic well-being, and the blessings of liberty, not only for this generation, but for posterity.

The overriding U.S. national security interest perennially is survival under conditions that preserve our independence, geographic integrity, fundamental institutions, and honor, while maintaining a high degree of political, social, economic, and military viability. A compelling corollary interest is universal peace, an aspiration articulated by President Nixon in his 22 January 1970 State of the Union message: "When we speak of America's priorities, the first priority must always be peace for America and the world."[1] That fundamental desire later became the theme for his annual reports to the Congress, which pragmatically recognized that this "driving dream" would be "an adventure realized not in the exhilaration of a single moment, but in the lasting rewards of patient, detailed and specific efforts — a step at a time."[2]

Subsidiary security interests are many and varied. One, which dates back at least thirty years, to the onset of World War II, is to retain freedom of action as a global power. Others are regionally oriented. A viable Japan, friendly or at least neutral and commercially cooperative, currently is in our best interests. So is a stable balance of power in Europe and the Middle East. Readers could compile a fairly comprehensive series from open sources, and place them in rough order of priority.

U.S. National Security Objectives

The "central national security objective" of the United States, derived from our generalized interests and spelled out by former Defense Secretary Melvin R. Laird, is "the prevention of war."[3] A number of subordinate goals can be deduced from the President's public statements, of which the following four are representative:

> Discourage armed attacks on the U.S. or against other areas deemed essential to our well-being.
>
> Deal effectively with transgressors if deterrence fails.
>
> Assist selected allies in preventing or defeating insurgency.
>
> Ensure uninhibited transit rights for Free World nations on international waters and airways and in outer space.

U.S. NATIONAL SECURITY POLICIES

Guidelines for attaining such objectives are contained in U.S. national security policy. Expurgated versions are open to the public in President Nixon's annual reports to the Congress, entitled *U.S. Foreign Policy for the 1970's*. Those precedent-shattering blueprints unquestionably should be required reading for all students of U.S. grand strategy. Half a dozen excerpts, from the first volume, published on 18 February 1970, demonstrate the broad policy coverage of those documents:

> [On Strategy] We must know what our real options are and not simply what compromise has found bureaucratic acceptance. Every view and every alternative must have a fair hearing.
>
> [On Force Posture] American weaknesses could tempt would-be aggressors to make dangerous miscalculations.
>
> [On Regional Priorities] For the foreseeable future, Europe must be the cornerstone of the structure of a durable peace.
>
> [On Collective Security] We cannot expect U.S. military forces to cope with the entire spectrum of threats facing allies or potential allies throughout the world.
>
> [On Arms Control] There is no area in which we and the Soviet Union — as well as others — have a greater common interest than in reaching agreement with regard to arms control.
>
> [On Strategic Dialogue] The United States and the Communist countries must negotiate on the issues that divide them. . . ."[4]

Over-all, the President's statements confirm that U.S. national security policy still is defensive, and that protection of the homeland understandably still ranks Number One. In place of "superiority," our military posture now is predicated on deliberately ambiguous "sufficiency," adequate (hopefully) to keep multiple options open across the whole spectrum of war, while avoiding overextension.

U.S. GRAND STRATEGY 1783–1968

Henry Kissinger, the twentieth-century U.S. Talleyrand, quickly squashed speculation that President Nixon's edicts comprise a politico-military "cookbook." They map a master menu, not detailed recipes. Nevertheless, the general concepts outlined therein set the stage for a U.S. strategy whose background is described beautifully by General Earle G. Wheeler, a former Chairman of the Joint Chiefs of Staff. A precis of his thoughts is worth reviewing.

As he sees it, the United States, from its inception through 1968, successively pursued three distinct grand strategies, each tailored to suit a specific need.

Western Hemisphere Defense

The first, based on a policy that shunned entangling alliances, persisted 115 years, from the Peace of Paris in 1783 until the end of the nineteenth century. It gave us time to grow. General Wheeler emphasized that to term that strategy *isolationism* misses the mark. Its architects shrewdly assessed the situation and concluded that the balance of power existing in Europe, combined with the Royal Navy's command of the seas,

75

assured our national security. "I have long believed," Wheeler wrote, "that balanced forces abroad permitted our early enunciation of the Monroe Doctrine."

Ad Hoc Interventionism

The second strategy, "*ad hoc* interventionism," began to emerge about 1898 and persevered for 50 years. It reflected revised policies that advocated direct U.S. participation in global affairs. We acquired property and increased interests in the Far East after the Spanish-American War, while retaining traditional concerns for Europe. Strong sea power was an obvious prerequisite for showing the flag around the world and for countering alien forces afloat that already were beginning to challenge Britain's naval supremacy. The resultant heavy reliance on what we now would call a single "weapons system," the U.S. Navy, proved sound in the Pacific for several decades, but the absence of a sturdy standing Army precluded timely application of American combat power in Europe during both World Wars.

The Containment of Communism

The third strategy, predicated on policies of containing communism and achieving a more stable world order, surfaced during the second Truman administration and was refined by Presidents Eisenhower, Kennedy, and Johnson. General Wheeler summarized the principal components:

> First, we [had to be] prepared to participate more directly and forcibly in any balancing of power that was to occur in Europe.
>
> Secondly, we [were] the principal nation of the West able to project our power into the Pacific to bring influence to bear on developments there.
>
> Finally, if anyone was to halt either the crude postwar drives of Communist power — or its more subtle later forms — that "anyone" [had to be] us.[5]

That strategy evolved in two distinct stages, massive retaliation and flexible response.

Massive Retaliation

The introductory stage, which spanned the 1950s, relied first on a U.S. nuclear monopoly, and later on overwhelming nuclear superiority, to awe communist aggressors and alleviate external threats. Very modest U.S. general-purpose forces, reconstituted after the disgraceful demobilization that followed World War II, were deployed well forward. They acted largely as "trip wires" which, if disturbed, would trigger a devastating reprisal by our Strategic Air Command (SAC). A series of regional and bilateral alliances were concluded around the Free World, each dominated by the United States and supplemented by expensive military assistance programs. Conventional power played important parts in the over-all strategic concept, but the principal ingredient unquestionably was nuclear deterrence, which sought to discourage hostile actions against ourselves and our allies by promising unacceptably devastating reaction.

The threat of massive retaliation contributed to a shaky balance of power, but only for the worst case. Nevertheless, General Wheeler paid that approach the highest accolade of the professional: "For its period and its purpose, it worked. The strategy deterred major war."[6] Even now, when Soviet nuclear capabilities approach parity with — some say surpass — those of the United States, massive retaliation still forms an important option of our second-strike general war strategy.

Unfortunately, the spectre of nuclear devastation failed to discourage the outbreak of lesser conflagrations kindled by communism along the rim of Asia from Malaya to Korea in the 1950s. A too-rigid approach to strategy and excessive confidence in a single "weapons system" — this time incredible aerial firepower — once again displayed deficiencies. It was like arming policemen with howitzers.

Flexible Response

In consequence, U.S. grand strategy was modified early in the Kennedy administration to cope with all levels of aggression, thus inaugurating stage two, the era of "flexible response." This postulate, preserved by President Johnson, presupposed a need for the ability to apply controlled force decisively across the full spectrum of war at times and places of our own choosing, in such fashion that the opposition would not be able to adjust.

Three features stood out. First, the new philosophy was predicated on general-war retaliatory forces that could wreak "assured destruction" on the enemy in event the communists chose the path of unbridled aggression. Beneath that nuclear umbrella, the U.S. military establishment was charged with maintaining capabilities that could cope simultaneously with major conflagrations in Europe and in Asia, while holding sufficient assets in reserve to handle a minor contingency elsewhere (the so-called 2½-war strategy). Finally, we recognized a requirement to repress revolutionary wars, and devoted increasing efforts in that direction. Collective security arrangements continued. They emphasized training programs for allies, but the United States concomitantly took on increasing responsibilities as a "world policeman," who theoretically might be called on to settle all sorts of disputes.

With such ambitious undertakings planned or in progress, flexible response soon became an expensive way to do business. A base-line force was built up and the defense budget expanded, but whether ends ever matched means was contestable. The Joint Chiefs, who used different time and force measurements than McNamara's aides, argued that the Secretary depended on too small an active establishment for the military commitments he stood ready to take on. Furthermore, they felt it was unrealistic to count on mobilizing and deploying reserve divisions quickly enough to serve as a backstop. U.S. strategy was in constant dispute, not because the means were *unavailable,* but because they were *unattainable* at a price the American public was willing to pay. Minimum acceptable levels for general-purpose forces therefore never were reached.

CONTEMPORARY STRATEGIC CONCEPTS

Changes in the Strategic Environment

The Nixon administration is trying to resolve that dilemma. The national security interests of the United States remain similar, but our compulsion to confront communism around the clock and around the globe has diminished. Henceforth, our strategists plan to concentrate on those areas where *salient* interests are at stake. The President himself best spells out how changes in the strategic environment have affected our approach:

> In the era of American predominance, we resorted to American prescriptions as well as resources. In the new era, our friends are revitalized and increasingly self-reliant while the American domestic consensus has been constrained by 25 years of global responsibilities. Failure to draw upon the growth of others would have stifled them and exhausted ourselves. Partnership that was always theoretically desirable is now physically and psychologically imperative.

> In the era of overwhelming U.S. military strength, we and our allies could rely on the doctrine of massive retaliation. In the new era, growing Soviet power has altered the military equation. Failure to adapt to this change could lead to confrontations which pose an agonizing choice between paralysis and holocaust. Strength that served the cause of peace during a period of relative superiority needs new definitions to keep the peace during a period of relative equality.

> In the era of Communist solidarity, we pursued an undifferentiated negotiating approach toward Communist countries. In the new era, we see a multipolar Communism marked by a variety of attitudes toward the rest of the world. Failure to respond to this diversity would have ignored new opportunities for improving relations. Negotiation with different Communist countries on specific issues carries more promise.

> Finally, in the new era, unprecedented challenges beckon nations to set aside doctrine and focus on a common agenda. A new global partnership could promote habits of working for the world's interests instead of narrow national interests.[7]

Strategic Planning Guidance

Defense Secretary Laird declared that U.S. national security planning during President Nixon's regime must satisfy the following criteria:

> Preservation by the United States of a sufficient strategic nuclear capability as the cornerstone of the Free World's nuclear deterrent.

> Development and/or continued maintenance of Free World forces that are effective, and minimize the likelihood of requiring the employment of strategic nuclear forces should deterrence fail.

> An International Security Assistance Program that will enhance effective self-defense capabilities throughout the Free World, and, when coupled with diplomatic and other actions, will encourage regional security agreements among our friends and allies.[8]

Salient Features of U.S. Strategy

Strength, partnership, negotiation, and realistic deterrence form the new framework of U.S. grand strategy. Capabilities embodied in the old catchwords "credible deterrence," "collective security," and "flexible response" all are still present, but are interpreted in different ways.

U.S. strategy for the 1970s stresses the need for seven salient features:

1. A concept of strategic sufficiency.

2. A strong conventional capability buttressed by increased burden sharing and improved defense capabilities of other Free World nations.

3. Adequate peacetime general purpose forces for simultaneously meeting a major Communist attack in either Europe or Asia, assisting allies against non-Chinese threats in Asia, and contending with a contingency elsewhere.

4. Smaller U.S. active forces, with great emphasis to be given to their readiness and effectiveness, including modernization.

5. A reemphasis on maintaining and using our technological superiority.

6. Increased international security assistance for the defense needs and roles of other Free World nations.

7. A new approach to U.S. military manpower, based on a goal of Zero Draft and an All-Volunteer active force, with increased reliance on National Guard and Reserve forces.[9]

Within that framework, numerous specific strategies take shape, constantly shifting in structure and emphasis, devised for different levels of warfare under different conditions in different parts of the world. There are separate concepts for general nuclear war and for lesser confrontations. Some are slanted toward the U.S.S.R. and Red China. Others register on Europe, the Middle East, East Asia and the Western Pacific, the Indian Ocean, Africa, and Latin America.

Secretary Laird differentiated precisely between NATO and the Orient, for example:

> In NATO/Europe, U.S. national security strategy for the 1970's must include the objective of maintaining a strong NATO deterrent in Western Europe, including its northern and southern flanks, against a wide range of possible Soviet and Warsaw Pact initiatives, short of strategic nuclear exchanges. Such initiatives could span a continuum, from border incursions and military backed political threats to a full-scale conventional or tactical nuclear attack, including conflict at sea.

> In Asia, our continuing nuclear superiority vis-à-vis the Chinese can contribute significantly to deterrence of Chinese nuclear attacks, or conventional attacks, on our Asian allies, and would be strengthened further with an area ballistic missile defense effective against small attacks. However, there is a need for our Asian friends and allies to strengthen their conventional forces, both to defend themselves against non-Chinese attacks and, in regional conjunction, to build a defensive capability which would give Communist China increased pause before initiating hostilities. At the same time, we will maintain adequate forces to meet our commitments in Asia.[10]

CONTINUOUS CONFLICTS OF OPINION

Regardless of its content or how it was concocted, every strategy creates critics who question what it means, what support is required, what its strengths and weaknesses are, and what might be done to save the day if it goes sour. This is particularly true in the United States, where appraisals by dedicated, knowledgeable individuals who are genuinely concerned with national security mingle with opinions expressed by vindictive or irresponsible parties who have personal, political, or economic axes to grind. In either event, caustic critique is a healthy adjunct that compels policy-makers, planners, and practitioners alike to justify their handiwork to detractors and, perhaps equally important, to themselves.

In the United States, critics run the gamut from extreme liberals to extreme conservatives, with kaleidoscopic shades in between. Disputes among them arise primarily because of differences in their individual assessments of national interests and objectives, evaluations of the threat, alignments of national priorities, their penchant for taking risks, and their personal philosophies, all of which condition their approaches to strategy.

Some commentaries are circumscribed. Others are catholic. Samuel P. Huntington, respected Professor of Government at Harvard and Associate Director of the Harvard Center for International Affairs, recently published a short but searching analysis in the latter category.

In his estimation, deteriorating American power has become "the preeminent feature of international politics." Our global hegemony is crumbling. In the new environment, he says, "the criterion for U.S. involvement [overseas] . . . is not who suffers from aggression, but who benefits from it. *The overall object is not to deter aggression, but to maintain a balance of power* [emphasis added]," in which no country or coalition of countries can exercise universal suzerainty. In most cases, "governments can fall and boundaries change with little damaging impact on U.S. interests." The implications for U.S. alliances are manifest.

Military power, Huntington contends, is increasingly an instrument of negotiation — the "bargaining chip" concept already is seeing extensive service. Military "sufficiency" but numerical inferiority thus may no longer suffice. Parity (at least) with opponents may prove imperative. Counterinsurgency, he suggests, is passé. *Counterintervention* concepts and capabilities will become more important in maintaining a balance of power.[11]

Such assertions, and others like them, bear careful consideration. The remaining chapters in Part III of this book dissect the elements of U.S. grand strategy and highlight prominent alternatives. Each reader must decide for himself what is sound, what is suspect, and what courses this country should follow.

11 Concepts of Deterrence

We are come to make a choice between the quick and the dead. That is our business. Behind the black portent of the new atomic age lies a hope which, seized upon with faith, can work our salvation. If we fail, then we have damned every man to be the slave of Fear. Let us not deceive ourselves: We must elect World Peace or World Destruction.

BERNARD M. BARUCH
Speaking before the United Nations
14 June 1946

The idea of deterrence is as old as war itself, but it emerged as the preeminent element of a modern nation's grand strategy only after the implications of general nuclear war began to take hold. Deterrence is not a strategy for war. It is a strategy for peace, designed to convince the opposition that aggression is the least attractive of all alternatives. Deterrence does not restrain the enemy physically. It restrains him psychologically.

CARDINAL CONSIDERATIONS

Deterrence Delimited

International conflicts occur when their instigators anticipate that risks will be low in relation to gains. They may also result from impulse. Effective deterrence must discourage war on either count, under conditions that call for Type I, Type II, or Type III deterrence, which deal with direct attacks, extremely provocative acts — such as assaults on allies — and aggressive adventurism, respectively.[1] This chapter concentrates on Types I and II, the highest priorities.

To understand the process fully, strategists should constantly bear the following skein in mind:

Who deters . . . . *whom* from what *actions (alternatives)*, by what *threats* and *counteractions* in what *situations* and *contexts,* in the face of what *counterthreats* and *counter counteractions* . . . . and *why* does he do it?[2]

To begin with, deterrence can be discharged positively or negatively, by promising punishment or denying rewards. In either event, it is based on a naked threat (there can be no deterrence if contemplated consequences are kept secret), backed by the assurance that decisive, automatic, and inexorable action will be taken when warranted. The portent of retribution need not be exclusively physical. Political, economic, social, and other sanctions sometimes suffice, or may buttress military might. Finally, if honorable alternatives are not left open, deterees could react like cornered beasts.

The goal of deterrence is to induce stability, a state of equilibrium which encourages prudence on the part of opponents who face the possibility of war. Stability does not signify the ability of belligerents to inflict equal damage on one another. Instead, it reflects their ability to visit unacceptable punishment on each other should deterrence fail. The concept of stability thus implies that *neither* party enjoys a rational first-strike option.

Essential Elements of Credibility

No idle threat can deter for long. Threats must exude credibility, an amalgam of capabilities and intentions, which gives clear evidence that they not only can, but will, be carried out in extremity. Bombast without credibility, far from deterring, can create exactly the opposite effect if its recipient calls the bluff.

The military capabilities needed to deter general war derive mainly from numbers and types of nuclear weapons; relatively invulnerable delivery systems; a professional state of readiness; and responsive command and control mechanisms. Capabilities never are static. They constantly shift (usually slowly, but sometimes suddenly) in response to changes in the strategic situation, particularly those related to training, technology, and numerical sufficiency. Capabilities are not entirely tangible, but they still can be determined with a respectable degree of objectivity.

Intentions, which are merely states of mind, must be measured subjectively. Deterees attempting to judge the authenticity of threats would be wise to weigh the opposition's interests and objectives against his temperament and will. National character, the personalities of leaders, their past practices, and the degree of public support they enjoy all are part of the equation. Vital interests normally lend credence to deterrent threats, but not if their promulgator is plagued by pusillanimity, vacillation, and domestic dissent.

Perhaps most important of all, the *deterrer* himself must believe that he not only has power, but also has the propensity to apply it, if he hopes to convince deterees of his credibility.

Caveats

Calculations concerning enemy capabilities and intentions never can be precise. At least three phenomena therefore lend some credibility to nuclear-deterrent threats, even when logic suggests that chances of implementation are slight.

82

The first of these was christened "the residual fear of war" by Herman Kahn, who postulates that in circumstances surrounding general nuclear war, the mind is likely to retreat from pure logic and heed instead lingering suspicions that the threat might indeed be carried out.[3]

"Deterrence through uncertainty," addressed by Kissinger in *The Necessity for Choice,* deals with doubts concerning the outcome of any attack and the probable response. The latitude for overestimating friendly capabilities, underestimating enemy capabilities, and misinterpreting enemy intentions are contributing factors. Prospective aggressors may thereby be discouraged from adventurism.[4]

"The threat that leaves something to chance," which occupies a full chapter in Schelling's *Strategy of Conflict,* deals with unforeseen complications which may accrue, all efforts to the contrary by both sides. Intervention by third parties and imperfect decision-making processes exemplify eventualities that could create results grossly disproportionate to those desired or required.[5]

In sum, neither laws of probability nor mathematical machinations can "prove" the credibility of deterrence. Too many qualifications are unpredictable and unquantifiable.

Reciprocal Deterrence

Deterrence is a "two-way street" that involves threats, counterthreats, a competition in risk-taking, and a war of nerves. As a result of the interaction, one party, all, or none may be deterred. Harkabi elaborates on that theme:

> The deterrent threat [sometimes] becomes a demonstration of willingness to follow through to the bitter end. This is what has been termed *brinkmanship,* the art of intentionally forcing crises to the brink of hostilities in order to compel the other side to retreat. . . . Either side may stretch deterrence too far and bring war about precisely because it is aware that the other cannot rationally be intending to go to war. We thus arrive at the next paradox: The danger of war lies precisely in the certainty of each side that the other will not initiate a nuclear holocaust.[6]

The "rationality of irrationality," described by Herman Kahn, sometimes plays a part in this pageant.[7] Shrewd bargainers, feigning a touch of madness, may announce an irrevocable commitment, expecting adversaries to back down. Should the threat work it would be rational, even though only a lunatic ever would carry it out. Unfortunately, the game would end in disaster if both sides used that strategy. If, however, as Bertrand Russell postulated, one party were willing to risk general war and the other were not, the former would be victorious in all negotiations, and ultimately would reduce the opposition to impotence. "No proud nation," he predicted, "will long acquiesce in such an ignominious role. We are, therefore, faced, quite inevitably, with the choice between brinkmanship and surrender."[8]

That statement may be a bit overdrawn, but it underscores the complexity of mutual deterrence.

DETERRENT DOCTRINES

Two schools of strategic thought, one certain that deterrence is permanent, the other that it is precarious, shape the doctrines of minimum and maximum deterrence (*see* Chapter 5 for basic philosophies). A brief summary and comparison of the two extremes and the most prominent compromise solutions illustrate alternative approaches.

Minimum Deterrence

Minimum deterrence is predicated on the proposition that general nuclear war would culminate in disaster for all parties concerned. Therefore, even a few thermonuclear weapons of a single type, targeted against cities, should be adequate to guarantee perpetual stability. Fifty warheads is a typical figure. "Overkill" capabilities reputedly would generate oppressive financial drains. Further, there is no need for large yields or great accuracy, since cities comprise soft, area targets. Adherents of this approach willingly accept inferiority in numbers of weapons, technical sophistication, and destructive power, secure in the belief that their scheme — the soul of simplicity — would succeed.

One apparent anomaly exists. Many advocates of this doctrine admit that mutual deterrence at the general-war level might, in fact, encourage limited wars. They therefore acknowledge a need for considerable capabilities to cope with lesser conflicts.

Minimum deterrence seems wholly unrealistic to detractors, who condemn its devotees for mingling "shocking naiveté" with "burning missionary zeal," the worst possible combination.[9] Disparagers claim that proponents habitually underestimate or overlook complexities in the strategic environment that might invalidate their conclusions: the possibility of human or mechanical error; the accuracy, reliability, and survivability of delivery systems; the quality of warning networks; the extent of active and passive defenses; and the status of alert forces.

As derogators see it, the deterrent value of 50–100 weapons is nearly nil. A superior foe could smother those numbers with one surprise first-strike salvo. Even if the delivery systems were virtually invulnerable, like ballistic-missile submarines on station, some weapons would abort, be neutralized en route, be off target, or otherwise fail to accomplish their missions. Such a small arsenal never could hope to saturate enemy antiaircraft and antiballistic-missile defenses. Moreover, minimum deterrence would provide no war-fighting prowess whatsoever. Any country espousing that strategy thus would be compelled to relinquish the initiative permanently. In tit-for-tat city-trading escalation, the enemy would hold all the trump cards, could persist until the defender went bankrupt, and would still retain a fearful reserve for use in future coercion.

Maximum Deterrence

Maximum deterrence, postulated on a "splendid" first-strike posture and minimum general-purpose forces, presupposes that the assumptions underlying minimum deterrence are false. Nuclear weapons do not automatically assure stability. The degree of devastation acceptable to the enemy cannot be predicted precisely. War-fighting capabilities are imperative. Champions of maximum deterrence therefore demand a high assurance that they would be able to disarm the opposition, limit damage to their own homeland, seize the initiative in emergency, and retain freedom of action thereafter.

To satisfy those objectives, partisans of maximum deterrence prescribe overwhelming numerical and technological supremacy; diversified offensive weapons systems with yields and accuracy needed to atomize hard targets; and a sound defense. Oddly enough, however, extremists of this persuasion are just as inflexible in their own way as the minimists — they oppose limited war capabilities altogether, and would rely on the threat of massive retaliation, backed by overwhelming nuclear superiority, to deter *minor* as well as major provocations.

Nevertheless, realists agree that there is no such thing as absolute deterrence. The Law of Diminishing Returns takes over. Bernard Brodie put this well, when he wrote:

> It is a fair surmise that the increase in deterrent effect is less than proportional to the increase in magnitude of potential destruction. . . . The human imagination can encompass just so much pain, anguish or horror. The intrusion of numbers by which to multiply given sums of such feelings is likely to have on the average human mind a rather dull effect. . . .

> Governments, it may be suggested, do not think like ordinary human beings, and one has to concede that the *maximum possible deterrence* which can be attained by the threat of retaliatory damage must involve a power which guarantees not only vast losses but also utter defeat. . . . [However,] it is likely that considerably less retaliatory destruction than that conceived under "maximum possible deterrence" will buy only slightly less deterrence.[10]

Maximum deterrence theories have been damned on political, military, and budgetary grounds. Disbelievers maintain that stability would be sacrificed to no useful purpose. A first-strike capability might prompt pessimistic opponents to preempt. An endless arms race would be inevitable, as each side sought to assure a survivable force that could weather a surprise attack. Arthur Waskow, writing ten years ago, augured that "constructing the weapons systems and shelters to support such a strategy would distort the free society we are pledged to support."[11] Finally, the absence of realistic ways to deal with minor provocations would undermine the credibility of any threat, resulting either in the proliferation of local wars, any one of which might escalate to unmanageable proportions, or the irresponsible application of force to the ultimate disadvantage of the wielder.

Compromises

Between the maximum and minimum poles lies a procession of possibilities that borrow peculiarities from one or both and inject additional ingredients. The four outlined below in ascending order of intensity have been described at length by numerous authorities. Herman Kahn and his associates have done so particularly well.[12]

Finite Deterrence
Finite deterrence affords a better buffer than minimum deterrence. It too features a counterpunch strategy and urban targeting, but strives for capabilities that are more

convincing. Finite deterrence, therefore, covers multiple contingencies that significantly increase requirements for deliverable weapons. Nuclear sufficiency presumably would be assured by 500 to 1,000 warheads, enough to provide a potent physical punch. In its purest form, finite deterrence often emphasizes arms control, takes cognizance of political, fiscal, social, and ethical considerations, is nonaggressive, and still is relatively simple. To avoid reciprocal fear of surprise attack, where each side imputes aggressive intentions to the other, it deliberately underplays defense and scrupulously abstains from accumulating war-fighting repertoires.

Mostly Finite Deterrence

Mostly finite deterrence adds adaptability to the finite foundation. It augments available retaliatory forces and charges significant elements with the defense of civilian populations and property. If deterrence fails, tit-for-tat or other controlled war strategies could be accommodated, and "excessive" collateral damage from counterforce attacks could be avoided. Mostly finite deterrence with respect to one potential adversary might well represent a credible first-strike capability against others, even though countervalue weaponry and philosophies still prevailed. The upper end of this category blends with a more muscular posture sometimes called "partial damage limiting."

Counterforce as Insurance

Counterforce as insurance improves flexibility markedly. Versatile targeting is feasible; "minor" nuclear provocations and blackmail by upstart states could be handled with more facility; active damage-limitation measures are enhanced; and opportunities for restrained reprisals and more credible escalation threats might improve intrawar deterrence. Most certainly, counterforce as insurance introduces genuine war-fighting capabilities not available from minimum, finite, mostly finite, or partial damage-limiting strategies.

Credible First Strike

Credible first-strike possibilities, near the upper end of the scale but below maximum deterrence, include calculated preemption and preventive war. Each capitalizes on counterforce capabilities of all kinds, offensive, defensive, active, and passive. Whether any first-strike options are worthy of serious consideration, other than against outrageously overmatched opponents, has been open to question. Most realistic first-strike concepts are predicated on near certainty that all or most of the enemy's retaliatory forces could be nullified or neutralized simultaneously. That condition does not pertain between superpowers, given the present state of technological art, and Bernard Brodie, a pioneer nuclear-war theorist, predicts with confidence that no easy solutions will soon be forthcoming:

> The degree of advantage that was until recently thought to accrue to the side making a surprise strategic attack — where it could hope to wipe out the retaliatory force of the opponent with near impunity — is gone, and is not likely to return among opponents no more disparate in power than the United States and Soviet Union.[13]

U.S. DETERRENT STRATEGIES IN THE PAST

Controversy over the U.S. approach to deterrence has raged since 1946, when President Truman suggested that "the atom's power . . . . can be used as an overriding influence against aggression and reckless war."[14] Chancellor Hutchins of Chicago University, who expressed outrage at the very thought of using nuclear weapons as a threat, typified those who set the stage for subsequent debate.[15]

The problem originally seemed straightforward. At first, the United States had an absolute monopoly on nuclear firepower. No country posed a significant threat to the continental United States until the 1950s, when the Soviets, in rapid succession, exploded a multimegaton thermonuclear bomb, unveiled the makings of a hitherto nonexistent long-range aerial strike force, and — even before the Sputnik episode in 1957 — clearly demonstrated the technological prowess needed to produce intercontinental ballistic missiles. Even then, only the U.S.S.R. posed a threat of general war. Only one delivery system, long-range bombers, was available to either side. Cataclysmic catastrophe seemed the inevitable consequence if nuclear weapons were used. Sophisticated concepts were unknown. Professor Albert Wohlstetter's "The Delicate Balance of Terror," which first called attention to a wide range of deterrent and war-fighting possibilities, was not published until 1959.[16]

The United States, feeling its way in unfamiliar territory during those early years, placed the highest possible premium on deterrence. All the prerequisites for a credible first strike were present for perhaps the first decade, but in keeping with tradition, this country refused to exploit that advantage, elected a second-strike strategy, and proclaimed that policy to the world. The American people presumably were not then, and are not now, psychologically or politically prepared to launch a preventive or preemptive nuclear attack, no matter how attractive those alternatives might appear.

In January 1954, Secretary of State John Foster Dulles officially christened the prevailing concept of "massive retaliation," which promised to punish transgressors "instantly, by means and at places of our own choosing."[17] * The supporting force structure included mixed capabilities designed to limit damage to the United States while inflicting intolerable pain on the opposition. The primary threat was aimed at the Soviet population and production base, but clear U.S. superiority in nuclear combat power also vested that version of "counterforce as insurance" with the capacity to win a general war if deterrence failed.

---

* Massive retaliation never was intended "to turn every local war into a general war," as Secretary Dulles made clear on 19 March 1954, testifying before the Senate Committee on Foreign Relations. There simply should be a capacity — he emphasized the word *capacity* — for massive retaliation. Admiral Arthur W. Radford, then Chairman of the Joint Chiefs of Staff, gave the same assurance: "Our planning does not subscribe to the thinking that the ability to deliver massive atomic retaliation is, by itself, adequate to meet all our security needs. It is not correct to say we are relying exclusively on 1 weapon, or 1 service, or that we are anticipating 1 kind of war. I believe that this Nation could be a prisoner of its own military posture if it had no capability, other than one to deliver a massive atomic attack."[18] Regardless of the intent, however, our general-purpose forces were poorly prepared to fulfill flexible roles.

When President Kennedy took office, the emphasis shifted sharply to the counterforce side of the ledger, as exemplified by Defense Secretary McNamara's famous speech at Ann Arbor:

> Principal military objectives, in the event of a nuclear war stemming from a major attack . . . . , should be the destruction of the enemy's military forces, not of his civilian population. . . . We are giving a possible opponent the strongest imaginable incentive to refrain from striking our own cities.[19]

The comparative simplicity of a counterforce strategy in those days soon dissolved, as both the United States and the Soviet Union acquired larger, more diversified strike forces and instituted multiple passive defense measures. When he recognized that the probability of eradicating all or most enemy offensive forces had disappeared, McNamara reversed his field dramatically. By 1964, just two years after the Ann Arbor address, he embraced finite-deterrence concepts. The new aim was "to ensure the destruction, singly or in combination, of the Soviet Union, Communist China, and the Communist satellites as national societies."[20] His position soon solidified. By 1968, the annual Defense Department posture statement asserted unequivocally that the objective was

> to deter deliberate nuclear attack upon the United States and its allies by maintaining, continuously, a highly reliable ability to inflict an unacceptable degree of damage upon any aggressor, or combination of aggressors, at any time during the course of a strategic nuclear exchange, even after absorbing a surprise first strike.
>
> . . . the capability for assured destruction must receive the first call on all of our resources and must be provided regardless of the costs and the difficulties involved. Damage limiting programs, no matter how much we spend on them, can never substitute for an Assured Destruction capability in the deterrent role. *It is our ability to destroy an attacker as a viable twentieth century nation that provides the deterrent, not our ability to partially limit damage to ourselves.* [Emphasis added.][21]

The United States thereafter retained a credible capability against many military targets — hardened facilities, including enemy missile silos, ballistic-missile submarines submerged at sea, and mobile ICBMs are notable exceptions — but the emphasis has been heavily countervalue for several years, and counterforce concepts have fallen into disrepute.

Stark finite deterrence was supplanted by mostly finite deterrence, which began to blend into a partial damage-limiting posture in the late 1960s, when President Johnson decided to deploy a thin area defense against ballistic missiles. That trend was arrested in May 1972, at least temporarily, when the United States and the U.S.S.R. agreed to restrict their respective ABM deployments to a pair of sites in each country, as a result of the Strategic Arms Limitation Talks (SALT) (*see* Chapter 22).[22]

CONTEMPORARY U.S. DETERRENT STRATEGY

The rigidity of U.S. deterrent strategy in 1969 led President Nixon to ask an oft-quoted rhetorical question shortly after he assumed office:

Should the President, in the event of a nuclear attack, be left with the single option of ordering the mass destruction of enemy civilians, in the face of the certainty that it would be followed by the mass slaughter of Americans? Should the concept of assured destruction be narrowly defined, and should it be the only measure of our ability to deter the variety of threats we may face?[23]

In answer to his own question, President Nixon has sought to add alternatives. His most conspicuous efforts have been politico-military initiatives related to strategic arms limitations. The results seem promising in some respects, but revolutionary changes await a technological breakthrough that would enable U.S. antisubmarine-warfare elements to locate, track, and destroy ballistic-missile submarines, or the evolvement of a hard-target kill capability for Minuteman III and Poseidon missiles. Either eventuality would make it possible (although not necessarily desirable) to reinstitute a counterforce-as-insurance approach to deterrence. Both developments would give this country the makings of a credible first-strike option.

12 Strategic Retaliatory Concepts

Look out for the wasps if you stir up their nest.

ARISTOPHANES
Lysistrata

Deterrence is solely a psychological barrier. War-fighting depends on action. Strategic capabilities and concepts contribute to both. They lend credibility to one and focus to the other.

ELEMENTS OF THE U.S. SECOND-STRIKE STRATEGY

Retaliatory Timing

The U.S. second-strike strategy for general nuclear war cannot be executed until after armed aggression begins against this country. Two timing options nevertheless remain open for our decision-makers: reciprocal operations could be triggered before or after enemy ordnance exploded over friendly territory.

Option I was in effect for about four years, beginning in 1957, when a sizeable number of SAC bombers first were placed on alert. All of our retaliatory forces presented soft targets to the enemy at that time (none of our ICBMs were in silos until 1961), and our vulnerability to a surprise first strike seemed excessively high. Hard evidence concerning the size, disposition, technical characteristics, and daily activities of Moscow's missile forces was sketchy. Payload and accuracy data were particularly hazy. If we waited until the first mushroom clouds began to blossom over SAC air bases and ICBM sites, massive retaliation might have misfired. To compensate, the United States therefore subscribed to a launch-on-warning strategy.

However, launch-on-warning at that time would have involved a high probability of miscalculation. The U.S. alert system was primitive (satellite sentinels were nonexistent) and signals sometimes were ambiguous. Neither the President nor the nation was anxious to incinerate Soviet cities unnecessarily. Consequently, following review in the early 1960s, the United States returned to a genuine second-strike strategy, despite its obvious disadvantages.[1]

Force Diversity: The Triad

Diversifying delivery means is a better way to improve force survivability. It vastly complicates enemy offensive/defensive planning, and reduces the likelihood that this country could be shocked by technological surprise — the opposition would have to achieve a series of R&D breakthroughs to gain first-strike mastery over multiple weapons systems with significantly different characteristics.

The U.S. strategic retaliatory force comprises a Triad of intercontinental ballistic missiles, manned bombers, and submarine-launched ballistic missiles. It may eventually become a Quadrad, if cruise-missile submarines are added to the inventory, a proposal now undergoing debate. Each component incorporates unique capabilities, measured in terms of reliability, range, accuracy, penetration potential, pre- and post-launch survivability, simplicity, adaptability, responsiveness, control, research and development prospects, and cost. Each has shortcomings, but in combination, the three segments complement each other nicely.

Intercontinental Ballistic Missiles

Our 54 Titan and 1,000 Minuteman missiles, most of which are on constant alert, capitalize on quick reaction (a matter of seconds), plus great speed over a ballistic path, which could put them on target in the U.S.S.R. or Red China thirty minutes after the decision to launch. Unfortunately, missile accuracy depends on exact geodetic target data, missiles cannot be recalled in flight, and post-strike reconnaissance would be required to determine whether any given warhead reached its target. The pre-launch survivability of our ICBMs presumably is good at present, but Soviet "heavy" missiles fitted with multiple independently targeted reentry vehicles may soon pose a significant threat.[2]

Manned bombers

The 400 B–52 and 60 FB–111 bombers of the Strategic Air Command, assigned as unit equipment in operational squadrons,* can vary tactics, axes of attack, altitudes, and penetration corridors, and can consciously avoid confirmed or suspected enemy defenses. Only manned bombers can seek out targets whose precise location is not known, determine whether they have already been neutralized, and strike if necessary. Best of all, bombers can be launched on warning, since recall procedures are almost ironclad. Nevertheless, aircraft too have flaws. Flight times are measured in hours, not minutes. Bases and bombers on the ground both are soft targets, particularly vulnerable to bombardment by Soviet SLBMs, and the U.S.S.R. owns a sophisticated air defense network.[3]

Tactical air elements, land- and carrier-based, augment the power of SAC's long-

---

* Heavy B–52 losses over North Vietnam in December 1972 reduced the total inventory of those aircraft, but not the number assigned to squadrons.

range bombers although, strictly speaking, they are not part of the Triad.* Since their geographic dispositions, reaction times from commitment to time-over-target, and performance characteristics vary radically from those of heavy bombers, these aircraft markedly increase the number of options available. In addition, tactical aircraft are ideal for attacking mobile missiles and radars, and engaging targets of opportunity.

Submarine-Launched Ballistic Missiles

Submarine-launched ballistic missiles, fired from constantly shifting, submerged platforms, constitute the most elusive weapons system yet devised, and therefore the least vulnerable. Those at sea are almost impossible to target reliably, given the current state of the art. The United States currently has forty-one nuclear-powered submarines committed to this role, each armed with sixteen missiles (total 656). Thirty-one boats eventually will be equipped with Poseidon missiles, the successors to Polaris, tipped with MIRV warheads. This leg of the Triad has become increasingly important in recent years because of its survivability, but Polaris submarines also have assorted weaknesses. A maximum of half are on station at any given time. At least one-fourth are in port, where they are sitting ducks. The remainder, en route to or from home stations, might not be immediately responsive. Trident (formerly designated ULMS for Undersea Long-range Missile System) promises to solve several problems, but it is not scheduled for deployment until 1978.[4]

The Triad's Survivability

In combination, components of the Triad confront potential aggressors with highly complicated scheduling problems.[4]

Assume, for example, that an enemy planned to use low-yield SLBMs against soft U.S. airfields and high-yield ICBMs against our hardened missile silos. Present-generation Soviet SLBMs, with ranges that vary from 750 to 1,750 statute miles, would have to be fired from positions near our shores. Their flight times would consume six to ten minutes or so, depending on the distance between launch areas and targets. ICBMs would be en route about half an hour.

If all enemy missiles were launched concurrently, our warning system would detect incoming SLBMs too late to save our bombers, which are on fifteen-minute strip alert, but hostile ICBMs would still be at least twenty minutes from impact. The Minuteman and Titan force thus would have plenty of time to take flight, provided SAC received the signal to fire. If, on the other hand, the opposition triggered its ICBMs early enough to arrive over U.S. targets simultaneously with SLBMs, we would have ample time to flush our bomber force, which could be recalled if the warning proved false.

Our Polaris/Poseidon fleet would be largely immune, regardless of enemy attack plans.

---

* "Strategic" (as opposed to "tactical") weapons systems, including nuclear bombs, warheads, delivery means, and ancillary equipment, are designed specifically to destroy the enemy's war-making capacity during general war or to so degrade it that the opposition collapses. Tactical aircraft are not procured specifically for such purposes, but those dedicated to the SIOP (*see* pages 96–7) are targeted against the Soviet homeland.

92

Force Capabilities

Ever since the decision in favor of a countervalue strategy based on assured destruction was made early in President Johnson's administration, U.S. strategic retaliatory forces have been tailored primarily to prevent nuclear wars, rather than wage them if they erupt. As a result, none of our ICBMs or SLBMs have been created expressly for use against hard targets constructed to withstand prodigious amounts of nuclear blast, heat, and radiation. Titan II carries a large warhead, but lacks adequate accuracy. Minuteman has better accuracy, but its yields are comparatively small. Neither Polaris nor Poseidon possesses a potent enough punch. The latter, like the MIRVed Minuteman III, is intended to increase target coverage and improve penetration probabilities against a sophisticated ABM defense.[5]

Whether those deficiencies should be rectified has been under consideration since President Nixon took office in 1969. Most recently, the Defense Department requested $20 million to cover research and development costs for nuclear warheads with increased yields and improved accuracy, which would afford Minuteman and Poseidon missiles the wherewithal to destroy hard targets.[6] That petition was rejected, but the matter continues to attract attention.[7]

Oddly enough, official efforts to accrue a counterforce capability against ballistic-missile submarines submerged at sea never have evoked much opposition by domestic critics. The Department of Defense is vigorously pursuing antisubmarine warfare (ASW) programs, for which the Congress has appropriated roughly $1.9 billion since 1969.[8]

Increased counterforce capabilities would increase U.S. flexibility in at least three ways, although the impact on stability would be uncertain.

Limit Damage
While it is not possible to *obviate* damage, given the current status of technological art, counterforce operations could *attenuate* it under certain circumstances by eroding the enemy's available firepower, through preemption *or* a second strike. Herman Kahn spells out the considerations succinctly:

> When one examines the possible effects of thermonuclear war carefully, one notices that there are indeed many postwar states that should be distinguished. . . . Both very sensitive and very callous individuals should be able to distinguish (and choose, perhaps) between a country which survives a war with, say, 150 million people and a gross national product (GNP) of $300 billion a year, and a nation which emerges with only 50 million people and a GNP of $10 billion. The former would [still be a rich and mighty nation]. . . . able to restore a reasonable facsimile of the prewar society; the latter would be a pitiful remnant that would contain few traces of the prewar way of life.[9]

Limit Escalation
Symbolic and exemplary attacks, overtures against the enemy's allies rather than his homeland, and talionic (tit-for-tat) exchanges illustrate some uses proposed for strategic nuclear weapons short of full-scale general war. In each case, actions against

military targets probably would generate less animosity than strikes against cities, and thus seem to proffer greater possibilities for controlled conflicts.

Handle Emerging Nuclear Powers

The proliferation of nuclear weapons among countries other than the United States and the Soviet Union has already begun. Whether the spread will continue is unknown. The multilateral problems posed are significantly different than those generated by bilateral U.S.-U.S.S.R. relationships. Assured destruction, for example, may not be the most effective way to deter or deal with potential aggressors like Red China, whose predominantly rural population is widely dispersed. The ability to disarm such countries may someday be the only protection against nuclear blackmail.

Force Size

A second-strike strategy is an expensive proposition. It costs billions to amass sufficient retaliatory assets to survive a massive surprise attack and still inflict grievous wounds on the enemy. The key question is: how much is enough?

Basic Considerations

Arguments for and against numerical superiority, parity, and "sufficiency" are specious unless placed in perspective. The fact that Side "A" has twice as many launch vehicles, three times as many warheads, or four times as much gross megatonnage as its opponent may be meaningful in one strategic context, but meaningless in others.

The size of America's ICBM and SLBM inventories has remained constant for several years, as a result of decisions made in the 1960s, when this country was wedded to finite deterrence, with minor modifications. Our strategic bomber fleet has declined.[10]

Four factors dictated those determinations: a countervalue strategy; assured-destruction policies; the threat; and the characteristics of available delivery systems.

Countervalue Strategy This country's retaliatory concepts evolved through several stages during Secretary of Defense McNamara's regime, as noted in the preceding chapter. By February 1965, when he delivered his posture statement before the House Armed Services Committee, the cornerstone of U.S. general-war strategy was "the deterrence of a deliberate nuclear attack against either the United States or its allies." U.S. leaders believed that this country and the Soviet Union had the capacity "to destroy one another" and that, if war occurred, disaster was inevitable. The resultant prescription for predominantly countervalue targeting put a lid on our force structure.

Assured-Destruction Policy Assured-destruction requirements to satisfy stated deterrence objectives fluctuated over the years. In the final analysis, McNamara judged that destroying from 20 to 25 percent of the Soviets' population and half of their industrial capacity would suffice.[11]

The size force needed to accomplish that chore depended first of all on the number, types, and locations of aiming points in the U.S.S.R., together with related enemy defenses. The quantity of U.S. launch vehicles was deemed far less important than the number of separately targetable, serviceable, accurate, reliable warheads. That conjecture caused the United States to MIRV existing missiles in response to burgeoning

Soviet offensive capabilities, instead of increasing its inventory of bombers and ballistic missiles. Moreover, absolute power, rather than relative strengths of opposing forces, was considered crucial. "Excess" strength (overkill capability) was considered unnecessary and undesirable.

The Threat   Force levels also correlated closely with estimates of the threat, which took cognizance of the extent, weight, and presumed effectiveness of a surprise first strike on U.S. retaliatory elements. Such prognostications never can be precise, but as McNamara put it, "they are not unmanageable":

> By postulating various sets of assumptions [often exceedingly controversial], ranging from optimistic to pessimistic, it is possible to introduce into our calculations reasonable allowances. . . . For example, we can use in our analysis both the higher and lower limits of the range of estimates of the number of enemy ICBMs and long-range bombers. We can assign to these forces a range of capabilities as to warhead yield, accuracy, reliability, etc.[12]

Delivery Systems   The vulnerabilities of each delivery system in relation to the threat create drastically different force requirements. There is a close connection, for instance, between the numbers of land-based missiles deployed by a defender and the numbers of weapons needed to destroy them. If all other things were equal, which they are not, the ratio would be one offensive ICBM per enemy silo. In practice, several weapons for each target may be mandatory to ensure the desired probability and degree of success. Contrarily, the electromagnetic pulse from one weapon might engage several targets simultaneously. One launch vehicle with MIRV capabilities could do the same. Nevertheless, there still is a direct relationship between the ICBM strength of adversaries. That is not so for submarines submerged at sea. Their survivability does not depend on the size of opposing nuclear strike forces.

Disputations

America's strategic retaliatory force levels are disputed by their architect as well as their detractors, for different reasons.

McNamara himself flatly stated in 1968:

> Our current numerical superiority over the Soviet Union . . . . is both greater than we had originally planned and more than we require. In the larger equation of security our superiority is of limited significance, for . . . . the Soviet Union, with its present forces, could still effectively destroy the United States, even after absorbing the full weight of an American first strike.[13]

Senator George McGovern, the Democratic presidential candidate four years later, concurred:

> While sufficiency for deterrence cannot be readily determined, there is at least one commonsense top limitation on the size of the nuclear force . . . . and that is the number of targets worth attacking.

> In the case of the Soviet Union, some 34 percent of the population and 62 percent of the industrial capacity is concentrated in 200 cities, almost all of which would be destroyed by a like number of one-megaton equivalents. Doubling the number of

> deliverable warheads would only add another six percent to the number of people lost, and another ten percent to the amount of industrial capacity demolished.
>
> [Comparable calculations were produced for Red China.]
>
> It is logical to conclude therefore that the guaranteed capability to deliver 200 one-megaton equivalents on separate targets in both the Soviet Union and China accomplishes at or near the maximum the United States can expect from the strategy of deterrence . . . . The United States plainly keeps many multiples of the maximum practical deterrent even after discounting for weapons that might fail or be lost to an initial attack.[14]

Disbelievers in assured destruction, who prefer a more versatile strategy, deplore the trend from unqualified U.S. numerical ascendancy vis-à-vis the U.S.S.R. to parity and, in some cases, inferiority. Among them is President Nixon, who has repeatedly expressed concern over the changing strategic balance. His misgivings prompted serious efforts during SALT I to negotiate a five-year injunction against the continued augmentation of Soviet SLBMs and intercontinental ballistic missiles. There was no mistaking the seriousness of that matter, as the U.S. delegation made clear: "If an agreement providing for more complete strategic arms limitations were not achieved within five years [that is, by 1977], U.S. supreme interests could be jeopardized."[15]

Centralized Planning: The Siop

Meticulous planning is mandatory if abstract theories and concepts are to be translated satisfactorily into concrete programs and available forces are to be orchestrated successfully.

Prior to 1960, each major U.S. command with a strategic nuclear capability prepared its own retaliatory plans, without formal regard for targeting undertaken at other headquarters. That indisputably created timing conflicts, inefficient allocation of weapons, duplication of effort, and unnecessary hazards for friendly forces.

As a result, Secretary of Defense Thomas S. Gates directed that all general-war strike planning be centralized. To accomplish that task, the JCS formed the Joint Strategic Target Planning Staff (JSTPS). Because the Strategic Air Command had the greatest nuclear targeting expertise at that time and the necessary machinery for strategic retaliatory planning, the JSTPS was collocated with SAC headquarters in Omaha, Nebraska, and CINCSAC was appointed Director of Strategic Target Planning (DSTP) as a corollary duty. The Joint Chiefs of Staff now deal directly with that single point of contact on matters concerning general nuclear war planning.

The JSTPS maintains its own specialized intelligence base, guides the collection process that keeps it current, and undertakes technical analyses, including the identification of desired ground zeroes (DGZ) — see Figure 3. All activities culminate in the Single Integrated Operational Plan (SIOP), the U.S. strike plan for general nuclear war, which is to be executed only if deterrence fails.

Representatives from all commands that allocate assets participate full-time in preparing the SIOP. In addition, two separate study groups assist. The Strategy Panel, an in-house organization, is dedicated to SIOP tactics and strategy. It investigates

FIGURE 3
The Joint Strategic Target Planning Staff

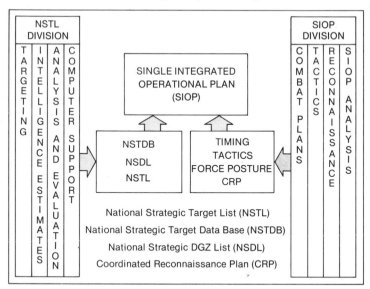

Courtesy of Mark D. Mariska and **Military Review**

prospective targets, the impact of new weapons systems, and their optimum employment. The Scientific Advisory Group, comprising military and civilian scientists, addresses specialized subjects, such as nuclear burst phenomena, weapons effects, and certain foreign weapons anomalies. Liaison between the JSTPS, the Departments of State and Defense, and the U.S. intelligence community further facilitates the compilation of a coordinated final product.

According to Mark D. Mariska, who authored the most illuminating treatise on the JSTPS that has reached unclassified print, the SIOP, constantly under revision, is analyzed and war-gamed under many conditions. The resultant contingency plan, reviewed and approved by the Joint Chiefs of Staff, gives the United States a flexible, rapid reaction capability:

> In some ways, it is surgically precise. Necessarily complex, complicated and tedious in preparation, the SIOP is straightforward and simple in execution, and it provides the President with many options regardless of the circumstances surrounding plan initiation.

> The SIOP applies, of course, only to preplanned operations in a general nuclear war environment. It is virtually impossible to [prepare for post-SIOP actions].[16]

Positive Control

Positive control over U.S. strategic retaliatory forces has always been official U.S. policy.

Strategic Control

Control problems can be incredibly complex during crisis situations preceding war. They could be critical during and after a nuclear attack, when the President (or his duly designated successor) would need to ascertain who did what under what circumstances, assess the damage, select the most appropriate response, communicate decisions to appropriate agencies, and initiate follow-up actions, all in a matter of minutes, under immense pressure.

A National Military Command System (NMCS) assists the National Command Authorities (NCA)* in those demanding tasks. The NMCS eventually will be integrated into a more sophisticated Worldwide Military Command and Control System (WWMCCS), which will provide improved service to a larger list of customers.

The National Military Command Center (NMCC), manned round-the-clock and housed in the Pentagon, is the focal point of the NMCS. The NMCC is tied directly to the White House Situation Room, the State Department Operations Center, the CIA Indications Office, the U.S. Intelligence Board National Indications Center, the United Nations Military Mission, the Office of Emergency Preparedness National Warning Center, and other key organizations. The NMCC therefore is in a paramount position to collect, evaluate, and disseminate the data needed to manage crises or prosecute a nuclear war. However, the NMCC being a soft target, fixed and mobile alternate command posts also serve the NCA. They afford complementary, but reduced, facilities.

The normal chain of command runs from the Chief Executive to the Secretary of Defense, then through the Joint Chiefs of Staff to commanders of unified and specified commands in the continental United States and overseas. However, the channel of communications for time-sensitive operations such as the SIOP is from the NCA through the Chairman of the Joint Chiefs of Staff (in the NMCC), thence directly to "executing commanders."[17] The latter are not specifically identified. If circumstances permitted, orders probably would be addressed to CINCSAC, who controls Minuteman and our long-range bombers, and to CINCs in the Atlantic and Pacific, who control Polaris/Poseidon missiles and tactical aircraft that have general war missions. In emergency, the NCA could contact individual ICBM sites, ballistic-missile submarines, and bomber bases. Communications networks are intermeshed, so that message traffic could be routed over alternative avenues if parts of the system failed to survive a nuclear attack.

Tactical Control

Procedural and technological controls are continually being improved to eliminate any likelihood that misunderstood directives or maliciously falsified orders could result in an unwanted war.

---

* JCS Pub. 1 lists the President, Secretary of Defense, the Joint Chiefs of Staff, and their authorized alternates as the NCA. DOD Instruction 5100.30, which delineates procedures for the WWMCCS, states that "the NCA consists only of the President and the Secretary of Defense or their duly deputized alternates or successors." The latter document must take precedence. However, the NMCS *does* serve the Joint Chiefs as well as the NCA, and the WWMCCS will do so later.

General Thomas S. Power, a former SAC Commander, explained some of the constraints imposed on strategic aircraft. After reaching the positive control point outside enemy territory,

> bombers return to their bases *unless* they receive coded voice instructions to proceed to their targets. The "go code" can be given only upon direct orders of the President, and it must be authenticated by officers at each of several levels of command and by more than one member of the bomber crew. Coordinated action by several crew members is also required to arm nuclear weapons after the "go code" has been received and authenticated.[18]

Safety measures for missile systems were simple in the early days, when boosters and fuels were stored separately. Preparation time was so lengthy that probabilities of an accidental or unauthorized launch were nearly nil. However, Titan II and Minuteman can be fired in a matter of moments, and once aloft, can be destroyed in flight, but cannot be recalled. Joel Larus describes Minuteman precautions in *Nuclear Weapons and the Common Defense*. A launch control commander and his deputy, at a control center physically separated from the silos, tend each flight of ten missiles. To complete the countdown, they must activate locks that are spaced at least ten feet apart. One man cannot turn both keys simultaneously. Perhaps even more important, the Air Force screening, selection, and evaluation process for personnel who control, handle, or have access to nuclear weapons systems eliminates (as far as possible) paranoids, the impulsive, and other misfits most prone to unreliability.[19] Similar safeguards apply to Titan and Polaris/Poseidon operations.

THE CONTINUED EVOLUTION OF U.S. RETALIATORY CONCEPTS

President Nixon, in his 1972 report to the Congress, accorded strategic nuclear forces first priority in the scheme of U.S. national defense. They must provide the primary deterrent against atomic attacks on the United States or its allies, convince aggressors that major provocations would cause them to risk unacceptable escalation, and minimize enemy opportunities for intimidation or coercion.[20]

Whether the contemporary U.S. conceptual framework affords a solid base from which to satisfy those objectives is the subject of debate within the Administration and without. The second-strike strategy, the emphasis on assured destruction and associated weaponry, the Triad, force requirements, planning, and control procedures all are the object of caustic criticism. Only the decision to discard launch-on-warning has been conceded anything approaching a favorable consensus.

13 Strategic Defensive Concepts

In war, the defensive exists mainly that the
offensive may act more freely.

ALFRED THAYER MAHAN
A lecture on naval strategy, 1911

Mahan's straightforward assertion seems slightly anachronistic in the Atomic Age, which has altered classic offensive-defensive relationships. Defense, for example, has traditionally been portrayed as nonprovocative, but in general war situations, it could be dangerously destabilizing. A tight defense, even one coupled with unpretentious offensive assets, could constitute a credible first-strike capability. Further, defense influences deterrence differently than it affects war-fighting.

DIFFERING VIEWS OF NUCLEAR DEFENSE

The desirability of strategic defense has been in dispute for well over a decade. The resultant complications are bewildering, as Figure 4 suggests. Those who accept defense as a necessary aspect of national security find favorable implications wherever they look. Those who reject it find misfortune.

Possony and Pournelle, in their treatise on *The Strategy of Technology,* identify two primary arguments against strategic defense, each with theoretical and economic implications:

> The basic theoretical argument against defenses is that they might work. By so doing, they reduce the casualties that would be incurred in a nuclear war, and thus make that war more "rational" or possible. . . . According to this theory, the American and Soviet populations are hostage to each other, and ought to be. . . .

> The second theoretical argument against defense, often made by the same people who suggest the first argument above, is that the system will *not* work [emphasis added]. Instead, all the defense systems will do is force each nation to construct strategic offensive forces that can penetrate the enemy defenses. . . .

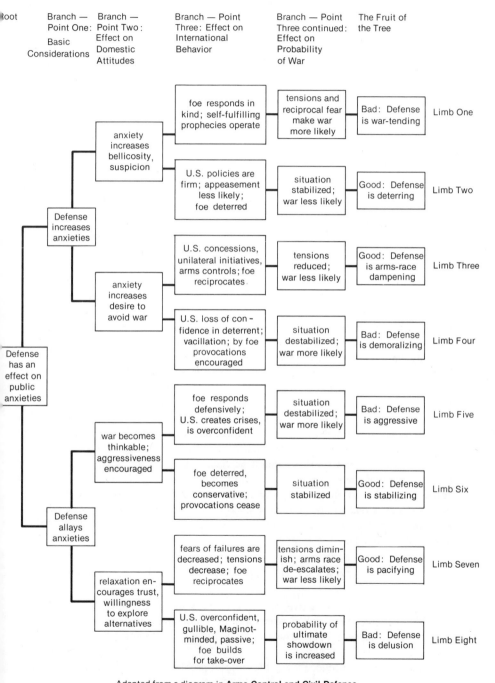

FIGURE 4
A Tree of Arguments Related to Strategic Defense

Adapted from a diagram in **Arms Control and Civil Defense,**
edited by D. G. Brennan. The Hudson Institute, 1963.

> The primary technical-economic arguments are, first, that [a sound system is inconceivable], or that we simply cannot afford a system that will work. . . . A second school contends that this argument is probably true, but that even if it were not, we would be better off using the money to construct new Strategic Offensive Forces, on the basis that the aggressor will be more easily detered by the prospect of [annihilation] than by the possibility that his attack will not be successful.[1]

Disbelievers in strategic defense place total faith in deterrence. They depend on the threat of mutual assured destruction. Others are of a different persuasion. Dr. Donald G. Brennan of the Hudson Institute coined the acronym "MAD" for mutual assured destruction, because he believes it to be "almost literally mad." It is mad to deliberately establish a strategy in which millions of innocent civilians would be exterminated if deterrence failed.[2]

Possony and Pournelle decry the absence of defense on conceptual, technological, budgetary, and moral grounds. In their view, which is widely held, wilfully prolonging the "balance of terror" runs counter to the Judeo-Christian ethic. They concede that leakproof defenses may be a practical impossibility, but nevertheless maintain that pervious defenses, which provide partial protection for the nation, are infinitely preferable to none. At the very least, they would complicate enemy strategy and tactics. Better still, fears of small-scale, accidental, unauthorized, exemplary, or nuisance attacks would diminish or disappear. Continuing R&D programs in the field of strategic defense would help this country to grow technologically, a practical necessity in any long-term struggle for survival. Even the arms race predicted by pessimists could hold some positive promise: as mutual inventories of offensive weaponry increase, destructive possibilities might well progress to the point that general nuclear war would be logically improbable. In fact, serious escalation in spending for strategic offensive arsenals should *de-escalate* the conventional arms race. If the costs "are really not high enough to accomplish that result, then they have been exaggerated." If they are, the United States is in a better economic position to compete than the Soviet Union.[3]

Superimposed on the controversy over whether to defend at all is the issue of *what* to defend — counterforce targets, countervalue targets, or both. Protecting land-based missiles and bombers, while leaving the people exposed, would suggest a second-strike deterrent strategy, and therefore might be stabilizing. Retaliatory capabilities would be enhanced, but the nation's vitals would still be vulnerable. Conversely, protecting cities, not retaliatory forces, could be construed as provocative. There is no need to defend weapons that will be used for aggressive pupuses. Defending strategic offensive arms *and* the population could connote clear evidence of intentions to accrue a credible first-strike capability.

U.S. STRATEGIC DEFENSIVE PHILOSOPHY

U.S. strategic defensive measures, whether active or passive, have served two purposes, sometimes separately, sometimes in combination: to preserve a savage second-strike capability, and/or to protect the population, production base, and national institutions.

Strategic defense produced few philosophical problems in the 1950s, when manned bombers constituted the only intercontinental nuclear threat. Both the United States and the Soviet Union met that challenge head-on with conventional, time-tested methods. However, ballistic missiles introduced complications before the decade was over. By the mid-1960s, the architects of our deterrent strategy, which was based on mutual assured destruction, had largely discarded strategic defense. We should not be under the illusion, Defense Secretary McNamara indicated, that damage-limiting ploys, regardless of how extensive they might be, could prevent either the United States or the U.S.S.R. from eradicating the other. In his opinion, improved offensive capabilities could always outstrip the defense, at a fraction of the cost.[4]

As time went on, he ameliorated that position slightly, acknowledging that population defense against a second-rate nuclear power (such as Red China) seemed feasible. Defense might also "offer a partial substitute for the further expansion of our offensive forces" if a greater-than-expected Soviet threat emerged. On one point, however, he remained adamant to the end. A comprehensive defense of cities against attacks by the U.S.S.R. would "be a futile waste of our resources."[5]

President Nixon concurred with the latter conclusion, after an intensive review of his predecessor's philosophies and practices. Moreover, whereas President Johnson had decided to install a thin area defense for U.S. cities, which could be modified to serve as a shield for our ICBMs, Nixon reversed the emphasis.[6] Within four years, he also helped engineer an antiballistic-missile treaty with the Soviets which effectively eliminated most future protection for our urban centers.[7] In short, the concept of mutual assured destruction has now been institutionalized by three successive administrations, despite recent and official rhetoric to the contrary. Contemporary U.S. strategic defensive posture reflects that trend.

U.S. STRATEGIC DEFENSIVE POSTURE

Active Defense

Antiaircraft Defense

Working hand-in-glove with our neighbors to the north, we set about installing an air defense system in the 1950s. It was, and still is, planned and operated by a closely knit, combined organization commanded by an American with a Canadian deputy. The North American Air Defense Command (NORAD), as it is now called, divided the entire continent above the Rio Grande into defense areas and exercised operational control over all participating forces.

The resultant arrangement comprised a comprehensive surveillance network, plus point and area defenses. Since the only dangerous avenue of enemy approach was from the north, Alaskan radar stations and the Distant Early Warning (DEW) Line were draped from the Aleutians to Iceland as an outer alert perimeter. The Mid-Canada and Pine Tree Lines were positioned closer in, augmented by a generous group of gap-filler radars, Navy picket ships offshore, USAF early warning and control aircraft, and the Texas Towers. Manned aircraft were charged with positively identifying "bogies," either visually or electronically. Interceptors furnished forward area defenses to engage and destroy confirmed enemy intruders. They were backed up by Bomarc cruise missiles deployed in our northeastern states and in southeastern Canada. Point defenses for high-value urban and industrial targets initially were provided by Nike batteries, which subsequently were supplemented by Hawk missiles with a low-level capability.

As time went by, our air defense system was allowed to deteriorate. The DEW Line has been cut drastically during the past decade. The number of search radars in the United States was reduced by nearly half during the same period. Gap-filler radars have disappeared. Picket ships and planes have been virtually discontinued, except for small patrols between Cuba and Florida. The remaining radar coverage creates a thin screen for our east and west coasts and along the Canadian border, but it has little depth. There is no electronic warning apparatus at all in the vast area between the mouths of the Mississippi and Colorado Rivers. The interceptor alert rate has been reduced and five squadrons of Bomarc missiles have been phased out. Modernization measures are lagging. In short, U.S. air-defense concepts appear sound, but the hardware is lacking.[8]

The causes can be traced to prevailing views of the threat. Official estimates credit the U.S.S.R. with just 140 heavy bombers, which are antiquated and are phasing out. The new Soviet Backfire bomber eventually may supersede them, but that is uncertain. Many influential observers currently doubt that the Kremlin would try to compensate by committing its 800 medium bombers in an intercontinental role, even if they were refueled en route.

Other authorities, including CINCNORAD, perceive a more serious threat. They are backed up by the Air Force Assistant Chief of Staff for Intelligence, who predicts that "the Soviets have definitely decided to maintain a credible air strike option against the CONUS."[9] However, such estimates, temporarily at least, have fallen from favor, and progressively fewer funds have been made available for improving U.S. air defense forces.

Antiballistic-Missile Defense

The U.S. shield against land-, sea-, and air-launched missiles thus far has been confined to an alert network.

The Ballistic Missile Early Warning System (BMEWS) is limited to three stations, one in Alaska, another in Greenland, and a third in England. Its surveillance fans cover all north polar approaches. The BMEWS promises to sound the alarm fifteen to twenty minutes before any ballistic-missile bombardment from the U.S.S.R. could burst on U.S. soil, depending on the elevation, trajectory, and target impact areas of the incoming ordnance. The BMEWS must discriminate between such diverse objects as enemy penetration aids and commonplace clutter on the radar screen, then compute range, course, and destination of warheads within seconds. Those capabilities are supplemented by over-the-horizon (OTH) radars located in Europe and the Far East, which currently can detect ICBM launchings anywhere on the Sino-Soviet landmass. Our 474N radars would afford six to ten minutes' advance notice of a sea-launched missile attack, but that brief notification is inadequate.

However, a new satellite-based sensor system "now provides high confidence, virtually immediate warning" of hostile SLBM and ICBM launches, including Fractional Orbit Bombardment System (FOBS) attacks. Space vehicles can be identified and tracked by USAF Spacetrack equipment and the Navy's Spasur, both of which tie into NORAD. The Space Defense Center provides continuous cataloguing.[10]

No U.S. antiballistic missile (ABM) sites are yet operational.

As a matter of principle, Defense Secretary McNamara vigorously opposed active ABM defenses throughout much of the Kennedy and Johnson administrations. He was irked at antagonists in the Armed Services, Congress, and the press, who accused him of playing dollar politics, and took steps to dispose of that indictment:

> It is alleged that we are opposed to deploying a large scale ABM system because it would carry the heavy price tag of $40 billion. Let me make it very clear that the $40 billion is not the issue. If we could build and deploy a genuinely impenetrable shield . . . we would be willing to spend . . . any reasonable multiple of that amount.[11]

The first reluctant steps in the opposite direction resulted from a significant shift in the strategic situation. When Red China began to emerge as a nuclear power, McNamara suddenly reversed his stand, conceding in late 1967 that there were "*marginal* grounds" for installing a modest ABM screen as a precaution against "miscalculation" or "irrational behavior" by Mao. But he predicted correctly that great pressures would be generated to expand that "relatively light and reliable Chinese-oriented ABM system into a heavy Soviet-oriented . . . system," and warned that "we must resist that temptation firmly."[12]

McNamara's proposed seventeen-site Sentinel program was suspended by President Nixon shortly after he took office, pending review. On 14 March 1969, Nixon announced his intention to proceed with a "modified Sentinel system," later redesignated Safeguard. Phased deployment of up to twelve sites was to be based on an annual reappraisal of the Soviet and Chinese Communist threats, as Figure 5 indicates.[13]

Safeguard objectives were to be threefold:

1. To protect U.S. land-based retaliatory forces against a direct attack by the Soviet Union.
2. To defend the American people against the kind of nuclear attack that Red China probably will be able to mount in the mid or late 1970s.
3. To protect the U.S. against accidental attacks from any source.[14]

President Nixon further described Safeguard as follows:

> We will provide for local defense of selected Minuteman missile sites and an area defense designed to protect our bomber bases and our command and control authorities. In addition, this new system will provide a defense of the Continental United States against an accidental attack and will provide substantial protection against [Red China]. . . . This deployment will not require us to place missile and radar sites close to our major cities [which the Sentinel program would have done, to the public's consternation].[15]

Phase I, comprising installations at Grand Forks AFB, North Dakota, and Malmstrom AFB, Montana, squeaked through the Senate by the narrowest of margins, and construction began. Scheduled readiness dates were October 1974 and early 1976 respectively. Congress subsequently authorized advanced preparations at Whiteman AFB, Missouri, and Warren AFB, Wyoming.[16]

Progress stopped on 26 May 1972, except at Grand Forks, when the United States and the Soviet Union signed an ABM treaty as an outcome of SALT I. Each party

FIGURE 5
Original Safeguard Phases and Options

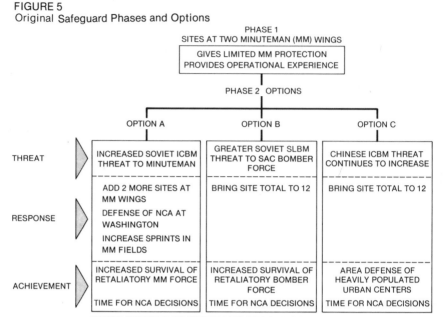

PHASE 1
SITES AT TWO MINUTEMAN (MM) WINGS

GIVES LIMITED MM PROTECTION
PROVIDES OPERATIONAL EXPERIENCE

PHASE 2 OPTIONS

	OPTION A	OPTION B	OPTION C
THREAT	INCREASED SOVIET ICBM THREAT TO MINUTEMAN	GREATER SOVIET SLBM THREAT TO SAC BOMBER FORCE	CHINESE ICBM THREAT CONTINUES TO INCREASE
RESPONSE	ADD 2 MORE SITES AT MM WINGS / DEFENSE OF NCA AT WASHINGTON / INCREASE SPRINTS IN MM FIELDS	BRING SITE TOTAL TO 12	BRING SITE TOTAL TO 12
ACHIEVEMENT	INCREASED SURVIVAL OF RETALIATORY MM FORCE / TIME FOR NCA DECISIONS	INCREASED SURVIVAL OF RETALIATORY BOMBER FORCE / TIME FOR NCA DECISIONS	AREA DEFENSE OF HEAVILY POPULATED URBAN CENTERS / TIME FOR NCA DECISIONS

POSSIBLE ADDITIONS TO THE ABOVE FULL DEPLOYMENT: ALASKA, HAWAII

renounced in perpetuity the right to erect an area defense of its homeland and agreed to restrict regional defenses to a pair of sites at least 800 miles apart, one centered on the national capital, the other on an ICBM field. The Malmstrom complex is being dismantled as a result. Whether an ABM installation eventually will cover the National Command Authorities and associated security apparatus at Washington, D.C., still is undetermined. In any event, antiballistic-missile defenses for this country will remain minimal for the foreseeable future.[17]

Passive Defense

Passive Protection for Retaliatory Forces
Passive defenses for U.S. counterforce targets are largely the responsibility of SAC and NORAD. Polaris submarines rely mainly on mobility to reduce their vulnerability.

Numerous techniques have been used alone or in combination to achieve the desired effect. The duplication and dispersion of sites are basic. So is the hardening, not only of ICBM silos, but of command, control, and communications centers as well, such as subterranean facilities for the National Command Authorities at Fort Ritchie, Maryland, and NORAD's nerve center, buried in the granite of Cheyenne Mountain, near Colorado Springs. The usefulness of hardening, however, has a limit, owing to the huge yields and improved accuracy of SS–9 missiles now in the Soviet inventory. The cost of drilling deep enough in bedrock, or pouring enough reinforced concrete, to protect Minutemen from direct hits or near misses is exorbitant.

Consequently, studies were undertaken to determine whether mobility by road, rail, or cross-country vehicles might be the key to ICBM survival. The so-called "shelter base" concept emerged, which contemplated creating multiple launch sites for every Minuteman and moving the missiles frequently. This would make it possible to play a gigantic "shell game," forcing the enemy to expend several nuclear weapons to guarantee a single hit. Some strategists suggest abandoning land-based missiles entirely in favor of weapons afloat, an opinion not likely to gain early acceptance, if for no other reason than expense. Proposals to put ICBMs on airborne platforms also exhibit serious shortcomings.

Passive defenses for aircraft take a different tack. To increase credibility, SAC has maintained a quick-reaction posture since 1957. Forty percent of all B–52s, FB–111s, and tankers normally are on continuous ground alert, deployed at many locations. Survivability was abetted in 1970 through the use of so-called "satellite bases," including civilian airfields, which permit increased dispersion in emergency and reduce the time needed to launch the force. In addition, a classified proportion of SAC bombers and tankers could be placed on airborne alert, twenty-four hours a day, seven days a week, in emergency. NORAD's squadrons also have dispersal plans.

Passive defense through mobility also is an option open to the National Command Authorities, whose National Emergency Airborne Command Post (NEACP), housed in three C–135 aircraft, is on constant strip alert at Andrews Air Force Base.*

Civil Defense

Passive security for countervalue targets, mainly cities, lies within the purview of civil defense. Four basic possibilities stand out: a low-key fallout shelter program to protect selected portions of the population; a comprehensive fallout shelter program applicable to the entire populace; fallout shelters, plus urban blast protection; and mass evacuation of heavily settled areas in event of a nuclear alert.

Only the first option ever enjoyed much emphasis, even during the civil defense heyday a decade ago, when President Kennedy briefly energized fallout shelter construction as a result of the U.S.-Soviet confrontation over Berlin. Panicky preparations continued for roughly two years. Get-rich-quick shelter manufacturers sprang up like mushrooms. Official publicity pushed the program well, but not very wisely, as Arthur Schlesinger recalls:

> As the Defense Department had first conceived the problem, each family was to dig for itself. To advance the cause the Pentagon hired Madison Avenue specialists to prepare a shelter instruction booklet intended for distribution to every householder. . . . [Unfortunately], it seemed to be addressed exclusively to the upper middle class—to people owning houses with gardens or basements; there was nothing in it for people who lived in tenements. . . . Moreover the tract assigned the protection of the population to private enterprise.[18]

That "do-it-yourself" family shelter proposal was a disaster. Before long, the Defense Department rewrote its pamphlet and a federal program was inaugurated, supple-

---

* Soon will be converted to modified Boeing 747s, as the Advanced Airborne Command Post (AABNCP).

mented by state and local efforts, to earmark existing sites in urban areas and stock them with emergency supplies. Even so, when the Cuban missile crisis ensued only five buildings out of 1,083 that met the prescribed criteria for fallout shelters in Washington, D.C., reportedly had been provisioned with food and first-aid articles.[19] Subsequent efforts improved the situation substantially, but the whole effort lost momentum rapidly after 1962, despite strong efforts by civil defense workers to convince Congress and the public that fallout shelters would be a cheap form of insurance against lethal or incapacitating radiation (*see* Figure 6).[20]

FIGURE 6
Benefits of Fallout Shelters

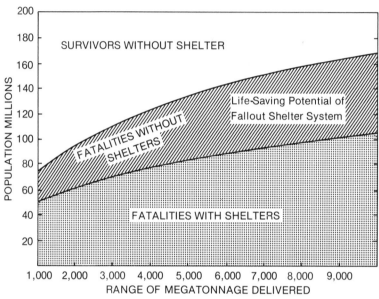

Blast shelters to provide protection against overpressures exceeding 250 pounds per square inch could be built, but the cost — perhaps ten times as much as for fallout shelters — has been branded prohibitive. If adequate alert notice were assured, which it is not, mass evacuation theoretically might empty key cities, except for caretaker service. However, the problems would be astronomical. Imagine motivating, moving, feeding, housing, and ministering to millions of able-bodied citizens (let alone the infirm) for an indefinite period, and relocating them permanently, if necessary.

Political, military, moral, technical, psychological, and philosophical theses have been advanced, pro and con, but in the final analysis, civil defense, like air defense, languishes largely because the American public discerns no immediate threat. That attitude is reflected by their Congress, which has become progressively disenchanted with prospects of spending substantial sums to prepare for an event that may never take place. Federal appropriations for fiscal year 1963 were barely half those for the preceding year. Since then, the residue has been sliced by roughly one-third, not counting depreciation in the purchasing power of the dollar.

STRATEGIC SUMMATION

The confusion of claims, counterclaims, semantic tricks, logic traps, and other calculated ambiguities regulated to general nuclear war has persisted for many years. Clarification is essential, but most rethinking is predicated on theories at least a decade old. The job of aspiring strategists now is to weigh the various cases, separate the sensible from the nonsensical, add their own innovations, and come up with some fresh, imaginative concepts.

14 Flexible Response as an Element of U.S. Strategy

'Tis the part of a wise man to keep himself today
for tomorrow, and not venture all his eggs in one
basket.

MIGUEL de CERVANTES
Don Quixote

THE GENESIS OF FLEXIBLE RESPONSE

The concept of flexible response, which has been articulated as a primary underpinning of U.S. military strategy for more than ten years, first saw the official light of day as *A National Military Program* conceived by General Maxwell D. Taylor, then Army Chief of Staff, approved by Wilber M. Brucker, Secretary of the Army, and published as a position paper on 1 October 1955. It was triggered by Taylor's belief that:

> Massive Retaliation as a guiding strategic concept has reached a dead end and that there is an urgent need for a reappraisal. . . . In its heyday, massive retaliation could offer our leaders only two choices, the initiation of general nuclear war or compromise and retreat. From its earliest days, many world events have occurred which cast doubt on its validity and exposed its fallacious character. Korea, a limited conventional war fought by the United States when we had an atomic monopoly, was clear disproof of its universal efficacy. The many other limited wars which have occurred since 1945 — the Chinese civil war, the guerrilla warfare in Greece and Malaya, Vietnam, Taiwan, Hungary, the Middle East, Laos, to mention only a few — are clear evidence that, while our massive retaliatory strategy may have prevented the Great War — a World War III — it has not maintained the Little Peace; that is, peace from disturbances that are little only in comparison with the disaster of general war. . . .

> The strategic doctrine which I would propose to replace Massive Retaliation is called . . . the Strategy of Flexible Response. This name suggests the need for a capability to react across the entire spectrum of possible challenge, for coping with anything from general atomic war to infiltrations. . . . The new strategy would recognize that it is just as necessary to deter or win quickly a limited war as to deter general war.

110

> Otherwise, the limited war which we cannot win quickly may result in our piecemeal attrition or involvement in an expanding conflict which may grow into the general war we all want to avoid.[1]

That thesis, which stresses multiple options rather than any single weapons system, strategic concept, or combination of allies sounds commonplace enough today, but it was highly provocative and controversial at the time, and still confronts strong opposition in some quarters. Similar ideas were advocated during that same period by respected intellectuals, including Henry Kissinger, but supporters in the armed services (other than the Army) were precious few. When Taylor's proposal came to a vote by the Joint Chiefs during a strategy conference in March 1956, it was rejected.

The rebuff was short-lived. General Taylor served his term as Army Chief of Staff and retired in 1959, but was recalled to active duty by John F. Kennedy two years later, became the President's personal military advisor, and shortly thereafter was elevated to the pinnacle as Chairman of the Joint Chiefs of Staff. Flexible response was in.

ARGUMENTS AGAINST FLEXIBLE RESPONSE

The opposition to flexible response reflected parochial service interests, with associated axe-grinding, but genuinely different approaches to defense policy and strategy were also involved.

Budgetary Objections

The defense budget was at the root of inter-service rivalry, because it directly controlled roles and missions (*see* Chapter 21). As General Taylor put it:

> Percentages from Fiscal Year 1955 to Fiscal Year 1959 had been about 46 per cent for the Air Force, about 28 per cent for the Navy and Marine Corps, and some 23 percent for the Army, with the remainder of the budget going to the Department of Defense itself. In the vital area of funds for the purchase of new equipment, which controls the rate of modernization, the Air Force in this period had consistently received some 60 per cent of the available resources, the Navy and Marine Corps about 30 per cent and the Army about 10 per cent.[2]

And, he concluded:

> Not only are [the resultant] military programs ponderous and hence difficult to redirect, but there are powerful service and economic forces committed to the maintenance of their *status quo*. I feel sure that the continued emphasis on Massive Retaliation and on the requirements of general war arises as much from the practical difficulties of overcoming this inertial momentum and of resisting these external forces as from any real conviction as to the rightness of the orthodox strategy.[3]

Budgetarily, the Air Force obviously was in the best position to benefit from the status quo, and its leaders predictably fought the new strategy, which threatened to reduce its share of the fiscal pie. However, the desperate competition for cash left no service entirely untainted. Allegations persisted that flexible response was nothing more than an Army hoax to improve its power position, apparent altruism notwithstanding. Tom Schelling, reminiscing ten years later, recollected that attitude:

> In the late fifties, the Navy realized that its weapons were not good at doing what the Air Force was being funded to do under the strategy of massive retaliation. The Navy therefore had to think of a reason why alternative strategies were better for the nation as a whole — and they settled on the Army's new strategy of flexible response. The Army, for its part, had developed the strategy because it had to come up with a theory of limited war or go out of business.[4]

Conceptual Objections

More germane than the exposition above were substantive disagreements with the logic of flexible response.

One basic conclusion reached by most proponents of flexible response, was that general nuclear war between two antagonists, neither of whom possessed an invulnerable first-strike capability, was unthinkable as a deliberate policy decision, unless survival was at stake and no acceptable alternatives were available. From that belief sprang the "firebreak concept," which postulates that opportunities for conventional limited wars would greatly increase within such parameters, since minor acts of aggression would not warrant a massive nuclear response. The precise level of the nuclear threshold cannot be defined, since it would vary with circumstances.

Maxwell Taylor's conclusion that massive retaliation offered U.S. decision-makers no other choice than "general nuclear war or compromise and retreat" drew derision from the likes of General Nathan Twining:

> The argument has been made that . . . the United States must face either humiliation or annihilation. Here we have either/or again. This argument is not in the best interests of the United States for two reasons: first, it is not true. Second, the implication of facing annihilation is a reflection of the defeatist attitude that no one can win a nuclear war. If the enemy thinks that America thinks it faces annihilation, he will naturally push our country to the wall.
>
> You can bet your bottom dollar that the [opposition] does not share the view that no one can win a nuclear war. But it is precisely what they want America to believe. They do not believe it, and they are preparing to win it.[5]

Equally cogent was the conviction held by supporters of massive retaliation that U.S. power in limited wars should be applied at points of decision, not dissipated in inconclusive actions. John Foster Dulles enunciated that view very well in his 12 January 1954 address to the Council on Foreign Relations:

> Local defense will always be important. But there is no local defense alone which will contain the mighty land-power of the communist world. Local defenses must be reinforced by the further deterrent of massive retaliatory power. A potential aggressor must know that he cannot always prescribe battle conditions that suit him.[6]

112

In short, members of the massive retaliation school believe that the best way for this country to handle limited wars is to engage the primary enemy directly and decisively, instead of fighting proxies. Of course, that position implies a willingness to risk general nuclear war and, in the estimation of President Kennedy and his successors, the ends rarely would justify such means.

Finally, massive-retaliation advocates contended that the very foundations of flexible response were specious, because the United States had enjoyed highly versatile capabilities for years. Twining again acted as a spokesman:

> U.S. military forces have had the capacity for flexible response all along. No sane man believes in driving a tack with a sledge-hammer. The nation has not had to. What this nation has lacked has been the political nerve at times to use what it has had.
>
> Now I do believe, as I have said before, that our military land and sea forces did need numerical strengthening in forward areas, *but not for the purpose of building up our capability to win a non-nuclear war*, but for the purpose of on-the-spot commitment of national prestige. The concepts are vastly different. [Emphasis added.][7]

Not everyone saw it that way, most particularly President Kennedy and Robert McNamara, who put flexible response into effect as a pillar of U.S. military strategy, along with credible deterrence and collective security.

The term *flexible response* was dropped from the Nixon-Laird lexicon, but the concept is still in effect, and it still creates a need to cope with all levels and scopes of conflict. Although flexible response is commonly associated with limited war, it applies equally to general nuclear war, where massive retaliation remains as *one* potential option.

FORCE REQUIREMENTS

To implement the strategy of flexible response, General Taylor recommended fundamental changes in the U.S. military posture. As first priority, he recommended steps "to modernize and protect the atomic deterrent force," while concurrently augmenting "our limited war, counter attrition forces to offset the . . . preponderant Soviet forces on the ground." Next, he sought "carefully selective provision for continental air defense, for the requirements of full mobilization, and for survival measures to hedge against the failures of deterrence." Alterations in the types and numbers of forces within each category, the character and extent of their equipment, the nature of their deployment at home and overseas, reaction times (which involve strategic mobility means), and sustainability all were essential if the theory was to have meaning and substance.[8]

Secretary McNamara, who was Secretary of Defense at the time, shaped the transitional process:

> When I entered the Defense Department in 1961, several basic considerations were becoming clear. We had to improve our strategic nuclear forces even as we fit them into our new understanding of their place in the balance of power, and we had to increase greatly the emphasis on our conventional forces. . . .

113

As a start we increased the purchase of conventional weapons, ammunition and equipment, expanded the Navy's ship-maintenance program, ordered construction of more amphibious transports, and modified Air Force tactical fighters to improve their non-nuclear delivery capability. In addition, we stepped up the pace of training; began revamping the Army Reserves; added personnel to the Army and its Special Forces, as well as the Marine Corps and its Reserve; increased airlift capability; and intensified non-nuclear military research and development.[9]

The Influence of Contingency Operations

The size of the force was conditioned by prevailing philosophies concerning contingency operations. McNamara spelled out Kennedy-Johnson views as follows:

> The over-all requirement for general-purpose forces is related not so much to the defense of our own territory, of course, as it is to the support of our commitments to other nations. Each of these commitments gives rise to contingencies for which we must plan. This does not mean that we will ever be confronted by forty-odd South Vietnams simultaneously, however . . . and while we cannot expect to meet all the contingencies simultaneously, neither can our opponents. Our policy has been to set the size of the general-purpose forces so that we can simultaneously meet the more probable contingencies.[10]

From that rationale we derived the "2½-war strategy," which called for capabilities to counter major concurrent challenges in Europe and the Orient, while retaining ample reserves to put out a minor brushfire elsewhere. Great improvements were realized, but that unrealistic goal, whose limits always were fuzzy, never was reached.

The Influence of Force Deployment

Just how the U.S. military establishment should be deployed to cope with contingencies was a continuing matter of controversy. McNamara explained the official decision:

> The central question here, of course, is the ability to move quickly to meet possible threats, conceivably at widely separated points in the world. There are essentially two main approaches. The first is to maintain very large conventional forces stationed around the globe near all potential trouble spots. The second is to maintain a smaller central reserve of highly ready forces, supported by the means to move them promptly wherever they might be needed. . . . Both the relative feasibility and desirability of the second have greatly increased during the last decade.[11]

Option I, full-scale forward deployment, is very expensive in terms of money, manpower, and materiel if applied to "all potential trouble spots." However, forces in position to react rapidly if and when crises arise have greater deterrent and war-fighting values than distant reserves. Option II, the "fire brigade" approach, reduces over-all requirements, but it also reduces responsiveness. Conditions in combat areas, particularly the loss of ports and airfields to early enemy actions, might delay the timely insertion of reinforcements. Moreover, reserves based in the continental United States must depend heavily on supplies and duplicate sets of equipment prepositioned overseas, which are costly, difficult to maintain, and are subject to seizure or destruction by the enemy.

A substantial body of opinion therefore believes that Options I and II both represent undesirable extremes which degrade, rather than upgrade, flexibility. Greater versatility is obtainable from compromise solutions that limit forward deployment to *selected* critical areas and, at the same time, maintain sizeable CONUS-based reserves, which could reinforce or cover lesser contingencies as required.

THE IMPACT OF VIETNAM

As the war in Vietnam developed, U.S. flexibility began to regress.

It is probably safe to say that the military machine we committed to that conflict in 1965 was the most professional general-purpose force the United States had ever fielded at the onset of a war, and it stayed that way for several years, but at terrible cost. Secretary McNamara exulted, for instance, that "the very stability of our NATO contribution during that period is a significant example of the flexibility we developed."[12]

In fact, the U.S. Seventh Army was stripped clean as early as 1966 to satisfy needs in Vietnam. As a result of "business-as-usual" defense policies (*see* Chapter 29), green lieutenants commanded companies in Europe, where seasoned captains had before; there was a critical shortage of experienced NCOs; troop units were chronically understrength; the modernization of materiel slackened, and in some cases ground to a stop. Helicopter production, for example, was earmarked almost exclusively for Vietnam. Morale, training, and combat effectiveness in Europe inevitably atrophied. The Navy and Air Force suffered similar setbacks. Rotation bases were virtually destroyed, leaving no ready reserve. Had we been confronted with additional serious outbreaks anywhere else in the world — the Middle East, in particular was a powder keg throughout that period — we had very few military means with which to meet them, without threatening nuclear war.

For all practical purposes, this country had swung full circle in less than a decade. The choice once again was between humiliation and an inappropriately harsh response, neither of which would be in our national interest. The *Pueblo* and EC-121 incidents off North Korea in 1968 and 1969 confirmed that grave provocations, such as armed attacks on U.S. ships and aircraft in international waters or airspace, might provoke no military retaliation at all. One reason was our inability to follow through, should the situation spark another limited war.

THE PRESENT STATUS OF
FLEXIBLE RESPONSE

Debits

A shrinking defense budget severely constrains this country's ability to apply force flexibly in support of its global strategy, wherever and whenever that should prove desirable:

115

We lack sufficient general-purpose forces to satisfy our modest "1½-war" strategy. We have drastically reduced the size of our military establishment, but have not modernized the residual forces to compensate.

We rely increasingly on centralized strategic reserves, but lack the means to deploy them expeditiously.

We emphasize burden-sharing by allies, but continue to chip away funds earmarked for military assistance.

Our regional strategies all depend heavily on freedom of the seas, but the naval forces which must maintain control are progressively deteriorating.

Our contingency operations depend on active and reserve forces in combination, but Army National Guard divisions are not combat ready.

Flexible response suffers from other ailments not associated with the budget. Our assured-destruction strategy for general war rather rigidly restricts combat options if deterrence should fail. At the limited war level, "graduated response" and "flexible response" have been considered interchangeable. General LeMay addressed the resultant problems:

> This doctrine has a fine-sounding ring to it, but as practiced it is "graduated" but *"inflexible."* It is graduated in that force is brought to bear against the enemy in increments which never seem quite enough to do the job, and "inflexible" because we fail to apply force at places and times of our choosing where we can profit by our strength and exploit enemy weaknesses.[13]

Credits

Insufficient financial support and frequent misapplication of the theory have kept flexible response from flowering militarily, as originally conceived, but fortunately "a capability to react across the entire spectrum of possible challenge" operates on many levels, of which the military level is not necessarily the most important. President Nixon, in tandem with Dr. Kissinger, has gone a long way toward reestablishing strategic flexibility politically, economically, and psychologically. Dialogues with the Soviet Union, Communist China, other opponents, and our allies bear that out. Several pluses have already resulted, in the President's opinion:

> 1. *The Soviet Union.* We have succeeded in giving a new momentum to the prospects for more constructive relations through a series of concrete agreements which get at the cause of the tension between our two countries. . . .
>
> . . . we agreed on a treaty barring weapons of mass destruction from the ocean floor.
>
> . . . we broke the deadlock which had developed in the talks on limiting strategic arms. . . .
>
> . . . we agreed on a draft treaty prohibiting the production or possession of biological and toxic [chemical] weapons.
>
> . . . we and our British and French allies reached an agreement with the Soviet Union . . . to reduce the danger of Berlin once again becoming the focus of a sharp and dangerous international confrontation.

116

. . . we agreed on a more reliable "Hot Line" communication between Washington and Moscow, and on measures for notification and consultation designed to reduce the risk of an accidental nuclear war.

2. *The Peoples Republic of China.* We have ended a 25-year period of implacable hostility, mutually embraced as a central feature of national policy. Fragile as it is, the rapprochement between the most populous nation and the most powerful nation of the world could have greater significance for future generations than any other measure we have taken [recently]. . . . It will represent a necessary and giant step toward the creation of a stable structure of world peace.[14]

President Nixon also cited several "breakthroughs" with our allies, including the palliation of economic threats to unity and the evolution of greater politico-military autonomy for our partners.[15]

A better balance between military and non-military flexibility nevertheless is still in order. In the final analysis, direct and indirect approaches must be intermixed, in cold war situations as well as hot, "to exert desired degrees and types of control over the opposition through threats, force . . . diplomacy, subterfuge, and other imaginative means." Only when *all* available tools are brought to bear in the most ingenious fashions can the concept of flexible response contribute most effectively to national security.

15 U.S. Concepts of Collective Security

Let every nation know, whether it wishes us well
or ill, that we shall pay any price, bear any
burden, meet any hardship, support any friend,
oppose any foe to assure the survival and the
success of liberty.

PRESIDENT JOHN F. KENNEDY
Inaugural Address, 1961

America cannot — and will not — conceive *all* the
plans, design *all* the programs, execute *all* the
decisions and undertake *all* the defense of the
free nations of the world.

PRESIDENT RICHARD M. NIXON
State of the World Message, 1970

CLASSICAL AND WORKING DEFINITIONS

Conflicting concepts of *collective security* begin with disagreements over what the term means.

Purists interpret collective security as "a global security system based on the agreement of *all or most states* to take common action against any nation that illegally breaks the peace" [emphasis added]. According to that rather narrow explication, "only two collective security systems — those of the League of Nations and of the United Nations — have been attempted in the modern world."[1] A. F. K. Organski fleshes out that concept as follows:

> The whole idea is based upon the correct assumptions that peace can best be preserved by a preponderance of power, that the combined strength of all the nations except a single aggressor would always equal such a preponderance, and that an aggressor faced with such overwhelming force would give up, probably in advance.[2]

118

Unfortunately, the mandatory united front almost inevitably fails to materialize in the clutch, primarily because incompatible national and supranational interests prevent it. Stringent political, economic, social, psychological, and moral pressures preclude a universal consensus as to who the aggressor is and what action, if any, should be taken. In consequence, all but the most determined individuals dedicated to the whole impractical proposition of a global police force generally agree that the gap between ideal and reality may be unbridgeable.

Working definitions used by U.S. officialdom, including the Departments of State and Defense and the Joint Chiefs of Staff, therefore correspond more closely to Webster, who describes collective security as "the maintenance by common action of the security of all members of an association of nations." Since "an association of nations" may include many participants or be limited to two, even bilateral concords qualify.

DIFFICULTIES IDENTIFIED

The primary purpose of any collective security pact is to augment the national power of all participants. Sometimes that goal is attainable, sometimes it is not. Admiral Arleigh Burke, a former Chief of Naval Operations, explored the following pros and cons at the National War College.

To begin with, no alliance is any stronger than the interests that bind its members together. Such attachments are fragile and subject to change, particularly when the survival of one or more parties is imperiled, but not that of the others. Ironically, allies can almost always be counted on to deliver when their help is needed the least. When the pressure is really punishing, they may contribute too little, arrive too late, or never pitch in at all. That manifestation occasionally can be traced to a Machiavellian syndrome, but most often it simply reflects human nature. When the balance of power looks precarious, few national leaders like to risk being on the losing side if there is an acceptable alternative. Warning signs of queasiness and vacillation sometimes are visible well in advance, but not always. Prudent planners therefore never lean too heavily on outsiders to pull chestnuts out of the fire.

Despite precautions, alliances nevertheless may involve unwilling colleagues in highly volatile ventures that run counter to their national interests. Jordan, for example, was in no position to wage war against Israel in 1967, but her partnership with Egypt excluded all options once Nasser struck from the Sinai. Worse yet, common bonds can be maliciously exploited by unprincipled confederates. The U.S.S.R. routinely uses its associates as cat's paws, buffers, and pawns. Its leaders exhibit no compunction whatsoever about sacrificing third-country assets to attain Soviet ends or to defeat opposing ambitions.

ADVANTAGES ACKNOWLEDGED

The question often asked by full-fledged skeptics is: "If, when the chips are down, allies invariably look after their own interests, what useful purposes do coalitions serve?"

Collective security arrangements encourage the development of common strategic concepts, the publication of common plans, and the generation of common preparations that constitute the bases for coordinated action against common enemies. Potential benefits range from intangibles like goodwill and understanding to material advantages, such as maneuver room, base and overflight rights, intelligence support, and access to local labor. Every *quid* of course demands a *quo*. History suggests that the best way to make agreements work is for national leaders to promise no more than they *really* can deliver, but to produce a little extra whenever possible. All affiliates should understand the rules (implicit, as well as explicit, ones) from the start, so that minimum leeway is left for interpretation when the moment of truth arrives.[3]

HISTORICAL PERSPECTIVE

This country's historic aversion to entangling foreign alliances slackened only slightly during the first World War, when we joined forces with Britain and France to help "make the world safe for democracy." That foray was succeeded by a retreat to our North American sanctuary in the 1920s and 1930s. General Lyman L. Lemnitzer, reminiscing about those interwar years, wryly recalls a parade of senior speakers at the Army War College in 1939, who preached from the pulpit, "If we have to fight another war, for God's sake do it without allies!" Their prejudice was widely echoed by influential political figures throughout this land.

Nevertheless, the very next year, we were immersed in coalition warfare on a global scale. Before Pearl Harbor, U.S. collective security policy consisted largely of providing aid and comfort to Great Britain, China, and the Soviet Union, but once we became actively embrangled in World War II, the need for a common strategy immediately became apparent. Formulating one was no mean task, since the political objectives, philosophies, and postures of the sovereign partners were radically different. Compromise, a distasteful process to many Americans, was common. Our "shotgun marriage" was under constant strain, but the lessons learned were invaluable.

For the succeeding quarter century, which brings us to the present, collective security has been a pillar of U.S. grand strategy. It was first put to the test shortly after VJ day when, in rapid succession, the Soviets began turning the screws along their southern periphery and in Eastern Europe. Hopes that the United Nations would secure peace in the postwar world soon dissolved, as the U.S.S.R. unveiled a string of vetoes which effectively hamstrung the Security Council. By 1947, when it was evident that Britain no longer could fulfill its traditional role in world affairs, the United States stepped into the breach.

The Truman Doctrine, expounded before a joint session of Congress on 12 March 1947 and enacted on 22 May that year, dealt specifically with Greece and Turkey, but it set the stage for subsequent collective security actions on a comprehensive scale:

> . . . totalitarian regimes imposed upon free peoples, by direct or indirect aggression, undermine the foundations of international peace and hence the security of the United States. . . . I believe that it must be the policy of the United States to support free peoples who are resisting subjugation by armed minorities or by outside pressures.[4]

CURRENT U.S. DEFENSE COMMITMENTS

During the period 1947–1954 we signed eight mutual defense pacts, both bilateral and multilateral, with forty-two countries, as shown in the table on pages 122 and 123 prepared by the Department of State.

Our 1951 defense ties with Japan were replaced by the present treaty in 1960. The United States, though not a member, also consented to cooperate with the Central Treaty Organization (CENTO), which consists of Great Britain, Turkey, Iran, and Pakistan. In addition, we concluded defense pledges or agreements with something like thirty other countries.

The resultant worldwide collective security system bound us to defend Latin America and almost every noncommunist state along the Sino-Soviet rim. In some cases, formal documents specify the obligations of all parties in great detail. In others, commitments are implied. The difference may be academic in given sets of circumstances.

U.S. MILITARY AID PROGRAMS

To buttress the military capabilities of its allies, the United States has maintained multiple military assistance programs (MAP) since 1947.

In the beginning, these were mainly grants, which encompassed free arms, equipment, training, and services for so-called "forward defense countries" along the Soviet frontier. Greece and Turkey were the first recipients. The famous Marshall Plan, which had military aspects, followed shortly thereafter. However, as Europe recovered from World War II and other states improved their capacity for self-help, we gradually substituted direct sales and credits in many instances, thereby converting giveaway programs to sources of revenue, which helped alleviate balance-of-payment problems. More than thirty nations still receive grants, but most outlays are very small, and are limited largely to training. South Korea, Turkey, and Cambodia currently get the most sizeable gifts (aside from Vietnam and Laos, which are included as a special category in the Department of Defense budget).

U.S. military aid to real, imagined, and potential allies expanded remarkably in the early 1950s, stimulated by the formation of NATO and by the Korean War. Eventually, MAP embraced numerous underdeveloped and/or emerging nations in Latin America, Africa, and Asia, whose relationships to U.S. national security were tenuous or nonexistent. MAP costs skyrocketed to almost $4 billion annually in fiscal year 1953, but subsided sharply soon thereafter. However, the incremental totals over the years have been enormous — grant aid alone has exceeded $35 billion since 1950[5] — and the entire aid endeavor has been subjected to increasingly caustic Congressional criticism for several years.

The climax came on 29 October 1971, when the Senate temporarily scuttled almost all of our foreign aid programs by refusing to authorize new funds. President Nixon immediately mounted a rescue operation. Whether or not his counteroffensive was responsible is debatable, but on 4 November a modified bill reinstated sufficient funds to satisfy existing commitments, pending a comprehensive review.

CURRENT U.S. DEFENSE COMMITMENTS

TREATIES

Multilateral Treaties

Inter-American Treaty of Reciprocal Assistance (Rio Pact 1947)

United States	Dominican	Nicaragua
Argentina	Republic	Panama
Bolivia	Ecuador	Paraguay
Brazil	El Salvador	Peru
Chile	Guatemala	Trinidad
Colombia	Haiti	Tobago
Costa Rica	Honduras	Uruguay
Cuba*	Mexico	Venezuela

* Cuba was excluded from the Rio Pact in 1962.

North Atlantic Treaty (1949)

United States	Italy	Greece (1952)
Belgium	Luxembourg	Turkey (1952)
Canada	Netherlands	Federal Repub-
Denmark	Norway	lic of Germany
France	Portugal	(1955)
Iceland	United Kingdom	

Security Treaty between the United States and Australia and New Zealand (ANZUS 1951)

Southeast Asia Collective Defense Treaty (SEATO 1954)

United States	Pakistan	South Vietnam*
Australia	Philippines	Cambodia*
France	Thailand	Laos*
New Zealand	United Kingdom	

Bilateral Treaties

Mutual Defense Treaty with the Philippines (1951)
Mutual Defense Treaty with South Korea (1953)
Mutual Defense Treaty with China (Taiwan) (1954)
Treaty of Mutual Security and Cooperation with Japan (1960)

* South Vietnam, Laos, and Cambodia are not signatories of SEATO but were included under treaty's defensive provisions in a protocol to the treaty. Cambodia has rejected the protection of SEATO. Laos has declared it will not "recognize the protection of any alliance or military coalition including SEATO" in the 1962 Geneva Declaration on the Neutrality of Laos. The United States and other nations agreed also in the Geneva Declaration to "respect the wish of . . . Laos not to recognize the protection of any alliance or military coalition, including SEATO."

CURRENT U.S. DEFENSE COMMITMENTS

CONGRESSIONAL RESOLUTIONS

There have been five Congressional resolutions since 1945. Each of these has been requested by the President to mobilize Congressional support at times of foreign policy crisis. The five resolutions follow. Dates of the joint resolutions refer to the day they were signed into law. The date for H Con Res 570 is the day the resolution was cleared by Congress. It did not require the President's signature and does not carry the force of law.

- Formosa resolution, H J Res 159, Jan. 29, 1955, covering Formosa (Nationalist China) and the Pescadores Islands against "armed attack" from Communist China.
- Middle East resolution, H J Res 117, March 9, 1957, proclaiming U.S. policy to defend Middle East countries "against aggression from any country controlled by international communism."
- Cuban resolution, S J Res 230, Oct. 3, 1962, to defend Latin America against Cuban aggression or subversion and to oppose the deployment of Soviet weapons in Cuba capable of endangering U.S. security.
- Berlin resolution, H Con Res 570, Oct. 10, 1962, reaffirming the U.S. determination to use armed force, if necessary, to defend West Berlin and the access rights of the Western powers to West Berlin.
- Vietnam resolution, H J Res 1145, Aug. 10, 1964, known as the Tonkin Gulf resolution, authorizing the President to use armed forces to repel attacks against U.S. forces and affirming U.S. determination to defend any SEATO treaty member or protocol state (this includes Vietnam) requesting assistance.

EXECUTIVE AGREEMENTS

The United States has entered defense arrangements by executive agreement with the following countries:

Denmark	1951	Iran	1959
Iceland	1951	Turkey	1959
Spain	1953	Pakistan	1959
Canada	1958	Philippines	1959, 1965
Liberia	1959		

POLICY DECLARATIONS, COMMUNIQUES

The State Department's 1967 compilation of U.S. commitments includes 34 Executive Branch policy declarations and communiques issued jointly with foreign governments. The following areas and nations are covered by these pledges: Latin America (Monroe Doctrine), Berlin, Iran, India, Jordan, Israel, Thailand, South Vietnam, the Republic of China and the Philippines. With the exception of India, these policy declarations and communiques cover nations which also have received U.S. pledges under treaties, executive agreements or Congressional resolutions. India received a pledge in 1954 from President Eisenhower that the United States would act to prevent Pakistan from using U.S. military aid against India.[5]

Courtesy of Congressional Quarterly Service. From *Global Defense: U.S. Military Commitments Abroad, 1969.*

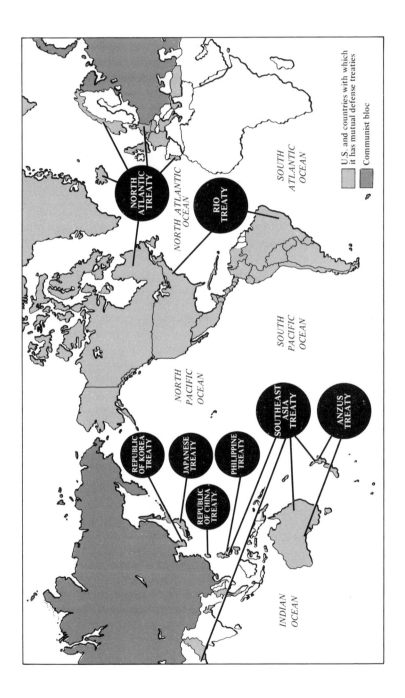

NORTH ATLANTIC TREATY

RIO TREATY

REPUBLIC OF KOREA TREATY

JAPANESE TREATY

REPUBLIC OF CHINA TREATY

PHILIPPINE TREATY

SOUTHEAST ASIA TREATY

ANZUS TREATY

NORTH ATLANTIC OCEAN

SOUTH ATLANTIC OCEAN

NORTH PACIFIC OCEAN

SOUTH PACIFIC OCEAN

INDIAN OCEAN

U.S. and countries with which it has mutual defense treaties

Communist bloc

Meanwhile, military assistance continues to be an important cog in U.S. collective security schemes.

Secretary of State William P. Rogers describes the current philosophy

> During a period marked by negotiation and by growing assumption of defense responsibilities by others [than the United States], a continued commitment to security assistance is essential. Such a commitment helps our friends maintain and increase their own security capabilities and raises the threshold at which our treaty commitments might be invoked. . . .

> Our security assistance is heavily concentrated in two areas where we have direct security interests and responsibilities — East Asia and the Middle East. . . .

> This program is an essentielement of the Nixon doctrine's emphasis on the primary responsibility of each nation for its own security. Thus a major objective . . . is to provide a foundation of stability during the adjustment period. The adjustment is greatest among East Asian countries. . . .

> A second major objective . . . is to preserve the balance of military power in the Middle East. . . .

> A third objective . . . is to strengthen the southern flank of NATO at a time of increased Soviet military presence in the Middle East and the Mediterranean. . . .[6]

CONTEMPORARY CRITICISMS OF COLLECTIVE SECURITY

Today, the whole U.S. concept of collective security is undergoing fundamental changes in response to sharp shifts in national temper that occurred during the decade between the two policy statements that introduce this chapter. The Executive Branch, Congress, military leaders, the news media, the academic community, independent "experts," and the public are actively embroiled in one of the most elemental and intense debates on national strategy since the United States emerged from seclusion during World War II. The key issues have been summarized by the Congressional Quarterly Service as follows:

> Does national security require that the United States maintain [masses of military personnel overseas? Must we retain a huge inventory of foreign bases?]. To what extent are these installations, designed and constructed primarily in the 1950's, relevant to the defense needs of the 1970's?

> Does national security dictate that the American taxpayer support a defense budget which is larger than the combined defense budgets of the next 17 nations with the largest defense expenditures (including the Soviet Union, Communist China, France, Great Britain, West Germany, Italy and Japan)?

> Do U.S. defense treaties . . . contribute to U.S. security or do they unavoidably involve the United States in costly wars where American interests are not at stake?

> Has the cost of maintaining worldwide commitments impeded the solution to domestic American problems by diverting economic resources from the problems of poverty, race relations, health, pollution and mass transportation?

125

What role have the costs and foreign expenditures of U.S. commitments played in contributing to America's balance-of-payments problems and to the threat to the stability of the dollar as an international currency? More generally, have U.S. commitments abroad placed an additional strain on the entire international financial system?

Does U.S. security, as well as U.S. payments problems, require this nation to become the leading arms merchant to the world? To what extent has the flow of American arms, particularly to underdeveloped countries, enabled rival nations to battle each other with a more sophisticated weaponry than would otherwise have been available? How many dictators throughout the world have used American weapons to suppress the legitimate demands of their own people? Which American defense interests have been at stake in these transactions?

Have the requirements of worldwide military planning and the role of covert intelligence operations removed decision-making on issues of peace and war from the elected and accountable representatives in Congress?

Finally, and above all, under what circumstances and for the benefit of which nations or governments should Americans be prepared to honor a pledge of defense by going to war?[7]

Numerous influential individuals, in private and public life, score collective security as a waste of time and money. Most of our allies, so the allegation goes, bleed this country white, physically and financially, to their benefit, but not ours. Japan, the world's third greatest industrial giant, is flayed as a flagrant example. Critics castigate the British for creating power vacuums in the Orient and Middle East, slur France for failing to support NATO, and scorn impotent Nationalist China. They sneer at South Vietnam, which still is struggling to stand on its own feet after more than a decade of U.S. assistance, dismiss CENTO and SEATO as weak reeds, and question the efficacy of security arrangements with Australia. Extremists would withdraw to a "Fortress America," abandoning all commitments to allies.

THE NIXON DOCTRINE

The President sees things somewhat differently. He rejects any "go-it-alone" policy as imprudent, for reasons expounded at the Air Force Academy in June 1969:

It would be easy, easy for a President of the United States to buy some popularity by going along with the new isolationists. But I submit to you that it would be disastrous for our Nation and the world. . . . Let us not, then, pose a false choice between meeting our responsibilities abroad and meeting the needs of our people at home. We shall meet both or we shall meet neither.[8]

The Nixon Doctrine, promulgated in August 1969 and since elaborated, spells out revamped collective security policies for the 1970s:

First, *the United States will keep all of its treaty commitments.* We will respect the commitments we inherited — both because of their intrinsic merit, and because of the impact of sudden shifts on regional or world stability. To desert those who have come to depend on us would cause disruption and invite aggression. It is in everyone's interest, however, including those with whom we have ties, to view undertakings as a dynamic process. Maintaining the integrity of commitments requires relating their tangible expression, such as troop deployments or financial contributions, to changing conditions. . . .

In contemplating new commitments we will apply rigorous yardsticks. What precisely is our national concern? What precisely is the threat? What would be the efficacy of our involvement? We do not rule out new commitments, but we will relate them to our interests. . . .

Second, *we shall provide a shield if a nuclear power threatens the freedom of a nation allied with us or of a nation whose survival we consider vital to our security.* Nuclear power is the element of security that our friends either cannot provide or could provide only with great and disruptive efforts. Hence, we bear special obligations toward non-nuclear countries. Their concern would be magnified if we were to leave them defenseless against nuclear blackmail, or conventional aggression backed by nuclear power. Nations in a position to build their own nuclear weapons would be likely to do so. And the spread of nuclear capabilities would be inherently destabilizing, multiplying the chances that conflicts could escalate into catastrophic exchanges. . . .

Third, *in cases involving other types of aggression we shall furnish military and economic assistance when requested in accordance with our treaty commitments. But we shall look to the nation directly threatened to assume the primary responsibility of providing the manpower for its defense.* No President can guarantee that future conflicts will never involve American personnel — but in some theaters the threshold of involvement will be raised and in some instances involvement will be much more unlikely. . . .

We will continue to provide elements of military strength and economic resources appropriate to our size and our interests. But it is no longer natural or possible in this age to argue that security or development around the globe is primarily America's concern. The defense and progress of other countries must be first their responsibility and second, a regional responsibility.[9]

Having enunciated those guidelines, the President outlined transitional difficulties:

Policy becomes clearer only in the process of translation into programs and actions.

In this process the Nixon Doctrine seeks to reflect the need for continuity as well as the mandate for change. There are two concurrent challenges:
— to carry out our new policy so as to maintain confidence abroad.
— to define our new policy to the American people and to elicit their support.
This transition from bearing the principal burdens to invoking and supporting the efforts of others is difficult and delicate. . . .

The challenge is not merely to reduce our presence, or redistribute our burden, or change our approach, but to do so in a way that does not call into question our very objectives. . . .

There are lessons to be learned from our Vietnam experience. . . . But there is also a lesson *not* to be drawn: that the only antidote for undifferentiated involvement is indiscriminate retreat.[10]

127

In short, the Nixon Doctrine is predicated on providing ample aid to friends so they can assume the obligations we relinquish, enhancing their national security and ours in the process. Paradoxically, U.S. influence should *increase* internationally as we *decrease* our presence overseas. Relations with allied governments should improve. Allied leaders should be less sensitive once they begin controlling their own destinies to a greater extent. And best of all (from our standpoint), they should be less prone to irresponsible policies, statements, and acts, which were fairly common when U.S. military power was present on the ground.

COLLECTIVE SECURITY TRENDS

No one expects the period of adjustment to be wholly trouble-free. One potential problem that bears careful scrutiny concerns future U.S. strategies for Europe and Asia, which will be examined individually in Chapters 16 and 17. Should our presence in those areas seriously diminish, the most likely candidates to fill the gap would be Germany and Japan, respectively, each of which has the manpower, education, industrial base, expanding economy, know-how, experience, and drive to do the job. Whether they would be willing to accept increasing regional security responsibilities — and whether their associates would be willing to let them — is a key question for the mid-range future. The implications in terms of U.S. national security are not yet clear, but the impact on regional and world stability, communist reactions, attitudes of our allies, and the combat capabilities of revised alliances all promise to be important considerations.

Whichever way this country turns strategically, it seems safe to say that collective security will continue to play a significant role. We may retrench, but it would be hard to imagine a flight from reality, in which the United States relinquished all claim to world leadership.

16 U.S. Strategy for Europe

NATO has often substituted plans for purpose
and hopes for substance.

HANSON BALDWIN
Strategy for Tomorrow

Europe presents the United States with a comprehensive strategic problem that bridges the entire conflict spectrum. It is not a strictly regional matter, nor is it strictly military. The following discourse concentrates on a single aspect: military strategy for NATO's Central Region, where U.S. national security interests are paramount and the potential peril to Europe is most severe.*

U.S. INTERESTS IN WEST CENTRAL EUROPE

West Central Europe, with which we have strong political, economic, military, technological, and cultural ties, rates second only to the United States in strategic importance among regions of the Free World. This country's leaders believe that NATO's security is inseparable from our own.

Most U.S. interests in Europe coincide with those of our NATO allies, but emphases differ. Europe's survival and independence, for example, would be *directly* endangered by Soviet thrusts through the Iron Curtain. Ours would not. Some choices that are seemingly open to us, therefore, are not open to the rest of NATO. That condition has complicated the formulation of an agreed NATO strategy since the mid-1960s, when burgeoning Soviet nuclear strike forces caused West Europeans to question whether the United States would risk general nuclear war to satisfy interests that are

---

* NATO's Central Region comprises the Federal Republic of Germany, France, the Low Countries, Luxembourg, and the United Kingdom. The Sixth Fleet is our only significant military force in the Mediterranean Basin. Its strength is predicated on U.S. interests in the Middle East, North Africa, and worldwide as well as our interests in NATO Europe. The United States maintains no military forces on the Scandinavian flank, where our interests are peripheral.

not immediately vital. If *Moscow* ever seriously entertained similar doubts concerning U.S. resolve, NATO's credibility could be shattered.

POTENTIAL MILITARY THREATS TO NATO

The one and only military threat to U.S. interests in Europe is posed by the Warsaw Pact.

Warsaw Pact Capabilities

Without significant warning, the U.S.S.R., in concert with its Warsaw Pact allies, could exercise the following military capabilities: inflict great damage on the continental United States with strategic nuclear weapons, as a prelude to war in Europe; invade Western Europe, using forces now in East Germany and Czechoslovakia; support conventional operations with tactical nuclear weapons, including intermediate and medium-range ballistic missiles (IRBM, MRBM) targeted against NATO forces, air-fields, ports, command and control installations, supply depots, and other assets; challenge NATO for air superiority over Western Europe; and seriously inhibit reinforcement and resupply from the United States by contesting NATO for control of intercontinental air and sea lanes. The Soviets could augment limited war capabilities listed above by injecting additional ready forces from European Russia, Poland, and Hungary, and/or by mobilizing its reserves.[1]

Soviet Intentions

Potential threats to NATO Europe, epitomized by the capabilities just enumerated, are tempered by Soviet intentions.

A premeditated attack on the United States seems unlikely as long as the Kremlin lacks a credible first-strike capability. The Soviet belief that "any military conflict . . . . between the opposing blocs in Europe would pose great danger of [uncontrolled] escalation"[2] makes the prospects for a deep invasion of NATO territory almost as implausible as is general nuclear war. Adventurism in the form of limited-objective incursions appears dubious for similar reasons — risks would be high in relation to anticipated gains. By process of elimination, *miscalculation* in time of crisis is considered the most probable military threat to peace in Europe.[3]

Soviet Doctrine for Regional War

If a *major* war should erupt, Soviet military doctrine suggests that the Warsaw Pact would have three main objectives: the destruction of NATO's armed forces; the rapid occupation of Western Europe; and the isolation of Europe from its U.S. ally.[4]

Unclassified analyses conclude that the Kremlin's concepts for conflict in Europe stress the early use of nuclear weapons in support of armored and airborne operations throughout the theater.[5] The Soviets probably would pursue nuclear warfare vigorously, since their ordnance offers little choice. Whereas NATO emphasizes large numbers of short-range, low-yield weapons, to be used against discrete military targets,

130

Moscow stresses longer-range, higher-yield, mobile missile systems which would be better suited against soft-area targets, such as airfields and logistic installations. Indeed, the Soviet force structure raises serious doubts that the U.S.S.R. could fight a limited nuclear war if it wanted to, much less one in which collateral damage and civilian casualties were minimized.[6]

NATO'S STRATEGIC GUIDELINES

NATO's Military Objectives

To satisfy its security interests despite potential threats, NATO seeks to deter all forms of Warsaw Pact aggression, from encroachment to general war, and to defend NATO territory without serious loss or damage, should dissuasion fail.

Strategists in Western Europe understandably stress deterrence even more than we do. Extensive hostilities on NATO soil would be "limited" from the U.S. standpoint, but could be catastrophic to our partners. Should war occur, *our* overriding objective would be to obviate damage to the United States. *Theirs* would be to safeguard Free Europe.

Those schisms in defense priorities shape opposing schools of thought, whose views differ regarding *what stance would best ensure deterrence, and where the war should be fought if battle were unavoidable.*

NATO's Military Policies

The fundamental policies that guide the military planning of NATO are summarized below.

DETERRENCE/DEFENSE	BURDEN-SHARING
Limited War	U.S. Provides:
Second Strike	Primary Nuclear Capability
Containment (not Rollback)	Most Sea Power
Flexible Response	Substantial Air Power
Forward Defense	Considerable Land Power
High Nuclear Threshold	Europe Provides:
Minimum Civilian Casualties	Most Land Power
Minimum Collateral Damage	Limited Nuclear Capability
Central Control	Limited Sea Power
Non-Provocative Posture	Substantial Air Power
Comprehensive Capabilities	Installations and Facilities
Lowest Credible Force Levels	
Heavy Reliance on:	
CONUS Reserves	
Mobilization	

As will be shown, there are several contradictions between policies and objectives, between various NATO policies, between official policies and West European proclivities, and between NATO policies and Soviet military doctrine. Strategic compromises and controversy thus are inevitable.

THE OUTLINE OF NATO'S MILITARY STRATEGY

America's strategic retaliatory forces, with their assured-destruction capability, provide the primary deterrent to general nuclear war between NATO and the Soviet Union, and hopefully would inhibit irresponsible escalation by the enemy, should regional combat occur.

NATO's strategy for limited war within the European theater contemplates a strong forward defense, to repel invaders immediately or to contain them as near the Iron Curtain as possible. That concept demands sufficient versatility to cope with aggression at the most appropriate level on the conflict scale, and to escalate under full control, if necessary. Nuclear weapons are held in reserve, ready for use whenever and wherever decision-makers decree. To execute its strategy successfully, the Alliance would have to gain and maintain air superiority over Western Europe and control selected seas. Should NATO's standing forces prove insufficient, stiffening would come from reserves.

In sum, NATO strives to deny the Soviets any hope of success unless they attack in such strength that compelling U.S. interests would be jeopardized and the risk of uncontrolled escalation would be great. We will now examine that strategy.

THE DEMISE OF MASSIVE RETALIATION

NATO's deterrent and defense posture originally was predicated on the threat of massive retaliation against the U.S.S.R. in event the Warsaw Pact provoked a war in Western Europe. That simple, relatively low-cost strategy sufficed as long as U.S. nuclear capabilities were markedly superior to Moscow's. As the Soviets strengthened their position, massive retaliation gradually lost credibility as a deterrent. Worse yet, if deterrence foundered, massive retaliation guaranteed a general nuclear war which NATO could not "win."

A sweeping strategic reappraisal therefore was sparked in the mid-1960s. Predominantly conventional defenses soon were deemed too expensive. Predominantly tactical nuclear defenses were deemed too unpredictable. Neither of those tacks could cope with a wide range of contingencies. After prolonged debate, a consensus eventually prevailed in NATO councils that the low-option, low-credibility, high-risk strategy of massive retaliation was imprudent. In December 1967, the Alliance therefore embraced the complex, costly strategy of flexible response, which could contribute credibly to deterrence and would afford multiple war-fighting options if a conflict erupted (*see* the table opposite for a comparison of NATO's old and new strategies).

THE ELEMENTS OF FLEXIBLE RESPONSE

Defense concepts facilitate combat operations. They also buttress deterrence. Flexible response thus serves a twofold purpose.

NATO's Strategic Options

	Massive Retaliation	Flexible Response
TYPE OF WAR		
Global; General	X	X*
Regional; Limited		X
MAIN THEATER OF OPERATIONS		
U.S.—U.S.S.R.	X	
Western Europe		X
MAIN OBJECTIVE		
Deterrence	X	
Defense		X
OPTIONS IF DETERRENCE FAILS		
Forward Defense		X
Available Forces Only		X
Reinforcement		X
Conventional Forces Only		X
Tactical Nuclear Assistance		X
Strategic Bombardment	X	X
SPECIAL REQUIREMENTS		
U.S. Nuclear Superiority	X	
U.S. Nuclear Sufficiency		X
Local Air Supremacy		X
Sea Control		X
Strategic Mobility		X
Mobilization		X
FORCE REQUIREMENTS		
Specialized	X	
Comprehensive		X

* General war is the last-resort option of flexible response.

Conventional Response

The way in which NATO deploys its military power before D-Day is critical. Forces concentrated for conventional combat could expect unprecedented casualties if the enemy launched a nuclear war. Forces dispersed to escape the effects of nuclear weapons would be poorly prepared for classic defense. Compromise solutions are ill-suited for either environment.

NATO presently is disposed for conventional combat, on the presumption that if war resulted from miscalculation, the Soviets would withhold nuclear weapons during the opening stage. Any surprise attack would be met, and repulsed if possible, by forces presently in place. If those elements alone were unable to stem the tide, they would strive to buy time for NATO to reinforce, make calculated decisions concerning escalation, or negotiate a solution.

To accomplish those missions, NATO must cover a defensive front that stretches 500 straight-line miles from the Baltic to the Austrian border, as can be seen on the accompanying map.

Three strategically significant avenues of approach are available to the Warsaw Pact. The northernmost comes to a dead end at Hamburg, a shallow but lucrative goal. The most dangerous invasion routes traverse the broad North German Plain, part of a 1,000-mile corridor that cuts through NATO's center sector in transit from Russia to France. The third thoroughfare, in the south, follows the Fulda Gap through rugged uplands from Thuringia to the Rhine.

NATO's much criticized dispositions athwart those three avenues result from historical accidents rather than from strategic design. In large part, they parallel British, French, and American occupation zones at the end of World War II. The *Bundeswehr* now shares responsibility with forces from Britain and the Low Countries for the critical North German Plain, but the mighty United States, on the southern flank, still guards the most easily defended terrain. Amending maldeployments, by shifting U.S. ranks to the north or holding them in mobile reserve, might make military sense, but the cost of moving would be immense, and the diplomatic implications perhaps unbearable. No such action is in the offing.

The prescription for forward defense originally was a *political expedient* to ensure wholehearted participation by West Germany, which has persistently rejected any proposition that arbitrarily cedes German ground.[7] The objective, therefore, has always been to block major attacks and stabilize the situation quickly.[8]

That task is imposing. The present line of contact would be difficult to defend, particularly along the flat northern plain, and prohibitions against deliberate delaying actions leave NATO forces little latitude. Nevertheless, forward defense has been a *military necessity* since 1967, when de Gaulle evicted NATO from France. The first sharp Soviet surge would sever friendly supply lines, which presently radiate from Bremerhaven, Rotterdam, and Antwerp, then run closely behind and parallel to the prospective front. Airfields also would be overrun.

NATO no longer could defend in depth, even if forward positions proved pregnable. The Alliance formerly could have fenced with the foe all the way to the Pyrenees, if necessary, along established lines of supply and communication. At West Germany's waist, the theater now is barely 130 miles wide, less than one-third the distance from Los Angeles to San Francisco. Maneuver room for armies is at a premium. NATO forces and facilities are fearfully congested. Every lucrative military target, including command and control centers, airbases, ports, and supply depots, is within reach of Soviet IRBMs and MRBMs. An enemy breakthrough would compel NATO to retreat across Belgium toward Dunkerque or south toward the alpine wall. Even if France

invited NATO back in emergency, few advantages would accrue, since facilities there have deteriorated or been dismantled.[9]

NATO's freedom of choice obviously would be constricted under present circumstances, and decision times compressed. How long the Atlantic Alliance could hold along the Iron Curtain would depend on a host of variables, including — but not restricted to — the nature of the conflict (nuclear or nonnuclear), the scale of the Soviet attack (comprehensive or limited objectives), the amount of warning (hours, days, or weeks), the capabilities of opposing forces, NATO's will, and the weather. If strong enemy elements cracked through the crust, our main line of resistance could be enveloped, unless friendly forces regrouped behind the unfordable Rhine, the first major defensible terrain feature to the rear.

Tactical Nuclear Response

If purely conventional defenses crumble, NATO plans to use tactical nuclear weapons, after consultation. The time, place, and circumstances under which the Alliance would "go nuclear" have deliberately been left vague to complicate enemy planning.[10]

A *low* nuclear threshold would improve NATO's ability to sustain a strong forward defense, but a *high* threshold would be salutary for several reasons.

Severe civilian casualties and collateral damage would be difficult to avoid if tactical nuclear weapons were exploded in large numbers. Limited target-acquisition capabilities make it technically impossible to deliver ordnance infallibly onto stationary targets, let alone onto military forces on the move. Moreover, in a war for survival, the temptation to engage "suspected" targets would be high. Numerous deaths from accidental fallout probably would follow, even if both sides agreed to abstain from surface detonations.

Controls would be tenuous at best. Nuclear weapons could be administered very selectively — for defensive purposes only; on NATO territory only; against military targets only; using air bursts only or atomic demolitions only; and low yields only — but none of those restrictions would be as readily distinguishable by the enemy as the "firebreak" between nuclear and conventional combat. Since the first side to disregard arbitrary restraints might accrue a decisive advantage, the pressures to escalate would be enormous.

Manpower requirements for tactical nuclear warfare might *exceed* those for conventional combat. NATO's forward defense forces would have to be strong enough to make the enemy mass. Otherwise, Soviet assault troops would present few profitable targets. However, friendly formations would also suffer from nuclear attack, and attrition rates would be high. Eventual ascendancy thus might be attained by the side with the greatest reserves of materiel and trained manpower.[11]

Reinforcement

NATO has few readily accessible reserves. All major ground combat forces are "on line." Available fighter squadrons have been judged insufficient to perform assigned tasks. In exigency, the early augmentation of elements now in place therefore would be imperative.

This country's air-ground reinforcements comprise three categories: dual-based forces, garrisoned in the United States, but dedicated to NATO; other active duty forces earmarked for NATO in emergency; and selected segments of our National Guard and Reserve.

These forces exhibit varying degrees of readiness. Some tactical fighter, reconnaissance, and airlift units, for example, could be en route to Europe almost immediately, others in less than ten days.[12] Army National Guard divisions would require significantly greater warning to receive personnel and equipment fillers, complete team training, and deploy. If the war terminated in, say, ninety days, only those elements mobilized and positioned well before that time would count. The remainder would be ineffective, no matter how impressive they might look on paper.

Reinforcements in the United States are less vulnerable to preemptive attack than those in Europe, and their rapid introduction into the theater in emergency could lend credence to NATO's resolve. However, distant reserves are a poor substitute for forces that are on hand, familiar with their missions, and attuned to the terrain. Equally important, it might be politically inexpedient to reinforce during time of tension. Such steps could *provoke,* rather than prevent, a war.

Massive Retaliation

If all other measures appeared inappropriate, NATO could still resort to massive retaliation against the Soviet homeland. Should that come to pass, the United States no longer would be primarily concerned with military support for its European allies. It would be struggling for survival.

ADDITIONAL DEMANDS

NATO's strategy of flexible response depends on several capabilities that were of reduced moment when massive retaliation was in vogue: air supremacy; sea control; strategic mobility, both airlift and sealift; and command/control arrangements for directing a regional war.

Air Supremacy

Freedom of action on the ground demands dominance in the air. How best to prosecute campaigns for air supremacy produces a quandary. Strikes against air bases in East Germany would engage enemy air power at its source, but would invite heavy losses from antiaircraft defenses and would risk rapid escalation. Limiting aerial combat to skies over West Germany would confine the conflict, but would forfeit initiative to the foe, and would compound civilian casualties and structural damage in NATO territory.

The duration of the air war would influence attrition. The 1967 Israeli raids against Egyptian airfields indicated how devastating a short conventional clash can be. Nuclear combat could multiply losses by several orders of magnitude, particularly if Soviet ballistic missiles struck our installations. The number of serviceable aircraft remaining to NATO after air issues had been decided would strongly condition the course of land battles.

Sea Control

Reinforcement and resupply, now high-priority projects, call for secure lines of communication from Western Europe to North America and the Middle East.

In the absence of armed escorts, allied shipping would be plagued by "very heavy losses," according to Admiral Elmo R. Zumwalt, Chief of Naval Operations, "starting with those which occur [on D-Day] as a result of interdiction by Soviet submarines operating in the Caribbean and on the West Coast of Africa." Essential avenues would have to be kept open indefinitely "against a maximum Soviet naval interdiction effort." Failure to do so "could result in the collapse of [NATO's] defense, due to POL and other logistical starvation, even if the land battle were to stabilize."[13] Protracted antisubmarine warfare operations would be essential before NATO could reduce losses to "manageable proportions."

Controlling the entire Atlantic Basin would be a practical impossibility. Therefore, NATO practices defense in depth. During time of war, its fleets would take advantage of geographic "choke points," such as the Greenland-Iceland-Faeroe gaps, the Turkish Straits, Gibraltar, and the Baltic bottlenecks, to help confine enemy naval forces.

Strategic Mobility

To function effectively, NATO must be able to move immense numbers of men and amounts of materiel from the United States to Europe on a continuing basis.

The throughput capacity of ports and airfields at both ends would be adequate, *provided installations in Western Europe remained reasonably intact.* Peacetime aerial ports would be supplemented in emergency by other military airfields suitable for transport aircraft and, if necessary, by civilian facilities — subject to political approval and the tactical situation. Benelux seaports that presently serve NATO would continue to do so in war. Either Rotterdam or Antwerp alone has sufficient capability to handle U.S. needs.[14]

Airlift resources are adequate to accomplish assigned missions. If war erupted without warning, only part of our military aircraft would be readily available, but analyses based on current airlift operations and the average daily disposition of airframes indicate that initial requirements could be handled. The entire U.S. air fleet would be fully committed for a considerable period, but no serious shortcomings are anticipated.[15]

The real question mark concerns sealift. Marine divisions, a few Army troops, and more than 90 percent of all U.S. supplies and equipment would have to be transported in ships.

Existing sealift assets reputedly are inadequate, both qualitatively and quantitatively, to that massive task. In the mid-1970s, our strategic force of government-owned and long-term chartered dry-cargo vessels will be limited to three roll-on/roll-off (RO/RO) craft. To meet wartime needs, we would have to rely almost exclusively on U.S. commercial shipping, which could be mobilized on presidential authority. However, even if all responded affirmatively, assembling the requisite ships would be a time-consuming process, since assets normally are widely scattered. Moreover, much of our Merchant Marine faces bloc obsolescence and is unsuitable for military purposes.

Break-bulk, dry-cargo vessels are being replaced by new container ships, which are larger and faster but are ill-adapted for transporting tanks, self-propelled guns, cargo trucks, and other out-sized equipment. We might receive some assistance from our NATO allies, but shortages would remain severe.[16]

Command and Control

NATO's strategy of flexible response features a complex command and control apparatus, comprising the personnel, equipment, communications, facilities, and procedures needed to plan, direct, coordinate, and control military forces and operations. Alternate command posts and redundant communications enhance survivability, but much of the system constitutes "soft" targets that would be particularly susceptible to destruction in event of nuclear war.

The multinational nature of the Alliance, combined with the obligation of members to consult in time of crisis, gives rise to other weaknesses. NATO's military command structure is not only complicated — it operates differently in peacetime than it would in war. Whether procedures presently in effect would be amply responsive is disputatious. That is a crucial point. NATO's ability to act expeditiously if and when the time comes to cross the nuclear threshold could be the key to survival.

FORCES RELATED TO STRATEGY

Flexible response requires more conventional power than does massive retaliation, but NATO's numerical strength has declined considerably since the Alliance adopted a versatile strategy. France, which once provided roughly 20 percent of the aggregate, withdrew its forces from NATO control in 1967. The United States has repeatedly cut its contribution, and might do so again. Only the Federal Republic of Germany provides more power than it did six years ago.[17]

The impact of the reductions the United States has already made has dulled NATO's deterrent. Our partners are strengthening their establishments somewhat, and could do more at reasonable expense, but there seems to be no substitute for a powerful U.S. presence. American armed forces in Europe are more respected than those of lesser allies, and more impressive than distant reserves. They play symbolic, plus practical, roles. Only the *Bundeswehr* could take their place properly, but increased German militarism would instigate instability on both sides of the Iron Curtain. Consequently, further U.S. cuts outside the framework of mutual and balanced force reductions (MBFR) could cause NATO to readopt massive retaliation for lack of realistic alternatives. Even as it stands, NATO's deterrent is underpinned primarily by uncertainty, rather than by sound military capabilities.

NATO's defense posture is no better than its deterrent. Its troops are spread very thinly. Four and one-third divisions in the U.S. zone, assisted by two armored cavalry regiments, cover a 250-kilometer (155-mile) front, approximately twice the desired distance. We have *no* divisions in reserve.[18] The "sufficiency" of U.S. air forces is less easily gauged, but war games, computers, and other techniques reportedly indicate that "our entire force structure" is inadequate.[19] Some essential objectives thus are beyond the reach of NATO's standing structure.

139

In the final analysis, a successful defense of Free Europe would be contingent on the early introduction of U.S. air-ground reinforcements, but their readiness is questionable and their timely arrival would be adversely affected by strategic mobility problems. NATO's strategy of flexible response therefore will be dubious until force deficiencies are corrected.

THE POLITICAL LEAVENING

Military conclusions must always be qualified by *political* considerations. At this writing, neither the United States nor its NATO allies believe that a shooting war is imminent.[20] Our future force posture very properly will reflect the value that U.S. decision-makers assign to American security interests in Europe, the degree of concern with which they view the changing threat, and their willingness to take risks. An accurate assessment of Soviet intentions obviously is imperative. Those intentions can change instantaneously. NATO's capabilities cannot.

17 U.S. Strategy for East Asia and the Western Pacific

Prior [to World War II], the western strategic frontier of the United States lay on the littoral line of the Americas with an exposed island salient extending out through Hawaii, Midway, and Guam to the Philippines. That salient proved not an outpost of strength but an avenue of weakness along which the enemy could and did attack. . . . All of this was changed by our Pacific victory. Our strategic frontier then shifted to embrace the entire Pacific Ocean which became a vast moat to protect us. . . . We control it to the shores of Asia by a chain of islands extending in an arc from the Aleutians to the Marianas held by us and our free allies. From this island chain we can dominate with sea and air power every Asiatic port from Vladivostok to Singapore and prevent any hostile movement into the Pacific.

GENERAL OF THE ARMY
DOUGLAS MACARTHUR

Speaking before a joint session of Congress 19 April 1951.

HISTORICAL PERSPECTIVE

During the interwar period from 1919 through 1938, U.S. strategic thought concentrated almost exclusively on potential conflict arising from anticipated Japanese aggression against American interests and territory in the Far East. For all practical purposes, there was no other impending peril. The Kaiser had just been defeated and deposed. Communism was a budding menace, but the Bolsheviks still were in a poor position to attack the United States.

Strategic challenges confronting this country have not been so simple or straightfor-

141

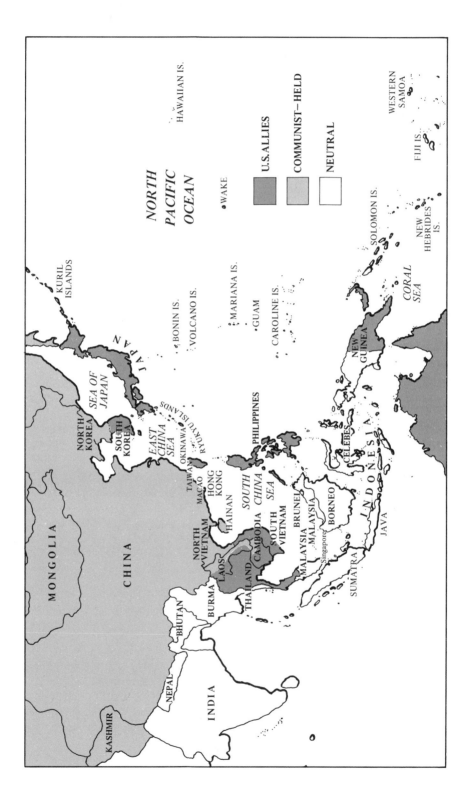

NORTH PACIFIC OCEAN

U.S. ALLIES

COMMUNIST—HELD

NEUTRAL

WAKE

HAWAIIAN IS.

WESTERN SAMOA

FIJI IS.

NEW HEBRIDES IS.

SOLOMON IS.

CORAL SEA

KURIL ISLANDS

JAPAN

SEA OF JAPAN

NORTH KOREA

SOUTH KOREA

BONIN IS.

VOLCANO IS.

MARIANA IS.

GUAM

CAROLINE IS.

EAST CHINA SEA

OKINAWA

RYUKYU ISLANDS

TAIWAN

MACAO

HONG KONG

PHILIPPINES

NEW GUINEA

MONGOLIA

CHINA

HAINAN

NORTH VIETNAM

SOUTH CHINA SEA

SOUTH VIETNAM

CELEBES

INDONESIA

LAOS

CAMBODIA

THAILAND

BURMA

BRUNEI

MALAYSIA

MALAYSIA

BORNEO

Singapore

SUMATRA

JAVA

BHUTAN

NEPAL

INDIA

KASHMIR

ward since, and may never be so again. The global threat in succeeding years grew more sophisticated, taking shape in such a way as to shift primary emphasis from the Orient, except for the period when we were preponderantly preoccupied with Southeast Asia in general and Vietnam in particular.

U.S. INTERESTS IN THE AREA

Even so, the United States retains significant national concern for the Pacific Basin and adjacent Asia. Roughly half of all mankind lives in lands bordering that greatest of oceans. The United States and the Soviet Union are the world's most powerful nations. Red China is the most populous. Japan has the third-ranking economy in the world. Four of our states sit on the Pacific's eastern rim. Hawaii is lodged in the middle. American Samoa, Guam, Wake, Johnson, and Midway, plus the Howland, Baker, and Jarvis Islands, are U.S. dependencies. The Pacific Trust Territories, which we have administered for the United Nations since the end of World War II, blanket more than three million square miles. In addition, we have a series of national security ties with numerous East Asian nations, some sentimental or traditional, others formalized by treaty (see Chapter 15).

However, U.S. interests need to be put in perspective as a prelude to strategy formulation. Dr. Edwin O. Reischauer, a long-time student of the Far East and U.S. Ambassador to Japan from 1961 to 1966, handles that task astutely:

> It would be hard indeed to make any case for immediate vital American interests in Asia. . . . The United States has neither geographic nor ideological borders with China; our trade with Asia [even with Japan] is trifling in our national economy; we have no lifelines in Asia; we are far away and many times more powerful than the whole of Asia. Clearly we have no vital national interests that can be immediately and directly threatened by Asians.

> Then what are our interests in Asia? Our first interest in Asia is as a major part of a now unitary world that we are trying to help toward peace, stability, and prosperity. . . . Our second great interest is in Asia's future. Someday the Asian half of the world will probably have much more relative power than it does today. . . . We have a great stake in that future Asia — far greater than in the Asia of today. . . . We have a third interest in Asia, and this is simply our own moral imperative to help those who need help.[1]

And since none of those interests or the objectives derived therefrom are compelling in his opinion, he advises that:

> We should therefore be the most relaxed of all nations in facing the problems of Asia, and thus best able to muster the patience, tolerance, and long-range foresight that are required.[2]

THE FRAMEWORK OF U.S. STRATEGY

Interpreted in that light, our "Europe first" strategy makes a lot of practical sense. In Asia, the United States does well to adopt an indirect strategic approach that relies less on direct military participation than has our strategy in the recent past.

Political diversity, geographic differences, and the nature of the threat in East Asia and the Western Pacific all conspire to create a far more complex matrix than we face in Europe. For example, there is no single, semicohesive agency like NATO to work through. There is no single, easily identified direction from which to anticipate attack along the enormous perimeter that demarks communism from our allies and the Third World. South of that periphery, subversion and insurgency prevail to a far greater extent than they do in NATO territory, but fortunately pockets of unrest in Indochina or the Philippines do not necessarily influence the fate of Taiwan, Korea, or Japan directly, as similar discord in West Germany would affect the rest of Free Europe. Contiguous lines of conventional defense thus are absent. It is not possible to formulate a single, cohesive strategy to cover the whole region. Separate U.S. sub-strategies must address individual areas, like Southeast Asia, the Philippines, Taiwan, Japan, and Korea.

THE NIXON DOCTRINE APPLIED

Nevertheless, certain fundamental guidelines apply.

The Guam Doctrine (now called the Nixon Doctrine) outlines the current U.S. formula for common defense in East Asia and the Western Pacific. Its primary theses recognize that the new forces rising in that region are wholly unlike those we contended with in the years after the Second World War:

> The old enmities of World War II are dead or dying. So are the old dependencies of the post-war era. . . .

> Asian states are stronger. They are able and determined to play a larger role in shaping the international structure of their region.

> They are joining together in regional structures which make them more independent of, and therefore more influential on, the policies of the greater powers.

> Each of the major powers of the Pacific region — Japan, the U.S.S.R., the Peoples Republic of China, and the United States — is faced with difficult decisions in adjusting its policies to the new realities in East Asia. . . .

> However, the new strength in Asia is a fact, and it requires a different and more restrained American approach, designed to encourage and sustain Asian regionalism, Asian self-reliance, and Asian initiatives.[3]

In molding a new strategy for the Orient, predicated on the realities enumerated above, President Nixon noted the need to strike a careful balance:

> If we do too little to help [our Asian associates] — and erode their belief in our commitments — they may lose the necessary will to conduct their own self-defense. . . . Yet, if we do too much, and American forces do what local forces can and should be doing, we promote dependence rather than independence. . . . [However,] weakness on our part would be more provocative than continued U.S. strength, for it might encourage others to take dangerous risks, to resort to the illusion that military adventurism could succeed.[4]

144

The Nixon Doctrine has been widely construed to mean "no more Vietnams," but in fact it is deliberately vague enough to evoke multiple interpretations by journalists, politicians, communist spokesmen, and even members of the President's own staff. The statement nowhere stipulates that there is a different policy for the Pacific islands than for the Asian mainland. Nowhere does it identify the type of threat that would trigger U.S. military reaction. There is no clear-cut delineation between formal treaties and other forms of alliance, or between types of U.S. assistance. Consequently, the concept affords great flexibility. It not only keeps the opposition guessing, but its calculated ambiguity means all things to all men among the friendly nations concerned.

Most conspicuously, the Nixon Doctrine avoids drawing a line, as many believe Secretary of State Dean Acheson did in his fateful speech to the National Press Club on 12 January 1950. At that time, he diagramed an insular defense perimeter from the Aleutians through Japan and the Ryukyus to the Philippines, excluding Formosa and all outposts on the Asian continent. "So far as the military security of other areas of the Pacific is concerned," he said, "it must be clear that no person can guarantee these areas against military attack."[5] Whether that disclosure encouraged adventurism by the Kremlin and its North Korean puppets may never be known, but it seems a strong coincidence that communist forces surged south across the 38th parallel toward Seoul barely six months later.

TREATY OBLIGATIONS

Most of the treaty obligations that this country vows to honor in Asia have edges as fuzzy as the Nixon Doctrine. Unlike the NATO agreement, which insists that an armed invasion against one member "shall be considered an attack against them all" (and be met by force if necessary), the SEATO pact binds each participant merely "to meet the common danger in accordance with its constitutional processes." Any aggression less than an overt attack calls for nothing more decisive than consultation.

The U.S. interpretation of obligations imposed by such accords obviously has been altered since General MacArthur, who was not a national policy-maker, despite his frequent pronouncements, delivered the following judgment in his farewell address to the Congress on 19 April 1951:

> . . . *under no circumstances* must Formosa fall under communist control. Such an eventuality would at once threaten the freedom of the Philippines and the loss of Japan, and might well force our western frontier back to the coasts of California, Oregon, and Washington.[6] [Emphasis added].

The United States is committed to the defense of Formosa just as firmly in the 1970s as it was in MacArthur's day. Any attempt by Red China to seize the island through massive invasion almost certainly would be met by U.S. military might. However, there are many other conceivable circumstances in which the application of U.S. military power would prove inappropriate, even though Nationalist China eventually might "fall under communist control."

South Korea also is being charged with substantially increased responsibilities for its own national defense, which strongly influences the security of neighboring Japan. The number of American forces permanently based in the Republic of Korea is being reduced as a result of that shift in strategy. As President Nixon put it:

> The level of U.S. forces in Korea had come to be viewed as a symbol of our commitment. . . . To a considerable extent, the symbol had become more important than the substance, for it inhibited critical examination of the threat, and of the capacity of local forces to deal with it. Yet it was clear that the situation in Korea had greatly changed since the decision was made in 1954 to maintain the U.S. military presence there at two combat divisions.[7]

The most likely contingency which could provoke the use of a physical American shield for any ally in Asia would be an unacceptable military gambit by Communist China. However, the likelihood is very low. The Chicoms presently are preoccupied with what they perceive to be a serious threat along their long northern border with the U.S.S.R. It is not in their best interests to undertake armed aggression against neighboring Free World nations that might evoke intervention by the United States. Further, their budding association with this country might play a very real part in maintaining a regional balance of power — why sabotage that possibility at any early date?

FORWARD-DEPLOYMENT PROBLEMS

In standing by its commitments throughout East Asia and the Western Pacific, the United States still must rely on the forward deployment of selected land, sea, and air forces to attain any acceptable degree of responsiveness. That requirement necessitates a network of overseas bases for staging and operating purposes. Supply, maintenance, medical, and other facilities are needed to support U.S. and allied general-purpose forces of all services under a wide variety of circumstances.

However, the strategic situation has shifted significantly since MacArthur penned the lines that introduce this chapter. The advent of accurate, long-range ballistic missiles, the emergence of Soviet sea power, the continued rise of Red China, and the changing U.S. role in world affairs, to mention only a few recent developments, have injected considerations that were unknown in 1951. As a result, the locations and functions of our bases and associated force levels currently are under review. So are the U.S. national security interests and objectives that make them meaningful.

Some installations probably will prove to be essential, regardless of scenario. Others obviously will not. The status of several crucial bases, such as Yokosuka Naval Base and the skein of airfields in Japan, major holdings on Okinawa, and facilities at Subic Bay and Clark Air Force Base in the Philippines, is the subject of chronic controversy. Assets such as those contributed significantly to our war effort in Vietnam, and could prove equally advantageous in the future if this country continues to play a prominent role in Asian security affairs. Unfortunately, opposition groups in the host nations often exert strong pressures to oust us. Continued efforts to correlate U.S. and allied interests in this regard are a vital element of our grand strategy.

Installations in Korea, Taiwan, and Thailand thus far have escaped serious contention in those countries, but are under fire at home by factions that advocate a radically reduced U.S. presence overseas. A good many facilities almost certainly will be relinquished in coming months, as the Nixon administration has already announced.

146

In consequence, high-priority studies are in progress to ascertain the impact of progressive withdrawal eastward across the Pacific. If retrenchment should prove essential, Guam would assume a greater role in strategic planning, as would bases elsewhere in the Marianas, Marshalls, and Carolines. Eviction from those Trust Territories would be a serious blow. Australia, which is strategically situated and friendly to the United States, is likely to figure more prominently in future U.S. planning. Pearl Harbor, of course, has marvelous accommodations, but it is a long way from Asia.

Wherever we position our advance forces and facilities, it will be incumbent on the First and Seventh Fleets to safeguard sea lines of communication that are essential to effective operations anywhere west of the Golden Gate. The U.S. Navy has been almost unopposed in that endeavor since World War II, but the competition promises to become increasingly stiff as Soviet and, perhaps later, Chicom "blue-water" capabilities increase.

GREAT-POWER RELATIONSHIPS

Relationships among the prime movers in East Asia and the Western Pacific will have enormous influence on U.S. strategic decisions as the decade progresses.

Perhaps most important of all is the future alignment and role of Japan in the defense of Free Asia. Whether that potentially powerful country joins the United States as a full-fledged partner working toward common goals, chooses a strictly neutral course as Red China gains strength, drifts away as an independent force, or actively collaborates with communists could make all the difference.

A corollary concern involves coming associations between the United States and Red China. President Nixon spelled out guidelines for that undertaking as follows:

We shall deal with the Peoples Republic of China:

— Confident that a peaceful and prospering China is in our own national interest;
— Recognizing that the talents and achievements of its people must be given their appropriate reflection in world affairs;
— Assured that peace in Asia and the fullest measure of progress and stability in Asia and in the world require China's positive contribution;
— Knowing that, like the United States, the Peoples Republic of China will not sacrifice its principles;
— Convinced that we can construct a permanent relationship with China only if we are reliable — in our relations with our friends as well as with China;
— Assuming that the Peoples Republic of China will shape its policy toward us with a reciprocal attitude. . . .

We will look for ways to begin reducing our differences. We will attempt to find some common ground on which to build a more constructive relationship.

If we can accomplish these objectives, we will have made a solid beginning.

Over the longer term, we will see whether two countries — whose histories and cultures are completely different, whose recent isolation has been total, whose ideologies clash, and whose visions of the future collide — can nevertheless move from antagonism to communication to understanding.

147

On January 20, 1969 in my Inaugural Address, I defined our approach toward all potential adversaries:

"After a period of confrontation, we are entering an era of negotiation.

"Let all nations know that during this Administration our lines of communication will be open.

"We seek an open world — open to ideas, open to the exchange of goods and people — a world in which no people, great or small, will live in angry isolation.

"We cannot expect to make everyone our friend, but we can try to make no one our enemy."

When I spoke those lines, I had the Peoples Republic of China very much in mind. It is this attitude that shaped our policy from the outset. . . . It is in this spirit that I go to Peking.[8]

Relationships between the Soviets and the Chinese Communists may prove decisive in this regard. It seems most unlikely that they could reforge a cohesive bloc in the foreseeable future. Even active Sino-Soviet cooperation currently seems remote. The outbreak of serious hostilities between those two would create serious strategic problems for this country.

Finally, we must appraise probable interactions between the United States and the U.S.S.R., which has truly emerged as a Pacific power. Our official evaluation of the Russian role suggests that:

[the] Soviet Union wishes to see our influence diminished, and yet fears that diminution as enhancing the possibility of expanded Chinese influence. At the same time, it has to consider that a lesser American influence could contribute to a normalization of relations between ourselves and Mainland China, and might permit and encourage a focus of Chinese energies not possible under the present realities.[9]

In response to such interplay, U.S. strategists are seeking a stable, four-way balance of power in the area, with the United States, the U.S.S.R., Red China, and Japan as the corners.

18 U.S. Strategy for the Middle East

Vietnam is our most anguishing problem. It is
not, however, the most dangerous. That grim
distinction must go to the situation in the Middle
East with its vastly greater potential for drawing
Soviet policy and our own into a collision that
could prove uncontrollable.

RICHARD M. NIXON
25 February 1971

HISTORICAL PERSPECTIVE

America's strategic connections with Europe date to the sixteenth century.
We have been a Pacific power since the days of Commodore Perry. By way of contrast,
our involvement in the Middle East is strictly neoteric.

The British, French, and Russians have contested that area since the Napoleonic
Wars, but U.S. influence was not deterministic until 1946, when President Truman's
hard-line stand caused Stalin to back out of northern Iran. That was a most propitious
time. All competitors had been discredited as imperialistic, and the United States,
entering on a white horse with banners flying, was widely admired and respected, not
just by Iran, but by Turkey and the Arab states as well.

U.S. INTERESTS IN THE MIDDLE EAST

Our primary national interests were three. Whether they were, or are, compulsory still is open to debate.

Interest One, which bore on the other two, was our quest for a free and independent
Middle East. At the time, that aspiration, in turn, was tied directly to a fundamental
U.S. national security objective: to maintain a balance of power by containing commu-
nism. That goal still is transcendental, as the following policy statement by President
Nixon indicates:

> America's interest in the Middle East — and the world's interest — is that the global
> structure of peace not be allowed to break down there. . . . Any effort by any major

149

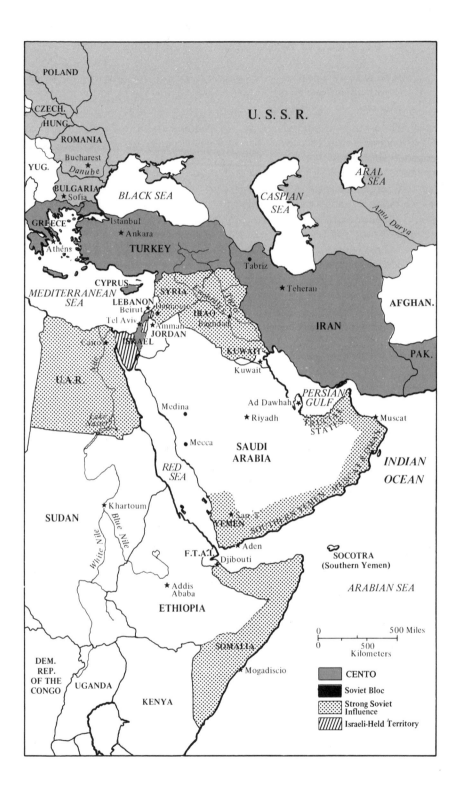

POLAND

CZECH.

HUNG.

ROMANIA

Bucharest
*
Danube

YUG.

BULGARIA
★Sofia

BLACK SEA

U.S.S.R.

*CASPIAN
SEA*

*ARAL
SEA*

Amu Darya

GREECE

Istanbul

★Ankara

TURKEY

Athens

*MEDITERRANEAN
SEA*

CYPRUS

Tabriz

★Teheran

AFGHAN.

LEBANON   SYRIA

Beirut

Tel Aviv

Cairo

ISRAEL

Amman

JORDAN

Damascus

IRAQ

Baghdad

IRAN

PAK.

KUWAIT

Kuwait

*PERSIAN
GULF*

U.A.R.

Lake Nasser

Medina

Ad Dawhah★

★Riyadh

TRUCIAL
STATES

★Muscat

*INDIAN

OCEAN*

• Mecca

SAUDI
ARABIA

*RED
SEA*

SUDAN

★Khartoum

White Nile

Blue Nile

SOUTHERN YEMEN

SOCOTRA
(Southern Yemen)

YEMEN

San'a'
★

ARABIAN SEA

F.T.A.I.

• Aden

Djibouti

★Addis
Ababa

ETHIOPIA

0   500 Miles

0   500
Kilometers

DEM.
REP.
OF THE
CONGO   UGANDA

SOMALIA

★Mogadiscio

KENYA

	CENTO
	Soviet Bloc
	Strong Soviet Influence
	Israeli-Held Territory

power to secure a dominant position could exacerbate local disputes, affect Europe's security, and increase the danger to world peace. We seek no such position; we cannot allow others to establish one.[1]

Interest Two was in a continuing supply of Middle East oil to the Free World, not just as a moneymaker and secondary source for this country, but because our NATO allies and Japan are heavily dependent on it. Between 1946 and 1950, the Middle East petroleum output soared from 700,000 to 1,750,000 barrels daily, a growth rate of roughly 26 percent per annum, versus less than 7 percent for all other regions. The area's oil industry steadily increased in importance during the next fifteen years, surpassing the United States as the number one producer in 1965. The region presently claims almost two-thirds of the planet's total proven reserves.[2]

Interest Three was in the Suez Canal. Since the lion's share of Middle East oil transited that sluiceway in the 1940s, and a heavy proportion continued to do so even after all pipelines were installed, the desire to keep the canal in hospitable hands was compelling. Other economic and military considerations reinforced that interest.

THE INFLUENCE OF ISRAEL ON U.S. STRATEGY

This country's sponsorship of Israel shattered our promising beginning in the Middle East, disaffected 100 million friendly Arabs from Muscat to Marrakesh and, to one degree or another, sabotaged all three of our key interests, together with supporting objectives. Without making any attempt to judge whether that U.S. decision was right or wrong, it is fair to say that emotion and a moral commitment supplanted calculated reason in the formulation of a foreign policy that to this day shapes our strategy for that strife-torn area.

On 14 May 1948, Zionist leaders proclaimed the new Israel. Within minutes, President Truman recognized Ben-Gurion's provisional government as "the *de facto* authority." Three days later, a cynical Kremlin followed suit, tendering *de jure* recognition for somewhat different reasons. The British Mandate terminated at midnight, and regular troops from Egypt, Transjordan, and Iraq invaded the infant Israel at dawn on May 15th. The Levant has not known one moment of real peace since.

THE CURRENT STRATEGIC ENVIRONMENT

Perhaps nowhere else on earth are the seeds of potential global destruction as well nourished as in this cockpit for proxy wars. With lines between the United States and the U.S.S.R. firmly drawn in Europe, the contest has spilled over to the Middle East, where the Arab-Israeli conflict creates some king-sized headaches. Most particularly, in President Nixon's words:

It has drawn the Soviet Union and the United States into close military association with the combatants, with all the danger that poses to world peace.

It has caused the disruption of normal US relations with a number of Arab countries. This, in turn, has increased the already excessive Arab dependence on Soviet support, and therefore their dangerous vulnerability to excessive Soviet influence.[3]

151

He then went on to explain that his administration faced a frustrating choice.

> We could have elected to stand aloof . . . on the theory that our diplomatic intervention would only serve to complicate further an already excessively complex problem.
>
> We rejected that course. We did so for three reasons. First, the stakes involved are too high for us to accept a passive role. Second, we could see nothing resulting from our restraint but the steady deterioration of the situation into open war. Third, it would have been intolerable to subordinate our own hopes for global peace and a more stable relationship with the Soviet Union to the local — if severe — animosities of the Middle East.
>
> Therefore — with no illusions about the difficulties or the risks — this Administration embarked upon a major and prolonged effort to achieve a peaceful settlement.[4]

The hydra we attack has one head labeled "the Arab-Israeli conflict"; another is labeled "intra-Arab differences," primarily those perpetuated by Palestinians; yet another is labeled "opposing U.S./Soviet interests." Each of those heads must be cut off before we can attain the objective set by President Nixon.

U.S. AND SOVIET STRATEGIES

The U.S. strategy designed to secure a peaceful settlement in the Middle East in no way parallels our approach either in Europe or East Asia.

U.S. Collective Security Policy

The Soviet Union has tried to use collective security as an offensive tool in this arena. U.S. collective security arrangements are strictly defensive.

In contrast with Europe and the Orient, where NATO, SEATO, and a substantial number of bilateral pacts are in effect, the United States has no treaty obligations anywhere in the Middle East, except for its NATO ties with Turkey, which serve a European purpose.

The closest we have ever come to a security pledge in the Middle East was House Joint Resolution 117, signed into law on 9 March 1957 and promptly dubbed the Eisenhower Doctrine. Its text declares:

> If the President determines the necessity thereof, the United States is prepared to use armed forces to assist any such nation or groups of such nations requesting assistance against armed aggression from any country controlled by international communism: *Provided,* that such employment shall be consonant with the treaty obligations . . . [and] the Constitution of the United States.[5]

To retain maximum freedom of action, no precise area boundary or listing of recipients was included in the resolution. The Eisenhower Doctrine was invoked on 15 July 1958 during the Lebanon crisis, and has not been exercised since.

However, H.J. Resolution 117 did form the basis for three bilateral executive agreements — one with Turkey, one with Iran, and one with Pakistan. Those identically worded documents, signed at Teheran on 5 March 1959, fit within the framework of

CENTO, an effete institution that looks much better on paper than it is in fact. They innocuously oblige the United States "to take appropriate action" in event of aggression against any of the contracting parties.

In addition, our Executive Branch — beginning with the U.S.-British-French Tripartite Declaration of 25 May 1950 — has recorded a number of policy statements, issued jointly with officials of Israel, Jordan, and Iran, which reaffirm (and in some cases reinforce) the formal, written agreements outlined above. J. William Fulbright and other members of the Senate Foreign Relations Committee disparage the "upgrading" of commitments in this way. In 1967, they expressly asked the Department of State whether the United States in fact had a national obligation to shore up Israel or any of the Arab States, either militarily or economically, in the event they were jeopardized by invasion or internal subversion. The reply, written in August that year, two months after the "Six-Day War," declared:

> President Johnson and his three predecessors have stated the United States interest and concern in supporting the political independence and territorial integrity of the countries of the Near East. *This is a statement of policy and not a commitment to take particular actions in particular circumstances* . . . [emphasis added].[6]

The Indirect Strategic Approach

Both this country and the U.S.S.R. have scrupulously avoided a direct, armed confrontation in the Middle East. Military power thus far has been used exclusively for political and deterrence purposes. The United States maintains no military cantonments of any kind in the Arab States or in Israel. Our three Air Force installations in Turkey are affiliated with NATO. A few specialized support elements complete our total complement in that country. We have no war-fighting capability in the area, beyond that afforded by our Sixth Fleet in the Mediterranean. Soviet armed might also is mainly afloat. Russian troops once manned some air defense units between the Suez Canal and the Nile, notably fighter-interceptor squadrons and SA-3 missile sites, but Egypt's President Anwar Sadat expelled them in the summer of 1972. Indirect strategic approaches thus are paramount.

Sadat's decision to reduce the Soviet presence in Egypt was a serious setback to Moscow's ambitions, but the Kremlin nevertheless continues to work through indigenous representatives in pursuit of its long-range goals in the Middle East, which still appear to be ever-increasing political, economic, and perhaps military, influence leading to domination and control over the entire area and adjacent waters. The Politburo probably has no real desire to eradicate Israel, without which there would be little incentive for Arabs to acquiesce in Soviet demands, but it is in Moscow's interest to keep the pot boiling.

The Impact of Military Aid

The result has been an arms race, with the U.S.S.R. first tipping the balance of power, then this country trying to restore it. Most of our military assistance understandably

153

has gone to Israel. However, we also have bolstered selected Arab States when by doing so we could further our interest in strategic equilibrium: Iraq in 1954; Jordan in 1957, 1965, and again in 1970; Saudi Arabia on a continuing basis (administered by a permanent military mission); plus token amounts to Lebanon, Syria, and Yemen. All materiel delivered to Israel, including F-4 fighter planes, has been purchased — that country has never been a recipient of U.S. grant aid. Moscow has concentrated its efforts in Egypt. It supplies lesser quantities, fewer types, and poorer-quality arms to Iraq and Syria.

The impact of military aid provided by both sides should be appreciated in its broadest context. Merely tallying numbers can create false impressions. Israel has a far greater capacity than the Arab States for absorbing modern hardware, tactics, and techniques, by virtue of superior leadership, education, organization, and methodologies. Its unity of purpose, unity of effort, and unity of command are in no way duplicated in the Arab World, whose burning hatred of Zionism curiously fails to create cohesion.

INFLUENCES IN THE MEDITERRANEAN AND INDIAN OCEAN

Obviously, neither U.S. nor Soviet strategies for solving the Arab-Israeli impasse operate in a vacuum. Their successes or failures are generally contingent on power relationships around the world, and specifically contingent on regional developments in the Mediterranean, the Indian Ocean, and the Persian Gulf. Soviet finagling in all three areas, British retrenchment east of Suez, Chinese Communist subversive activities on the fringe, and our own future role in those regions all have implications.

The importance of the Mediterranean, especially its Levantine reaches, is manifest. Without that lifeline, the ability of the United States to apply force or the threat of force in furtherance of its Middle East policies would be negligible. Unhappily, the security of that artery, long taken for granted, comes increasingly into question, as Hanson Baldwin explained in his perceptive *Strategy for Tomorrow:*

> In the Eastern Mediterranean the major Soviet advantage is its increasingly strong position in the contiguous nations.
>
> Russian ships are welcome in many of the principal ports . . . Yugoslavia is a communist state — albeit an independent one — which welcomes periodic visits from Russian ships and aids and abets many, though not all, Soviet foreign policy gambits. In strong contrast, there are only two countries, Italy and Greece, where the US Sixth Fleet can be assured of a relatively quiet visit. . . . Gradually, the ports of the area have been shut to the US flag. . . .
>
> The Russians manage and operate a shipyard in Alexandria, and Soviet naval vessels regularly use Alexandria and Port Said for overhaul and refueling.[7]

Turkey, long one of our staunchest allies and guardian of the critical straits that control Soviet egress from the Black Sea to the Mediterranean, has become increasingly ambivalent in recent years. The offshoot has been closer Turkish contacts with the U.S.S.R. and looser Turkish connections with the United States. This by no means implies that the Turks are likely to fall under Soviet domination, but their cooperation with this country in event of an Arab-Israeli crisis is no longer certain.

Instability in the Persian Gulf affords opportunities for increased Soviet activities in that vital area as well, now that the British are withdrawing. Russian efforts have been tied to infiltration tactics throughout the Indian Ocean, with special attention to Aden, Southern Yemen, and Somalia, which proffer the possibility of ideal bases from which to dominate all movement from Europe to South and East Asia via the Suez Canal. Using Aden and the People's Republic of Yemen as a springboard, the Soviets are attempting to subvert the Sultanate of Muscat and Oman, competing in a small way with Chinese Communists. They also have been seeking footholds in the former Trucial States, which have formed a federation known as the Union of Arab Emirates. Small wonder that a good number of well-informed observers perceive a grand pattern of Soviet encirclement that, if it succeeds, eventually will ring the entire Middle East. Hanson Baldwin reflected that thinking when he wrote:

> In short, Soviet communist penetration of the Saudi Arabian Peninsula capitalizes on local conflicts, but its program is long-term, definite and deliberate. As one diplomat put it, "The Russians have a positive expansionist policy in the gulf and the Arabian Peninsula, while the British are pulling out, and the Americans are doing nothing."[8]

For these reasons, if for no others, continued closure of the Suez Canal is a contentious matter.

Militarily, a closed canal is in our interest, since the Soviet Navy faces serious support problems in the Indian Ocean. Free access to the Mediterranean would help solve them. The Kremlin may resolve such shortcomings anyway in coming years, by establishing advanced bases along the rim of East Africa and South Asia, but that will be a lengthy process entailing diplomatic arrangements and considerable construction.

Economically, a closed canal seems to favor Soviet purposes. The Free World, which depends so heavily on Middle East oil, has adjusted fairly well to the stoppage, but at great expense. Its members would welcome a shorter route, for dry cargo as well as for petroleum.

Politically, the closed canal stands as an important inhibitor to diplomatic agreements that could lead to a comprehensive settlement of Arab-Israeli problems. If opening that waterway would in any way expedite an equitable and final solution, U.S. security interests probably would be well served, despite strategic disadvantages.

THE QUEST FOR PEACE

President Nixon concisely described U.S. efforts to stabilize the situation in 1970, when "the intensity of the [Arab-Israeli] conflict had . . . reached the critical level." Artillery duels were a daily ritual along the Suez Canal. Israeli air power struck deep into Egypt. Fedayeen raids provoked increasingly daring retaliation. And Moscow kept fanning the flames. "Obviously," as the President saw it, "the situation was once again about to go out of control":

> On June 19 [of that year] therefore, the United States launched an initiative to get both sides to:
> — reestablish the ceasefire.

155

—observe a military standstill in an agreed zone on both sides of the Israel-UAR ceasefire line.

—agree on a set of principles as the basic starting point for Arab-Israeli talks under the auspices of Ambassador [Gunnar] Jarring [the UN Secretary General's Special Representative].[9]

That overture, calculated to stop the shooting and start the talking, embodied an essential element of U.S. grand strategy for the Middle East, namely negotiation. We received precious little cooperation from communists in the Kremlin or their Arab associates. Although President Nixon publicly proclaimed on 31 July 1970 "that neither side is to use the cease-fire period to improve its military position,"[10] the Soviets and the United Arab Republic cynically disregarded that provision. They completed a massive air defense buildup west of the Suez Canal before complying. An armed clash was averted, but the situation remained insecure.

The subsequent estrangement of Egypt from the Soviet Union, which was by no means a clean break, improved matters somewhat, from our standpoint at least. Moscow's credibility among Arab and unaligned nations was shaken. A pillar of the Kremlin's military strategy for the Middle East had sagged. And best of all, the possibilities of a direct showdown between the United States and the U.S.S.R. were much reduced. Peace perhaps was no nearer than before, but open warfare seemed farther away, until Sadat began bristling again in 1973.

Some armchair strategists with no official responsibility say that the ultimate way out is simple: dump Israel, and our difficulties will disappear. After all, one argument goes, we extricated ourselves from Vietnam when it became evident that the game was not worth the candle, and a vastly better case can be built for U.S. interests there than in Israel.

Those conclusions may be correct, but it is clear that the U.S. government will not adopt any such course in the foreseeable future. General Earle G. Wheeler stated the administration's position perfectly when he was Chairman of the Joint Chiefs of Staff:

> The Joint Chiefs of Staff, I assure you, can add up real estate, populations, and oil reserves. . . . The arithmetic of abandoning Israel is self-evident. But United States strategy is never a pure exercise in arithmetic.[11]

His words suit U.S. strategic sentiments.

19 Counterinsurgency Concepts

I know of two types of warfare: mobile warfare
and positional warfare. I never heard of
revolutionary warfare.

GENERAL DE GAULLE
Quoted by Bernard B. Fall in *Street Without Joy*

Charles de Gaulle's acid comment, reportedly made in the early 1950s before the French debacle at Dien Bien Phu, characterizes national decision-makers who do not appreciate the unique nature of revolutionary war.

COUNTERINSURGENCY PROBLEMS IDENTIFIED

Unlike other conflicts, insurgencies are primarily political and social acts that constitute war long before military manifestations surface. As such, they demand a treatment that mingles force with suasion in very special ways. Even during Phases II and III (*see* Chapter 7), conventional counterinsurgency operations that center on seizing critical terrain and besting battalions in battle exhibit serious shortcomings. The elusive enemy cedes ground readily and rarely deigns to stand and fight, except at times and places and in circumstances of his own choosing. Governments need an integrated politico-military-economic-social-psychological scheme that capitalizes on their credits and exploits the insurgents' liabilities.

There apparently is no "best" way to counter all revolutions. Both strategies and tactics must be tailored to specific situations, which vary remarkably. However, successful solutions in the past have had several common denominators.

COUNTERMEASURES DURING PHASE I

Almost everyone agrees that an ounce of prevention is worth a pound of cure. Revolution, like cancer, can be coped with best if detected and treated early. That is easier said than done, since the insurgents' initial intrusion usually is low-key. Radicals on the fringe of respectability are hard to recognize. Their activities are subject to misinterpretation and, once identified, may be deliberately ignored by fatuous functionaries. Frequently only the police and a few politicians realize the threat. Furthermore, since the apparent danger during incipient stages almost invariably seems insignificant in comparison with recommended responses, transmitting any sense of urgency to the general populace takes some doing.

Therein lies a serious dilemma. If stringent and selective countermeasures are implemented early, subversion generally can be squelched. However, the regime risks charges of "brutal repression," which could damage its reputation, both domestically and internationally, and might even lead to its downfall. Moreover, the revolutionary movement almost certainly will revive at a later date in even more virulent form, unless serious efforts are made to expunge its underlying causes. When subversion is allowed to blossom into a full-blown insurgency, the justification for relentless retaliation eventually becomes clear, but by that time national survival is at stake.

David Galula, a retired French army officer who wrote at Harvard's Center for International Affairs several years ago, portrayed several broad courses of action that are open to counterinsurgents during the incubation stages of any insurrection.[1]

Direct Action

Direct action against rebel leaders, the most obvious procedure, may pay off in short order, *provided* it can be taken within the law and without fanfare. The first condition is very often violated, even in countries that cherish civil rights. The most democratic governments are sorely tempted to dispense with legal frills when dealing with terrorists and guerrillas, on the grounds that due processes are cumbersome and constitutional safeguards are inapplicable. The amendment of local procedures is often an agonizingly slow project (it took nearly ten years to ban the U.S. Communist Party after proceedings were instigated). That situation aggravates tendencies to bend existing rules.

Officials who yield to the temptation to do so almost invariably pay a stiff price. Widespread arrests, preventive detention, mandatory death penalties for bearing arms, harsh prison terms for lesser offenses, the suspension of habeas corpus, and the denigration of other civil rights are bound to be opposed by much of the populace. Oppressed insurgents therefore expect automatic assistance from well-meaning but ill-advised zealots, who try to turn trials into sounding boards for the revolutionary cause. Measures to prevent that from happening may evoke even greater repression. If they do, the incumbents will almost invariably discredit the very apparatus they seek to support, and simultaneously will encourage lawlessness among their constituents.

Countersubversion

Trusted agents can insinuate themselves into the insurgent apparatus, report on its activities, and sow seeds of dissent in its innermost organs. The FBI has used infiltration techniques to perfection against homegrown communists, the German-American Bund, Black Panthers, and the like. Such steps are most effective during early stages, when many members of the underground are potential "generals" trying to recruit a few "privates." Countersubversion becomes progressively more difficult as the malignancy spreads.

Indirect Action

Indirect actions aimed at attenuating or eliminating conditions that enable revolutions to flourish afford further possibilities. If the insurgents' cause can be discredited or taken over by the government, the crisis will collapse. Examples of success unfortunately are rare. So are cases in which a regime instituted timely and effective programs to shore up its position, eliminate corruption, strengthen the bureaucracy, reinforce the police and armed forces and, above all, build a political machine at the grass roots. President Ramon Magsaysay of the Philippines succeeded marvelously on the island of Luzon in the 1950s, when he undercut the Hukbalahap movement and usurped its cause, but not many national leaders have such acumen. Most of them are too intent on maintaining the status quo.

Efforts to seal off outside assistance hold considerable promise if the sources of insurgent support are geographically isolated from the area of operations, as was the case in the Philippines, Indonesia, and the Congo. Blocking reinforcements and supplies at their points of origin manifestly is the most satisfactory method, if such a strategy can be pursued without provoking hostile responses from major unfriendly powers. Stopgap measures applied along logistic lines like the Ho Chi Minh Trail are less effective, but nevertheless they help.

Prerequisites for Early Success

None of those ploys is likely to prevail alone. Prospects are much improved when they are used in-concert. Whatever combination is chosen, it must be implacable and positive. Sir Robert Thompson lays out five basic principles which he suggests are prerequisites to success.

The first of these is the need to frame clearly defined national objectives, whose essence must be to "establish and maintain a free, independent and united country which is politically and economically stable and viable. . . . The insurgency may demand priority, but it cannot be treated in isolation."

Next, the government must have a comprehensive plan that compels revolutionaries to *react* rather than act. Flexibility is the key. Close and continuous coordination among all agencies involved is compulsory, or crucial considerations may "fall through the cracks."

Third, the revolutionary infrastructure must be the top-priority target. "If the subversive political organization at A can be eliminated, then the guerrilla units at B and C, being short of supplies, recruits and intelligence, will be steadily reduced by a process of attrition" (*see* Figure 7).

Fourth, Sir Robert says, the government should secure its best developed areas at all costs as the conflict begins to heat up. That is where most of the people are, and the economic base. Controlling those assets will help limit the insurgents' absorptive capacity and inhibit their rapid expansion.

Finally, counterinsurgents should operate within the law, as previously discussed.[2]

FIGURE 7
Revolutionary Relationships

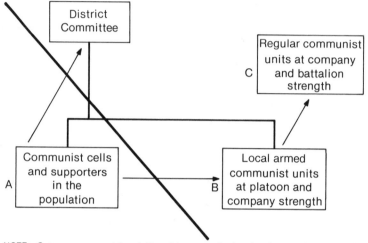

NOTE: C may or may not be stationed in every district, but is moved in to reinforce B for specific operations. The diagonal line symbolizes the separation between subversive elements in populated places and guerrilla forces in the countryside.

Adapted from a diagram in **Defeating Communist Insurgency** by Sir Robert Thompson, Praeger Publishers, Inc., 1966.

COUNTERMEASURES DURING PHASES II AND III

Once the use of force begins to predominate in revolutionary war, the pattern changes, as Galula describes:

> [By that time,] the insurgent has succeeded in building his political organization. He directs either an elite party leading a united front, or a large revolutionary movement bound to the cause. Although his actions other than subversion are overt, he operates clandestinely.
>
> The country's map reveals three sorts of areas: the "red" areas, where the insurgent effectively controls the population and carries out guerrilla warfare.
>
> The "pink" areas, in which he attempts to expand; there are some efforts at organizing the populations and some guerrilla activity.
>
> The "white" areas, not yet affected but nevertheless threatened; they are subjected to the insurgent's subversion but all seems quiet.
>
> Confusion is prevalent in the counterinsurgent's camp. There is a realization that an emergency exists, but the feeling of crisis is more widely spread in government circles than among the population of the white and even the pink areas. The true allegiance of every citizen is open to doubt.[3]

160

Decisive action by the regime is imperative at this juncture if the situation is to be salvaged. Galula's solution is summarized below:

Regaining control over and voluntary support from the people are the goals. Ejecting organized guerrillas from key areas by military maneuvers contributes to their fulfillment, but *keeping* them out is more important.

No lasting gains can be registered in that regard unless the masses cooperate. To that end, national leaders should strive to rally the loyal minority and convert the neutral majority, then play them off against the malcontents. This course is feasible only if the counterinsurgent contingent offers better prospects than do the rebels.

However, the loyal minority will never lend active support nor will the neutrals be swayed unless they are absolutely assured that the home team has the means and moxie to win. "When a man's life is at stake, it takes more than propaganda to budge him. . . . Political, social, economic, and other reforms, however much they ought to be wanted and popular, are inoperative when offered while the insurgent still controls the population."

Government forces (police, paramilitary units, and hard-bitten regulars) thus must protect the populace from the whole spectrum of depredations perpetrated by insurgent military elements, guerrilla units, or "goon squads" that gun down local leaders, impress young men into revolutionary service, levy taxes without compensation, occupy private homes uninvited, and drain off meager food supplies. Once the people recognize that the incumbent regime will protect them and has their best interests at heart, they usually begin to furnish counterinsurgent forces with timely, accurate intelligence, which must precede effective operations against the enemy's infrastructure and military units.

Perhaps most important of all, counterinsurgent forces must constantly bear in mind that Rome was not built in a day. Initiating overly ambitious projects invites failures and frustrations that undermine confidence and the will to continue.[4] Robert Thompson emphasizes that

> A thoroughly methodical approach to the problem, which may appear rather slow, encourages a steamroller outlook which provides the people with faith in ultimate victory. By preparing for a long haul, the government may achieve victory quicker than expected. By seeking quick military victories in insurgent controlled areas, it will certainly get a long haul for which neither it nor the people may be prepared.[5]

How can counterinsurgents pull all the pieces together to produce pragmatic programs?

There is no school solution, but Galula's strategy to combat rampant insurgency in "red" areas serves as a useful model:

1. Destroy or expel insurgent armed forces.
2. Occupy cleared areas militarily to maintain security.
3. Institute population control measures.
4. Destroy the insurgent infrastructure.
5. Hold local elections.
6. Test the resultant leadership; eliminate dead wood.
7. Organize a national political movement.
8. Win over or mop up insurgent remnants.

Some steps obviously could be conducted concurrently. Others could be skipped in "pink" or "white" sectors. Galula concedes that the whole concept might prove invalid if applied too rigidly to a particular case, but it provides a practical point of departure.[6]

U.S. COUNTERINSURGENCY CONCEPTS

Matters reviewed thus far in this chapter represent works that first saw print in the late 1950s and early 1960s, before the United States became deeply embroiled in Vietnam. In 1963 the U.S. Army's Special Warfare Center published a *Counterinsurgency Planning Guide,* based on similar material. Section headings in that publication blanketed everything from interests and objectives to clear-and-hold operations, intelligence activities, organizational requirements, psychological warfare, national development, and civic action.

However, there was many a slip between the cup and the lip when it came to translating theory to practice in Vietnam, our only experience to date with people's revolutionary war. U.S. policy-makers failed to differentiate adequately between actions and orders that are appropriate to governments under fire and those that pertain to supporting powers. Relationships between helpers and the helped thus were distorted. Undue emphasis on counterguerrilla operations and glamorous Green Berets left an almost fatal socio-political blind spot in U.S. doctrine for many years. Materialistic, action-oriented Americans, organized, trained, and equipped for conventional combat, were slow to realize that no outsider can win a revolutionary war; that minds can prevail over matter; that measureable results may not be decisive; that simple solutions sometimes are superior to science and technology; and that no amount of money can buy victory if the strategy is insufficient. Last, but certainly not least, institutional inertia created conditions that were almost impervious to change.

As a result, budding U.S. doctrine for combating insurgency began to take shape belatedly, after numerous false starts and interludes of indecision. Fortunately, a few disasters helped to clear fuzzy minds.

Lessons Learned

Criteria for U.S. Involvement
The U.S. Policy on Internal Defense in Selected Foreign Countries (FIDP), promulgated by President Johnson on 23 May 1968, defined our national interests, established priorities, and passed primary responsibility for coping with revolutionary wars from the United States to beleaguered governments. The Nixon administration's reaffirmation of the FIDP on 10 July the following year was summarized by the State Department as follows:

> The President has made it clear that the nature of our assistance to nations threatened by internal subversion will hereafter depend on the realities of each separate situation. In some cases, assistance in economic and political development may be enough. In other cases, aid in the form of training and equipment may be necessary. But the job of counterinsurgency in the field is one which must be conducted by the government concerned, making use of its popular support, its resources, and its men. Large scale

intervention from abroad is, of course, something else again, and must be considered against the backdrop of the total obligations and interests of the American people.[7]

Shortly after the FIDP was published, a message went from Washington to the field setting forth criteria for U.S. involvement in counterinsurgency efforts. To begin with, there must be a *significant* (not necessarily vital) U.S. security interest in the area. There must be a bona fide threat to that interest. The country concerned must be ready, willing, and able to act in its own behalf and absorb U.S. assistance. And appropriate aid must be unavailable from other sources, such as a former mother country. The thrust is wholly compatible with the Nixon Doctrine.

Within that broad policy framework, integrated deterrence, defense, and development doctrines have a reasonable chance to gel.

Organizational Adjustments

At one time, U.S. operations in Vietnam were a three-ring circus that featured military maneuvering in the center ring. Nation-building and pacification efforts were subordinate and disassociated. American agencies proliferated like rabbits, with everyone and no one in charge. The lack of coordination was appalling. An organizational overhaul was imperative.

Robert W. Komer, an architect of the Vietnam pacification program from 1967 to 1970 and the first head of Civil Operations and Revolutionary Development Support (CORDS) in that country, reached the following conclusions:

> Perhaps the chief *organizational* lesson that can be learned from Vietnam is the limited capacity of conventional government machinery (both U.S. and local) for coping flexibly with unconventional insurgency problems. Unified management of political, military and economic conflict will produce the best results, both where policy is made and in the field. Where major active insurgencies must be dealt with, special ad hoc machinery . . . should be set up early in the day [emphasis added].[8]

Such words were well taken. We now emphasize single managership and integrated organization at all echelons, beginning with the national government of the host country. In Indochina, the top position was occupied by a general officer but, if needs arise elsewhere, it could just as well be filled by a civilian. In Vietnam, a unified civil-military chain of command ran down through regions, provinces, and districts. Indigenous officials, assisted by U.S. advisors, were the key program executors at each level. That system seemed to work reasonably well, and could be adapted for use under different circumstances.

Operational Policies

Contemporary U.S. counterinsurgency policies generally correspond closely with the teachings of Thompson, Galula, and their strategic counterparts. Timely action, attainable goals, command emphasis, sustained security, and the eradication of revolutionary causes rather than symptoms are prominent ingredients. We finally recognized that there was no "other war" in Vietnam, as was popularly claimed — military operations on one hand, and political, economic, social, and psychological operations on the other were all part of the same package. That revelation should stand us in good stead elsewhere.

163

Pedestrian approaches are outdated, and the need for adaptability is observed. Once again, Komer acts as the informant:

> Despite George Santayana's axiom that those who fail to learn from history are condemned to repeat it, too often learning the lessons of the last war means that we tend to prepare for the next one on the same model. . . . The next "revolutionary war" in which U.S. interests might be at risk may not be a rural-based one like in Vietnam but essentially urban-based, for example.
>
> Perhaps the key *operational* lesson to be learned from Vietnam is the paramount need for flexible adaptation to the particular situation. Though this seems self-evident, it is not all that simple . . . [emphasis added].[9]

Lessons Not Learned

The Role of Negotiations

Negotiations take on a special meaning in revolutionary environments. Robert Thompson reviews the implications succinctly:

> There seem to be [just] three circumstances under which a communist revolutionary movement may be prepared to negotiate: to secure international recognition of a victory, to prevent a complete defeat, and to open another front. . . .
>
> When a country is on the defensive and is fighting solely for its continued existence and survival there is . . . nothing to negotiate. . . .
>
> In a war of this nature less than victory means defeat because one concession automatically undermines the foundation for resisting the next, until either a vital issue is conceded or . . . the will to resist collapses. Both North and South Vietnam understood this very well, hence the complete intransigence on both sides.[10]

Willingness to negotiate is a pillar of U.S. foreign policy, but our diplomatic history, like our military experience before Vietnam, was mainly in the conventional context. In consequence, our attempts to negotiate a solution to revolutionary war in Southeast Asia met with repeated disappointments, and may have prolonged hostilities.

Whether gambits in 1973 will be advantageous remains to be seen, but many students of counterinsurgency are pessimistic. Hanoi's politburo probably welcomed negotiations beginning in the autumn of 1972. Peace talks at that time camouflaged their military defeat, gave the revolutionaries a much-needed breathing spell and the opportunity to reopen other fronts. The palavering, which proceeded for months without Saigon's direct participation while the countryside was still hotly contested, made no clear provisions for a political settlement. As a result, it placed our partner's vital interests in peril. It is too early to tell whether peace on the agreed terms will serve *our* interests, but whatever the outcome, negotiating under those circumstances was a high-risk proposition.

Institutional Fickleness

Even before U.S. military participation in Vietnam ended, our official concern for counterinsurgency waned. Revolutionary war was no longer fashionable. The U.S. government and military establishment turned their attention once again to more familiar topics. Colonel Harry E. Ruhsam, U.S. Army (Retired), explored some of the ramifications when he was with the National War College Strategic Research Group. His findings can be encapsulated as follows:

Mechanisms created to cope with counterinsurgency matters have already been dismantled, or are withering away. The supra-cabinet-level Special Group (Counterinsurgency) and the National Interdepartmental Seminar, our two senior agencies with policy, plans, and coordination responsibilities, have been disbanded; the State Department, which monitors the FIDP, displays undisguised disinterest; counterinsurgency organs within the Office of the Joint Chiefs of Staff have atrophied, and are largely preoccupied with other matters; the Army's John F. Kennedy Center for Special Warfare at Fort Bragg, North Carolina, has been redesignated the Center for Military Assistance; and counterinsurgency, once mandatory in the curriculum of every U.S. service school, now is a moribund subject. Doctrinal disputes remain unresolved. Roles and missions cry for clarification. Counterinsurgency training suffers, for civilians and military alike.

Unless that trend is reversed, our embryonic expertise in this crucial field of endeavor will vanish, and the lessons learned at great cost in blood and national treasure will be lost.[11]

PART IV

SPECIAL CONSIDERATIONS

20 The Impact of Geography

Knowledge of the country is to a general what a
musket is to an infantryman and what the rules
of arithmetic are to a geometrician. If he does
not know the country he will do nothing but
make grave mistakes.

FREDERICK THE GREAT
Instructions to His Generals

Misguided strategists who misinterpret, misapply, or ignore the crushing
impact of geography on national security affairs learn their lessons painfully, after
squandering national prestige, lives, and treasure. The most famous names are represented: Churchill got his comeuppance on Gallipoli's rocky shores; Hitler later lost
his bullheaded bout with the Russian winter; and Khrushchev sullied his name by
staking a claim in inaccessible Cuba.

Strategic masters manipulate the physical environment, exploit its strengths, evade
its weaknesses, acknowledge constraints, and contrive always to make nature work for
them, instead of against them.

GEOGRAPHIC FACTORS IDENTIFIED

Webster defines geography as "a science that deals with the earth and its life;
especially, the description of land, sea, air, and the distribution of plant and animal
life including man and his industries with reference to the mutual relations of these
diverse elements." For practical purposes, however, strategists can narrow that hodge-
podge to ten basic considerations which, properly interpreted, would enable them to
estimate the probable influence of environment on plans and operations:

1. Space relationships ⎤
2. Primary land forms ⎥   Physical
3. Climate   ⎥   geography
4. Natural vegetation ⎦

167

5. Resources, including agriculture/forestry	
6. Industries	
7. Population size and pattern	Economic/Cultural
8. Distribution of critical activities	geography
9. Transportation networks	
10. Communications networks	

Lesser included aspects, like local relief and drainage, weather, and characteristics of urban clusters, usually are of greater concern to tacticians than to strategists, who deal primarily with systems and patterns, rather than details.

The factors listed above constitute geographic inputs to national power, which influence the ways that political, military, and other forms of power can be applied. They must be analyzed in global, regional, *and* local contexts if their full significance is to be appreciated.

STRATEGIC VIEWS OF THE GLOBE

The classic schools of strategic thought, maritime, continental, and aerospace (*see* Chapter 3), appraise geographic settings in sharply different ways. Three early spokesmen — Mahan, Mackinder, and de Seversky — advanced concepts that still illustrate the basic divergences displayed by their philosophical descendents, even though details outlined by that trio have since been altered to reflect current circumstances.

Maritime

Alfred Thayer Mahan, an unabashed champion of military might, focused his attention on the hydrosphere, the aqueous envelope that covers three-fourths of our earth's epidermis. Before the turn of the twentieth century, he contended that any country or coalition strong enough to command the high seas could control the world's wealth and thereby dominate the earth. As the principal prerequisites, he saw a powerful navy with operating bases at home and overseas, complemented by a massive merchant marine. For maximum effectiveness, Mahan's theory depends on several essentials identified in his treatise *The Influence of Sea Power Upon History.* A centrally situated strategic position, which combines secure land boundaries with access to one or more bodies of open water, tops his list. Those basic geographic attributes must be coupled with a coastline that features deep-draft harbors and defensible shores. Next, no nation can carry out seafaring strategies on a grand scale unless its people have an affinity for salt water and an aptitude for commerce. Finally, governmental policies must actively exploit all environmental advantages to promote power afloat.[1]

Continental

Halford J. Mackinder, who followed Mahan by just a few years, emphasized the strategic importance of land masses as opposed to the seas. His study, "The Geographical Pivot of History," published in 1904, recognized central Eurasia as the hub of the universe (*see* accompanying map). The original Pivot Area, whose confines corre-

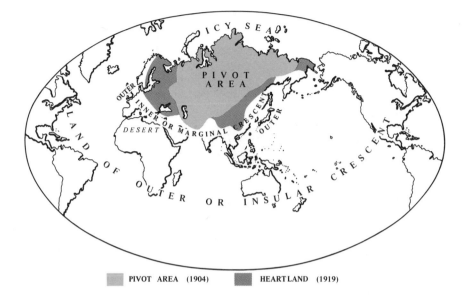

PIVOT AREA (1904)   HEARTLAND (1919)

sponded closely with those of Asiatic Russia, reputedly afforded great mobility for ground forces, but not a base of power in terms of teeming population or intrinsic treasures. Consequently, Mackinder eventually added a good deal of Eastern Europe to the Pivot Area, which he redesignated the Heartland. His ultimate outline therefore embraced lands that afford a happier marriage of mobility and power. The remainder of Europe and Asia constituted an Inner, or Marginal, Crescent, sometimes known as the Rimland. The Americas, Africa south of the Sahara, Australia, and large islands like Britain, Japan, and Indonesia, comprised an Outer, or Insular, Crescent. As the concept evolved, Eurasia and Africa in combination came to be called the World-Island. From that total theorem Mackinder derived his primary postulation:

> Who rules East Europe commands the Heartland.
> Who rules the Heartland commands the World-Island.
> Who rules the World-Island commands the World.[2]

Aerospace

The advent of air power threw in a third dimension. Alexander P. de Seversky proposed a competing theory, based on the premise that complete air supremacy, not just local or temporary air superiority, is possible. His book *Air Power: Key to Survival,* written in 1950, before the existence of ICBMs, discounted overseas bases as "untenable," downgraded the importance of naval and land combat, and stated unequivocally that "the manifest destiny of the United States is in the skies." His view of the globe, based on a polar projection, visualized the East-West confrontation across the Arctic Ocean, not across the Atlantic and Pacific (*see* map on page 170). He drew a blue circle around the United States, demarking the 5,000–mile strike radius of contemporary bombers.

169

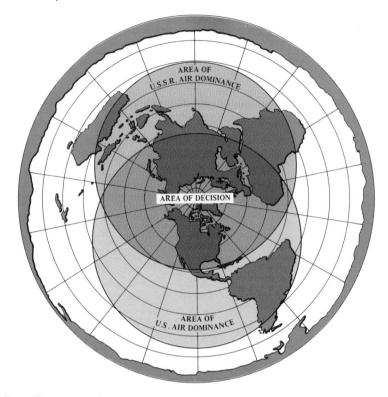

A yellow ellipse, demarked by similar bounds, was centered on the Soviet Union. The two overlapped at the Area of Decision,

> where the struggle for mastery of the whole air ocean will be unfolded. . . . Any investment we make today in the yellow zone with the intention of assuring a flow of strategic supplies in wartime is sheer waste. It is as unrealistic as would be investment for the same purposes by the Soviet Union in our blue zone. Common sense demands that we channel economic preparedness only into the zone we can successfully defend.[3]

THE NEED FOR INTEGRATED VIEWS

The truth of the matter is, none of the media just addressed offers a panacea, although some influential strategists still persist in pushing one approach to the exclusion of others. Maritime strategies, for example, are ideal for extending national influence over wide areas, as the Soviets are demonstrating today, but they are not likely to cripple resourceful countries like the United States and Red China. Whosoever rules the Heartland (*any* heartland, not necessarily the one described by Mackinder) would be constrained from commanding the rest of the world if he lacked the ability to project a potent punch beyond his particular land mass. Aerospace operations depend heavily on terrestrial fulcrums. Like Archimedes, airmen need a place to stand before they can even try to move the world. Candidates for modern great-power status need the flexibility to function effectively in all three environments.

170

CORE AREAS AND CRITICAL TERRAIN

Regardless of which school they subscribe to, strategists find that strategies founded on force or the threat of force almost invariably focus on geography.

Offensive strategies seek to dominate or destroy the opposition's vital assets, which usually can be plotted on a map. Even intangibles like national will and morale can be tied to population density. Defensive strategies are designed to protect those same national properties.

Most vital assets fall in one of the economic/cultural categories listed at the beginning of this chapter, including national institutions and armed forces, which qualify as "critical activities." Critical terrain features constitute prospective objectives or targets — industrial installations, transportation nodes, command/control centers, and the like. Strategists commonly lump those features together to form core areas. Europe, for example, contains a continental core that comprises most of France, Germany, Belgium, and Holland, where we find the political, military, industrial, commercial, financial, transportation, telecommunications, and cultural heart of the Northeast Atlantic community. Each country contains one or more subordinate cores, which vary tremendously in number, size, and composition. Large lands like the United States and the U.S.S.R. support several apiece, which are highly diversified. The primary Soviet core, encompassed by the Leningrad-Odessa-Kuznetsk triangle, can be divided into half a dozen subsidiaries: Moscow, the southern Urals, and the entire Donets Basin are examples. The Baku oil fields, Baikal developments, and the Soviet Far East are some of the satellites around the primary core. At the other end of the spectrum are small countries, such as Singapore, that contain a single strategic area.

Choke points, such as Gibraltar and Suez, owe their importance solely to strategic position. Other critical terrain features have strictly transitory value. The normally worthless real estate that facilitated U.S. island-hopping campaigns across the Central and South Pacific beginning in August 1942, demonstrated that premise perfectly. Most Americans had never heard of Bougainville, Buna Mission, or Biak before World War II, but all emblazoned their names in history because they proffered convenient positions at particular points in time and space. Cities, by way of contrast, have great innate value. Small wonder that they figure prominently in strategic planning and as pawns of war. Capitals in particular can be real plums. Consider Copenhagen or Havana, each of which contains a quarter or more of its country's total population and a huge proportion of the national entity. If those heads were killed, the bodies would surely die.

SPACE RELATIONSHIPS

Space relationships concern the location, size, and shape of great land masses and oceans, seen as slick surfaces stripped of all physical features. The effects of distance, direct contact, boundaries, and dispersion all strongly influence the accessibility and vulnerability of core areas.

Distance

All arguments to the contrary, distance still is a factor to be reckoned with under most circumstances. The continental United States are safer from physical invasion today than they were in the eighteenth century, since no hostile force in the world can effectively bridge the watery miles that separate us from potential aggressors. Red China, Asia's awkward giant, poses a significant threat to Soviet troops in the Far East, but Chinese armies are not about to overrun the far-off Russian heartland. Only when we talk about aircraft and missiles does the screening effect of distance begin to break down.

Direct Contact

Accessibility and vulnerability depend as much or more on direct contact between offensive forces and objective areas as they do on distance. Every time we contemplate doing battle in Budapest, Bratislava, or Berlin, we perceive how great our disadvantage would be in comparison with the Red juggernaut, which could generate combat power rapidly at the point of decision and sustain it over short, internal lines. Prospects for mutual troop withdrawals from areas of East-West confrontation are clouded by the same sort of dilemma. The communists could fade back a few miles *overland* in Europe or Asia and return in a matter of hours. U.S. forces would have to retrench all the way to North America, or to other remote bases, separated from the crisis areas by several thousand miles of air or water.

Of course, the difficulties are not all on one side. The Soviets have similar problems. So do the Chinese. It is no accident that thus far they have neither fought wars in, nor shown much success in dominating, any areas not contiguous with the Iron or Bamboo Curtains. In Cuba, the Congo, and other hot spots, the communists have backed down. Even their support for "peoples' wars" and "just wars of national liberation" has suffered. Success has been registered mainly around the Red rim, where subversives and insurgent bands could be easily supplied and reinforced.

Boundaries

Man-made boundaries also influence access. Take the matter of privileged sanctuaries, those curious by-products of modern limited war, which permit inferior antagonists to live by the ancient adage, "He who fights and runs away, lives to fight another day." Manchuria, Laos, North Vietnam, and Cambodia all served as communist safe-havens at one time or another during the Korean and Indochinese wars. No obstructions prevented the United States from lancing those irritating boils whenever it chose — the only barriers were political prohibitions and lines on the map.

Dispersion

Strategically significant dispersion is largely contingent on the amount of land available to any given country, including holdings beyond its boundaries. However, total territory is not always an accurate index. Cadaverous Chile, 2,650 miles long and nowhere more than 250 miles wide, is four times the size of circular Uruguay in terms of area, but the smaller country, calipered from east to west, has double or treble the depth. Six Brobdingnagian-sized nation-states — the U.S.S.R., Canada, Red China, the

United States, Brazil, and Australia — lay claim to approximately half of the world's land surface, excluding ice-bound Antarctica, yet the core areas of all but two are woefully concentrated. Relocating basic elements of national power to compensate for such conditions, as the Soviets did early in World War II, can be a costly, time-consuming process. Sometimes it cannot be done at all.

TOPOGRAPHY

Physiographic considerations also are important in determining accessibility, since they give specific shape and substance to space relationships.

Land forms are the basic stage whereon each pageant plays. Lofty mountains, hills and dales, plateaus and lowland plains all in turn are modified by a bevy of variables. Bonneville's salt-encrusted flats and Okefenokee's watery wastes both may be basically horizontal, but their surfaces exhibit geographic extremes. Likewise, sere spires in the Sahara and neighboring Sinai only faintly resemble sequoia-covered slopes in the rain-drenched Sierra Nevadas. The military implications that derive from those differences are strikingly dissimilar.

Depending on the lay of the land and the point of view, topography shapes strategic obstacles or corridors.

Core areas in European Russia and Western Siberia, for example, are shielded by mile after forbidding mile of taiga in their northern and eastern quadrants, while rugged ranges, deserts, and inland seas bar the way from south and west. The best invasion routes, which served Hitler and Napoleon, sweep in from Poland, but even those must bypass 40,000 square miles of desolate bog centered on the city of Pinsk. In short, the U.S.S.R. is almost ideally situated for defense, except against attacks from aerospace.

That condition contrasts sharply with NATO's preserve, which is penetrated by a well-defined corridor comprising the North German Plain, Belgium, and all of western France.

LINES OF COMMUNICATION

Any discussion of avenues must differentiate between natural and man-made. Roads, railways, inland waterways, airfields, and deep-water ports, alone or in combination, are essential to modern military power. Deficiencies incur liabilities, as illustrated by our frustration when we faced the need for a quick buildup in logistically impoverished Vietnam at the end of a 10,000-mile line of communication. A skimpy road and rail net inhibits the Chinese Communists from shifting armies and associated assets from one point to another along their borders. The U.S.S.R. reluctantly relies on the ribbon-like and highly vulnerable Trans-Siberian Railway as its primary means of reinforcing or resupplying rapidly in the Far East. Aerial avenues of approach can complement continental or maritime routes under certain circumstances, but are unacceptable substitutes when it comes to extensive, sustained operations.

CLIMATE

Having noted the impact of space relationships and physical features on

173

accessibility and vulnerability, we must also mention weather and climate. Campaigns in the arctic, deserts, tropics, and temperate climes call for separate types of warfare.

Extreme temperatures, winds, and precipitation in particular can have great strategic consequences that affect the timing, conduct, and support of military operations. History is replete with accounts of armies mired in mud axle-deep to a ferris wheel, fleets blown off course, and bombers as helpless as gooney birds, grounded by gales or fog. Two examples suffice.

Climatic regimes caused by the north-south mountain chain that forms the backbone of Vietnam condition all military machinations in Indochina. When the Northeast Monsoon buffets Annam's beaches and turns coastal plains to quagmires from mid-October until early March, Cambodia and Laos are dry. When the Southwest Monsoon takes over from May to September, the reverse occurs. Operations must be scheduled accordingly.

Halfway around the world, Russian weather paints a different picture. Jubilant Germans who spearheaded Operation Barbarossa in June 1941 had no conception of the mud or cold they would soon encounter. By November, some crippled columns of trucks and tracked vehicles were cemented in place like Greek friezes. Before Christmas, small arms, lubricants, and radiators froze solid. Butchers' axes rebounded like boomerangs from horsemeat as solid as stone. Butter was sliced with saws. Such details may seem tactical, but the strategic consequences were tremendous.

Nuclear warfare is just as sensitive to weather conditions as are conventional conflicts. Strategically catastrophic consequences can occur as the aftermath of radioactive fallout in particular, which is responsive to winds.

Enormous amounts of debris are sucked up the stems of mushroom clouds produced by subsurface, surface, and low-air bursts of nuclear weapons. The heaviest, most contaminated chaff rains down near ground zero within minutes after the blast, but winds aloft waft a deadly mist of particles hundreds or thousands of miles before they sink back to earth. The size, shape, and potency of the resultant fallout patterns differ drastically, according to wind speeds and directions. Hot spots and skip zones may occur at random within each radioactive fan because of terrain shadows, crosswinds, or local precipitation.

Figure 8 illustrates fallout peculiarities recorded following the Boltzmann and Turk nuclear test shots, which were conducted at different times from the same tower in the Nevada desert. One fallout concentration drifted generally northeast, the other northwest. Boltzmann displayed a 500 MR/HR (milliroentgens per hour) hot spot nearly seventy miles from ground zero, almost atop a 1 MR/HR contour; Turk developed no such deviation.

The prediction of such erratic fallout patterns depends on the availability of wind-structure data from ground level into the stratosphere, since forecasters must allow for variations in direction, speed, and shearing at different levels. However, even under ideal circumstances, the process is subject to substantial error.[4]

NATURAL RESOURCES

Finally, no coverage of geographic constraints would be complete without at least alluding to natural resources, animal, vegetable, and mineral.

FIGURE 8
The Relationship of Fallout to Wind

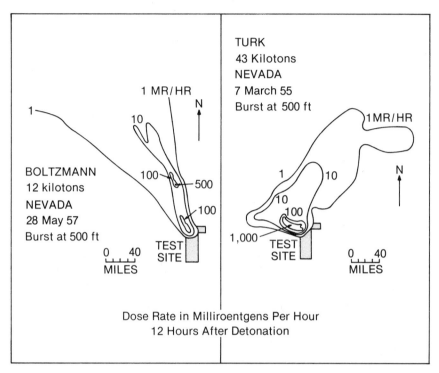

Dose Rate in Milliroentgens Per Hour
12 Hours After Detonation

National power in the twentieth century depends on a diversified economic base, but as chance would have it, the world community is divided inequitably into "have" and "have not" nations. Every country has shortages, but some are much worse off than others. Many states augment their assets peacefully through political and economic manipulations. Those that seek to alleviate shortages by coercive means are the source of serious strategic problems.

Food is the irreducible essential, followed by raw materials and the means for converting them to usable goods. Hans J. Morgenthau mentioned those matters in his *Politics Among Nations:*

> Regardless of the other assets of national power which are at [a country's] disposal . . . . permanent deficiencies in food compel it to act in its foreign policy from weakness rather than from strength. . . .

> What holds true of food is of course also true of those natural resources which are important for industrial production and, more particularly, for the waging of war. . . . It is not by accident that the two most powerful nations today, the United States and the Soviet Union, are most nearly self-sufficient in the raw materials necessary for modern industrial production, and control at least the access to the sources of those raw materials which they do not themselves produce.

175

As the absolute importance of the control of raw materials for national power has increased in proportion to the mechanization of warfare, so certain raw materials have gained in importance over others. . . . Only a few years ago the control or lack of control of uranium deposits was entirely irrelevant for the power of a nation. . . .

The example of uranium illustrates, however, the importance of another factor for the power of a nation — industrial capacity. The Congo has vast deposits of high-grade uranium. Yet, while this fact has increased the value of that country as a prize of war and, therefore, its importance from the point of view of military strategy, it has not affected the power of the Congo in relation to other nations. For the Congo does not have the industrial plant to put the uranium deposits to industrial and military use. . . .

Since victory in modern war depends on the number and quality of highways, railroads, trucks, ships, airplanes, tanks, and equipment and weapons of all kinds, from mosquito nets and automatic rifles to oxygen masks and guided missiles, the competition among nations for power transforms itself largely into competition for the production of bigger, better, and more implements of war. . . .

Thus it is inevitable that the leading industrial nations should be identified with the great powers, and a change in industrial rank, for better or for worse, should be accompanied or followed by a corresponding change in the hierarchy of power.[5]

Japan, which has recently emerged as the world's third-ranking industrial giant and, in the minds of many, the world's third superpower, presents an interesting anomaly: the country combines immense peacetime strengths with what may well be incurable wartime weaknesses. Economic insufficiency virtually dictated Japanese strategy during World War II — where and when Premier Tojo could strike, and how long he could play the game. Nothing much has changed in the past thirty-five years. In fact, Japan's dependence on foreign trade has increased. As a result, Nippon still suffers from the same fatal flaw that foretold her military disaster in the 1940s, namely inadequate sources of indigenous foodstuffs and raw materials, including fuels for power, iron and nonferrous metals, graphite, potash, cotton, and salt.

In short, only a few huge nations now have the economic potential for great military-power, and indispensable underpinning for national security. It will take revolutionary technological changes to alter that situation

THE DYNAMICS OF CHANGE

One admonition. Contrary to popular myth, geography fluctuates eternally in response to seasonal, cyclical, and random change. No strategist can ever complete an analysis, stamp it "approved," and stash it on the shelf. Alterations in national interests, objectives, policies, the situation, or technology of the day can conjure up whole new sets of geographic equations.

21 Characteristics of Armed Forces

> Some things a country wants it can take, and
> some things it has it can keep, by sheer
> strength, skill, and ingenuity. . . . Forcibly a
> country can repel and expel, penetrate and
> occupy, seize, exterminate, disarm, disable,
> confine, deny access, and directly frustrate
> intrusion or attack. It can, that is, if it has enough
> strength. "Enough" depends on how much an
> opponent has.
>
> THOMAS C. SCHELLING,
> *Arms and Influence*

Policy-makers who overcommit available combat power can get their countries in deep trouble. As they concoct concepts and plans, professionals therefore carefully consider the capabilities and limitations of their own armed forces, present and projected, active and reserve. In addition, they evaluate the forces of enemies and allies.

Sound assessments demand a broad working knowledge of military machines: their composition, organization, and balance; roles and missions; personnel strengths; states of training; arms and equipment; logistic systems; locations and dispositions; mobility means; coordination, command, and control.

COMPOSITION, ORGANIZATION, AND BALANCE

To exercise the full range of military might, countries must have armies, navies, air forces, and marines, organized and balanced to suit their particular needs. Each service displays singular attributes. None could shoulder all burdens alone. Nations suffering from quantitative or qualitative deficiencies thus are disadvantaged.

Schoolboys chortle over rude jokes about the nonexistent Swiss Navy, but in fact it is no laughing matter — an important element of national power is missing. The Federal Republic of Germany, now the strongest country in Western Europe, could never be more than a regional threat, unless it added intercontinental ballistic missiles to its military inventory. Japan lacks many accoutrements. Among all the modern military powers, only the United States deploys diversified land, sea, and aerospace combat forces that can function effectively in every environment, together with the logistic apparatus required to provision them in distant theaters.

For various reasons, the armed forces of our chief competitors exhibit significant structural shortcomings that limit their range of strategic options. The Chinese Communists, who concentrate on gigantic ground armies to the prejudice of air power, a deep-water navy, mobility means, and supporting establishments, exert conventional pressures only along their borders. Even the Soviet Union, which maintains a sophisticated, three-service array of military might, is minus the carrier-aircraft and amphibious capabilities needed to seize sizeable footholds on remote shores and the wherewithal to support large-scale land operations far from its Eurasian base.

ROLES AND MISSIONS

The structure of any military establishment, of course, must be predicated on assigned roles and missions.

The Key West Conference

The Joint Chiefs of Staff hammered out primary and collateral functions for our Army, Navy, Air Force, and Marines during a four-day period in March 1948 at the famous Key West Conference, convened by the first Secretary of Defense, James Forrestal. His aim was to resolve paralyzing rivalries among the services, to eliminate wasteful and inefficient duplication of effort, and to weld a truly effective team. Should each of the four services be authorized its own separate air arm? Should the Marine Corps, which had burgeoned to six divisions and 478,000 men in World War II, emerge as a second land army? Indeed, should there be a Marine Corps at all? Who should be responsible for air defense of the United States, which involves both ground and air forces? Who should be charged with developing joint doctrine, equipment, and procedures related to airborne operations? Those were the kinds of sticky questions addressed at Key West.[1]

Broad, basic decisions were forthcoming from that confrontation and the less well publicized followup at Newport, Rhode Island, in August of that year. The Air Force, for example, recognized the right of the Navy to develop aerial weapons systems needed to carry out its mission, and to engage inland targets that influence naval operations. They further conceded that, in certain circumstances, it might be beneficial for the Navy to participate in all-out air campaigns. In return, both parties agreed that the Air Force should exercise exclusive prerogatives in the realm of strategic bombardment. The Army retained its traditional roles, with emphasis on sustained ground combat.[2]

At best, the Key West Agreement was an uneasy compromise. The Navy Department emerged organized and equipped to cope militarily in a maritime milieu, with balanced, self-contained land, sea, and air components. Generally speaking, the Navy was a satisfied and staunch defender of the status quo, with only one serious bone of contention unresolved: the use of nuclear weapons, which still were instruments of the Air Force alone. This posed problems related to the scope of strategic offensive operations and grand strategy. The Army's discontent ran deeper. In Forrestal's words, it had become a "catch-all for the unwanted and unglamorous jobs."[3]

Subsequent clarifications of Key West decisions eliminated some ambiguities and sources of discord. Other irritants continue to crop up in response to changes in national security objectives, policy and strategy, tactics, and technology. Perennial debates over the merits of service unification, the scope of Army aviation programs, and that melange of misgivings related to alleged usurpation or duplication of service functions by the Department of Defense are representative. As each issue is resolved, a more cohesive force results.

Despite disagreements, the four services fundamentally complement one another, rather than compete. A brief discussion of characteristic capabilities and limitations serves to illustrate.

Army Roles and Missions

Our Army has the primary responsibility for conducting prompt and sustained combat operations on land, with the aim of imposing the nation's will on hostile populations and territories for protracted periods. It is designed specifically to close with and defeat major enemy ground forces and to secure, occupy, defend and, if necessary, govern strategic areas. On request, it provides massive logistic and administrative support for sister services. In addition, the Army assists in U.S. domestic security missions when the occasion arises. However, the Army exhibits significant deficiencies. It depends on the Air Force and Navy for much of its aerial fire power, long-range reconnaissance, and air defense, plus all of its strategic mobility.[4]

Navy Roles and Missions

The U.S. Navy obviously is lord of a specialized domain. No other service is as well suited to conduct sustained operations at sea, seek and destroy the enemy's naval forces, suppress his commerce far from land, control vital ocean areas, and protect U.S. maritime lines of communication. No other service is prepared to move the mass tonnages overseas that routinely are handled by sealift. Carrier-based air power presents the opposition with a constantly shifting target. It takes advantage of positions otherwise unavailable for U.S. initiatives. Probably the Navy's most glaring limitations are its ultimate dependence on installations ashore, with their numerous inherent shortcomings and vulnerabilities, and its inability to project power far inland, other than with aircraft and missiles.[5]

Air Force Roles and Missions

The Air Force, late-comer among the four services, also operates in a distinctive environment. It no longer has a monopoly on general-war strike forces, but still is the only service that has strategic air warfare as a primary function. Moreover, its tactical air assets, unlike those of the Navy and Marine Corps, are organized expressly to gain

179

and maintain general air supremacy, to influence areas inland, and to conduct close combat, interdiction, airlift, and aerial logistic operations in support of the Army. Equally important, our Air Force is best adapted to cope with air defense problems facing the continental United States, although it receives invaluable assistance from the Army and Navy in that crucial endeavor. Its salient shortcomings include reliance on fixed bases of operation and heavy dependence on other services for important aspects of logistic support.[6]

Marine Corps Roles and Missions

The U.S. Marine Corps, organized, trained, equipped, and psychologically conditioned as an elite air/ground team, specializes in amphibious operations. Marines feature adaptability and responsiveness. Battalion landing teams afloat in the Mediterranean and Caribbean, for example, permitted the United States to inject ground forces quickly at points of decision during the Lebanon and Dominican Republic crises. Marines serving with the various fleets are ideal for showing the flag, seizing and/or defending advanced naval bases, and conducting land operations along a littoral that is essential to naval campaigns, but they have to rely heavily on Army support for deep or prolonged missions, such as those the Corps undertook during World War I, in Korea, and in Vietnam.[7]

The Balance of Service Power

The relative ascendance of one service over the others depends to a high degree on the worldwide situation and national strategy. During the era of massive retaliation, the United States underscored nuclear air power, then stressed general-purpose forces during the era of flexible response. The emphasis again is in flux.

PERSONNEL

Quantitative Features

George Washington and Maurice de Saxe independently expressed the view, widely repeated today, that *good* armed forces, not *big* ones, win wars. That premise is valid to a point, beyond which it begins to lose perspective — a good big man almost always will whip a good little one. Moreover, small forces usually lack flexibility and quickly spread too thin. Conversely, however, it is possible for armed forces to be overly large. Extravagant size can drain human, material, and financial resources, degrading, rather than enhancing, national security.

Mobilization potential may add to active strength, although some strategies, most notably those associated with general nuclear war, depend preponderantly on forces in being. The effectiveness of "Christmas help" varies markedly from country to country, depending on the reserve and call-up systems. Israel and Switzerland, which maintain small standing armies, are envied internationally for their ability to man the ramparts in record time with highly skilled reserves, although both would suffer severely if compelled to siphon civilians from the domestic economy for protracted periods. Less-well-organized countries lack the machinery to expand rapidly in the clutch, as evidenced by Ethiopia's courageous but chaotic response to the Emperor's edict when Mussolini invaded in 1935:

> Everyone will now be mobilized, and all boys old enough to carry a spear will be sent to Addis Ababa. Married men will take their wives to carry food and cook. Those without wives will take any woman without a husband. Women with small babies need not go. The blind, those who cannot walk, or for any reasons cannot carry a spear, are exempted. Anyone found at home after the receipt of this order will be hanged.[8]

Qualitative Features

Raw-strength figures frequently are misleading. Manpower *effectiveness* is equally important. National traditions and temperament, whether warlike, pacific, neutral, or apathetic, provide one index. Discipline, loyalty, aggressiveness, and general morale, including attitudes toward military service, provide another. Native intelligence, education, age, physique, vigor, hardiness, adaptability, aggressiveness, grace under pressure and, above all, leadership, typify traits that demark the manpower pool of one nation from that of another. The lust for battle that loomed so large in the Zulu nation was not present among the peoples of ancient Phoenicia, and still is missing among their descendents.

Training and battle experience shape different final products. Nearly every flag officer now in the U.S. Navy, for example, is a veteran of World War II, the last conflict that enabled major powers to test a wide variety of naval concepts under combat conditions, including mid-ocean fleet operations. Those same men have continued to hone their tools for more than twenty-five years, off the coasts of Taiwan, Korea, the Levant, and Vietnam, and in the Caribbean. Some see that as a great benefit in comparison with unblooded skippers in the burgeoning Soviet Navy. Others, who either discount or disparage any apparent advantage, intimate that we are accruing the wrong experience.

FIREPOWER

The cutting edge of available forces, active and reserve, is firepower. To get "the biggest bang for the buck" and concurrently avoid overcommitting friendly forces, strategists must understand the relative capabilities, limitations, and vulnerabilities of complete weapons *systems* — the marriage of destructive power with delivery vehicles and means of control.*

---

* Many modern weapons systems are quite complicated. Our Safeguard antiballistic-missile system, for example, combines nuclear explosives with short-range, high-acceleration Sprint missiles designed for endo-atmospheric interception. Long-range Spartan counterparts are engineered to engage targets in space. Perimeter-acquisition radars are charged with detecting distant incoming ICBMs. Multi-function array radars take over intermediate tracking tasks. And finally, missile-site radars, aided by ancillary equipment, compute intercept points, launch Spartans and Sprints, as appropriate, and guide them to their targets.

181

As a rule of thumb, massive firepower permits modest military establishments to prevail over larger forces that are less well endowed but, as always, there are caveats. The destructive potential of nuclear, biological, and certain chemical weapons is so great, and their total repercussions are so unpredictable, that rational men hesitate to use them, even when decisive applications seem apparent. Lesser limitations abound.

STAYING POWER

Firepower in the field, aloft, or afloat, is dramatic evidence of any nation's military posture, but it would be ineffective without a stable administrative base and solid logistic support to give it staying power. The Chinese Communists, hard pressed to supple their front-line forces in Korea because of logistic inadequacies, never were able to sustain any major offensive for more than a few days at a time. Viet Cong and North Vietnamese *military* strategies in Indochina were similarly constrained. Conversely, the conspicuous U.S. logistic tail, which chronically draws fire from Congress and the press, provides all the necessities of life (as well as untold luxuries). However, its sheer size and complexity sometimes create strategic problems almost as severe as those caused by insufficiency.

Not the least of those difficulties relate to strategic mobility. The United States, being remote from most objective areas overseas, must rely heavily on airlift and oceangoing transport to move the necessary masses of men, materiel, and supplies to and between theaters of operation in an expeditious, economical, and efficient manner.

Troops and high-priority items currently are handled almost exclusively by air, which offers responsiveness, suppleness, and speed. The Military Airlift Command (MAC) maintains a comprehensive system, comprised of multipurpose airframes, a network of departure, en-route, and recovery bases, multiple routes, inflight refueling capabilities, and a stock of war readiness materials, that makes it possible to meet recurring requirements and emergencies with minimum waste motion. Important augmentation is derived from commercial contract carriers and reserves that routinely work with our active forces. However, there are limitations since, within the present state of the art, airlift still is quite sensitive to weather and cannot move mass tonnages or outsize items on a grand scale. Deploying a force to contact without being able to sustain it would sow the seeds of disaster.

Consequently, more than 95 percent of all U.S. military bulk cargo bound for Europe or the Orient, including aviation fuel for MAC, moves by sea. A nucleus fleet of "in service" ships crewed by civilians — the only such craft in our Navy — provides a small force in being and hypothetically affords the basis for expansion in time of national emergency. The U.S. Merchant Marine traditionally provides reinforcements, but today its antique vessels face "bloc obsolescence," and cannot carry the load. As a result, we place extraordinary dependence on U.S.-owned, but privately-operated, commercial carriers that fly foreign flags and are manned by alien crews who owe this country no allegiance. Serious strategic shortcomings are inherent in such an arrangement.

The Soviets and Chinese, whose military operations thus far have been confined exclusively to the Eurasian land mass and adjacent waters, define strategic mobility needs largely in terms of railway rolling stock and motor transport. Aircraft play a significant, but secondary, role. Like the United States, both countries have vulnerabilities. Land lines of communication are at least as susceptible to interdiction as those by sea or air, since terminals are immobile and the intervening routes lack flexibility.

COMMAND, CONTROL, AND COMMUNICATIONS

The combat effectiveness of national armed forces depends on cohesive action. Failure to fuse the various sources of military might can have sorrowful consequences. In an effort to attain the greatest degree of unity, some countries, such as Canada, have evolved a single service. Others, patterned after Prussia, place great store in a professional general staff.

Each of the U.S. military departments and services organizes, equips, and trains its own forces for specific combatant roles, coordinating with other parties as required. This means that the Army, Navy, Air Force, and Marine Corps develop their own tactical and technical doctrines. Responsibilities for joint doctrines, which involve two or more services, are assigned by the Secretary of Defense, who considers recommendations by the Joint Chiefs of Staff.[9]

Military activities supporting U.S. grand strategy, including combat operations, are carried out by six unified commands* with regional responsibilities: Alaska Command (ALCOM); Atlantic Command (LANTCOM); European Command (EUCOM), which covers the NATO area, Africa north of the Sahara, and much of the Middle East; Pacific Command (PACOM), whose purview for planning purposes extends from our own west coast through the Indian Ocean and includes most of Asia; and Southern Command (SOUTHCOM), which is oriented toward South America. The Continental Air Defense Command (CONAD), which has functional *and* area aspects, covers the United States. Each unified command amalgamates forces from two or more services. The Strategic Air Command (SAC), the sole specified command, is structured for functional purposes, and is manned almost exclusively by the Air Force. In all cases, the chain of command runs from the President, as Commander-in-Chief, to the Secretary of Defense, then through the Joint Chiefs of Staff directly to the unified and specified commands.

Every system of command and control has its own peculiarities, ours included. Strategists should beware of organizational pitfalls as they go about planning. Problems multiply and intensify in coalitions, which demand the ultimate in coordination if the desired results are to be achieved. The alliance between Tojo and Hitler, for example, suffered considerably from the absence of cohesion. There never were any combined operations, no common plans, no appreciable exchange of supplies, no integrated chiefs of staff. Granted that distance was a great inhibitor, but tighter relationships surely could have been welded. Lack of a combined U.S.-South Vietnamese command structure also caused serious shortcomings. By contrast, the Anglo-American Combined Chiefs of Staff in World War II and the multinational United Nations Command in Korea were somewhat more successful.

---

* *See* Appendix I for definitions of unified and specified commands. Strike Command (STRICOM) was replaced by the Readiness Command (REDCOM) in January 1972. REDCOM, unlike other unified commands, has no geographic or operations responsibilities.

Organization is only one aspect of command/control. Lieutenant General Robert F. Sink, one-time Commander of XVIII Airborne Corps, identified another when he quipped, "If you ain't got communications, you ain't got nothin'!" Great men who lack communications only command their aides.

Communications must be responsive, survivable, *and secure* to be optimally effective, as the Japanese learned to their sorrow during World War II. U.S. successes in cracking their codes crippled Nippon's ability to operate in secret and contributed conclusively to our final victory in the Pacific.[10]

Fortunately (or unfortunately, as some see it), the United States owns and operates the world's best communications network. Instantaneous touch between high-level decision-makers and key commanders at home and overseas usually is possible. The advantages are apparent, but so are the liabilities. The temptation for superiors to dabble directly in the affairs of subordinates can be irresistible, sometimes with serious detriment.

MILITARY POWER IN PERSPECTIVE

Klaus Knorr, Princeton's professor of international affairs, sums up the gist of this chapter very well:

> There are neither theoretical guidance nor empirical apparatus for measuring and comparing, and essentially predicting, the combat strength of . . . different states. The only known measurement test which is accurate is the test of battle. Of course quantitative comparisons of infantry divisions, aircraft wings, naval vessels, missile launchers and military personnel can be made. . . . [But studying statistical data] on the armed forces of Israel and the United Arab Republic . . . would have left us completely unprepared for the outcome of the Arab-Israeli war in 1967. . . . The main problem arises from the fact that the presence of qualitative factors makes quantitative comparisons often inconclusive. . . . It would have been equally difficult to compare, before the event, the fighting strength of North Vietnamese regulars and U.S. Marines south of the Demilitarized Zone.[11]

Well said. Combat effectiveness is a compilation of many things, some of which can and some of which cannot be precisely calculated. That is just one of the reasons why strategy formulation always has been and always will be an art as well as a science.

22 The Influence of Arms Control

Armed readiness is not an end in itself; it is simply one method of protecting our national security. Similarly, arms control is another method of obtaining the same objectives. . . . Under certain circumstances, one method may be superior to the other.

MARK E. SMITH III
and CLAUDE J. JOHNS, JR.
American Defense Policy

Arms control measures influence strategy in ways that bear directly on U.S. national security, and perhaps on our national survival. How best to go about the business of limiting arms is an eternally contentious matter. This chapter points out opportunities as well as pitfalls to provide perspective.

ARMS CONTROL DESCRIBED

Most believers in arms control, as differentiated from proponents of general and complete disarmament, are pragmatic men who agree that wars likely are inevitable, for the foreseeable future. Consequently, they concur that an injunction against all instruments of war would not only be unattainable at present, but would also be undesirable. Society, as they see it, therefore must find ways of attenuating or eliminating any possibility that violence might destroy this planet or sizeable portions of its population.

Arms-control measures generally apply two or more of the following restraints: the retardation or prevention of nuclear proliferation; emphasis on defensive rather than offensive weapons systems and strategies; limitations on arms production and arms commerce; restrictions on nuclear testing; prohibitions on placing weapons in orbit; the reduction of nuclear stockpiles; and tension-reducing ploys, such as thinning out opposing forces and establishing nuclear-free zones.

185

CURRENT U.S. ARMS CONTROL POLICY

The present U.S. position concerning arms control was outlined concisely by President Nixon in his 18 February 1970 report to the Congress:

> There is no area in which we and the Soviet Union — as well as others — have a greater common interest than in reaching agreement with regard to arms control.

> The traditional course of seeking security primarily through military strength raises several problems in a world of multiplying strategic weapons.

> Modern technology makes any balance precarious and prompts new efforts at ever higher levels of complexity.

> Such an arms race absorbs resources, talents and energies.

> The more intense the competition, the greater the uncertainty about the other side's intentions.

> The higher the level of armaments, the greater the violence and devastation should deterrence fail.

> For these reasons I decided early in the Administration that we should seek to maintain our security whenever possible through cooperative efforts with other nations at the lowest possible level of uncertainty, cost, and potential violence.[1]

NUCLEAR ARMS CONTROL MEASURES

Nuclear weapons have been our prime preoccupation since the first fireball burst over Hiroshima. Since then, this country has stressed strictly defensive general-war postures, has limited the types of hardware in its inventory and the size of its warhead stockpiles, has severely curtailed opportunities to test existing or projected systems, and restricted the circumstances under which we would employ nuclear weapons.

Nuclear Testing

The Uninspected Test Moratorium

The uninspected moratorium on nuclear testing from 1958 to 1961 is not listed as an achievement by the U.S. Arms Control and Disarmament Agency (ACDA). It provoked violent reactions such as that registered by General Nathan F. Twining, U.S. Air Force (Retired), Chairman of the Joint Chiefs of Staff during most of that period:

> Following the tacit agreement of 1958, [the United States] was maneuvered into endless meetings with the U.S.S.R. . . . Consistently [we] came back with nothing but a compromised and weakened U.S. position for the next round of discussions. . . .

> In 1961, Russia, by unilateral action, abrogated the "gentlemen's agreement" . . . [accomplishing] a series of nuclear tests of great sophistication, technological depth, and vast military significance. . . .

> This nation was not prepared to resume an effective and sophisticated nuclear-weapons testing program. . . . During the time of the moratorium, we lost our Pacific bases

186

for nuclear testing, lost the trained nuclear teams, lost the motivation in nuclear laboratories, and lost the capacity for producing meaningful and up-to-date plans. Consequently, I am convinced that the decision to accept the uninspected nuclear-test moratorium in 1958 was a great strategic mistake. . . .[2]

Many informed individuals today take issue with that statement. However, even those who claim that it is grossly overdrawn generally concur that Soviet duplicity should have been expected, and that the United States therefore was negligently unprepared.

The Partial Test Ban Treaty

Our next significant experience involved the partial test ban treaty of 5 August 1963, which prohibits nuclear detonations in the atmosphere, in outer space, and under water. Fortunately, we had learned a few lessons by that time. President Kennedy supported that pact after plumbing four questions:

1. Did the U.S.S.R. have, or could it achieve, a significant military advantage the United States would be unable to overcome if it signed the treaty?
2. Would clandestine Soviet testing have a seriously adverse effect on the relative balance of military power?
3. Could the United States recoup without undue delay if the U.S.S.R. defaulted or our interests were imperiled?
4. If the first two answers were unfavorable, could we glean ample compensation in other ways?[3]

No insurmountable difficulties were identified. The Joint Chiefs of Staff concluded that the treaty would restrain nuclear proliferation, reduce international tensions, and "should contribute to the fundamental objective of the U.S. Armed Forces; namely, the deterrence of war and maintenance of peace on honorable terms."[4] Those features were deemed important enough to offset predictable technological liabilities.

Nevertheless, some observers still have reservations. As a direct result of the limited test ban treaty, the United States presently pursues a general-war strategy predicated on nuclear weapons which never have been proven in practice. Delivery vehicles have been tested to satisfaction using dummy warheads. Weapons have undergone endless underground experiments. Complete packages meet rigorous standards when subjected to simulations. But the fact remains that integrated systems have yet to be tried under realistic conditions. In addition, numerous contingency effects, such as those related to communications blackouts caused by nuclear blasts in space, never have been properly probed. The resultant risks to U.S. national security are deemed slight by responsible officials, but their conclusions perforce are calculated using incomplete evidence.

Nonproliferation

Nuclear proliferation problems were nonexistent from 1945 to 1950. Americans enjoyed a monopoly of deliverable nuclear weapons during that period. For the succeeding fifteen years, our general-war strategy was concerned exclusively with the Soviet Union, which posed the only nuclear threat. That situation changed in October 1964, when Red China detonated its first nuclear device. Peking followed up with a multimegaton thermonuclear burst in the spring of 1967, and demonstrated an active interest in developing delivery systems. France and Great Britain also own nuclear capabilities, but fortunately they are aligned with the United States. As other nations acquire nuclear weapons, we clearly will be confronted with sharply different strategic planning problems than we face today, particularly if the countries concerned are known enemies or states with erratic behavior patterns.

The Nonproliferation Treaty

The Treaty on the Non-proliferation of Nuclear Weapons, which went into effect on 5 March 1970, has been signed by ninety-seven nations. Seventy countries have acceded to or ratified that treaty. Significantly, states such as Israel, India, and Brazil, which have the ability to join the "Nuclear Club" on fairly short notice, are not signatories. Japan and the Federal Republic of Germany signed, but have not ratified, the treaty.[5] The two superpowers, plus Great Britain, have publicly promised "to seek immediate Security Council action to provide assistance, in accordance with the Charter, to any non-nuclear-weapon state party to the treaty . . . that is a victim of an act of aggression or an object of a threat of aggression in which nuclear weapons are used."[6] Nevertheless, no nation is likely to abstain indefinitely from acquiring its own capability if, in the opinion of its leaders, national interests dictate otherwise.

The Nuclear Multilateral Force

In its efforts to prevent the spread of nuclear weapons, and simultaneously to provide some semblance of equal partnership in the defense of NATO Europe, the United States proposed a nuclear Multilateral Force (MLF) in the early 1960s. That proposition raised two very thorny problems: *which* of our allies should have a finger on the trigger, and *under what conditions?* Ambivalence on both counts by all parties caused the program to founder from the start. The prospect of German participation caused almost as much consternation in Western Europe as it did in the Soviet Union. That attitude, combined with U.S. reluctance to relinquish control, led to such tight restrictions that the coequal status originally sought simply failed to materialize. Our NATO teammates in fact never gained access to a U.S.-provided nuclear capability which could respond to *their* decisions in time of crisis. Far from engendering a feeling of cooperation, the Multilateral Force fostered distrust, dissatisfaction, and further eroded Europeans' confidence that the United States would risk general war to guarantee *their* security if our own survival were not clearly at stake.[7]

Nuclear-Free Zones

"Nuclear-free zones" are geographical areas where nuclear weapons are *prohibited by international agreement.* For some time, only Antarctica, outer space, and the seabed were so designated. The first serious attempt to apply this principle to inhabited lands was made in 1957, when Adam Rapacki, then the Prime Minister of Poland, proposed that Central Europe be declared a nuclear-free zone. He failed, because NATO and Warsaw Pact strategies both were predicated in part on the use of nuclear firepower, and neither side was willing to sacrifice that flexibility.

Subsequent suggestions related to other regions have been rejected because of strategic inequities and the disparity of national interests among world powers. The United Arab Republic, for example, understandably opposed Africa as a nuclear-free zone because Israel is in Asia, and thus would be excluded. To date, Latin America, where the use of nuclear weapons seems quite unlikely, is the only populated area established as a nuclear-free zone — a treaty to that effect was signed in 1967. However, Latin American countries are the sole signatories, and only the United States and the United Kingdom have signed the accompanying protocol "designed for ratification by the nuclear powers who . . . agree not to use or threaten to use nuclear weapons against a party to the treaty."[8]

The United States created a de facto free zone in Korea in 1950 *without resorting to any international agreement,* when President Truman refused to atomize the Chinese, despite considerable pressure by influential circles. Presidents Johnson and Nixon applied duplicate decisions to Indochina. In each instance, those choices influenced U.S. strategic concepts for limited war.

Strategic Arms Limitation Talks

The greatest arms control emphasis today, in both the United States and the U.S.S.R., rests with the Strategic Arms Limitation Talks (SALT). President Nixon outlined the U.S. approach in his foreign policy statement of 18 February 1970:

> We first laid out preliminary models of possible strategic arms limitation agreements. We compared these both with each other and with the situation most likely to prevail in the absence of an agreement. . . .
>
> [We] surveyed our intelligence capability to monitor the other side's compliance with a curb for each weapons system; the precise activities that would have to be restricted to ensure confidence in the effectiveness of the limitation; and the impact of limitation on U.S. and Soviet strategic weapons programs.[9]

Phase I of the negotiations, commonly called SALT I, culminated on 26 May 1972. At that time, the United States and the U.S.S.R. announced a treaty, which limits their present and projected antiballistic-missile systems, and an interim agreement that puts a five-year freeze on selected strategic offensive force levels (*see* table below). Both countries are free to improve authorized forces qualitatively, provided that no new technological developments, such as lasers, are introduced. Each signatory has the right to withdraw from the treaty or agreement should "extraordinary events" jeopardize its supreme interests, and we have made it clear that if comprehensive strategic offensive arms limitations are not concluded during the five-year freeze period, "U.S. supreme interests *could* be jeopardized" [emphasis added].[10]

The Antiballistic Missile Treaty
The United States and the U.S.S.R. must limit their antiballistic-missile installations to one site defending the national capital and another covering an ICBM field. Neither site may exceed 100 ABM launchers, each with a single interceptor missile. Radar

189

INFLUENCES OF SALT I ON U.S. AND
SOVIET STRATEGIC FORCES

Weapons System	United States	Soviet Union
ABM Sites		
Current		
Operational	0	1
Under construction	1	0
Projected 1977*	3	1
Planned	12	?
Effect of SALT I freeze	2	2
ICBM Launchers		
Current	1,054	1,618
Projected 1977*	1,054	2,868
Effect of SALT I freeze	1,054	1,618
Maximum conversion allowed by SALT I**	1,000	1,408
Ballistic-Missile Submarines		
Current		
Operational	41	25
Under construction	0	16–18
Projected 1977*	41	80–90
Effect of SALT I freeze	41	41–43
Maximum conversion allowed by SALT I**	44	62
SLBM Launchers		
Current	656	560
Projected 1977*	656	1,200
Effect of SALT I freeze	656	740
Maximum conversion allowed by SALT I**	710	950
Strategic Bombers		
Current	460***	140
Projected 1977*	460***	140
Effect of SALT I freeze	Not applicable	Not applicable
Maximum conversion allowed by SALT I	Not applicable	Not applicable

  *   Before the freeze imposed by SALT I
  **   If obsolescent ICBMs and/or SLBMS are converted to modern SLBMs
  *** In operational squadrons

support is severely restricted. Excess installations under construction must be dismantled or destroyed.

The United States will retain its ABM site at Grand Forks, North Dakota. Operations there are scheduled to begin by mid-1975. Preparations at Malmstrom, Montana, and Whiteman, Missouri, have stopped. No decision has yet been made to build a complex centered on Washington, D.C. The U.S.S.R. currently defends Moscow with sixty-four ABM missiles. Should the Soviets choose to establish companion coverage for an ICBM cluster, it must be located at least 800 miles from their capital city — which would place it east of the Urals.

ABM systems based at sea or in aerospace are forbidden, as are mobile land-based models, rapid reloading facilities, and ABMs with MIRV warheads. Antiaircraft missile systems may not be converted to ABM roles. Finally, neither the United States nor the U.S.S.R. may transfer ABM components to allies or otherwise deploy ABM elements outside their own national boundaries.[11]

The Interim Agreement on Strategic Offensive Arms

Intercontinental Ballistic Missiles The interim agreement, as amplified by its accompanying protocol, bars both countries from *initiating* ICBM-launcher construction after 1 July 1972. No light ICBMs or heavy models deployed before 1964 may be converted into launchers for heavy ICBM types deployed at later dates.

Those restrictions will not affect U.S. general-war retaliatory capabilities, since this country has no up-to-date heavy ICBMs and had no plans to augment its land-based missile force during the five-year period from mid-1972 to mid-1977. However, the Soviets were building ICBMs at an estimated rate of 250 per year. Without the freeze, their arsenal could have numbered nearly 2,870 launchers by 1977, as compared with 1,000 Minutemen and 54 Titans for the United States.

Ballistic-Missile Submarines and SLBMs SLBMs and modern ballistic-missile submarines (typified by U.S. Polaris and Soviet Y-class models) must be limited to those that were operational or under construction on 26 May 1972. ICBMs deployed before 1964 and SLBMs on obsolescent Soviet G- and H-class submarines may be converted to SLBMs on modern vessels on a one-for-one basis. The United States is authorized a maximum of 710 SLBMs and 44 modern boats; the Soviet ceiling is 950 and 62 respectively. Modern SLBMs on *any* type submarine will be counted against those totals.

As was the case with ICBM launchers, the United States had no programs to augment its ballistic-missile submarine force during the freeze period. The U.S.S.R., however, was building eight or nine new boats annually. If the freeze had not gone into effect, its complement of modern submarines might well have been more than twice as large as ours by 1977.

Other Systems The interim agreement does not address long-range bombers, land- and carrier-based tactical aircraft with strategic missions, or sea-launched cruise missiles.[12] The status of such weapons systems will be discussed during Phase II of the Strategic Arms Limitation Talks (SALT II).

Agreed Interpretations and Unilateral Statements

Both the ABM treaty and the interim agreement contain clauses that are subject to differing interpretations. Three items are of particular strategic importance.

The terms *heavy ICBMs* and *light ICBMs* have not been defined. The United States construes *heavy ICBMs* to mean missiles comparable to the Soviet SS-9, even though it did not differentiate that precisely in its published unilateral statement.

Moscow reserves the right to increase its modern ballistic-missile submarine holdings "correspondingly" if continued submarine construction by our European allies causes

191

NATO's total to exceed 50 submarines or 800 SLBMs. The United States demurs. The Soviets favor liquidating all U.S. overseas bases for ballistic-missile submarines. This country objects. Forward deployment bases at Holy Loch, Scotland, Rota, Spain, and in Guam permit us to retain roughly half of our submarines on station at all times. A substantially lower percentage is presently judged unacceptable.[13]

The Basic Consequences of SALT I

SALT I negotiators sought mutual restraint in the nuclear-arms race and accepted mutual vulnerability, "not on the basis of trust," as Dr. Kissinger put it, "but on the enlightened self-interest of both sides."[14]

The United States apparently will retain a 3:1 margin of superiority over the U.S.S.R. in total numbers of bombs and warheads, even if the Soviets begin deploying MIRVs during the freeze period. The Russians will exhibit a 3:1 superiority in gross megatonnage, owing largely to their SS-9 assemblage. A condition of rough parity in total delivery vehicles pertains, if U.S. tactical aircraft with strategic missions are counted.[15]

Whether this country will continue to satisfy its strategic force "sufficiency" criteria under those conditions is a matter for conjecture. Skeptics contend that SALT I impinges seriously on our deterrent posture and our ability to wage a general nuclear war if deterrence should fail. Architects of the accords believe the opposite. They submit that SALT I created a strategic situation far more favorable to U.S. national security than otherwise would have prevailed. Only time will tell which presumption is most accurate.

NONNUCLEAR ARMS CONTROL EFFORTS

Nonnuclear arms control efforts presently receive less publicity than do the critical steps described above, but many measures, including the Washington-to-Moscow "hot line" and peaceful uses of outer space and the ocean floor, have sweeping strategic ramifications. International traffic in conventional arms and munitions, the mainstays of limited war, is cause for concern, but has been allocated a fairly low priority. In addition, this country exhibits considerable interest in curtailing prospects for chemical and biological warfare. It has unilaterally renounced the use of biological and toxic weapons, and destroyed all such stocks. On 10 April 1972, the United States and the Soviet Union both signed an international bacteriological warfare convention that serves a similar purpose, and also pledges participants to seek companion controls dealing with chemical weapons.[16]

Mutual and balanced force reductions in Central Europe merit special mention. Secretary of State Rogers addressed that matter in Brussels on 6 December 1969:

> For many years NATO has given serious study to the difficult question of how security in Europe, now sustained by a high balance of armaments, could be maintained at a lower and less expensive level of arms on both sides. Since June 1968, it has explicitly stated its belief that mutual force reductions could significantly contribute to lessening of tensions.[17]

President Nixon's guidelines to U.S. negotiators counseled caution, as the following policy extract indicates:

The principal objective should be a more stable military balance at lower levels of forces and costs. Therefore, reductions should have the effect of enhancing defensive capabilities, so as to diminish the incentives for attacking forces. Even if defensive capabilities were not actually improved, force reductions, as a minimum, should not create offensive advantages greater than those already existing. Yet, reductions would tend to favor offensive capabilities, since attacking forces could concentrate while reduced defensive forces were compelled to spread along a given line.[18]

Those goals have been exceedingly elusive. Deleting stipulated percentages of U.S. and Soviet forces, for example, would favor the communists, who have substantially greater numbers of troops, aircraft, and divisions in the European theater than we do. The larger the reduction, the greater the disparity. The United States would find it difficult to regenerate combat power in emergency, since its elements would have to be repositioned in North America. Soviet forces would withdraw a few miles overland to Western Russia. Problems of inspection and verification have yet to be resolved. And finally, initiatives such as the Mansfield Resolution, which recommended unilateral diminution of U.S. military strength in Europe, would make mutual and balanced force reductions academic.

Such dilemmas obviously must be resolved if solid progress is ever to be registered. The prognosis is pessimistic.

THE ARMS CONTROL OUTLOOK

Few officials, or private citizens for that matter, are neutral or moderate when it comes to arms control. The entire subject arouses passionate emotions. Some critics feel that the United States emphasizes arms control far too much. Others feel that we do too little. With few exceptions, however, responsible individuals generally agree that reciprocal, effectively monitored measures are in the national interest, and should play an important part in national defense strategy. Present policy bears that out.

193

23 Economic and Fiscal Constraints

Brother, can you spare a dime?
Panhandler's plea during the depression

Ideally, national security interests are the bases for objectives which, within policy guidelines, shape strategy. Grand strategy in turn generates military force requirements. Assets then are allocated to satisfy needs.

THE COMPETITION FOR RESOURCES

That Utopian sequence rarely occurs in real life. National security interests inevitably compete with other wants and wishes, foreign and domestic, for money, manpower, and materiel. The emphasis continually shifts on a sliding scale of priorities. Except in times of dire emergency, Free World countries in particular tend to tailor their strategies and supporting forces at the lowest possible levels, glossing over or assuming away many potential threats. The trick is to walk a tightrope between excessive defense expenditures that emasculate political, economic, social, scientific, and ecological programs on one hand, and deficient defense expenditures that actively endanger national security on the other.

The demands that defense makes on economic resources are tremendous. Costs continue to skyrocket at an exponential rate, aggravated by inflation, which undercuts buying power (annual inflationary increases of 4 to 5 percent have been the rule in this country during recent years). According to the latest edition of *World Military Expenditures,* the international community devoted $208 billion to armed forces in 1970, a new record, and the outlay was expected to reach $216 billion in 1971.[1]

Trends in the United States afford a prime example. An M-4 tank in World War II cost the taxpayer something like $70,000. The controversial Main Battle Tank (MBT), scrapped during its developmental stage, would have cost ten times that much. The B-29 that blasted Hiroshima had a $640,000 price tag, in contrast with our forthcoming B-1 manned bomber, which will run at least $40 million a copy. A nuclear-powered aircraft carrier, complete with air wing, is valued at $1.5 billion.

194

Moreover, those figures merely reflect purchase prices. Research, development, operat-ing, and maintenance costs make such goods immensely more expensive.*

THE ECONOMIC POWER BASE

The economic power base, which provides the wherewithal, constitutes a matrix of industry, commerce, trade, finance, and natural resources, including those related to energy. Skilled manpower and organization provide direction, know-how, and impetus.

Just assessing the present and projected capacity of any economy to produce pre-scribed goods in prescribed quantities and of prescribed qualities during prescribed periods is a complicated proposition. The Gross National Product (GNP) is a superfi-cial indicator. Many countries, for example, choose to produce guns instead of butter. Growth rates for investment volume and the production of capital goods can be equally misleading: shipyards and furniture factories have significantly different impacts on power potential. The same could be said for electric power, oil and steel production, or the numbers of scientists and engineers. Oskar Morgenstern, a noted economist, would base his estimates on the allocation "of resources for future expansion of the whole economy, the particular growth rate of industries important for defense, the rate of use of materials by the military effort," and similar considerations.[2]

ENDS RELATED TO MEANS

How to slice up the economic pie most effectively has been, and always will be, debatable. Even the United States, an economic giant with a trillion-dollar GNP, faces practical limitations, as described by James M. Roherty in *Decisions of Robert S. McNamara:*

> The phenomenon of technological acceleration on an unprecedented scale might strike some as belying scarcity of resources. Quite on the contrary, the world of the decision-maker is "a world in which resources are limited." The fact of a luxury of choice counterposed against a dearth of resources demands that choices be made under the constraint of economy.[3]

A good many men in the field of U.S. defense management, whose views are ex-pounded by Roherty, insist that national security objectives and supporting strategies must be geared to monetary costs:

> The selection of the best alternative — it may be only a "good" alternative — is done

---

* Admiral Thomas H. Moorer, Chairman of the Joint Chiefs of Staff, tells an amusing anecdote related to this subject when he reminisces about his days as an ensign: "We had, among other things [in 1933], an aircraft called F-4, which was selling for about $30,000. . . . Today we also have an F-4, used by the Navy and Air Force, which weighs more and costs more than an entire squadron in those days. Furthermore, the F-4 today will fly faster straight up than [its ancestor] would go straight down!"

195

on the basis of an *economic criterion*. Strategies are merely ways of using resources; technology tells us, in turn, what strategies are possible. But economy does not turn out to be simply a third element in a problem that will be subjected to a higher test. Economy is the test; economy decides. . . . While Hitch [Charles J. Hitch, McNamara's comptroller] has insisted that "judgment is always of critical importance in . . . choosing the alternatives to be compared, and *selecting the criterion*," it is invariably a matter of choosing *the most appropriate economic criterion*.[4]

That approach to strategy formulation puts the cart before the horse, according to disbelievers. They grant that strict standards should be applied to the end use of every dollar, but preach that imperative national security interests, not the manipulation of money, should be the prime consideration. We allocated roughly 40 percent of our GNP to defense needs in 1943 and 1944, they say, without any serious consequences, as opposed to 8 or 9 percent in recent years. Certainly, we could split the difference over a protracted period, if necessary, to counter serious threats. To vindicate their views, members of that group cite Secretary McNamara, the principal proponent of "cost effectiveness," who readily acknowledged that "the United States is well able to spend whatever it needs . . . on national security."[5]

Hans Morgenthau lays out the fundamental problem:

Good government . . . must start by performing two different intellectual operations. First, it must choose the objectives and methods of its foreign policy in view of the power available to support them with a maximum chance of success. A nation that sets its sights too low, foregoing foreign policies well within the reach of its power, abdicates its rightful role in the council of nations; the United States fell into that error in the interwar period. A nation may also set its sights too high and pursue policies that cannot be successfully executed with the available power; this was the error which the United States committed during the peace negotiations in 1919. As Lloyd George put it: "The Americans appeared to assume responsibility for the sole guardianship of the Ten Commandments and for the Sermon on the Mount; yet, when it came to a practical question of assistance and responsibility, they absolutely refused to accept it." A nation may try to play the role of a great power without having the prerequisites for doing so, and will court disaster, as Poland did in the interwar period. Or, being a great power, it may embark upon a policy of unlimited conquest, overtaxing its strength; the unsuccessful world-conquerors, . . . [like] Hitler, illustrate that point.[6]

Matching realistic ends with attainable means is a vexing matter under the best of circumstances. Businessmen predicate their estimates on profits and losses expressed in dollars and cents. Defense decision-makers have no such advantage. They must pit objective costs against subjective values.

What price tag, pray tell, can be placed on any given national interest? What premium can be placed on human life? No sound answers are forthcoming. "As a result," Oskar Morgenstern contends, "the Congress and the people (not to mention the Bureau of the Budget!) look hypnotized at the monetary figures alone and are completely at sea when it comes to the real assessment, i.e., the value of . . . weapons systems for the defense of the country."[7] That bemusement is likely to persist until some genius devises a better yardstick.

196

U.S. RESOURCE ALLOCATION PROCEDURES, 1945–1960

Two schools of budgetary thought — "traditional" and "active management" — have been evidenced in the United States since World War II. Both have the same point of departure: the President submits his proposed defense budget to the Congress which, exercising its rights under Section 8, Article I of the Constitution, appropriates such monies as it sees fit to "raise and support Armies . . . provide and maintain a Navy . . . [and] to provide for organizing, arming, and disciplining, the Militia." However, the two schools go about that process in sharply different ways.

The Traditional School

Defense Budget Practices

The "traditional" school, at work during the Truman and Eisenhower years, is described by Alain C. Enthoven and K. Wayne Smith in their book *How Much is Enough?:*

> Defense budgets at that time represented essentially predetermined, arbitrary ceilings in the sense that they did not follow from decisions about strategy, military needs and weapon systems. . . . The President, relatively early in the budget cycle, provided guidance to the Secretary of Defense on the size of the defense budget which he thought economically and politically feasible for the next fiscal year. The problem was that this figure was usually arrived at by simply estimating the government's total revenues, then deducting fixed payments (such as interest on the national debt and payments to veterans), the estimated costs of domestic programs, and expenditures on foreign aid. Whatever "remained" was then allocated to the military. The strategic implications of these budget guidelines were not explicitly and systematically considered. Once the President had decided on an acceptable defense budget, the Secretary of Defense then determined and enforced a fixed percentage among the Services. Largely because the fractions set in each year's budget guidelines were an extrapolation of the fractions in the previous budget, from 1954 to 1961 the allocations remained remarkably constant. . . . Each Service in turn fixed allocations among its various components in accordance with its internal institutional pressures and its own interpretation of the guidance on national strategy and priorities infrequently set forth by the National Security Council in a paper called Basic National Security Policy (BNSP).[8]

That system had some predictable defects.

The Joint Chiefs of Staff played no part in budget formulation, since they were assigned no clearly defined role by the Secretary of Defense. General Maxwell D. Taylor, writing at that time, painted the following picture:

> Each Service [prepared] its budget in isolation from the others. Although many earnest discussions of uniservice needs took place between the Secretary of Defense, the Department Secretaries, and their Chiefs of Staff, at no time to my knowledge were the three service budgets put side by side and an appraisal made of the fighting capabilities of the aggregate military forces supported by the budget. This so-called "vertical"

(rather than "horizontal") approach to building the budget . . . accounts in a large measure for the inability thus far to develop a budget which keeps fiscal emphasis in phase with military priorities. It is not an exaggeration to say that nobody knows what we are actually buying with any specific budget.[9]

A lack of financial discipline, coupled with ego-oriented service desires, contributed to budgetary nonsense in many cases. President Eisenhower confirmed that contention in May 1953, shortly after he took office:

> Words like "essential" and "indispensable" and "absolute minimum" become the common coin of the realm, and they are spent with wild abandon. One military man will argue hotly for a given number of aircraft as the "absolute minimum," and others will earnestly advocate the "indispensable" needs for ships, tanks, rockets, guided missiles, or artillery, all totalled in numbers that are always called "minimum." All such views are argued with vigor and tenacity, but obviously all cannot be right.[10]

Many exaggerated estimates could be traced to ingrained service conservatism, which urged guardians of national security to hedge against uncertainty. The resultant evaluations frequently took undue cognizance of "greater than expected threats" that depicted enemies ten feet tall. Inflated requirements were the consequence.

To make matters worse, parochially oriented service demands often bore little relation to any considered scheme of priorities. When Congress directed Secretary of Defense Neil McElroy to choose between the Army's Nike Hercules and the Air Force's Bomarc for continental air defense, he polled the services with predictable results: the Army opted for Nike, with interceptor support, but no Bomarc; the Air Force elected interceptors and Bomarc; and the Navy concluded that neither Nike nor Bomarc was needed.[11]

Small wonder, then, that open-ended force requirements chronically clashed with fixed funds. In the absence of agreement among the several services as to how those funds should be allocated, the Secretary of Defense and his staff "hewed away the fat," which invariably included requests for items that everyone knew could not be accommodated within the predetermined budget ceilings.

The Impact on Defense Planning

The impact on rational planning was devastating. Secretary McNamara later reviewed the situation in these terms:

> We can imagine many different kinds of wars the United States must be prepared to fight, but a war in which the Army fights independently of the Navy, or the Navy independently of the Air Force, is not one of them. Quite obviously, the coordination of the planning of the four services makes eminently good sense on the narrowest military grounds. . . .
>
> [Unfortunately,] the three military departments had been establishing their requirements independently of each other. The results could be described fairly as chaotic: Army planning, for example, was based primarily on a long war of attrition; Air Force planning was based, largely, on a short war of nuclear bombardment. Consequently, the Army was stating a requirement for stocking months, if not years, of combat

198

supplies against the event of a sizable conventional conflict. The Air Force stock requirements for such a war had to be measured in days, and not very many days at that. Either approach, consistently followed, might make some sense. The two combined could not possibly make sense. What we needed was a coordinated strategy seeking objectives actually attainable with the military resources available.[12]

Equally important, strategic planning was projected far into the future, but defense budgeting was hand-to-mouth, one year at a time. Piecemeal financing of that sort, which dealt only with the tip of the iceberg, was disastrous. Since total costs were never known (operating and maintenance costs, plus those related to research, development, and procurement), the budgetary implications of program decisions were unpredictable. Numerous projects were started without any real probability that they could be completed. Overcommitments led to costly cancellations and delays that could have been circumvented by long-range financial planning.

U.S. RESOURCE ALLOCATION PROCEDURES, 1961–1968

The Active Management School

Since 1961, the "traditional" school has been usurped by the "active management" school, which interlocks national security interests, objectives, policy, strategy, force posture, and defense budgets somewhat more closely. Once again, Enthoven and Smith provide the description:

> In reaction to the failings of the system used in the 1950's, President Kennedy decided there would be no arbitrary budget ceilings on the defense budget. The President's two basic instructions to Secretary McNamara were to "develop the force structure necessary to our military requirements without regard to arbitrary budget ceilings" and to "procure and operate this force at the lowest possible cost." McNamara's idea was that the nation's foreign policy, military strategy, military forces, and defense budget would be brought into balance, and Service and JCS proposals would be considered on their merits on a case-by-case basis.[13]

The McNamara Reforms

Secretary McNamara took the helm determined to centralize authority and to assume the role of active decision-maker, rather than to act as judge, umpire, or arbiter. DOD civilians began to participate in the strategy process to an extent unheard of in the past — so much so that they frequently were accused of undercutting the Joint Chiefs of Staff.

A formal Planning-Programming-Budgeting System (PPBS) was introduced. For the first time, the Secretary of Defense was able to make integrated decisions. Also for the first time, it was possible to identify specifically where money was going, since defense requirements were addressed by agency and branch of service, and were further broken down within two functional categories. Research, development, and military assistance were common to both:

199

Strategic Forces
General-Purpose Forces
Intelligence and Communications
Airlift and Sealift
Guard and Reserve Forces
Central Supply and Maintenance
Training, Medical, etc.
Administration and Associated Activities
Unfunded (-) Current Service Retirement Pay

Military Personnel
Operations and Maintenance
Procurement
Military Construction
Defense Family Housing
Other[14]

A Five-Year Defense Program (FYDP) was inaugurated to sum up *approved* programs for all DOD components. It provides continuity eight years into the future for forces and five years for resources, thereby relating input to output and force posture to strategy.

Systems Analysis Analyzed

McNamara's most maligned innovation was systems analysis, described by its advocates as "a reasoned approach to the problems of decision." This technique, which draws on various academic disciplines, mainly mathematics, economics, and statistics, is praised by some as a marvelous tool that substitutes science for "seat-of-the-pants" verdicts, and is reviled by others as an occult art that tries to quantify the unquantifiable. In fact, it is neither. Systems analysis simply isolates and examines relevant facts, logical propositions, and assumptions in ways that highlight alternatives, so that decision-makers can apply judgment sagaciously, and relationships between ends and means can be optimized.

One purpose of systems analysis is to guarantee the best possible trade-offs between cost and effectiveness. A typical display, related to weapons procurement, is shown in Figure 9.

If a weapons system plots at A, either the objective is too ambitious or more money is needed. If the system plots at B, a few additional funds would greatly increase effectiveness. D is the optimum objective, since increased effectiveness in relation to cost levels out beyond that point. If the system plots at E, diminishing returns have set in. The figure also identifies margins. At A or E, minor changes in funding would have an insignificant influence. At C, however, the addition or deletion of a few dollars would drastically improve or degrade effectiveness.

The results of such studies can be good, bad, or indifferent, depending on the intellect, education, experience, and biases of the analysts. The "garbage in, garbage out" adage applies to perfection. Ill-advised assumptions can completely distort conclusions. Nevertheless, systems analysis in conjunction with PPBS has provided a powerful management tool which holds great promise for the future.

200

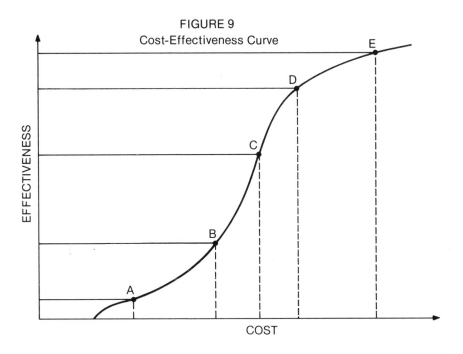

FIGURE 9
Cost-Effectiveness Curve

CURRENT U.S. RESOURCE ALLOCATION PROCEDURES

When the Nixon-Laird team took office, they overhauled the whole PPBS apparatus. The Secretary of Defense now issues tentative fiscal guidance early in the cycle, *before* force requirements are developed, covering a period five years into the future by major mission and support category for each of the military departments and defense agencies. Revised guidance is dispensed later, as required.

In addition, a Defense Program Review Committee (DPRC) has been established as an adjunct of the National Security Council. That body, presently chaired by Dr. Kissinger, includes the Under Secretaries of State and Defense, the Chairman of the JCS, Directors of Central Intelligence and the Office of Budget and Management, plus the Chairman of the Council of Economic Advisors. Perhaps its most important function is to resolve questions concerning resource allocation. That interdepartmental overview has proved to be a blessing.[15]

Other countries obviously have different arrangements, but no matter how today's strategists face fiscal and economic constraints, they must satisfy national security interests and objectives in ways that retain freedom of action and choice. Except in rare circumstances, the use of armed force constitutes the most expensive of all options. Perspicacious planners therefore should take full advantage of alternatives that feature the indirect approach to strategy.

President Nixon summed up this chapter best in the commencement address he delivered to graduates of the Air Force Academy on 4 June 1969:

IV Special Considerations

I have asked only for those programs and those expenditures that I believe are necessary to guarantee the security of this country and to honor our obligations. . . . I do not consider my recommendations infallible. But if I have made a mistake, I pray that it is on the side of too much and not too little. If we do too much, it will cost us our money. If we do too little, it may cost us our lives.[16]

24 Science, Technology, and Strategy

> The Technological War is the decisive struggle in the Protracted Conflict. Victory in the Technological War gives supremacy in all other phases. . . . Victory in the Technological War is achieved when a participant has a technological lead so far advanced that his opponent cannot overcome it. . . . The loser may know that he has lost, and know it for quite a long time, yet be unable to do anything about it.
>
> STEFAN T. POSSONY and J. E. POURNELLE
> *The Strategy of Technology*

Technological warfare is not the one "decisive" element that leads to victory in all manners of war. Technological warfare may not even be the decisive element needed to *win* the protracted contest between the United States and the Soviet Union. But without superior science and technology, that battle could be *lost*.

HARNESSING THE TECHNOLOGICAL REVOLUTION

Science and technology have had a profound influence on military strategy and strategic posture throughout the twentieth century. The first really great surge during World War I saw the advent of military aircraft and the use of submarines on a large scale. Subsequent spasms were provoked by World War II, which produced jet engines, rockets, radar, and nuclear weapons. The strategically useful marvels paraded since those days include nanosecond computers and data-processing devices, both associated with revolutionary changes in the storing, retrieving, and harnessing of information; satellite communications; orbital reconnaissance platforms; and multiple independently-targeted reentry vehicles (MIRV) with thermonuclear warheads.

The current technological explosion is diffuse, cumulative, accelerative and, to a considerable extent, self-sustaining. Man's mission is to harness and direct its energies

203

so that ideas are translated into substance at a rate that guarantees perpetual national security vis-à-vis the most potent threats. This takes talent, time, foresight, money, and concentration. In fact, the demands have become so extravagant that only the two richest and most powerful nations in the world, the United States and the U.S.S.R., are able to compete, other than in very specialized ways.

How to apply available resources most effectively is a contentious question, complicated by the fact that science and technology have grown so complex that it no longer is possible to categorize distinct disciplines or to arbitrarily separate basic from applied research. Physics merges into chemistry, the two tie directly to biology, then into genetics, with trails to physical, social, and behavioral studies, and so on. Science and technology continually feed on each other, leading to an endless chain of discoveries. This causes trouble at budget time when some participants in decision-making try to draw sharp lines between practical end products and esoteric exploration.

THE ROLE OF BASIC RESEARCH

Disagreements over the utility of *pure research* are basic. There is great resistance in some U.S. circles to allocating taxpayers' monies for such endeavors, accompanied by charges that funds are frittered away for the personal aggrandizement of ivory-tower scientists, universities, and congressional districts. Others view abstract science as an indispensable ingredient of the defense equation. Admittedly, the dedicated elite which plies that trade may seem impractical as it gropes for fundamental truths, but its members measure and predict the behavior of materials and forces in ways that add immeasurably to the corporate body of human knowledge, and thus hugely increase the probability that unforeseen but useful strategic consequences will emerge. The lack of directed effort that bedevils keepers of the coffers preordains a certain amount of "wheel-spinning," but creative freedom compensates over the long haul, as Herman Kahn and Anthony Wiener noted in their book *The Year 2000:*

> Interacting effects tend to be important not only because advances in one area are correlated with or spur advances in other areas, but also because various separate advances often allow for unexpected solutions to problems, or can be fitted together to make new wholes that are greater than the sum of their parts, or lead to other unexpected innovations.[1]

Advancement normally is incremental, resulting from the cumulative labors of many people with many ideas. Even on those rare occasions when a really momentous theorem derives, its full significance depends on multifaceted interpretation. No one in 1915, for example, forecast the monstrous military implications of Einstein's Special Theory of Relativity. The postulation by Maxwell that electromagnetic waves exist and their eventual discovery by Hertz led not to one application but to literally thousands that revolutionized communications.

THE ROLE OF APPLIED TECHNOLOGY

Applied science and technology seek specific goals, whereas basic research does not. The hard questions include:

204

What are the needs?
What stumbling blocks are involved?
What will programs cost in terms of time and money?
How many units are financially feasible?
Will the items be obsolete before they are built?
Will the results pay off in combat better than known alternatives?
What major alterations in military strategy and/or force structures are likely
   to ensue?
Are those changes acceptable?

TECHNOLOGICAL FORECASTING

The search for accurate answers involves technological forecasting for specified periods in the future, not by clairvoyance, but by blending realistic assessments
of forthcoming *requirements* with what presumably will be technically attainable
capabilities, so as to reach conclusions that can guide national leaders to sound *policy
decisions* in ways that make practical sense.

Such forecasting, as everyone involved is aware, is a very imprecise art. Kahn and
Wiener took heed of this phenomenon:

> It is often only in retrospect that . . . relations seem clear; our expectations and activity
> are often sporadic, eclectic, unintegrated, and startlingly incomplete. Thus a study in
> 1937 totally missed not only the computer but atomic energy, antibiotics, radar, and
> jet propulsion, nearly all of which had been around in principle and waiting for
> development. . . .

> Consider [they continued] the POLARIS missile system. The first POLARIS subma-
> rine — the George Washington — was launched in 1960; the forty-first, and last, was
> tested in 1967. It would have been almost impossible to argue in the early 1950s, at
> least before a hardheaded and scientifically knowledgeable audience, that such a system
> could be produced successfully within a decade. It took at least six technological
> innovations or breakthroughs, all of which seemed unlikely to be realized soon enough
> to be reliably useful in an early 1960s weapon system. These were (1) a nuclear
> propulsion system . . . (2) a solid fuel propellant for the missiles . . . (3) [an accurate]
> submarine navigation system . . . (4) a lightweight, reliable, and accurate inertial
> guidance system to be carried by the missile; (5) small [but powerful] nuclear warheads
> . . . and (6) successful design, procurement, and assembly of the ten million parts of
> the system, many of them complex and untested.[2]

Requirement Forecasting

Forecasting future needs is a complicated process geared to projected national security
objectives and the projected threat, both of which are subject to unanticipated alterations on a grand scale. Serendipitous results of basic or applied research sometimes
invalidate prospective patterns, creating imperative needs where none existed before.
No strategist in the 1930s would have been presumptuous enough to state an essential

military requirement for a bomb with a million times the destructive power of conventional high explosives. Project Manhattan *followed* the discovery of uranium fission, not vice versa.

Capability Forecasting

Attempts to forecast future capabilities can be just as exasperating as predicting requirements. Capability forecasting demands a careful analysis of trends related to the technical state of the art (which paradoxically might be the least crucial consideration), admixed with the quality and quantity of scholars emanating from institutions of higher learning, the character of civil-military technical interplay, and the national will to compete.

SPECIAL PROBLEMS

Educational Disaffection

The matter of education merits special mention, since the numbers, types, and relative competence of graduates in scientific and technical fields hold the key to future defense capabilities. The United States is passing through an unfavorable period in that regard. Politico-military developments, especially the Vietnam war, have estranged important academic institutions, with insidious long-range effects. Towers of strength in the realm of defense technology, among them MIT, whose top-notch Draper Laboratory developed the guidance system for Poseidon, Stanford, Wisconsin, and Cornell, have cut back defense research projects drastically in response to antimilitary pressure groups. Should that tendency continue unchecked, our country could lose vital contributions from a whole generation of aspiring young scientists now being indoctrinated in an "anti-defense" environment. In such event, this nation would forfeit its claim to technical supremacy in national security fields within the next one or two decades.

Industrial Disaffection

Similar trends are evident in industry. Bell Telephone Company, to cite a single example, has decided to reject any further contracts in the ABM field, after being a key cog in missile defense works for twenty-five years. The potential consequences with regard to future U.S. strategic capabilities are considerable, as Defense Secretary Laird implied in 1971:

> We can mobilize the manpower and production potential of this country in a relatively short period of time. Everyone must understand that we cannot similarly improve overnight our technological base. This . . . capability will only be available when needed if it is maintained, encouraged, and appreciated now as an essential national asset. Recent reductions in technological areas already have seriously affected our ability to sustain essential technological leadership.[3]

206

Official Apathy

However, even if this country continued to maintain scientific superiority, its advantage would not necessarily be decisive. Capabilities are useless without the will to use them. Once again, the United States exhibits disquieting tendencies, typified by reluctance to compete in potentially critical areas. The congressional decision to suspend further funds for developing a supersonic transport is a case in point. Lost in the debates was the ultimate issue: not whether the SST *could* or *should* be built, but rather *who* will build it and thus accrue technical expertise? Other, less well publicized, instances are fairly commonplace.

The Problem of Priorities

Future needs and capabilities must match attainable ends with available means in order of priority if unacceptable dissipation of energies and resources is to be avoided. This facet was addressed in a special study published by the Center for Strategic Studies at Georgetown University:

> To pursue the potential military application of each and every promising scientific and technological theory or development within the adversary's capability would be impossible, but to limit oneself only to those that one believes the potential enemy might find attractive would be too risky. To escape from the dilemma the policy maker must put priority on long lead time items in the most important fields, carefully considering the risks of delay and faulty decision making. At the same time he must continue to build an expanding base of technology that can both advance [his] own capabilities for new systems and reduce reaction time when a new weapon actually appears in the arsenal of the enemy. He must constantly look for military applications the potential enemy may not have recognized or may have failed to pursue. All of these investments must be compared against the expected value of other investments in new intelligence systems that might increase [his] warning time concerning progress on the other side.[4]

CONSERVATISM VERSUS SCIENCE

Klaus Knorr and Oskar Morgenstern have identified and discussed four kinds of constraint that tend to perpetuate quite conservative selections "from the menu of radically new ideas proffered by the scientists and engineers": economic, institutional, bureaucratic, and doctrinal.

Economic Constraints

Economic inhibitions were discussed in the preceding chapter, but one or two points bear elaboration here. Innovation is expensive, as everyone knows. Chancellors of the exchequer understandably are reluctant to shift funds from existing, known-quantity programs to promising but unproven replacements. As a result, weeding out obsolete and redundant items can be a painfully slow process. Further, in the United States at least, the application of cost-effectiveness studies may have acted as "too sharp a brake" on inventive genius, since the criteria against which revolutionary ideas must be measured are so imprecise that judgments often are grossly misleading.

Institutional Constraints

Institutional constraints to creativity are linked hand-in-glove with economic limitations. Existing weapons systems and associated supporting establishments have behind them strong vested interests in the Congress and in industry who opt for the status quo. The resultant inertia is anathema to freewheeling enterprise.

Bureaucratic Constraints

Bureaucratic roadblocks are characterized by a preference for doing accustomed things in accustomed ways, "and hence — without deliberation — for putting up undue resistance to innovation. . . . There is safety in sticking to the familiar, and risk of making mistakes in backing the radically new." Within bureaucracies, change can only occur with concurrent assent from multiple layers. Such collective endorsement is habitually slow in coming, even when the project under consideration is urgent. When proposals are unorthodox or daring, necessary support may prove impossible to muster.

Doctrinal Constraints

Doctrinal difficulties are related to strategy, as Knorr and Morgenstern indicate:

> Prevalent military strategy favors inventions that fit, and tends to resist ideas that clash with it and require its revision. The temptation is to evaluate new ideas in terms of old practices. The ideas that get the green light are not usually the ones threatening to unbalance strong doctrinal attachments.

Small wonder that national leaders continually are accused of preparing to refight the last war — science and technology to a very real degree are deliberately bridled, and strategic thought lags substantially behind decisions to act.[5]

MANAGING TECHNOLOGY

Even the most magnificent inventions and innovations need champions with vision, energy, organizational ability, and politico-military connections.

The Wright brothers demonstrated the feasibility of powered flight by heavier-than-air craft at Kitty Hawk in December 1903, but the United States was compelled to rely on war planes of foreign manufacture throughout the First Great War because no one in this country exploited the possibilities. Dr. Goddard pioneered in the field of rocketry during the 1920s and 1930s, but German, not U.S., ingenuity put his and parallel theories to practical test during World War II. The brightest scientific brains in the business collaborated to produce the first atomic bomb, but without a Leslie Groves as prime mover, Project Manhattan never would have reached fruition expeditiously.

The managerial experts who link research on one hand with development on the other need not be inventive geniuses — they rarely are. Men like Werner von Braun are prominent exceptions. The prime prerequisites are a knack for understanding the "big picture," the determination to meet time and cost objectives, and a flair for attracting, motivating, and coordinating top talent so that all efforts are channeled into productive enterprise.

TECHNOLOGICAL COMPETITION RELATED TO THE THREAT

What are the strategic implications of science and technology to the United States in its present-day competition with other great powers?

The great danger in falling behind is the possibility of technological surprise, especially in the upper echelons of the conflict spectrum, where breakthroughs in space operations, nuclear weapons, exotic forms of power and propulsion, biological or bacteriological warfare, computer development, climate control, laser applications, and the like could create instantaneous and spectacular shifts in the world balance of power. Less flamboyant, but unexpected, enemy innovations could condition our capacity to function effectively. The chances of anticipating such eventualities are enhanced by being "ahead," since it is easier for U.S. experts to predict enemy R & D activities accurately if they know what is possible. If our opponents could see technological horizons totally beyond our reach, then reliable predictions might become impossible.

Hence, many responsible U.S. officials express concern that we no longer seem to be winning the technological battle. "Surprising as it may seem to Americans who are used to our technological superiority in defense, the U.S. will lose [out] to the Soviets in the next several years if present trends continue," says Dr. John S. Foster, Jr., the Pentagon's Director of Defense Research and Engineering. ". . . If this loss of leadership occurs in 3 or 4 years [a prospect which Defense Secretary Laird admitted exists],[6] we will face certainly an extremely expensive, perhaps an impossible, task if we choose to attempt to [recoup] even by 1985."[7] The strategic studies group at Georgetown University concurs:

> Achieving U.S. recognition of Soviet superiority would permit the U.S.S.R. to pursue a more aggressive foreign policy, to demand concessions from the United States on many issues long in contention, to inhibit U.S. resistance to communist inspired or exploited wars of liberation, to fracture Western alliances . . . and to attain greater support from the unaligned Third World. . . .

> If the Soviet Union does gain the edge in strategic systems, then the credibility of U.S. deterrent will be diminished or lost — politically, militarily, and psychologically. This kind of result of the technical conflict indicates that, given current and projected trends, there is every prospect that the Soviet technological challenge has developed into one of the most pressing long-term national security concerns.[8]

Not everyone agrees. Those convictions are opposed by apathy at one end of the scale and disbelief at the other. A strong body of opinion in the United States sees U.S. scientific and technological superiority as a destabilizing influence that contributes directly to an ever-increasing arms race. Its members contend that continued U.S.

209

supremacy would encourage Soviet suspicion and distrust, would block the building of political bridges, and thus would increase the likelihood of war. Some spokesmen advocate unilateral U.S. constraints on technological progress related to military power, in an effort to encourage a greater degree of U.S.-Soviet empathy.

Whatever views finally prevail, their validity is crucial. It is not too dramatic to suggest that our country's survival may be at stake.

25 National Character and Attitudes

> A prudent ruler ought not to keep faith wnen by
> so doing it would be against his interest, and
> when the reasons which made him bind himself
> no longer exist. If all men were good, this
> precept would not be a good one; but as they
> are bad, and would not observe their faith with
> you, so you are not bound to keep faith with
> them.
>
> NICCOLO MACHIAVELLI
> *The Prince*

Machiavelli's antithesis was Sir Galahad, who boasted, "My strength is as the strength of ten, because my heart is pure." That gallant knight may have overstated the case, but for good or evil, behavioral and emotional characteristics *do* have a direct bearing on the capabilities of nations as well as of individuals. Just how much influence such attributes exert, and in what ways, are considerations for strategists, who must figure effective methods to exploit those ethereal elements of national power.

This chapter dwells briefly on just three interrelated aspects: national character, will, and ethics, which separately and in concert condition every people's aptitudes and stomach for war.

THE INFLUENCE OF NATIONAL CHARACTER ON STRATEGY

Hans Morgenthau, a noted scholar, expresses the opinion that national character, which sets one people apart from another, exerts a "permanent and often decisive influence upon the weight a nation is able to put into the scales of international politics":

> National character cannot fail to influence national power; for those who act for the
> nation in peace and war, formulate, execute, and support its policies, elect and are
> elected, mold public opinion, produce and consume — all bear to a greater or lesser

degree the imprint of those intellectual and moral qualities which make up the national character. The "elementary force and persistence" of the Russians, the individual initiative and inventiveness of the Americans, the undogmatic common sense of the British, the discipline and thoroughness of the Germans are some of the qualities which will manifest themselves, for better or for worse, in all the individual and collective activities in which the members of a nation may engage. In consequence of the differences in national character, the German and Russian governments, for instance, have been able to embark upon foreign policies that the American and British governments would have been incapable of pursuing, and vice versa. Antimilitarism, aversion to standing armies and to compulsory military service are permanent traits of the American and British national character. Yet the same institutions and activities have for centuries stood high in the hierarchy of values of Prussia, from where their prestige spread over all of Germany. In Russia the tradition of obedience to the authority of the government and the traditional fear of the foreigner have made large permanent military establishments acceptable to the population.

Thus the national character has given Germany and Russia an initial advantage in the struggle for power, since they could transform in peacetime a greater portion of their national resources into instruments of war. On the other hand, the reluctance of the American and British peoples to consider such a transformation, especially on a large scale and with respect to manpower, except in an obvious national emergency, has imposed a severe handicap upon American and British foreign policy. Governments of militaristic nations are able to plan, prepare, and wage war at the moment of their choosing. They can, more particularly, start a preventive war whenever it seems to be most propitious for their cause. Governments of pacifist nations, of which the United States was the outstanding example until the end of the Second World War, are in this respect in a much more difficult situation and have much less freedom of action.[1]

At the opposite pole, A. F. K. Organski, a prominent interpreter in his own right, exhibits strong doubts, shared by many sociologists, regarding the deterministic properties of national character. He submits that three shaky assumptions underlie any such theory:

(1) That the individual citizens of a nation share a common psychological make-up or personality or value system that distinguishes them from the citizens of other nations, (2) that this national character persists without major changes over a relatively long period of time, and (3) that there is a traceable relationship between individual character and national goals. . . . If any of [these presumptions] turns out to be false, the whole theory is disproved.[2]

As for point one, he scoffs at popular analyses based on what he believes is dubious evidence unsubstantiated by scientific proof. Whether any given country's idiosyncrasies are good, bad, or indifferent, he suggests, is largely in the mind of the beholder. "Every nation has a relatively favorable stereotype of its own national character, a faintly hostile stereotype of the character of its allies, and a distinctly unflattering stereotype . . . of its enemies." He challenges the permanence of national personality quirks if, in fact, such exist, citing several examples, including the transformation of yesteryear's restless Vikings into self-satisfied Scandinavians and — more recently —

the stark contrast between Napoleon's dynamic followers and their defeatist descendents who folded before the Nazis five generations later.

Further, he questions whether there is any direct correlation between so-called national character and national goals. It could be argued, he contends, that an overwhelming desire to be recognized and accepted by the world community drove the Japanese to unbridled aggression in the 1930s and 1940s. When that failed, the *same* desire led to peaceful policies which featured a reluctance to arm at all. In short, Organski warns that strategists who plan to use national character as a practical index do so at their own risk.[3]

Regardless of which school one subscribes to, prudence must be applied in sorting out ambiguous virtues and vices. Special attention needs to be given subcultures, which sometimes reflect the main stream, but more often do not, with an eye to ascertaining their true import in any given society.

THE ROLE OF TRANSIENT ATTITUDES

Transient attitudes, as opposed to long-term character traits, represent the moods of the masses. These tend to vacillate from liberal to conservative, hawkish to dovish, emotional to logical, idealistic to realistic, rational to irrational, and back again. A pendulum effect frequently is evident, as the median majority is influenced periodically by extremists on either flank — witness the dispassion with which most Americans viewed the war in Vietnam during the early 1960s; their avid involvement in the mid-1960s; their disillusioned indignation in the late 1960s; and their drift back toward indifference in the early 1970s, after U.S. ground combat troops were withdrawn.

The Importance of National Will

Perhaps the most important moods translate into national will or morale, which most authorities agree is a vital element in the strategic equation.

The doughtiest contestants risk ruin if the spirit is willing but the flesh is weak, yet second-rate countries sometimes unseat colossi who lack national fortitude. In fact, Marshal de Saxe, exploring the mysterious sources of victory and defeat in his *Reveries on the Art of War,* concluded that "the solution lies in human hearts and one should search for it there." Clausewitz, writing 100 years later, found that most of the subjects discussed in his opus *On War* "are composed half of physical, half of moral, causes and effects, and we might say the physical are almost no more than the wooden handle, whilst the moral are the noble metal, the real, brightly polished weapon."[4]

If, indeed, every war, whether hot or cold, is nothing more nor less than a contest between opposing wills, the ultimate objective of every participant must be to break the foe's will, or bend it to suit his own purpose, so that armed clashes never erupt at all or, if they do, the opposition will soon capitulate. Lenin counseled that "the soundest strategy in war is to postpone [military] operations until the moral disintegration of the enemy renders a mortal blow both possible and easy." Communist strategies generally follow that advice. Those of the Western World in general, and of the United States in particular, generally do not.

213

The Manipulation of National Will

Destroying the enemy's resolution to resist is far more important than crippling his material capabilities. Brute force serves a useful purpose in certain circumstances, but the correlation between coercion and the collapse of national will is tenuous at best. On the contrary, studies of cause and effect tend to confirm that violence short of total devastation may *amplify* rather than erode a people's determination. The Battle of Britain buttressed British will in 1940. German atrocities helped crystalize Soviet resistance the following year, most notably in the Ukraine. French force failed to prevail against a materially inferior foe in Algeria. American bombing during the 1960s reinforced resolve in North Vietnam. Similar cases, from every period in history, could be cited.

In consequence, successful strategists consider alternatives which amalgamate political, economic, social, and psychological pressures in ways that supplement or supplant the application of military power. Where force and threats of force seek to degrade or demolish the enemy's will through fear, indirect approaches capitalize on enticement. Bargaining is especially effective. Rewards, perhaps in conjunction with punishment, can "bribe" recipients into altering their interests, objectives, and courses of action — greed is a powerful stimulus. Psychological warfare, properly applied, can sow seeds of serious doubt or convince dedicated belligerents that they are wrong. Even more exotic measures may be in the offing:

> If the ultimate purpose of total strategy is to destroy the will to resist, hallucinogenic drugs (LSD, marijuana, peyote, etc.) may provide the primary weapon. Military power, economic power, and persuasive power, after all, attack the will only obliquely; "pot" assaults it directly. What is more lethargic than a satisfied drug addict? . . . In addition to the strategic use of drugs, developments in genetics and biology suggest that real breakthroughs in the art of controlling men may lie in these areas. . . . The strategic use of hallucinogens, truth serum, and induced genetic mutations could make a tyrant the master of the world. The world of 1984 may be closer than we think.[5]

Far out? Not really. Communists did not create the drug crises that beset U.S. armed forces in Southeast Asia and, to a lesser extent, elsewhere beginning in the late 1960s, but if they failed to exploit that weakness, they missed a fine chance.

Of all the methods that can be used to reach a settlement by undermining enemy morale, coercion is the least likely to produce lasting results. Oppression may subjugate opposing wills temporarily, but it leaves a smouldering residue of resentment. Instances are legion in which one war almost inevitably led to the next because of such conditions. This shortcoming can be circumvented by obliterating the opposition, as was done at Ninevah and Carthage, but it is doubtful that such practices were profitable even then — Polybius noted 2,000 years ago that "to destroy that for which a war is undertaken seems an act of madness." Strategy should always strive to create conditions wherein the enemy's will conforms willingly to one's own. As a bonus effect, former foes sometimes turn into friends. Germany and Japan, our bitter enemies during World War II, now are important allies.

LEGAL AND ETHICAL RESTRAINTS

The commands and sanctions exerted by morals, mores, and law strongly constrain strategists in their attempts to formulate *desirable* courses of actions that also are *acceptable* to the people. Such restraints are most evident in free societies, where national leaders rarely can pursue their policies effectively without the approval, or at least passive acquiescence, of the public.

The fundamental question is: which means whereby one nation or coalition may impose its will on another are permissible and which are proscribed?

The Evolving Ethical Environment

In olden times, restrictions were exiguous or nonexistent. The "enemy" comprised every individual, male or female, old or young, combatant or noncombatant, who owed allegiance to or lived in the territory of antagonistic leaders. That concept began to change after the Thirty Years' War ravaged Europe. Thereafter, international conflict was conceived as a contest between opposing armed forces, rather than between populations. Avoiding "unnecessary" casualties among innocent bystanders or prisoners of war eventually became a bonded legal and ethical duty, spelled out by the Hague Conventions with respect to the Laws and Customs of War on Land (1899 and 1907) and by the Geneva Conventions of 1864, 1906, 1929, and 1949. Nearly every civilized nation adheres to those agreements in principle, if not in practice. Beliefs that war should be controlled and, if possible, outlawed as an instrument of foreign policy have led to the League of Nations, the Kellogg-Briand Pact, and the United Nations.

The Concept of Just War

Bellum justum, or Just War, concepts of the Middle Ages have undergone radical surgery. Just War originally was a justifiable vindictive act. "Blameless self-defense" was only one of the many allowable actions. Aggression was authorized if duly constituted authorities with the "right intention" deemed it the sole satisfactory way to maintain or restore order. Preventive or preemptive operations aimed at redressing wrongs, enforcing rights, and forestalling potential enemy initiatives were permissible. Thus, Just War was regarded as defensive, since it defended "justice," but justice was never defined. There was no more assurance in the fifteenth century than there is in the twentieth that humanity and virtue would coincide. Consequently, criticisms currently used so effectively against wars for "reasons of state" applied equally to many features of the classic Just War.[6]

Just War presently takes on different connotations than it did in medieval days. Contemporary international law does not tolerate offensive warfare in any guise as a means of righting wrongs, and aggression is no longer considered a legitimate method of altering the status quo.[7] Force is approved only as a last resort in the defense of one's territorial integrity or political independence; or in support of allies whose national sovereignty is jeopardized.

215

Modern War and Ethics

Changes in the nature of modern war, particularly the emergence of general nuclear war and mass military insurrections, place unusual strains on the established ethical structure.

General War

Means of mass-destruction, notably nuclear, chemical, and biological weapons, combined with concepts of total war, have created new and complicated ethical uncertainties. To abstain or not to abstain from using those tools simply on moral grounds is a fearful question. Michael Howard, in his *Studies in War and Peace,* advises that:

> The dilemma does not lie in a simple choice between, on the one hand, using nuclear weapons, and on the other risking the extinction of one's cultural pattern by political subjugation or nuclear destruction; though that choice in itself would not necessarily be an easy one to make. It lies rather in the choice — one open to a very few states — between possessing a nuclear armoury and the evident determination to use it, if only to deter such attacks against oneself; and deliberately depriving oneself of such a possibility, irrespective of what the effect of such self-denial might be on the plans and attitudes of other, potentially hostile states which might not be interested in following one's example. The first course will probably lead to a heightening of international tension and possibly one day to nuclear holocaust. The second is very likely to place one's state in an inferior position *vis-à-vis* those which make no such self-denying ordinance, in exercising influence on the international environment even in normal times, and may put it in a position of fatal inferiority in a situation of extreme conflict.[8]

Limited War

Whereas the risks of mass-destruction warfare have heightened moral concerns in some regards, compunctions against mass murder have been dulled at lower levels on the conflict scale. Limitations on killing, so marked earlier in this century, have slackened. Hans Morgenthau, for one, observes that the "very existence [of restrictions] in the consciences of political and military leaders as well as of the common people becomes ever more precarious and is threatened with extinction." He goes on to say:

> The Second World War has made . . . . methods of direct intervention [such as aerial bombardment] the most effective instrument for the destruction of a nation's productive capacity. The interest in the mass destruction of civilian life and property coincided with the ability to carry such mass destruction through, and this combination has been too strong for the moral convictions of the modern world to resist. . . .

> Warsaw and Rotterdam, London and Coventry, Cologne and Nuremburg, Hiroshima and Nagasaki are steppingstones, not only in the development of the modern technology of war, but in the development of the modern morality of warfare.[9]

Revolutionary War

Revolutionary war is intrinsically amoral. Ends are construed to justify any means. Ideological forces spark the same sort of fervor demonstrated during religious wars

216

in the sixteenth and seventeenth centuries. Morgenthau, speaking in a different context, articulated thoughts that apply perfectly to so-called "people's wars" and "wars of national liberation," in which the citizen no longer fights for

> the glory of his prince or the unity and greatness of his nation, but he "crusades" for an "ideal," a set of "principles," a "way of life," for which he claims a monopoly of truth and virtue. In consequence, he fights to the death or to "unconditional surrender" all those who adhere to another, a false and evil, "ideal" and "way of life." Since it is this "ideal" and "way of life" that he fights in whatever persons they manifest themselves, the distinctions between fighting and disabled soldiers, combatants and civilians — if they are not eliminated altogether — are subordinated to the one distinction that really matters: the distinction between the representatives of the right and the wrong philosophy and way of life. The moral duty to spare the wounded, the sick, the surrendering and unarmed enemy, and to respect him as a human being who was an enemy only by virtue of being found on the other side of the fence, is superseded by the moral duty to punish and to wipe off the face of the earth the professors and practitioners of evil.[10]

Conflicting Schools of Ethical Thought

Within the contemporary moral environment, conditioned by the nature of modern war, wide variations in approach to strategic problem-solving are evident.

Machiavelli's fine Italian hand, consciously or not, has guided the unconscionable for more than 400 years. He differentiated between personal and official codes of conduct and, in the name of the state, encouraged acts that would be contemptible if committed by private citizens. Parties in positions of power were given license to lie, cheat, or steal if necessary to accomplish their missions. According to his creed, might is right. Vice and virtue are on the same plane, gauged only by their ability to get the job done. Let "the masses judge the end [success] when it is reached, and not the means used." After all, he declared, "it is easy for strength to acquire a reputation, but not for a reputation to acquire strength."

> How praiseworthy it is that a prince keeps his word and governs by candor instead of craft, everyone knows. Yet the experience of our time shows that those princes who had little regard for their word and had the craftiness to turn men's minds have accomplished great things and, in the end, have overcome those who governed their actions by their pledges.[11]

At the other extreme, pacifists operate within the framework of a morality which believes that *no* ends justify the infliction of suffering and death, by whatever instrumentality. The Marquis of Queensberry Rules, they feel, should always be applied, regardless of the consequences.

The United States, dedicated to the Judeo-Christian ethic, seeks a middle ground that matches credible ends with civilized means in ways that place a premium on human dignity and life. Michael Howard outlines the options as follows:

> Where the decisions have moral implications they are likely to be complex and obscure. Seldom is a [strategist] fortunate enough to have a clearcut choice between an obviously

"good" or innocuous course of action and one equally obviously bad. His choice is likely always to be one between two evils. And for those with whom ultimate powers of direction and decision rest in great modern states, the implications of their decisions may well be vast; not only for their own peoples and their descendants, but for the whole of the world.[12]

SUMMATION

All told, national character and attitudes exert a demanding influence on the conduct of security affairs. The presence or absence of desirable qualities should be taken into consideration by strategists at every turn, with full appreciation for ambiguities and possibilities of change. Intangible though it may be, the temper of the people constitutes a crucial element of national power that often is decisive.

PART V

THE ROAD TO STRATEGIC SUPERIORITY

26 Characteristics of Successful Strategists

For many are called, but few are chosen.

MATTHEW 22:14

Creative thinkers are a "special breed of cat," no matter what their occupation—agriculture, astronomy, or the performing arts. Innovative strategists are no exception. If any one common thread runs through their diverse social backgrounds, temperaments, educations, and professional experience, it is individuality. Dissimilarity is their most common characteristic.

INNOVATIVE STRATEGISTS COMPARED

Thumbnail sketches of five strategic theorists who flourished during different periods in different environments and developed different strategic styles serve to drive home this point.

Clausewitz

Clausewitz epitomized the self-made man. Of formal education he had almost none. He joined the Prussian Army at age twelve, was commissioned within a few months, and thereafter devoted his entire life to the military service. By burning midnight oil, he eventually gained admission to the *Kriegsschule* (War Academy) in Berlin, where he became a protégé of Scharnhorst, who gained fame reforming the Prussian Army. Seventeen years later, after a distinguished career as a staff officer, Major General Clausewitz returned to the *Kriegsschule* as its director, and immersed himself in thoughts and writing. His efforts culminated in the magnum opus *On War*.

Kahn

Extroverted Herman Kahn, a civilian, differs extraordinarily in personality and professional background from the shy, sensitive soldier, Clausewitz. Kahn's three-year army

221

service terminated at the grade of sergeant. His education, extended in time, stressed mathematics and physics, odd starting points for a politico-military theorist. He built his reputation while working for the Rand Corporation, where he purveyed provocative scriptures, particularly those related to general nuclear war.

Lenin

Lenin also was the antithesis of career soldier Clausewitz. He never served a day in uniform, nor did he hold a steady job. Whereas Kahn was a steadfast scholar, Lenin was expelled from college in Kazan. Nevertheless, that brilliant Bolshevik eventually garnered a law degree from St. Petersburg University as a nonresident, after four years of solitary study. He mastered the works of Marx, Machiavelli, and Clausewitz, amalgamated their ideas and his own with Russian revolutionary tradition to form a new philosophy, and used the resultant tool to put a worldwide movement in motion.

Mao Tse-Tung

Mao Tse-tung, unlike any of the three above, was a hard-bitten field commander. As a boy, he rebelled against conventional Chinese educational institutions, which delayed his graduation from normal school until he was twenty-five. Instead of concentrating on customary canons, he stressed the romances and military history of China's classical kingdoms, social studies, and political thought. He was an assistant librarian at Peking University and taught briefly in Hunan, before dedicating himself to "the struggle." From the beginning, Mao pitted his brand of strategy against orthodox Marxists, supremely confident that his precepts would become dogma.

Douhet

Guilio Douhet, the soothsayer from Caserta, began prophesying on the future of air power five scant years after the Wright brothers first took flight. When his heretical views came in conflict with conservatives on the Italian General Staff, he was ignominiously grounded, court-martialed, imprisoned, and sacked for his continued criticism. Fortunately for the advocates of air power, Douhet was recalled to active duty after the Italian catastrophe at Caporetto vindicated many of his views. Neither education nor experience prepared that man for his remarkable role. He was simply an imaginative thinker.

COMMON CHARACTERISTICS IDENTIFIED

Despite the diversity in origins, upbringing, aptitudes, interests, character, races, creeds, and colors, there is considerable homogeneity among those five men. Like other sensational strategists throughout history, they generally were:

Brainy	Rational	Skeptical	Patient
Scholarly	Analytical	Open-minded	Self-confident
Inquisitive	Imaginative	Objective	Articulate

222

Persons engaged in the precarious process of selecting competent candidates for strategic "think tanks" should be well advised of the fact that not every acceptable applicant need exhibit *all* of those attributes, but he cannot lack many of them.

How to identify such intangible virtues is the sticky problem — they rarely are reflected in academic transcripts, personal histories, resumés, military "fitness" reports, or other personnel files. Most traces are buried between the lines. The best way to ferret them out is by personal interview, but even that is not foolproof. Cut-and-try methods must follow.

A brief review of requisite traits is in order.

Intelligence

Great native intelligence tops the list of desirable characteristics. No reliable statistics are available, but compelling arguments could be advanced to prove that nearly every strategic wizard is a genius, in the broadest sense of that word. Each is just as inventive in his own way as Thomas A. Edison or Alexander Graham Bell, even though the fruits of his mental labors are less material.

There is little evidence that brain power and formal education correlate closely, as our five biographies indicate. Graduate degrees and senior service college diplomas are merely useful indicators that the owner has a fairly high IQ, is literate, and has been exposed to research procedures.

Intellectual Activism

How well a person puts inherited intellect to work depends largely on his attitudes and habits. Much of the world's wit lies permanently fallow or is wasted on underachievers. Nearly every innovative strategist combines curiosity with receptivity.

Liddell Hart once wryly observed that "the only thing harder than getting a new idea into the military mind is to get an old one out." That indictment fits civilian strategists equally well. Freethinkers stand out. Their quest for fundamental truths invariably features enlightened skepticism, which leads them to challenge all premises, attack all shibboleths, search for variables, and explore alternatives. Uncle Remus was right when he warned, "It ain't the things you don't know what gets you in deep trouble. It's the things you knows for sure what ain't so!"

Objective strategists substitute reason for emotion as they systematically pick other men's brains, including those at polarized extremes. They recognize that the most outlandish points of view usually have *something* worthwhile to offer. The mission is to sift through the evidence, retain what seems useful, and discard the nonsense.

Analytical Acumen

Ungarnished facts are not enough. Interpretation provides strategic meaning, as Edward M. Collins pointed out in the introduction to his book *War, Politics, and Power:*

> [Clausewitz had] an inquiring and critical mind, rather than a creative one: he analyzed, understood and codified the methods of warfare which others had created. In so doing, he performed an enormously creative act, for he changed the future by seeing and

223

revealing to others the larger significance which lay below the surface of contemporary events.[1]

Nearly every successful strategist has the chess player's proclivity for thinking things through. He anticipates opponents' moves and his own responses. Judgment always is important, but it becomes critical when applied to questions that have no quantifiable answers, such as "how much is enough?" and "how great is the risk?" The gift of discernment in such instances often makes a critical difference.

Imagination, of course, is the soul of creative thinking. Unconventional individuals have been solving seemingly insoluble problems since Alexander sliced the Gordian knot. Douhet, for example, had no precedent to draw on, yet he divined ways to dodge the feckless strategies enshrined by Joffre and Haig. No one else invaded the third dimension in quite the same way as Douhet did, preaching how to project military power through the troposphere into the enemy heartland. His professional descendents will yet devise comparable concepts to take advantage of outer space, and perhaps will work in *other* dimensions as well.

Persistence

Inspiration is an independent, transient thing that answers neither beck nor call. Transcendental ideas may appear soon, they may appear late, or maybe not at all. Because the desired results frequently reflect products of accretion over a period of time, rather than spontaneous imagery, three other traits are beneficial: patience, confidence, and a thick skin. Most brainstormers suffer multiple failures for every success, in search of one or two ideas that count. Those who fear sarcasm or scorn are not likely to survive.

Eloquence

Finally, strategic thinkers who concoct new concepts must be supersalesmen if they expect to change the perceptions of those in power. The ability to communicate is crucial. The five figures described at the beginning of this chapter were not all top-notch toastmasters but, without exception, they were skillful writers, as were most of their famous strategic forebears. There may have been inarticulate prodigies who could have changed the face of the world but, if so, their schemes died unknown and unsung.

Perspective

If ever there was a field in which generalists are preferable to specialists, that field is strategy. Unlike scientific scouts who probe the frontiers of knowledge along fairly narrow fronts, strategic theorists need the broadest possible professional base. Depth in particular areas can be drawn from the detailed wisdom of experts in distinctive disciplines. If Herman Kahn had continued to specialize in mathematics and physics, he might have made his strategic mark, if he made it at all, writing about circumscribed subjects, like the theory of gaming. As it turned out, he ranged far and wide in the social sciences for more than twenty-five years, and significantly influenced strategic thinking on a number of levels.

Prescience

Last, but not least, no catalog of characteristics could ever be complete without reminding readers that fashioning progressive strategies, by definition, is a creative act. Master craftsmen appreciate right from the start that innate and induced qualities, like those described in this chapter, are imperative points of departure, but more than passing success demands that they be buttressed by the generous interspersion of *a priori* apperception, divine revelation, intuition, initiative, and good old-fashioned common sense.

27 Cultivating Creative Thought

Senior officials are chronically overburdened by
the urgent, very often at the expense of the
important.

HENRY A. KISSINGER

*Special Assistant to the President for National
Security Affairs*

Stellar strategic theorists throughout history almost invariably have enjoyed
two decisive assets not discussed in the preceding chapter: time to think and environments conducive to creativity.

HISTORICAL PRECEDENTS

Machiavelli had been dismissed from office by the Medici and banished to
the family farm near San Casciano when he wrote *The Prince* and *Discourses* during
the ensuing period of idleness.

Mahan produced many of his greatest works while cloistered at the Naval War
College for six years, undisturbed by the press of peacetime naval operations.

Mao's strategic concepts took shape in a Shensi cave at the end of the Long March,
while his Red Army regrouped, reinforced, resupplied, and retrained, far from the
worries of war.

CIVILIAN AND OFFICIAL COMMUNITIES COMPARED

The Civilian Community

The contemporary U.S. civilian community provides interested intellectuals
with a climate far more stimulating than those available to the trio above. The academic
world, governmental contract agencies, private research institutes, and industry offer
funds, facilities, and provocative forums for strategic research that open up horizons

226

totally beyond the reach of old-time theoreticians. The brief survey following merely highlights pertinent aspects.

Funds

Money may be the root of all evil, but it also is a blessing. Most major civilian endeavors dealing with strategic thought have been or are subsidized, in whole or in part, by federal financing or private philanthropy. Gene M. Lyons and Louis Morton summarize this nicely in their book *Schools for Strategy:*

> For the university centers and institutes, foundation support has been vital to giving them their place within the academic community. Without it, few of the programs would have come into existence or survived, for, with only one major exception, all were and still are largely dependent on funds from one or more foundations . . . [primarily] Carnegie, Ford and Rockefeller. . . .
>
> Government support for national security studies has been largely concentrated in specialized institutes set up by the military services — the RAND Corporation, by the Air Force; the Research Analysis Corporation, working almost exclusively for the Army; the Navy's Operations Evaluation Group; and the Institute for Defense Analyses, set up by the Department of Defense. But the government has also contracted with outside institutions for special military studies . . . [For example, contracts have been let and grants awarded] to scholars at Princeton, Harvard and Yale, to groups organized by the Washington Center of Foreign Policy Research, M.I.T., and Rutgers, to private research agencies like the Hudson Institute and the Stanford Research Institute, and to industrial firms like the Bendix Corporation and Arthur D. Little, Inc.[1]

Funds furnish basic research facilities where none exist and embellish those in existence. Dollars also provide much more, in the form of pay and emoluments, scholarships, fellowships, and the like. They underwrite special projects, contribute to constructive conferences, and finance related travel. Such benefits attract talent from all fifty states, plus great minds from abroad, representing diversified disciplines.

Intellectual Freedom

Abstract advantages help hold the quality allured by cash. Foremost among these is a wonderfully detached viewpoint, particularly in academia, which is divorced from operational life and unfettered by official responsibility. There is a built-in tolerance for failure. If concepts prove impractical today, something else is tried tomorrow.

Private citizens can publicly say or write what they think. The Constitution guarantees that right. Collaterally, they enjoy the equivalent of a direct channel to the President of the United States and his most trusted advisors through the publishing media. Nearly every authoritative strategic theorist in the academic world built his reputation on unclassified studies. Occupants of free-lance civilian "think tanks" have done likewise.

Freedom of action, combined with freedom of expression and the absence of any need to justify, defend, support, or conform to official policy, encourages flights of fancy and leads to creativity.

227

Continuity

Numerous influential intellectuals, who gravitated to the field of national security affairs in the 1950s, have been engaged ever since in the full-time study of strategy. Some, like Bernard Brodie, have had international reputations in that realm for nearly thirty years.

The continuous exchange of opinions among such a coterie, at once exciting and controversial, marks an important milestone in the strategy business. Most of the old masters conceived ideas in isolation. Few distinguished theorists can afford that luxury today. The scopes are too comprehensive and the problems too complex. Nearly every big-name brain truster, including Kissinger, Kahn, and Schelling, had help on the way to fame, and still functions as part of a team.

A spate of U.S. civilian strategic theorists has grown up professionally in that environment. In many regards, but most notably in the field of nuclear warfare, those seers have injected a variety of provocative concepts that stimulate the imagination and *compel disbelievers to think through the reasons why they disagree.* That contribution alone is priceless.

The Official Establishment

By contrast, the official establishment, which excels at crisis management, has been badly outclassed in the field of grand strategy.

Why?

Because its environment is inimical to creative thinking.

Frenetic Activity

To begin with, strategic planners in the Pentagon and Foggy Bottom ordinarily have scant opportunity to think. They are inundated with pressing problems. The pressure of ongoing operations routinely prevents much abstract contemplation or theorizing.

The favored few who *do* have time generally abuse it, partly because they have distorted values. Senior career officers too often equate dedication and devotion to duty with hours on the job, regardless of the circumstances. Hard-chargers boast that they work round-the-clock, seven days a week, scorning Saturdays, Sundays, holidays, and leave. Those public servants are wracked by guilt if they are not engaged from dawn until long after dark. They expect the same fever pitch from subordinates. There is rarely an opportunity to stand back, take a breather, and see the forest instead of its trees. The constant grind leads to mental stagnation.

The temptation thus is irresistible to put all projects on a crash basis, a modus operandi that is death to creative thought. Beethoven himself could not have promised to compose a masterpiece by 1530 hours on any given afternoon, even for the House of Hapsburg. Neither can strategic theorists deliver on set schedules.

Turbulent Career Patterns

A lack of continuity further restricts chances of success. Few military men or diplomats in America are exposed to more than one or two tours of duty in high-level plans or operations, the closest they ever come to strategic thinking, and even those stints are rarely consecutive. Their total exposure is limited.

Any hope of reversing that trend must be preceded by shifts in personnel policy. As it stands, officers with fifteen to twenty years' service are engaged in "punching tickets." In the armed forces, for example, the tickets needed for promotion to general or flag rank are commands at successive stages, preferably in combat; high-level staff duty, particularly in the Pentagon, "where the action is"; and diplomas from senior service colleges. In the struggle for recognition, where men must be seen to survive, quiet periods in meditation outside the main stream are anathema.

That state of affairs was well demonstrated at the National War College in December 1970, when the Commandant sought selected military and civilian volunteers from the student body to staff the infant Strategic Research Group for its inaugural year. The common rejoinder was, "that's the most exciting proposal I've ever heard, but I wouldn't touch it with a ten-foot pole!" Their rationale was clear. A pilot project of that sort (or, indeed, one firmly established), championed by no service chief and with no recognized status, could scarcely be construed as a steppingstone to an ambassadorship or a star. Many of the project's most enthusiastic supporters regretfully refused to risk professional ruin by being diverted even for a twelve-month period.

Autocratic Restrictions
Autocratic restrictions further fetter originality in the official establishment.

Military men and governmental employees serve a bureaucracy which almost reflexively resists opinions that "rock the boat" or fail to parrot party lines. Since multiple organizational layers usually separate "action officers" (at whatever echelon) from approving authorities, only a few revolutionary proposals make their way through the maze. Those that do generally are rendered unrecognizable by arbitrary amendments and compromise, often by individuals who do not bother to consult the originators.

Provocative ideas that eventually win recognition within the establishment rarely receive much publicity. That is a serious shortcoming, since innovations should be added to the corporate body of strategic knowledge, where they can be reviewed by a wide range of authorities, adapted, and improved. Unfortunately, regulations prohibit unclassified public pronouncements without prior policy review. "Undesirable" conclusions commonly are suppressed or censored. As a result, few prophets of change reach print before they retire. Generals Gavin, LeMay, Shoup, Taylor, and Twining have no counterparts on active duty.

PREREQUISITES FOR CREATIVITY

From that simplified comparison of two conflicting strategic environments, one of which encourages originality, the other of which does not, it is possible to distill a few cardinal principles for use by those who strive to generate and sustain chain reactions of creativity.

An Unregimented Regime

Time to think, devoid of avoidable distractions, is imperative. That time should not be rigidly budgeted. The set publication schedules and regular hours characteristic of bureaucratic establishments inhibit innovative thought. Routines that are just right for one individual may very well be stultifying to another.

229

At one end of the scale are clock-punchers, who limit their productivity to the period from eight-to-five during conventional forty-hour weeks. Few great minds function effectively under such restrictive regimes, which signal adherents to be creative only at specific times and places. At the opposite end are drudges, nailed to their desks hour after endless hour, whose jaded intellects reflect the futility of consistent close confinement and overcommitment. The brainiest men strain in vain for inspiration in such circumstances.

A high degree of freewheeling informality, tailored to individual idiosyncrasies, is infinitely preferable to either extreme. Inventive geniuses generally are immersed in their projects more or less continuously. They make contact with progressive ideas at odd intervals in the bedroom or bath, at breakfast, on the bus, or in the local bar. Day in and day out, they rack up more productive hours than their regimented counterparts, but at an adjustable pace.

Nevertheless, unlimited permissiveness obviously is unacceptable. *Some* pressure is essential. Even perpetual-motion machines need an impulse to get them started. The most dedicated, disciplined humans may procrastinate or devote undue attention to pedantic details unless they are reactivated as required.

Unfettered Research

Strategic theorizing is to strategic planning as basic scientific research is to applied technology. Creative thinkers, whose mission is originality, not current problem-solving, need much greater intellectual latitude than crisis managers. Directed approaches that specify *what* will be done under *what* conditions are "the kiss of death." The world would still be waiting for Einstein's Special Theory of Relativity if that project had hinged on directives from the Joint Chiefs of Staff, who are preoccupied with "practical" matters.

Unconventional Approaches

Nonconformance is to be prized, not punished. Supervisors should control strategic thinkers with a loose rein, encourage unconventional experimentation, and allow ample room for error. Pioneers who fear the consequences of failure are apt to be extremely conservative.

There is no substitute for rigorous peer reviews during the incubation stage of any strategic concept, but enforced compromise and committee solutions can cancel creativity just as surely as can castigation. Critique sessions therefore serve best when used simply to air opinions, expose weaknesses in arguments, and sharpen thought, leaving participants free to adopt or disregard all criticism. End products should be accepted, rejected, or altered arbitrarily *only by authorities at the top.*

Prolific Contacts

Innovative strategists profit immensely from the uninhibited interchange of ideas. They flower most effectively in an atmosphere that provides for open publication; active participation in scholarly forums as panelists, seminarists, or presenters of strategic research papers; and membership in professional societies. Continuous liaison between and among governmental agencies, public and private institutions, and individual strategists would benefit this nation by improving performance all around.

Professional Career Patterns

Finally, continued, cumulative, and progressive experience is essential. Only careerists can excel at this complicated endeavor. Candidates for fame and fortune in the field of conceptual strategy should periodically renew acquaintanceships with "real life," to broaden their perceptions, identify problems, and extend their base of knowledge, but they should not stray too long.

SOME CAUTIONS

Funds and facilities obviously are important, but their role in shaping strategic theory should not be overrated. Computers and other complicated, expensive pieces of equipment have limited utility — war games and operational analyses are prominent exceptions. Classified information, the sine qua non for planners, can impede rather than promote creative thinking. Imaginative, motivated, untrammeled brain power is the precious commodity.

28 What Is To Be Done?

Al ain't sellin' excuses. . . .
Al's sellin' whiskey.

Attributed to Frank Nitti
Al Capone's "enforcer"

It should be amply evident by now that strategy is a fascinating, educational, intellectually exciting game that anyone can play, amateurs for fun, professionals for profit — including the nation's profit — if they are adroit. There is plenty of room for theoreticians and operators, specialists, and general practitioners.

THE STRATEGIC PROBLEM

What is to be done?

Step one is to identify potentially crucial problems so that great minds can think about them. Thereafter, the need is to assess the implications, select, analyze, and compare courses of action, and decide which alternative is "right" under given sets of circumstances. Those processes are subjective, as an anonymous luminary in the Nixon administration once allowed:

> Before I was in office, I found nothing more boring, and infuriating in fact, than a high official who met with outsiders and told them that all choices had been considered, that the best possible policy was being pursued, and that if outsiders only knew as much as he did, they would of course come to the same conclusion. I am here to tell you that all options have been considered, the best possible ones have been chosen, and if you only knew as much as I do, we could dispense with the question period!

He was being facetious, of course. President Nixon and his advisors have done a monumental job reviewing U.S. grand strategy, but estimators in the White House, the National Security Council, the Departments of State and Defense, and the Joint Chiefs of Staff are mere mortals who *may* have overlooked some options and *certainly* were compelled to compromise on most decisions. Consequently, nearly every chapter in this book catalogs controversial issues, which could be resolved in many cases by refining or replacing existing strategic concepts.

232

THE IMPACT OF TRENDS ON FUTURE STRATEGY

No strategist is likely to achieve any breakthroughs unless he perceives the probable impact of major trends, regional and worldwide, on the course of events, and exploits the possibilities. Readers could readily quintuple the following list of representative international trends, each of which has significant strategic implications:

POLITICAL
The Sino-Soviet split
The proliferation of nations
The increased interdependence of nations
Changing concepts of sovereignty
The changing role of international organizations

ECONOMIC
The agricultural revolution
The widening gap between "have" and "have not" nations
The decreased value of U.S. dollars on the world market
The emergence of Japan as an economic superpower
The depletion of critical natural resources

MILITARY
Increased emphasis on arms control
The prevalence of revolutionary wars
The emergence of Soviet sea power
Increasing costs of military hardware
Multiple limitations on the use of force

SOCIAL
The population explosion
Rising expectations
Increased concern for human rights
Increased concern for ecology
Urbanization

SCIENTIFIC/TECHNOLOGICAL
Instantaneous, worldwide communications
The expanding use of computers
The emergence of laser technology
The energy crisis
The development of space technology

Many trends that ostensibly have obscure connections with national security are being plumbed from fifty directions by all manner of experts, whose study plans rarely include a *strategic* bent. Strategists must apply a special slant.

Take the growth of urban sprawl, for example. Will it alter contemporary schools of strategic thought and, if so, how? What will happen when expanding cities in Europe leave little room for the employment of mobile ground forces — latter-day Schlieffen

Plans will be highly impractical. What will happen when 90 percent of our people live in cities? Will strategic centers of gravity be in the rural regions that provide food or in the megalopoli? What will happen to strategic bombing theories? What will happen if urbanization undermines agrarian Asia's revolutionary power base? What new vulnerabilities will be associated with synthetic environments? How can we capitalize on them? How can we counter them?

Colonel Robert Leider, U.S. Army, a senior fellow with the National War College Strategic Research Group, addressed such matters in a monograph entitled *War by Other Means: Extending the Concept of Force.*[1] In a different vein, he explored *The Environmental Issue in International Relations,* and arrived at some startling conclusions:

> "Now everything is changed," Einstein is reputed to have said after the first atomic blast, "except the picture in men's minds of what their world is like." This contrast, between what is and what man's institutions strive for, may well be the root cause of the great difficulties that lie ahead.

> There will be an increase in conflict opportunities because the actions that stem from environmental contacts and environmental fears lead so readily to the clash of national goals and objectives. It may be well-nigh impossible to avoid collisions: potential opponents are driven by matters which they deem essential to survival; the issues are easily understood by the citizenry; and they appear in stark colors. . . .

> [Already] in the confrontation between the Soviet Union and the United States, the unequal skill . . . . in exploiting the new issue is readily apparent. The American involvement with ecology, rooted in prosperity, emphasizes esthetics and cleanliness. . . . The socialists, in contrast, look beyond the littered landscape and see the aspirations, fears, inequalities, conflicts, and contradictions inherent in the environmental issue. With practice based on long experience, they have learned to string these emotional consequences together, like a pontoon bridge, to gain another route to long-standing objectives. . . .

> As long as the Soviet Union views [environmental problems] as a political issue, the gains come easy against an adversary who declares [them] to be a sanitary problem . . . . there is every indication that Soviet propagandists will take the issue, as they appropriated such other Western concerns as "peace" and "democracy," and mold it to fit their own semantics and purposes.[2]

Opportunities for imaginative interpretations of current events are almost unlimited. The most unlikely subjects may lead to unusual insights, as demonstrated by Leider's revelations.

THE GAME STRATEGISTS PLAY

Like it or not, grand strategy is a game, which is played for the world's highest stakes. Actually, there are games within games, and they are all related. Every game is played simultaneously on the same big board. There is no limit to the number of players. The players can participate singly or form teams but, no matter how they split up, who is on which side is always ambiguous. No two players start with the same

234

sets of pieces. Equally important, every player places different values on his own pieces, those of his partners, and those of the opposition. No two players use the same rules. Whole piles of pieces, not just one at a time, can shift suddenly in any direction. No one needs to wait his turn. Players, pieces, values, opponents, and rules are all subject to unannounced change. And, of course, the game never ends.

Bearing those conditions in mind, strategy may be a game that anyone can play, but it is *not* a game that just anyone can play well. Only the most gifted participants have much chance to win a prize, as General Beaufre has advised:

> The strategist can place no reliance on precedent and has no permanent unit of measure to hand. Strategic thought must continuously take the facts of change into account, not only those of the foreseeable future but probable changes many years ahead. Strategy can no longer proceed by a process of firmly based objective deduction; it must work on hypotheses and produce solutions by truly *original thought.*

> This aspect of strategy is one which was hardly grasped at all up to recent years. For a long time evolution was so slow that it seemed reasonable to base decisions on past experience. . . . Now that it has been driven back upon hypothesis, strategy must play with time as it has come to do with space; it must discard rigid and dangerous hypotheses like some recent theories . . . which are based on a mathematical evaluation of *probabilities.* Instead it must be based on a whole gamut of *possibilities* and there must be organization to ensure that these possibilities are kept under review so as to sort out in good time those which are growing and turning into fact from those which are disappearing. . . .

> There can be no rules for the inventive ability required to work out a future solution to meet an estimated future situation using new or readapted tools. All that can be said is that there must be no routine about it. . . . [After all,] no artist has ever painted a picture by following a complete set of theoretical rules. All that he may sometimes do is check his work against certain rules to ensure that it [is *technically* correct].[3]

The entire purpose of this handbook is to assist that process. No attempt has been made to tell aspiring strategists *what* to think about grand strategy. The preceding chapters simply show them *how.* There are no pat answers or school solutions. There are only strategic tools, and those tools are now in each reader's hands.

PART VI

APPLIED STRATEGY

29 The Vietnam War: A Case Study In Grand Strategy

If the strategy be wrong, the skill of the general
on the battlefield, the valor of the soldier, the
brilliancy of the victory, however otherwise
decisive, fail of their effect.

ALFRED THAYER MAHAN
Naval Administration and Warfare

The protracted conflict in Vietnam, still so fresh in American minds, furnishes a ready-made vehicle for analyzing, interpreting, and comparing strategic interactions of the United States with allies as well as antagonists.

This case study methodically segregates and examines the fundamental strategic elements of both sides in that altercation, emphasizes the influence of each element on the other, then compares friendly and enemy patterns. If U.S. decision-makers had applied such procedures to problems in Vietnam, controlling factors might have stood out better *before,* not after, the fact.

The following text is keyed directly to eight bar graphs which plot U.S., South Vietnamese, North Vietnamese, and Viet Cong security interests, objectives, policies, and strategies on a twenty-two-year time scale that commences in 1950, the year Vietnam was proclaimed as a state. Hard data are still scarce concerning Soviet and Chinese Communist influences in Indochina. The roles of those countries therefore are noted wherever necessary for clarity, but they are not plumbed in depth.

The first fifteen years are compressed into five-year blocks. The remaining seven are illustrated individually. Dotted lines indicate formative or fading stages of development. Since the Republic of Vietnam (RVN) was not conceived until 1954, in response to the Geneva Agreements, the earliest entries for that country correspond with that date.

Each graph was prepared from public pronouncements made *at the time* by senior officials, including chiefs of state, their civilian staffs, and key military advisors.[1] Thus, 20–20 hindsight played a minor part in piecing together the study.

237

THE FRAMEWORK OF FRIENDLY STRATEGY

U.S. Interests

What interests drew the United States into Vietnam, and what interests kept us there?

Reams have been written on that subject. Opinions run a gamut from altruism to avarice, including some very ethereal explanations, such as the compulsion "to conquer hunger, illiteracy, and disease." Figure 10 offers a more realistic appraisal.

FIGURE 10
Friendly Interests

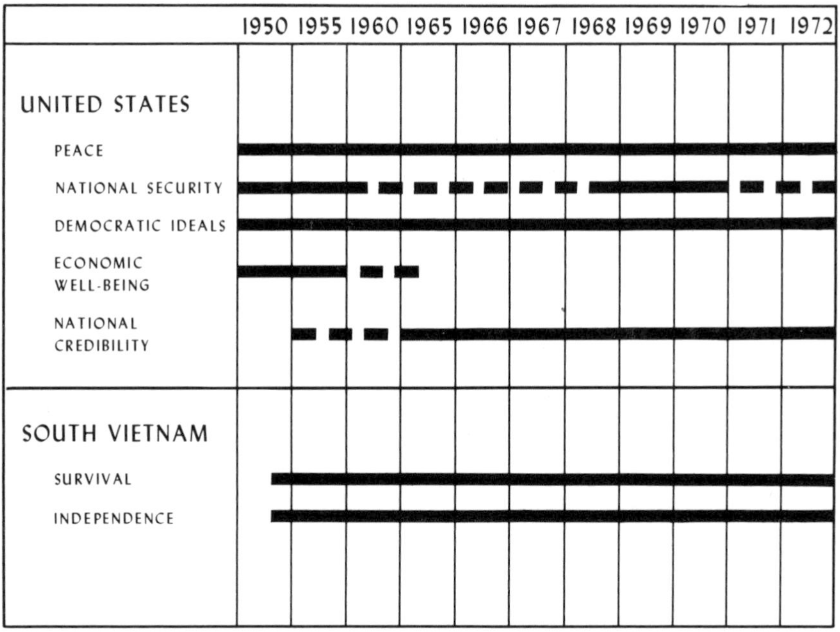

	1950	1955	1960	1965	1966	1967	1968	1969	1970	1971	1972
UNITED STATES											
PEACE											
NATIONAL SECURITY											
DEMOCRATIC IDEALS											
ECONOMIC WELL-BEING											
NATIONAL CREDIBILITY											
SOUTH VIETNAM											
SURVIVAL											
INDEPENDENCE											

Peace

Ubiquitous peace has been the overriding U.S. national security interest for at least three decades. It was our prime preoccupation throughout the Truman and Eisenhower administrations, was confirmed by President Nixon in his first State of the Union message, and has been reiterated by him in each annual foreign policy report to the Congress. All manner of U.S. initiatives in Indochina, unilateral, bilateral, and multilateral, both public and private, ranging from the 1968 bombing halt through our progressive troop withdrawals to the search for a comprehensive cease-fire, can be traced to a deep-seated desire for peace on the part of the United States.

National Security

That urge for peace took on a special connotation in the 1950s, when cumulative encroachment by international communism was nibbling the Free World to death. If the process was not halted, we concluded, U.S. survival ultimately would be at stake.

Our simplistic view of the threat dissolved in the subsequent decade. By 1962, the so-called monolithic communist conspiracy, calculating, cohesive, and coordinated by the Kremlin, was defunct. The Cuban missile crisis marked the last time that Russia threatened imminent armed aggression against a Free World country. The Sino-Indian border dispute that same year signalled the end of serious Chinese saber-rattling. Thereafter, Mao was tied down, first by domestic chaos, then by troubles with the U.S.S.R.

As always, there was a significant time lag between reality and realization, but those trends and their basic ramifications were clear to most informed persons by 1965. National security undisputably was a *valid* interest in Vietnam at that juncture, but in no way was it *vital.*

Paradoxically, national security interests not only enmeshed us in Vietnam — they later compelled us to pare our presence drastically. By mid-1968, domestic dissent, derived directly from the war in Southeast Asia, was tearing this country apart. President Nixon's options thus were severely restricted when he took office the following year. To counter divisive influences at home, he set about reducing U.S. ground combat participation to local security roles. American deaths from enemy action dropped to near zero by early 1972.

Democratic Ideals

Democratic ideals, as a U.S. national interest in Vietnam, were intertwined with our traditional belief in political self-determination. The abstract, moral, ideological conviction that freedom of choice is an inalienable right of man has prevailed from the beginning. Our yearning for democratic allies, not dictators, was a derivative consideration.

Economic Well-Being

American material well-being was frequently linked to interests in Southeast Asia during the Truman and Eisenhower eras, when the raw materials and agricultural products of that area were deemed indispensable to the Free World. References to "vital" economic interests are sparse after that period, since it became increasingly apparent that the resources in question were available elsewhere, or could be replaced.

National Credibility

Finally, national honor and prestige came into play. The impact of those interests was marginal when the United States took over responsibilities from the French in 1955, providing political, economic, training, and moral support for South Vietnam, but it intensified progressively. American credibility was really "on the line" after we committed combat forces in 1965. The whole world was waiting for the outcome, which would sharply influence our future foreign policy and alliance system. President Johnson met that challenge head-on. "If we are driven from the field in Vietnam," he said late that summer, "then no nation can ever have the same confidence in American promises or American protection. We will stand in Vietnam."[2] There was no change of mind during his administration.

239

President Nixon's evaluation four years later took a dissimilar tack. Henceforth, he said, in Vietnam as elsewhere, "we will respect the commitments we inherited . . . [but] maintaining the integrity of commitments requires relating their tangible expression, such as troop deployments or financial contributions, to changing conditions."[3] Consequently, he was unwilling to expend U.S. blood and treasure at the previous rates. Nevertheless, he made it clear that he would rather be "a one-term President" than see "America become a second-rate power and . . . see this nation accept the first defeat in its proud 190-year history."[4]

Military and Geographic Interests

The United States had no major military interests in Vietnam when we first became embroiled. Consequently, none show on the chart. We had no bases or direct alliances. Laos, Cambodia, and Vietnam were merely protocol partners of SEATO. There once were zealous attempts to justify U.S. involvement on the basis of geographic interests, centered mainly on the ability of militant communism to seal off Free World shipping routes that skirt South Asia. Since that could best be done from Singapore, Malaysia, or Indonesia, not from Vietnam, those interests were never compelling.

South Vietnamese Interests

The interests of South Vietnam, our protégé and ally, are in stark contrast to those of the United States. Successive governments of Vietnam were concerned with peace and prosperity, but two other interests were overriding: survival and independence, both irreducible and nonnegotiable. This in part explains the people's tenacity. Despite all the death, devastation, and disarray, they are still undaunted after nineteen years of subversion, terror, and armed combat. None of our interests remotely rivaled theirs in intensity, which led to dissonant purposes and policies when both parties came under pressure.

U.S. Objectives

The interests just elaborated spawned the objectives listed in Figure 11, which spelled out *what we were trying to do.*

With that in mind, note the erratic U.S. pattern. Only one goal made it all the way across the graph. Robert Shaplen, in his treatise *Time Out of Hand,* observed that "flexibility may be a virtue . . . but if it is pursued too long, if it fails to create a design and to achieve a sure purpose, it is little more, in the final analysis, than vacillation."[5]

Block Communist Aggression

The objective of countering communist aggression supported U.S. interests in "peace" and "national security," both of which lost their vital connotation early. Coincidentally, this aim contributed to the fulfillment of both RVN interests — survival and independence.

Countering communist aggression was initially associated with the Domino Theory, popularized by President Eisenhower but prevalent before and after his regime. A 1952 National Security Council document, later published in the *Pentagon Papers,* specu-

240

FIGURE 11
Friendly Objectives

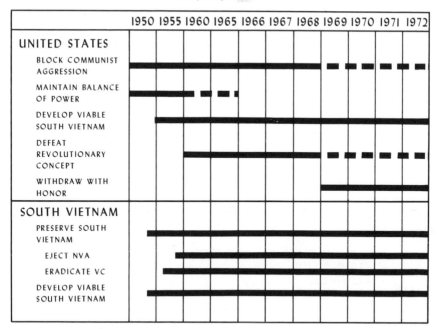

	1950	1955	1960	1965	1966	1967	1968	1969	1970	1971	1972
UNITED STATES											
BLOCK COMMUNIST AGGRESSION											
MAINTAIN BALANCE OF POWER											
DEVELOP VIABLE SOUTH VIETNAM											
DEFEAT REVOLUTIONARY CONCEPT											
WITHDRAW WITH HONOR											
SOUTH VIETNAM											
PRESERVE SOUTH VIETNAM											
EJECT NVA											
ERADICATE VC											
DEVELOP VIABLE SOUTH VIETNAM											

lated that failure to stem the communist tide in "any single country" of Southeast Asia could cause Free World dominoes to topple in the Middle East, ultimately "endanger the stability and security of Europe," imperil our "position in the Pacific offshore island chain," and "seriously jeopardize fundamental U.S. security interests in the Far East."[6]

Whether or not that estimate was ever correct, we had to block communist aggression if we were to buy time for nation-building, not just in Vietnam, but throughout mainland and insular Southeast Asia. As more than one on-the-spot pundit reported, regional leaders regarded a geopolitical buffer as indispensable if their newly independent nations were to attain political and economic stability. The Domino Theory was valid to them in the sense that, if South Vietnam fell, they would have to realign their policies drastically.

In any event, the need to stanch communist *insurgency* in this area ceased to be a consummate U.S. conviction sometime after 1969. It was still considered very important, but not enough so to warrant the continued commitment of U.S. ground forces. However, suppressing *conventional* communist aggression remained a solid American goal.

Maintain Balance of Power

Maintaining a balance of power between the free and communist worlds was a genuine U.S. goal as long as the vision of Sino-Soviet solidarity and Red Chinese power plays persisted. Thereafter, our perception changed. The United States still favors a balkanized Southeast Asia in which no single country enjoys hegemony, but the balance of

241

power in that area no longer seems to be a crucial consideration in the classic sense.

Develop Viable South Vietnam

Developing a free, independent, and viable South Vietnam related in one way or other to every U.S. interest. That objective was the key to our whole operation, and its dominance of the bar graph shows that U.S. leaders were always aware of that, even if sometimes subconsciously. Failure in this arena would permit the opposition to prevail eventually through subversion and skulduggery. Unless political, economic, and social institutions were established or revamped satisfactorily, unless basic causes of the revolution were eradicated, and unless the enemy infrastructure were rooted out, the Viet Cong would still be able to stage a strong comeback in the aftermath of an apparent Free World victory.

Despite the indispensability of this objective, our other aims seemed to be poorly coordinated with it for a good many years. Moreover, our methodology often was in question. For example, the U.S. quest for a sound South Vietnam was unduly influenced by our interest in democratic ideals. Robert Thompson put his finger on that problem when he wrote:

> It was assumed that, with a freedom of choice, democratic institutions and procedures would flourish and that the minority would be ready to tolerate the rule of the majority without question. . . . The American aim, as it developed, was far too ambitious for the circumstances.[7]

American efforts to assist nation-building in South Vietnam have been somewhat more successful since 1969 than in previous years, but the goal will not be satisfied until Saigon is able to stand solidly alone, without fear of collapse generated by internal pressures or invasion by immediate neighbors.

Defeat the Revolutionary Concept

"Defeat the revolutionary concept" first surfaced in 1961 as an objective during the Kennedy administration, when Khrushchev proclaimed communism's "sacred duty" to support "just wars of national liberation," and Mao's principles for "peoples' wars" were getting wide publicity. Secretary of Defense McNamara, in a memorandum to President Johnson three years later, identified the confrontation in Vietnam as a "test case."[8] General Earle G. Wheeler, Chairman of the Joint Chiefs of Staff at that time, echoed his view.[9]

When our determination to counter communism in Southeast Asia began to attenuate, that objective atrophied. True, it is still a consideration, but without marked emphasis. Few authoritative officials today publicly proclaim any U.S. compulsion to defeat the revolutionary concept. Success in such venture is infrequently linked with the Domino Theory, as it once was by General Maxwell D. Taylor, who concluded that failure might exert an "unfavorable effect upon our image [as far away as] Africa and Latin America."[10]

Whether we really had an urgent need to defeat the revolutionary concept is not yet known, despite rationalizations by minions from the far right to the far left in the U.S. politico-military spectrum who, for different reasons, assert that we *have* satisfied that objective. The proof will be in future events. If the Vietnam experience, for whatever reason, deters Red China and the U.S.S.R from encouraging, sponsoring, and supporting revolutionary wars elsewhere around the globe, we will indeed have defeated the revolutionary concept, *even if South Vietnam eventually falls.* Otherwise, our efforts will reflect some degree of failure.

Withdraw with Honor

The goal of withdrawing with honor neither complemented nor contributed to other U.S. objectives, with one exception: a diminution of U.S. presence and influence was imperative if we ever hoped to develop a self-sufficient South Vietnam. However, it did dovetail precisely with most of our *interests,* even though it seemed completely contrary to those espoused by the RVN.

South Vietnamese Objectives

The divergence of U.S. and South Vietnamese objectives sowed the seeds of distress. All four RVN goals were unequivocal, as might have been expected in light of the elemental interests from which they derived. As we became less and less completely committed, the resultant contradictions were wide open to exploitation by the enemy. Moreover, if our reduced aims eventually allowed us a greater degree of latitude, they allowed our ally almost none.

U.S. Policies

Policy permits a systematic, coordinated approach to the attainment of goals, but only if applied perspicaciously so that ends justify means and costs relate proportionately to gains.

The United States promulgated a plethora of policies during the twenty-two-year period from 1950 to 1972, but only those that shaped strategy, as opposed to tactics, are depicted in Figure 12. The most damning indictment is the absence of any continuum that contributed progressively and decisively to the attainment of the primal aim: the development of a stable South Vietnam. "A foolish consistency" may be "the hobgoblin of little minds, adored by little statesmen and philosophers and divines," but Emerson would be the first to acknowledge that *sensible* consistency could have worked miracles in these circumstances.

Contain Communism

When the United States first became involved, the principal U.S. policy was containment. Unhappily, that defensive tack took on a predominantly military connotation, which augered ill for the prosecution of a successful counterrevolutionary war. However, given that drawback, it inadvertently was a fortunate policy, for it coincidentally helped confine the conflict. North Vietnam was inviolate, except for aerial and naval bombardment. Her survival was never an issue. Ambassador Arthur J. Goldberg punctuated that policy at a plenary session of the United Nations in 1966, when he reinforced earlier utterances by other high-ranking officials: "We do not seek to overthrow the Government of North Viet-Nam. . . . We do not ask of North Viet-Nam an unconditional surrender or indeed the surrender of anything that belongs to it."[11] Subsequent statements confirmed that position.

FIGURE 12
Friendly Policies

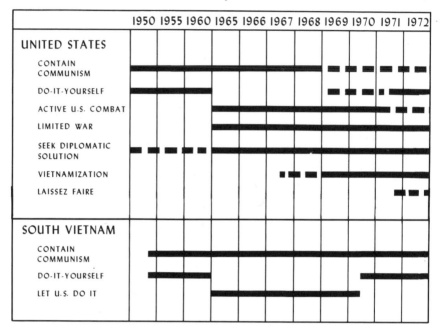

	1950	1955	1960	1965	1966	1967	1968	1969	1970	1971	1972
UNITED STATES											

Do-It-Yourself

Our early "Do-It-Yourself" policy, properly managed, might have produced a winner. Presidents Truman and Eisenhower were basically on the right track. John F. Kennedy continued that well-meaning trend by "giving Diem what he [needed] to win his own war."[12] However, the implementation machinery was faulty throughout those three regimes.

From the onset, short tours of duty constituted a serious deficiency. Except for a few general officers and civilians, the average length of service in the theater was between twelve and eighteen months, an insufficient period, as Shaplen said, "for anyone to learn and understand enough about the place and its people and to come to grips either with Vietnam as a country or with the American engagement there." He contrasted that "whole concept of swinging door diplomacy" most unfavorably with the British action in Malaya, where continuity was measured in many years — in some cases for the full decade of the emergency.[13] Institutional memory thus was chronically faulty. As wags are wont to observe, "The United States didn't accrue 20 years of experience in Vietnam. In many respects, it repeated one year's experience 20 times."

Partly in consequence, our aid policy and programs, predicated on imperfect understanding and shaped by unsound advice, came a cropper. When South Vietnam was established as a separate state, Diem requested and received assurances of U.S. *economic* assistance, but in fact President Eisenhower gave aid an unfortunate slant by stressing the development of abilities to resist revolutionary pressures "through military

244

means." Thus, as early as October 1954, we had already missed the point. "This," notes Robert Thompson, "coupled with the limitations imposed by Congress on foreign aid of a civil nature at that time, and the ready availability of surplus military material, resulted in the main emphasis of American aid being military. Even on the economic front, aid was oriented toward the problem of paying for a large [South Vietnamese] army."[14]

Military organization and training, in turn, reflected U.S. experiences in World War II and Korea, both of which were conventional conflicts conducted under radically different circumstances. That background helped to engender grossly misplaced emphases.

The great need from the early 1950s on was for local security, which demanded an effective police establishment, paramilitary adjuncts, and an integrated intelligence service. Instead, we created conventional South Vietnamese armed forces to fight conventional battles. There *was* a requirement to grapple with Viet Cong main forces and later with North Vietnamese regulars, but the absence of continuous grass-roots control nearly proved fatal.

Active U.S. Combat

If U.S. Do-It-Yourself policies had been keenly conceived, we might never have been compelled to choose between committing combat forces or accepting defeat. As it was, our counterinsurgency efforts went bankrupt in 1965. At that moment, action-oriented Americans breathed a sigh of relief. After ten years of passive participation, Uncle Sam's "hard chargers" at last could "get on with the war."

"Americanization" would have been acceptable as a stopgap, but in the long run, it was a strategic disaster. The "military war" assumed and retained top priority; our ally's armed forces were cavalierly shunted aside; corollary political and economic programs received little encouragement; and, predictably, the populace suffered. Probably no other policy could have prevented our success as surely as did Americanization.

Limited War

President Johnson's watchword was, "We want no wider war." A variety of political, economic, military, and geographic constraints were conscientiously applied, mainly to preclude the probability of armed intervention by the U.S.S.R. or Red China, but desired results often were elusive.

It proved almost impossible, for example, to limit the conflict politically, since revolutionary war by its very nature is an eminently political process. Diplomatic maneuvering took place on a global scale, usually to our detriment.

"Business-as-usual" measures were equally ill-starred. In an effort to damp down jingoism and excessive emotion, U.S. leaders decided not to declare war; not to mobilize the Reserve, the National Guard, or industry; not to impose any special controls, such as censorship or commodity rationing; to continue other U.S. defense commitments on a shoestring budget; and to sanction mass draft deferments. The upshot was that all efforts to enlist public support were enervated, the combat burden was borne by the "unlucky" few, irresponsible reporting by some members of the mass media ensued, we suffered from deficit spending and an unfavorable international balance of payments, and our security posture everywhere, other than in Vietnam, was undermined.

We had similar difficulties trying to limit the scope territorially. Our leaders allowed the opposition sanctuaries in Laos and Cambodia for many years (some such havens were never violated), and throughout the war we scrupulously avoided ground combat in North Vietnam. Nevertheless, our bombing campaigns extended the theater far beyond Southeast Asia, both politically and psychologically.

"Graduated response," sometimes called "piecemealing," brought U.S. military might to bear one step at a time. The purpose was to avoid the appearance of applying unbridled power against a minor antagonist, yet still crank the rack enough to convince the communists that salvation lay on the conference table. However, graduated response failed in both regards. First, public opinion at home and abroad looked on the mighty United States as a bully brutalizing a brave but outclassed opponent. Further, graduated response actually *strengthened* enemy resolve. North Vietnam learned to live with incrementally increased punishment in much the same way a cancer patient learns to live with pain that would be intolerable if inflicted instantaneously.

It has been said, in fact, that the bombing brought *us,* not Hanoi, to the conference table, prepared to settle for something less than our stated objectives.

Seek Diplomatic Solution

The search for a diplomatic solution had its policy roots in Franklin Roosevelt's days. The pitfalls that face counterrevolutionaries who choose to negotiate were perfectly prepared by the communists in Vietnam. Our eagerness to convene a conference was construed by the foe as a weakness, and prolonged the shooting war. In addition, it actively eroded the morale of our embattled ally, South Vietnam, whose survival and independence seemed, in the eyes of many Americans, to be expendable. The only U.S. goal that negotiation could satisfy under the conditions presented was "withdraw with honor," and even that was in doubt.

Vietnamization

Throughout the period 1965-1968, when the emphasis was on military operations, pacification and nation-building programs proceeded at a slow pace, reflecting their low priority. Yet Vietnamization alone was geared to South Vietnam's obligatory objectives, as well as to ours.

That policy had been in effect under other names for a number of years, with indifferent success. General Westmoreland gave it impetus in 1967, when he directed General Abrams, his new deputy, to expedite the upgrading of the ARVN. With the advent of President Nixon's administration in 1969, Vietnamization was broadened so that the RVN could accept increasing responsibilities and exert increasing authority in political, economic, and social spheres.

Those changes signalled a gradual return to "Do-It-Yourself," in keeping with the Nixon Doctrine, which stipulates that our allies must

> participate fully in the creation of plans and the designing of programs. They must define the nature of their own security and determine the path of their own progress. . . . We shall furnish economic and military assistance when requested in accordance with our treaty commitments. But we shall look to the nation directly threatened to assume the primary responsibility of providing the manpower for its defense.[15]

The Chinese Communists have understood that principle all along. They promise their Vietnamese constituents advice, support, and "spiritual atom bombs," but no reinforcements. Revolutions, Mao says, must be fought and won by indigenous elements.

As Vietnamization progressed, RVN policies started to assume a more independent shape, and became less prone to dangerous adventurism predicated on U.S. participation — repeated entreaties to march north are illustrative of hare-brained proposals in the past. Vietnamization also paved the way for American military disengagement. Our extrication was essential for many reasons, but U.S. public opinion unfortunately prompted so precipitate a withdrawal that improvements in Saigon's security posture could not keep pace.

Laissez Faire

As active U.S. ground combat tapered off in 1971, a new policy of reduced U.S. involvement emerged. In keeping with the Nixon Doctrine, we extend South Vietnam "assistance" against outright invasion by communist neighbors, although it is difficult to imagine circumstances in which the United States would re-engage its ground forces. The RVN must handle insurgencies largely within its own military means.

South Vietnamese Policies

South Vietnamese policies generally paralleled those of the United States, but they were simpler and far more consistent. Their policy of containment, for example, reflected interests in survival and independence, backed by unequivocal objectives that left little choice. The RVN policy entitled "Let-the-U.S.-Do-It" reflected the natural inclination of any individual or nation to let a willing collaborator do dirty work that seems to be in the beneficiary's best interests.

U.S. Strategies

Clausewitz once concluded that:

> The first, the grandest, the most decisive act of judgment which the Statesman and General exercises is rightly to understand the War in which he engages, not to take it for something, to wish to make of it something, which by the nature of its relations it is impossible for it to be.[16]

Revolutionary war is *not* a specialized form of limited war, as is so often surmised. It is a form of total war that occupies its own niche in the conflict spectrum. The term connotes conscious efforts to seize political power by illegal and violent means, deliberately destroying existing systems of government and social structure in the process. Conventional antidotes are inappropriate. Consequently, U.S. countermeasures, which were conventional, unintegrated, and mainly military, were poorly suited (Figure 13).

Conventional Concepts

Most senior members of the U.S. government and armed forces were rank amateurs

FIGURE 13
Friendly Strategies

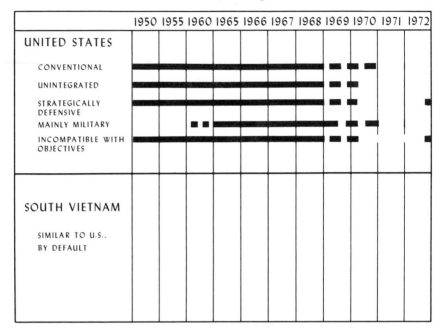

	1950	1955	1960	1965	1966	1967	1968	1969	1970	1971	1972
UNITED STATES											
CONVENTIONAL											
UNINTEGRATED											
STRATEGICALLY DEFENSIVE											
MAINLY MILITARY											
INCOMPATIBLE WITH OBJECTIVES											
SOUTH VIETNAM											
SIMILAR TO U.S., BY DEFAULT											

in the counterrevolutionary business until recently. Many still are. That allegation is not made disparagingly. Their training and experience with war were mainly military and *conventional*. They were too tied down with crisis-management and current problem-solving to study *unconventional* revolution. Results were foreseeably disappointing. As Robert Thompson put it:

> . . . in fighting according to their own concept of the war . . . the Americans had inflicted many battle defeats and enormous casualties on Viet Cong and North Vietnamese units but victory was . . . elusive . . . because they . . . failed to inflict a [strategic] defeat in accordance with the concept of People's Revolutionary War.[17]

In short, U.S. strategists suffered from a syndrome identified 200 years ago by Marshal de Saxe, who described the symptoms as follows: "In default of knowing what should be done, they do what they know."

Unintegrated Plans and Operations

There apparently was no combined U.S./RVN master plan until the United States began pulling out. Neither was there adequate politico-military machinery to coordinate programs and operations until very late in the day. Disjointed *strategic* schemes, therefore, grew like Topsy, while we experimented with the *tactics* of counter-insurgency.

Early in 1966, Shaplen discloses, "when the Americans sought to rationalize the program of rural development . . . there were no fewer than 39 different Vietnamese groups or agencies engaged in the attempt to bring reforms and benefits to the villages and to provide them with some degree of security."[18] Our organization was little better. The Commander-in-Chief, Pacific, in Hawaii, was responsible for the air war. The Commander, U.S. Military Assistance Command, Vietnam, was charged with conducting the ground war. Our ambassador in Saigon handled diplomatic matters. Bureaucratic ineptitude, inertia, and duplication, exacerbated by slipshod coordination, were rampant in several critical fields: intelligence collection, processing, and dissemination; military and economic aid; logistics. The President of the United States — not the President of South Vietnam — was in over-all charge.

Organizational anarchy would have been indefensible under any circumstances. In a revolutionary war, wherein the interests and objectives of the supporting and supported powers differed significantly, it was intolerable.

Strategically Defensive Approaches

American armed forces in Vietnam achieved an almost uninterrupted series of splendid tactical victories, but were consistently on the strategic defensive.

To quote Robert Thompson once again:

> It was never understood [before 1969] that nation building was the *offensive* constructive programme designed to strengthen the government's assets and eliminate its weaknesses, while the military operations were *defensive* and destructive designed to hold the ring . . . and, in so doing, to weaken the enemy's military assets. The programme which linked these two together was pacification. . . . The three programmes were tackled and regarded in precisely the reverse order of importance in relation to the objective and, in turn, the strategy. [Emphases added][19]

Actually, the requirements were understood by a good many U.S. officials, but they experienced great difficulty in making their voices heard.

Mainly Military Emphases

For several years, we fought two separate wars, one military, one political. Robert W. Komer, in fact, served as President Johnson's Special Assistant for the "Other War" in Vietnam during 1966 and 1967.

Make no mistake. The United States was driven to defend South Vietnam in 1965. It was the only way we could salvage the situation and provide a screen behind which productive programs could prosper. Characteristically, however, we put too many eggs in one basket. Excessive reliance on a conventional military approach slighted other available elements of U.S. power which should have been committed concurrently.

Overlooking Sun Tzu's sage advice that the "supreme importance in war is to attack the enemy's strategy," which in this case was revolutionary, the United States plunged into battle like a bull in a china shop. We overestimated friendly capabilities and underestimated the enemy's. Our enthusiastic application of armed force quickly generated an inconclusive objective: military victory on the battlefield. Once again, political objectives and military aims diverged to our detriment. Even if we had "bombed North Vietnam back to the Stone Age," as some extremists advocated, and made the Viet Cong run for cover, the best we could have hoped to accomplish was an undeclared armistice that would buy time for nation-building and pacification — which at the

249

height of our armed endeavor were receiving little stress. Without complementary actions in those fields to augment friendly assets while enemy causes and organization were being eradicated, our efforts went for naught. The revolution remained unscathed, costs soared, and consequences got completely out of hand.

The U.S. "search and destroy" strategy was a born loser on two counts: first, the Democratic Republic of Vietnam (DRV) was prepared to accept unconscionable costs to achieve its political goals; second, firepower and attrition on the battlefield in no way helped us to regain control over and voluntary support from the people. "Clear and hold" operations were much more befitting, but it took us a long time to appreciate that fundamental fact.

Distorted Objectives

While fundamental objectives were being slighted, nearly every basic interest of the United States, as expounded in the Preamble to our Constitution, was jeopardized, not to mention the specific interests tabled in Figure 10.

The way to a genuine offensive strategy, of course, was nation-building. President Eisenhower realized this. What he was after was "an independent Vietnam endowed with a strong government." Presidents Kennedy and Johnson concurred, but none of the early strategies contributed to that goal. The turning point came in 1969, when new leaders with fresh viewpoints began to put it all together. Our interests, objectives, policies, and strategies started to coincide — fourteen years late, but better late than never. Modest, but positive, results began to appear within a few months.

South Vietnamese Strategies

As noted in Figure 13, RVN strategies were similar to our own. They had little choice.

THE FRAMEWORK OF ENEMY STRATEGY

Enemy strategy can be outlined quickly, since it was simple, concise, and consistent throughout most of the period. The opposition knew what they wanted to do, they had the initiative, and they had a winning combination until quite recently.

Enemy Interests

North Vietnamese interests (Figure 14), backed by emotional causes like nationalism, anticolonialism, and anti-imperialism, were solid as a brick. Consequently, they afforded vastly better platforms for strategic planning than the mushy motivations that entrapped the United States. The first three entries on the graph probably were considered vital by headmen in Hanoi. The remaining two were compelling.

The interest in independence was satisfied in 1954, when Ho Chi Minh ousted the French. Since then, the primary interest has been political power, which pervades the struggle for suzerainty over all of Indochina. What the world has been watching is a war to determine colonial succession. Call it neo-imperialism on a very small scale, if you like.

Interests in communist ideology, the yearning for the solidarity of Vietnamese peo-

FIGURE 14
Enemy Interests

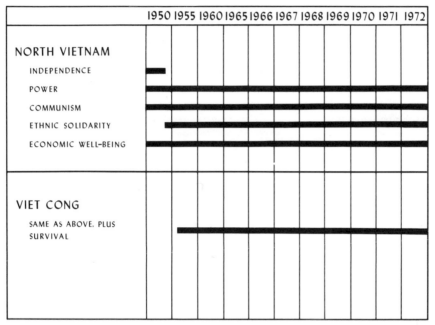

	1950	1955	1960	1965	1966	1967	1968	1969	1970	1971	1972
NORTH VIETNAM											
INDEPENDENCE											
POWER											
COMMUNISM											
ETHNIC SOLIDARITY											
ECONOMIC WELL-BEING											
VIET CONG											
SAME AS ABOVE, PLUS SURVIVAL											

ples, both north and south, and the urge for economic well-being that would result from a melding of the Mekong rice bowl with material assets in the Red River delta, are self-explanatory.

Viet Cong interests have always duplicated those of the DRV, with a single exception: VC actions have been directly related to physical survival since the situation heated up in 1957.

Enemy Objectives

Every DRV/VC aim (Figure 15) contributed conclusively to the satisfaction of vital interests.

Controlling and communizing all of Indochina have always been the foe's overriding objectives. Patrick J. Honey, a Reader in Vietnamese Studies at the University of London and a noted authority on this subject, cites a *Lao Dong* Party document captured by the French in 1952 as "the clearest statement" of North Vietnamese long-term goals: to wit, "to install communist regimes in the whole of Vietnam, in Laos, and in Cambodia."[20] After 1954, reunification thus was indispensable.

North Vietnamese and Viet Cong goals generally coincided, although emphases differed regarding the urgency of reunification. Some factions preached a need for solidarity. Others represented a strong tradition of southern separatism. As early as 1961, Douglas Pike, a U.S. Foreign Service Officer and student of Viet Cong policies and practices, detected three distinct VC attitudes:

251

FIGURE 15
Enemy Objectives

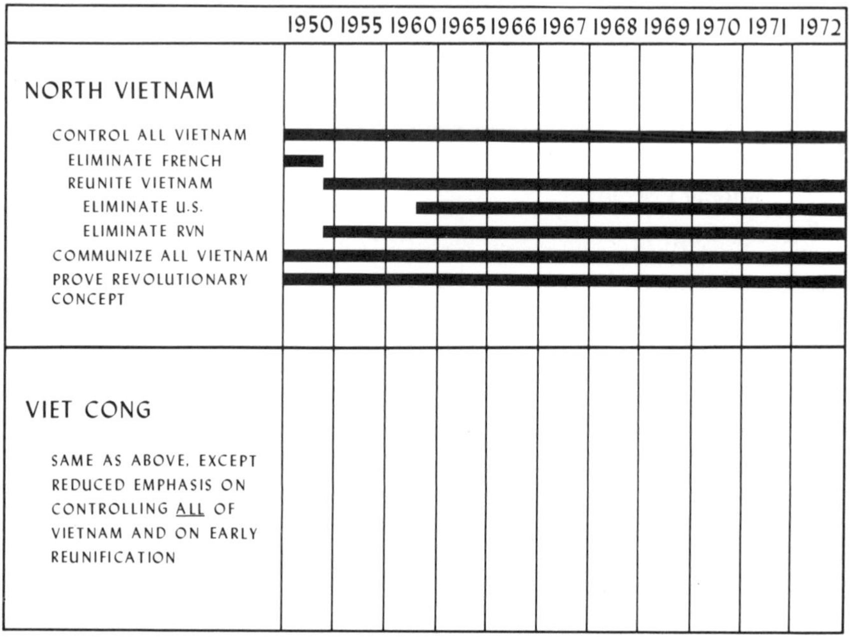

	1950	1955	1960	1965	1966	1967	1968	1969	1970	1971	1972

NORTH VIETNAM

CONTROL ALL VIETNAM
ELIMINATE FRENCH
REUNITE VIETNAM
ELIMINATE U.S.
ELIMINATE RVN
COMMUNIZE ALL VIETNAM
PROVE REVOLUTIONARY
CONCEPT

VIET CONG

SAME AS ABOVE, EXCEPT
REDUCED EMPHASIS ON
CONTROLLING ALL OF
VIETNAM AND ON EARLY
REUNIFICATION

> There were those who maintained that reunification must be pursued at all costs, those who favored it in principle but asserted that it was impossible to achieve, and those who opposed it on the grounds that it would mean absorption by the Northerners. . . . The division grew increasingly apparent in late 1964 and early 1965, when Radio Liberation spoke constantly in terms of "US withdrawal and the establishment of neutrality" while Radio Hanoi spoke constantly in terms of "US withdrawal, negotiation, and reunification."[21]

However, the People's Revolutionary Party (PRP), founded by Hanoi as a hard "inner pyramidal core" within the National Liberation Front (NLF), kept that sort of ideological isolationism well under control, and nothing much ever came of it. No schism, in truth, offered a very fertile field for *strategic* probes by friendly psychological warfare experts and propagandists.

Lao Dong Party Resolutions 12 and 13, issued in 1965 and 1966, respectively, laid out plans to match the U.S. troop buildup and defeat allied forces on the battlefield. Hanoi's Central Office for South Vietnam (COSVN) published Resolution 6 in 1968, calling for a quick military victory. Nevertheless, members of the communist high command were, and are, realists. They undoubtedly understood that they had little chance of defeating the United States decisively in armed combat. Therefore, they concentrated on courses of action designed to saddle us with exorbitant political, economic, social, and military costs, stoically accepting grievous wounds in return. The contest with the United States thus was a test of will, not a trial of strength.

Even so, a secondary objective was, in Robert Thompson's opinion, closely tied to "proving the revolutionary concept." Namely, beginning in 1965, "it would not be enough that the United States should just lose. They must lose stinking." The end thus served would be the disaffection of our allies, in Europe as well as Asia, whose faith in U.S. security guarantees would be seriously shaken. Pike appears to bear that out.[22] The strategic center of gravity selected was U.S./RVN resolve, which was attacked relentlessly, by blending armed aggression with psychological warfare.

Enemy Policies

Enemy policies (Figure 16) clearly corresponded with enemy aims. Reunification through referendum appeared possible during the days that followed the 1954 Geneva Agreements, which provided for countrywide elections not later than 20 July 1956. That prospect was eminently agreeable to the communists, whose potential for political manipulation seemed favorable. However, when the time came, President Diem reneged, because he feared that local VC leverage might preclude a proper plebiscite, despite all the high-sounding assurances about impartial supervision.

Reunification through force flowered as the DRV policy when it became apparent that political connivance had failed. The Viet Cong acquiesced, as evidenced by repetitious incantations over a period of years that "this revolution can and should be settled only by the use of revolutionary acts and the force of the masses to defeat enemy force. It absolutely cannot be settled by treaties and accords." Subterfuge remained as an adjunct.

FIGURE 16
Enemy Policies

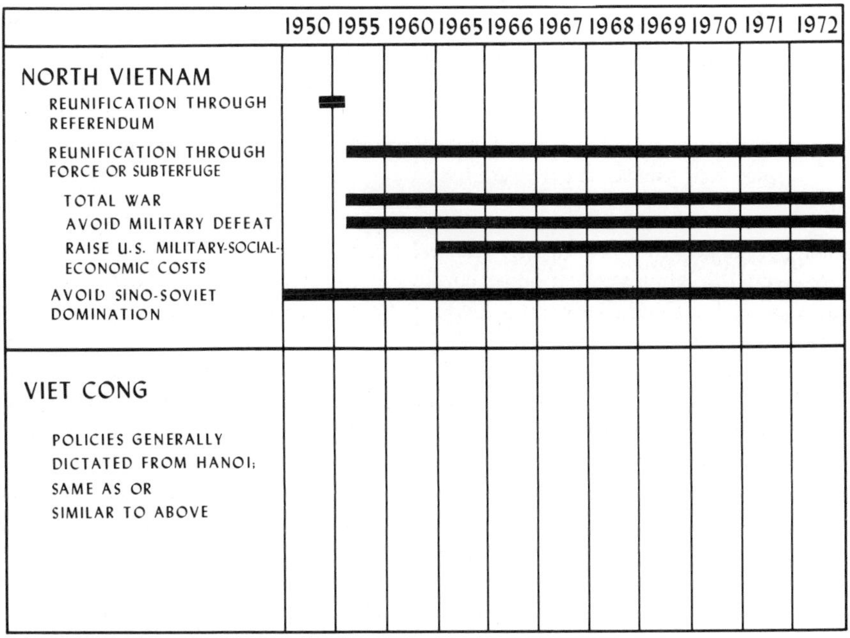

	1950	1955	1960	1965	1966	1967	1968	1969	1970	1971	1972
NORTH VIETNAM REUNIFICATION THROUGH REFERENDUM	▬										
REUNIFICATION THROUGH FORCE OR SUBTERFUGE		▬	▬	▬	▬	▬	▬	▬	▬	▬	▬
TOTAL WAR		▬	▬	▬	▬	▬	▬	▬	▬	▬	▬
AVOID MILITARY DEFEAT		▬	▬	▬	▬	▬	▬	▬	▬	▬	▬
RAISE U.S. MILITARY-SOCIAL-ECONOMIC COSTS				▬	▬	▬	▬	▬	▬	▬	▬
AVOID SINO-SOVIET DOMINATION	▬	▬	▬	▬	▬	▬	▬	▬	▬	▬	▬
VIET CONG POLICIES GENERALLY DICTATED FROM HANOI; SAME AS OR SIMILAR TO ABOVE											

253

That heavy-handed policy no doubt caused occasional embarrassment in Moscow, since it parroted the Chinese Communist party line, rather than that of the Soviets, who generally preferred a softer approach. For all intents and purposes, however, the DRV skillfully played both ends against the middle, with a high degree of success. Considering that Russia and China are perennially in competition with one another and both had vested interests in ejecting the United States from Vietnam, neither was eager to turn off the aid tap as a means of influencing Hanoi's posture.

The North Vietnamese had little to fear and everything to gain from those policies as long as a revolutionary environment existed in South Vietnam. Their survival and independence were never at stake, and they could stop the bloodletting at any time, if the pressure got too great. The worst that could happen would be military reverses that caused them to retrench from Phase III to Phase II or Phase I in the revolutionary war. Only the Viet Cong were in a truly ticklish situation, since their continued existence was always an issue, but even they could go underground if necessary, awaiting an opportunity to rise again.

Enemy Strategies

Over the years, enemy strategies (Figure 17), predicated on sound objectives and propelled by generally enlightened policies, were all the things ours were not: integrated, multifaceted (as opposed to predominantly military), and dynamic.

FIGURE 17
Enemy Strategies

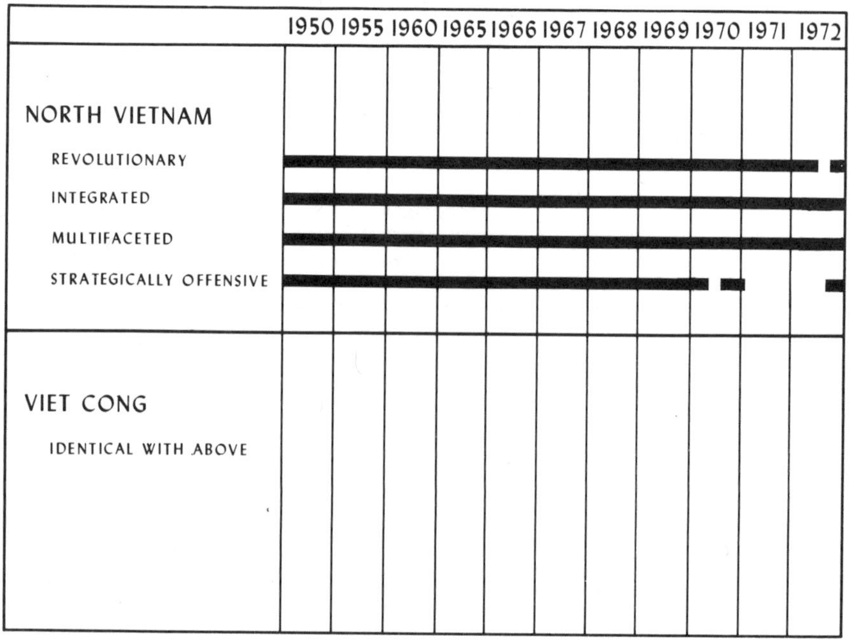

	1950	1955	1960	1965	1966	1967	1968	1969	1970	1971	1972
NORTH VIETNAM											
REVOLUTIONARY											
INTEGRATED											
MULTIFACETED											
STRATEGICALLY OFFENSIVE											
VIET CONG											
IDENTICAL WITH ABOVE											

The Strategic Pattern, 1950-1971

Revolutionary brain trusts seized the strategic initiative in the 1950s and refused to relinquish it, politically, psychologically, or militarily. Most strategically important confrontations in all three spheres consistently were at times and places of communist choosing. By applying multiple modes of power, they enjoyed great flexibility, outmaneuvering the United States with telling effect in Paris, in the United Nations, and here at home. Strategic surprise of the sort they achieved at Tet time in 1968 was never duplicated by the United States or South Vietnam (the Cambodian incursion was mainly tactical) and the communists constantly capitalized on our ignorance of revolutionary war.

As a result, a ninth-rate nation, in concert with a collection of motivated peasants, consistently outsmarted the world's preeminent superpower for at least fourteen years, and thereby produced a strategic classic.

The Tet offensive was a turning point. The communists scored a sweeping psychological victory in the United States, but the Viet Cong infrastructure suffered severely, and Saigon's will was strengthened. Productive U.S./RVN programs flourished the following year.

After 1969, DRV/VC ascendancy weakened. The United States and South Vietnam did more things right than wrong for a change, and seized the strategic initiative. Vietnamization progressed in many regards — military improvements were merely the most manifest. President Nguyen Van Thieu consolidated his position. By the end of 1971, it was evident that the doctrine of "People's War, People's Victory" was finally being discredited.

The Strategic Metamorphosis, 1972-1973

In response, North Vietnam launched a massive conventional onslaught with minimum assistance from the Viet Cong. That unorthodox ploy represented a radical departure from revolutionary precedent in at least two regards. First, traditional theory advocates that the indigenous population must provide the principal source of power to shape its own destiny. And second, the procession of events should progress through phases geared to the strengths and weaknesses of the conflicting sides. Provisions are made for a climactic offensive when conditions are ripe, but nothing approaching the apocalyptic war of attrition which DRV leaders planned to prosecute unceasingly until the opposition lay prostrate.

The timing of that "go for broke" bid was impeccable. The invasion was triggered at Eastertide 1972, *after* U.S. ground combat troops had been withdrawn, but *before* Saigon's army was completely ready. However, communist planners sadly misjudged the temper of their opponents and the tenor of the times. The initial surge was spectacular, but everything soon went wrong: the ARVN reeled, then recovered rapidly and mounted counteroffensives; air power broke the DRV spearheads and shattered DRV supplies; the U.S. mining of Haiphong harbor came as a total surprise; provincial capitals crumbled, but remained in friendly hands; droves of disenchanted supporters in South Vietnam deserted the communist cause; and, in contrast with enemy expectations, the American public held firm. Thieu emerged from the struggle stronger than ever. Vietnamization was vindicated.

By early autumn 1972, that reckless expenditure of men and materiel had garnered the DRV naught. North Vietnam was blocked on the battlefield, isolated from its Soviet and Chinese allies, scorned by world opinion, and faced painful problems at home. The initiative returned to the capitalist camp, politically, militarily, and psychologically. In the eyes of experienced observers, the communists had lost.[23]

At that dark moment, Hanoi's ruling quadrumvirate salvaged the situation by re-opening a quiescent political front. On 8 October 1972, it extended an olive branch in Paris.

Circumstances were close to perfect for psychological warfare. We were overconfident and caught unaware. Playing on our penchant for peace and proclivity for negotiations, the DRV Politburo proffered prospects for ending the endless agony immediately and exchanging prisoners of war. President Nixon and his strategic advisors were anxious to present the American people with a present just before the November election, or before Christmas, for that matter. Great optimism was expressed in a statement by Dr. Kissinger, our chief negotiator:

> The North Vietnamese for the first time . . . enabled us to accelerate the negotiations. . . . They dropped their demand for a coalition government. . . . They dropped their demand for a veto over the personalities and the structure of the existing [RVN] government. . . . They agreed for the first time to a formula which permitted a simultaneous discussion of Laos and Cambodia.[24]

Having laid the groundwork for a psychological offensive, Hanoi suddenly publicized that an accord had been reached and that its confirmation was imminent. The entire world was electrified by the following broadcast from Hanoi:

> By October 22, 1972, the DRV side and the U.S. side had agreed both on the full text of the "agreement on ending the war and restoring peace in Vietnam" and on a schedule . . . for the formal signing . . . on October 31, 1972.[25]

Then came the master stroke. In its very next utterance, North Vietnam put the onus on the United States to conclude a treaty (on communist terms) not later than the following week:

> But on 23 October, 1972, contrary to its pledges, the U.S. side again . . . demanded that the negotiations be continued for resolving new problems. . . This behavior of the U.S. side has brought about a very serious situation which risks . . . the signing of the agreement.[26]

The United States, but not South Vietnam, fell face forward into Hanoi's trap. Instead of placing that canard in perspective, we relaxed all pressures and pronounced that "peace is at hand. . . . What remains to be done can be settled in one more negotiating session . . . lasting . . . no more than three or four days."[27]

Elation prevailed in America and elsewhere. During subsequent sessions at the conference table, hopes were raised high. Banner headlines blared "President Confident On Peace" and "Optimism Mounts In Paris." Our prisoners in the "Hanoi Hilton" dutifully acted as pawns.

As the days dragged on without conciliation, frustration replaced euphoria. In exasperation, Kissinger explained that "a settlement was always [seemingly] within our

256

reach, and was always pulled [away] when we attempted to grasp it."[28] On 14 December, the peace talks collapsed. Each side blamed the other. Four days later the prodigious bombing recommenced, *with the United States cast in the role of "aggressor."*

Cynical enemy intellects had scored another strategic coup. World public opinion shamed this country once again; anti-war sentiment was resurrected in the United States; fresh impetus impelled Congressional movements to cut off funds for the conflict in Vietnam and to proscribe presidential war-making powers; and our hard-won detentes with Red China and the U.S.S.R. seemed to be shaken.

We eventually restabilized the situation, but by brute force, not finesse, with scant recourse to grand strategy. The enemy acquiesced to terms that rid the region of American military power but left their own power in place, and on 27 January 1973 a fragile cease-fire commenced. Phase III of the revolutionary war terminated for the second time in nineteen years, but the struggle continued, despite U.S. press pronouncements that "peace accords" had been signed.

Harry Reasoner, who presided over a CBS special review on that date, expressed a fitting epitaph for our strategic experience in Vietnam:

"We meant well."

U.S. STRATEGY APPRAISED

Strategic Successes

There *were* strategic benefits to the United States and the Free World from our involvement in Vietnam, critics notwithstanding.

We helped to suppress subversion and stabilize the political situation in South Vietnam, arrested external aggression long enough for RVN armed forces to improve their position immensely, and may indeed have destroyed the myth that wars of national liberation, substantially supported from the outside, will inevitably succeed. We provided neighboring nations an opportunity to put their houses in order, if they would — Indonesia's continuing freedom from communist influence is indicative of achievements in that arena. Peking and Moscow both have discovered that revolutionary wars under foreign control can run erratic courses that sometimes conflict with their interests, and that provisioning partisans can be a thankless task. Perhaps most important of all, the United States honored its commitments under great duress, despite the fearful price. That lesson, we hope, has not been lost on either our allies or our enemies.[29]

Strategic Failures

Unfortunately, our strategic debits far outweighed our credits. The pity is that most of our 46,000 dead, thousands of disfigured and disabled, billions of dollars "down the drain," and ruptured relations at home and abroad might have been avoided if we had formulated an effective strategy in 1955, when we took up the torch from France.

Failing that, we might still have kept our losses low if we had reviewed our national interests in Southeast Asia. Any claim to *vital* U.S. interests associated with survival

257

or economic well-being had been invalidated before this country committed combat forces in Vietnam, but our leaders, who lacked a systematic approach to strategic problem-solving, did not appreciate that fact. Once the first flush of excitement and spirit of adventure passed, such intangible interests as peace, democratic ideals, pride, and prestige became increasingly unsalable to the American public, which did not consider them worth the high cost in American lives. Therein lay the roots of domestic discord and the weakness of U.S. resolve.

Does that mean the United States should not have intervened in Vietnam?

Not necessarily. We still had *important* interests. But it was a clear indicator that the nature of U.S. commitments should have been more carefully considered and probable-cost-versus-prospective-gain ratios scrutinized more shrewdly at every step.

Once engaged in that treacherous conflict, we continued to pit a conventional strategy against an unconventional foe, and came off second best in every category, except body counts. An old military maxim advises "never reinforce a failure," but for fourteen years, most U.S. decision-makers, inexperienced in counterinsurgency matters, *did not know they were failing.* Many men in uniform still believe that firepower alone, if unfettered by artificial constraints, can "win" revolutionary wars. In truth, armed force cannot prevail unless complemented by calculated political, economic, social, and psychological campaigns.

Strategic Alternatives

Were there suitable strategic alternatives? Of course.

The bases for a sound doctrine and the ingredients for successful counterinsurgency operations by the United States and South Vietnam were present in 1955. At least some of our interests and those of the RVN seemed compelling at that time. They were not identical, but they were compatible. The only thing necessary was a common, sensible objective, with the emphasis on nation-building programs designed to eliminate or alleviate revolutionary causes. Remember, overt insurgent activities were virtually at a standstill then. Pacification was not yet a real problem. If, despite our best efforts, Diem refused to cooperate — an eventuality that was by no means preordained, since his interests were vital — we had enough fundamental information at hand and enough time to reevaluate our interests, objectives, policies, and strategies, reassess accompanying risks (using techniques displayed in this study), then modify methods or get out before costs exceeded gains.

If we had concentrated on emasculating the Viet Cong infrastructure and shoring up South Vietnamese interests in survival and independence during the period 1955 to 1959, the situation might well have been quite different by the time DRV troops marched south. With a less virulent Viet Cong movement to sustain and support them on "foreign" soil, those forces would have been hard pressed to survive. Armed counteroffensives, by the United States if necessary, would have enjoyed the moral blessings of free peoples around the world. Better yet, if North Vietnamese participation had not been part of a countrywide revolution, we would have stood a much better chance of defeating DRV divisions cost-effectively in semi-conventional combat, which is our forte. They would have been compelled to play a *U.S.* game in which *we* held the strategic initiative.

THE BIG PICTURE

Thus far, this case study has examined the Vietnam conflict as a regional phenomenon. To grasp its full meaning, we must place the American involvement in a global context.

The Principles of War are one convenient tool with which to evaluate strategic performance. Representative findings follow.

Purpose

The products of unprofitable U.S. strategies for Vietnam caused this great nation, temporarily at least, to lose its sense of purpose as the leader of the Free World.

Initiative

Reactionary U.S. strategies abdicated initiative to the enemy and posed for the American public the prospect of an endless war. The resultant weakening of our confidence and national will colors nearly every aspect of our foreign policy.

Flexibility

Arbitrary budgetary limitations, which took little cognizance of U.S. global commitments, destroyed the flexibility of our armed forces, except in Vietnam.

Concentration

Preoccupation with Vietnam caused U.S. leaders to lose perspective. Our national security priorities were so distorted that critical areas, such as Europe and the Middle East, were deprived of the concentrated energy and effort they deserved.

Economy

The horrendous financial burden brought about by misplaced military emphases in Vietnam caused this country to economize excessively on domestic programs, to our long-term detriment.

Maneuver

The United States was consistently outmaneuvered politically and psychologically in Paris, in the United Nations, and at home. Our freedom of action thus was sharply reduced, both domestically and internationally.

Surprise

Strategic surprise is always difficult to achieve in an open society. The interaction between senior U.S. officials and members of the mass media during the fracas in Vietnam developed unfortunate habit patterns, which magnify that problem.

Exploitation

The distressing experience in Vietnam, which sapped our urge to compete internationally, constrains administration efforts to exploit circumstances around the world which would gratify genuine U.S. national security interests.

Security

The decision to avoid censorship or other regulation of media reporting was deleterious to U.S. security. Unfavorably slanted news coverage constricted our courses of action, undermined the faith of allies, alienated the uncommitted, gave aid and comfort to our enemies, and helped unseat a President of the United States.

Simplicity

The Vietnam conflict never was explained to the American people in simple, straightforward terms that could be understood. Credibility gaps inevitably occurred, which had far-reaching foreign-policy implications.

Unity

Our strategic blunders in Vietnam divided this nation as have few other events in U.S. history. The public spectacle of our President, strong factions in Congress, and influential segments of society tugging in different directions gave heart to the enemy and caused friends to lose confidence.

Morale

Low morale on the U.S. home front, characterized by pacifist activities, strident dissent, mass-protest demonstrations, violence, and treasonable dealings with the enemy, degraded this country's credibility in the realm of international security affairs.

WRAP-UP

Vietnam serves as a tragic object lesson for future strategists. There *were* legitimate U.S. interests and aims. There *were* legitimate costs in lives and money. Unfortunately, the architects of our involvement never successfully matched costs with gains, not because they were indifferent, but because they lacked incisive instruments. Adhering to fundamentals might not have provided a panacea, but it would have made a more reasoned approach possible, without distorting national priorities.

To borrow a dictum from Clausewitz, applying the methodology presented in this case study may be simple, but not on that account very easy. Lieutenant General Richard G. Stilwell indicated as much when he reviewed the first draft of this chapter:

An inherent difficulty . . . in any strategic problem solving technique is the question of perceptions. Perceptions are subjective evaluations, usually arrived at with only limited available information, and are required to be translated into policy through the uncertain realm of domestic and international politics. Strategic programs, like other major policies in our society, are not the product of expert planners rationally determining the actions necessary to achieve desired goals. Rather, they are the product of controversy, negotiations, and bargaining among groups with different interests and outlooks. The process, with its many variables and uncertainties, I am afraid, is one that is not easily structured into a rational, disciplined process, nor susceptible to easy analysis with any assurance of acceptable reliability. *It is because of these very reasons and the importance of the subject area, however, that the process deserves careful study* [emphasis added].[30]

Not everyone agrees that we should heed fundamentals. Many concerned citizens feel that dispassionate strategists, who deal with such sterile abstractions as "interests," "objectives," "policies," and "principles," are wholly insensitive to the human suffering that issues from their calculated concepts. The world of strategy formulation, those critics contend, is spiritually, as well as geographically, worlds apart from the piles of decomposing corpses, mutilated survivors, disaster, and devastation that result from war.

That simply is not true.

Grand strategists who substitute sentiment for reason, or merely "muddle through," spill far more blood than they save in the long run. National interests, by definition, serve the needs and wants of people. Consciously considered objectives, policies, and strategies mark the only avenues to consistent success.

Our leaders understand that implicitly, but without some technique to trigger their reflexes, even the most professional sometimes lapse into bad habits. After one session of our National Security Council, so the story goes, cabinet officers scurried for their limousines. Kissinger tucked his huge notebook under his arm and strode down the hall. "Something nags at him," notes the narrator. "He mutters, half to himself, 'not one of us mentioned the national interest.' "[31]

APPENDIXES

I Strategic Terminology

ACCIDENTAL WAR — A war that occurs without deliberate design of competent national or international authorities.

ACTIVE DEFENSE — The use of armed forces to protect friendly assets. Means may include counteroffensives. *See also* Passive Defense

AEROSPACE — The earth's envelope of atmosphere and the space surrounding it, considered as a single realm for national security purposes.

AIM — *See* National Objectives and National Security Objectives

AIR SUPERIORITY — Dominance in the air to a degree that permits friendly land, sea, and air forces to operate at specific times and places without prohibitive interference by enemy air forces. *See also* Air Supremacy

AIR SUPREMACY — That degree of air superiority that permits friendly land, sea, and air forces to operate at will without effective interference by enemy air forces. *See also* Air Superiority

APPROACH — *See* Direct Approach and Indirect Approach

AREA DEFENSE — The protection of a geographic expanse, as opposed to particular points within that expanse. Area defense often is combined with point defenses. *See also* Point Defense

ARMS CONTROL — Explicit or implicit international agreements that govern the numbers, types, characteristics, deployment, and use of armed forces and armaments. *See also* Arms Limitation and Disarmament

ARMS LIMITATION — An agreement to prohibit quantitative or qualitative improvements in specific armaments or weapons systems. *See also* Arms Control and Strategic Arms Limitation Talks

ARMS RACE — Competition between two or more countries or coalitions of countries that result in the cumulative proliferation or accretion of weapons; an increase in the destructive power of weapons possessed by those parties; and/or the buildup of their armed forces, incited by convictions that

263

their national security objectives demand quantitative superiority, qualitative superiority, or both.

ASSUMPTION — A supposition concerning the current situation or future events, presumed to be true in the absence of positive proof to the contrary. Used for planning and decision-making purposes.

ASSURED DESTRUCTION — The ability to inflict unacceptable damage on a particular aggressor or combination of aggressors, even after absorbing a surprise first strike. Specifically, the capability upon which U.S. nuclear deterrence is predicated.

BARGAINING — *See* Strategic Bargaining

BLACKMAIL — *See* Nuclear Blackmail

BLACK PROPAGANDA — Information, ideas, doctrines, and/or special appeals whose source is deliberately misrepresented by the sponsor. *See also* Gray Propaganda, Propaganda, and White Propaganda

BUFFER STATE OR ZONE — A relatively weak country, combination of countries, or geographic expanse that physically separates two or more rival powers or coalitions. *See also* Demilitarized Zone

CAPABILITY — The ability of a country or coalition of countries to execute specific courses of action. Capabilities are conditioned by many variables, including enemy strengths, time, space, terrain, and weather. *See also* Intention

CATALYTIC WAR — War between two countries or coalitions of countries deliberately instigated by a third party.

CENTRAL WAR — A form of general nuclear war in which opposing great powers concentrate their attacks on each other's homeland. *See also* General War

CIVIL DEFENSE — Passive measures designed to minimize the effects of enemy action on all aspects of civil life, particularly population protection and emergency steps to repair or restore vital utilities and facilities.

CLANDESTINE (INTELLIGENCE, OPERATIONS) — Activities conducted surreptitiously, so that they are undiscovered by the opposition. *See also* Covert (Intelligence, Operations)

COALITION WAR — A conflict in which one or more sides comprise a group of allied nations banded together to attain or protect common national security objectives.

COLD WAR — A state of international tension at the lower end of the conflict spectrum, wherein political, economic, technological, sociological, psychological, paramilitary, and military measures short of sustained, armed combat are orchestrated to attain national objectives.

COLLATERAL CASUALTIES AND DAMAGE — Physical harm done to persons and property collocated with or adjacent to targets. Collateral effects may or may not be desirable, depending on circumstances.

COLLECTIVE SECURITY — Common actions by an association of two or more states to preserve the safety and well-being of the group.

COMBINED (FORCE, OPERATIONS, STAFF) — Organizations and efforts involving two or more allied countries. *See also* Joint (Force, Operations, Staff)

COMMAND AND CONTROL — An arrangement of facilities, equipment, personnel, and procedures used to acquire, process, and disseminate data needed by decision-makers to plan, direct, and control operations.

COMMITMENT — An obligation or pledge to carry out or support a given national policy. *See also* National Security Policies

CONFLICT SPECTRUM — A continuum of hostilities that ranges from subcrisis maneuvering in cold-war situations to the most violent form of general war.

CONTAINMENT — Measures to discourage or prevent the expansion of enemy territorial holdings and/or influence. Specifically, a U.S. policy directed against communist expansion.

CONTINGENCY PLANS AND OPERATIONS — Preparation for major events that can reasonably be anticipated and that probably would have a detrimental effect on national security; actions in case such events occur.

CONTROLLED COUNTERFORCE WAR — War in which one or both sides concentrate on reducing enemy strategic retaliatory forces in a bargaining situation, and take special precautions to minimize collateral casualties and damage. *See also* Controlled War

CONTROLLED WAR — A war waged in response to the continuous receipt and evaluation of information concerning changes in the situation, combined with the competence to adjust accordingly. *See also* Controlled Counterforce War

CONVENTIONAL (FORCES, WAR, WEAPONS) — Military organizations, hostilities, and hardware that exclude nuclear, chemical, and biological capabilities. *See also* Unconventional (Forces, War, Weapons)

CORE AREA — A continental, regional, or national cluster of geographic features, natural or man-made, of great strategic importance politically, economically, militarily, and/or culturally, the seizure, retention, destruction, or control of which would afford a marked advantage to one or more countries or coalitions of countries. *See also* Critical Terrain

COST EFFECTIVENESS — A condition that matches ends with means in ways that create maximum capabilities at minimum expense.

COUNTER CITY — *See* Countervalue

COUNTERFORCE — The concepts, plans, weapons, and actions used to destroy or neutralize selected military capabilities of an enemy. *See also* Countervalue

COUNTERINSURGENCY — Political, economic, social, psychological, military, and paramilitary concepts, plans, and actions used by a government to combat revolutionary war. *See also* Revolutionary War

COUNTERINTELLIGENCE — Activities designed to destroy the effectiveness of inimical foreign intelligence-collection programs and to protect a nation against subversion and sabotage. *See also* Intelligence and Subversion

COUNTERSUBVERSION — That aspect of counterintelligence designed to detect, destroy, neutralize, or otherwise prevent inimical individuals or groups from surreptitiously undermining the strength of a state. *See also* Counterintelligence and Subversion

COUNTERVALUE — The concepts, plans, weapons, and actions used to destroy or neutralize selected enemy population centers, industries, resources, and/or institutions. *See also* Counterforce

COVERT (INTELLIGENCE, OPERATIONS) — Activities conducted so that the opposition is unable to identify the sponsor. *See also* Clandestine (Intelligence, Operations)

CREDIBILITY — Clear evidence that capabilities and national will are sufficient to support purported policies.

CRISIS MANAGEMENT — Emergency actions taken by national leaders to control and/or terminate activities, foreign and domestic, which they believe jeopardize or seriously impinge upon important national interests.

CRITICAL TERRAIN — A single geographic feature, natural or man-made, of great strategic importance, the seizure, retention, destruction, or control of which would afford a marked advantage to one or more countries or coalitions of countries. *See also* Core Area

CUMULATIVE STRATEGY — A collection of individual, random actions that are unrelated but, in sum, eventually create crushing results. *See also* Sequential Strategy

DAMAGE LIMITATION — Active and/or passive efforts to restrict the level or areal extent of devastation during war. Includes counterforce operations of all kinds, as well as civil defense. *See also* Civil Defense and Counterforce

D-DAY — The day on which hostilities are scheduled to commence. *See also* M-Day

DEFEAT — Failure to attain stated national security objectives as a result of enemy intervention, or to protect national security interests successfully in the face of enemy action. *See also* Pyrrhic Victory and Victory

DEFENSE — Measures taken by a country or coalition of countries to resist political, military, economic, social, psychological, and/or technological attacks. Defensive capabilities reinforce deterrence, and vice versa. *See also* Active Defense, Area Defense, Civil Defense, Internal Defense, Passive Defense, and Point Defense; Deterrence; and Offense

DEFENSE IN DEPTH — Protective measures in successive positions along the axis of enemy advance, as opposed to a single line of resistance. Designed to absorb and progressively weaken enemy penetrations in preparation for counter operations. *See also* Forward Defense

DEMILITARIZED ZONE — An area in which military forces and installations of all kinds are prohibited by international agreement. *See also* Buffer State or Zone

DESTABILIZING — *See* Stability

DETENTE — Lessening of tensions in international relations. May be achieved formally or informally.

DETERRENCE — Measures to prevent, rather than prosecute, wars, using psychological, as opposed to physical, means. Deterrent capabilities reinforce defense, and vice versa. *See also* Defense, Extended Deterrence, Finite Deterrence, Graduated Deterrence, Independent Deterrence, Intrawar Deterrence, Maximum Deterrence, Minimum Deterrence, Mutual Deterrence, Type I Deterrence, Type II Deterrence, Type III Deterrence, and War-Fighting

DIRECT APPROACH — Any grand strategy in which the use of force predominates; any military strategy that depends primarily on physical pressure, as opposed to deterrence, surprise, or maneuver. *See also* Indirect Approach

DISARMAMENT — The reduction of armed forces and/or armaments as a result of unilateral initiatives or international agreement. *See also* Arms Control

DOCTRINE — Fundamental precepts that guide actions in support of national policy. It is authoritative, but requires judgment in application.

DOMESTIC INTELLIGENCE — Evaluated, interpreted data related to indigenous conditions and activities that threaten the internal security of a state. *See also* Intelligence

ECONOMIC POTENTIAL FOR WAR — The share of a country's total economic capacity that could be used to assist in waging war.

ECONOMIC WARFARE — The offensive or defensive use of trade, foreign-aid programs, financial transactions, and other matters that influence the production, distribution, and consumption of goods/services. Seeks to achieve national security objectives by augmenting friendly capabilities and diminishing or neutralizing enemy capabilities and potential. *See also* Sanctions

ENDS — *See* National Objectives and National Security Objectives

ESCALATION — An increase in the scope or intensity of a conflict. The increase may be deliberate or unpremeditated. *See also* Escalation Ladder

ESCALATION LADDER — Successive levels of intensity in the conflict spectrum. *See also* Conflict Spectrum and Escalation

ESTIMATE — An analysis of a situation or trend that identifies principal considerations, interprets them in light of national security objectives, appraises courses of action that might be taken in response, and recommends which course decision-makers should adopt.

EXEMPLARY ATTACK — The isolated engagement of a military target, civilian property, or a population center, designed primarily for psychological effect. It demonstrates a capability. The atomic attacks on Hiroshima and Nagasaki were exemplary. *See also* Symbolic Attack

EXTENDED DETERRENCE — The deterrent power of a country or coalition of countries projected to protect allies, neutrals, or its own forces on foreign soil. *See also* Deterrence

FINITE DETERRENCE — Deterrent power predicated on objective capabilities sufficient to satisfy precisely calculable needs under any conceivable circumstances. *See also* Deterrence, Maximum Deterrence, and Minimum Deterrence

FIREBREAK — A psychological barrier that inhibits escalation from one type of warfare to another, as from conventional to nuclear combat. *See also* Threshold

FIRST STRIKE — The initial offensive move of a war. When applied to general war, it implies the ability to eliminate effective retaliation. *See also* First Use and Second Strike

FIRST USE — The initial employment of specific powers during the conduct of a war. A belligerent could execute a second strike in response to aggression, yet be the first to employ nuclear weapons. *See also* First Strike

FLEXIBLE RESPONSE — A strategy predicated on capabilities to act effectively across the entire spectrum of war at times, places, and in manners of the user's choosing. *See also* Graduated Response

FORCE — The use of physical coercion to attain national security objectives. *See also* Violence

FOREIGN MILITARY SALES — Military assistance, including goods and services (such as training), which is purchased by the recipient country. *See also* Grant Aid and Military Assistance

FORWARD BASING — The peacetime deployment of military forces into foreign areas that are, or are contiguous to, actual or potential trouble spots.

FORWARD DEFENSE — Protective measures taken to contain and/or repulse military aggression as close to the original line of contact as possible. *See also* Defense in Depth

GENERAL AND COMPLETE DISARMAMENT — An extreme form of arms control that would reduce armed forces and armaments to levels sufficient simply for domestic security. *See also* Arms Control

GENERAL-PURPOSE FORCES — All combat forces not designed to accomplish strategic offensive or defensive missions, including command organizations, organic logistic elements, and related support units that are deployed or deployable as constituent parts of military or naval forces and field organizations. Examples are ground force maneuver elements; cruisers and destroyers; logistic commands; and reconnaissance aircraft. Some general-purpose forces may perform strategic functions — attack carriers and tactical aircraft that can deliver nuclear weapons are illustrative.

GENERAL WAR — Widespread armed conflict between major powers in which the national survival of one or more belligerents is in jeopardy. The term commonly connotes a global showdown between the United States and the Soviet Union, featuring strategic nuclear weapons and/or other mass-casualty producers. *See also* Central War, Spasm War, and Total War

GOALS — *See* National Objectives and National Security Objectives

GRADUATED DETERRENCE — A range of deterrent power that affords credible capabilities to inhibit aggression across all, or a considerable portion, of the conflict spectrum. *See also* Deterrence

GRADUATED RESPONSE — The incremental application of national power in ways that allow the opposition to accommodate one step at a time. Sometimes called "piecemealing." *See also* Flexible Response

GRAND STRATEGY — The art and science of employing national power under all circumstances to exert desired types and degrees of control over the opposition by applying force, the threat of force, indirect pressures, diplomacy, subterfuge, and other imaginative means to attain national security objectives. *See also* National Strategy

GRANT AID — Military assistance, including goods and services (such as training), for which the donor receives no reimbursement. *See also* Foreign Military Sales and Military Assistance

GRAY PROPAGANDA — Information, ideas, doctrines, and/or special appeals whose source is unidentified by the sponsor. *See also* Black Propaganda, Propaganda, and White Propaganda

GUERRILLA WARFARE — Military and paramilitary operations conducted in enemy-held or otherwise hostile territory by irregular, predominantly indigenous forces. May be conducted in conjunction with conventional military operations, or as an aspect of revolutionary war.

HARD TARGET — A target protected against the blast, heat, and radiation produced by nuclear explosions. The most effective hardening also shields against chemical and biological attacks. *See also* Soft Target and Target

HIGH THRESHOLD — An intangible line between levels and types of conflict across which one or more antagonists plan to escalate with great reluctance after other courses of action fail, or which they could be compelled to cross only if subjected to immense pressures. *See also* Low Threshold and Threshold

INCIDENT — A brief clash or other military disturbance involving minor forces.

INDEPENDENT DETERRENCE — Deterrent power under the sovereign control of a country.

INDIRECT APPROACH — Any grand strategy that emphasizes political, economic, social, and psychological pressures instead of force; any military strategy that seeks to throw the enemy off balance before engaging his main forces. *See also* Direct Approach

INFORMATION — Unprocessed data, regardless of type or derivation, that can be converted into intelligence. *See also* Intelligence

INFRASTRUCTURE — Organizations, fabrications, facilities, and installations that control and support military, paramilitary, and/or subversive activities.

INSPECTION — Periodic, on-the-spot verification procedures to determine compliance with arms-control agreements. *See also* Surveillance and Verification

INSURANCE — The prudential embellishment of capabilities as a hedge against such imponderables as inaccurate estimates of the situation, technological surprise, and unforeseen policy changes.

INSURGENCY — *See* Revolutionary War

INTELLIGENCE — Products resulting from the collection, evaluation, analysis, integration, and interpretation of information. *See also* Clandestine Intelligence, Counterintelligence, Covert Intelligence, Domestic Intelligence, Information, and Strategic Intelligence

INTENTION — An aim or design to carry out a specific course or action. *See also* Capability

INTEREST — *See* National Interests and National Security Interests

INTERNAL DEFENSE — The full range of measures taken by a government and its allies to safeguard its society from revolutionary activities. *See also* Internal Security

INTERNAL SECURITY — The state of law and order prevailing within a country. *See also* Internal Defense

INTRAWAR DETERRENCE — Deterrent power exercised during the conduct of a war to inhibit escalation by the enemy and/or to limit damage. *See also* Deterrence

JOINT (FORCE, OPERATIONS, STAFF) — Organizations and efforts involving two or more military services of the same country. *See also* Combined (Force, Operations, Staff)

JUST WAR — In the classic sense, conflict conducted by competent authorities with irreproachable motives to defend rights, rectify wrongs, and/or punish transgressors. Just War today connotes actions by a state to defend its own territory or the sovereignty of other nations beset by aggressors.

KEY TERRAIN — *See* Critical Terrain

LAUNCH-ON-WARNING — Retaliatory strikes, particularly those involving aircraft and ballistic missiles, triggered upon notification that an enemy attack is in progress, but before hostile forces or ordnance violate friendly soil.

LIMITED STRATEGIC WAR — A form of general war in which one or more belligerents exercise voluntary restraints to restrict casualties and/or damage. *See also* General War and Limited War

LIMITED WAR — Armed encounters, exclusive of incidents, in which one or more major powers or their proxies voluntarily exercise various types and degrees of restraint to prevent unmanageable escalation. *See also* Escalation, Incident, Limited Strategic War, and Proxy War

LINES OF COMMUNICATION — Land, sea, and aerospace routes essential to the conduct of international security affairs, particularly the deployment of armed forces and associated logistic support.

LOCAL WAR — *See* Regional War

LOGISTICS — Plans and operations associated with the design, development, acquisition, storage, movement, distribution, maintenance, evacuation, and disposition of materiel; the movement, evacuation, and hospitalization of personnel; the acquisition or construction, maintenance, operation, and disposition of facilities; and the acquisition or furnishing of services.

LOW THRESHOLD — An intangible line between levels and types of conflict across which one or more antagonists plan to escalate with scant regret, or which they would be compelled to cross quickly if subjected to pressures. *See also* High Threshold and Threshold

MASS-DESTRUCTION (WAR, WEAPONS) — Conflict and instruments of conflict capable of creating casualties and devastation indiscriminately on a colossal scale; particularly, chemical, biological, and nuclear weapons and warfare. *See also* Nuclear Delivery System, Nuclear Weapon, and Strategic Weapons System

MASSIVE RETALIATION — The act of countering aggression of any type with tremendous destructive power; particularly a crushing nuclear response to any provocation deemed serious enough to warrant military action.

MAXIMUM DETERRENCE — Diversified, survivable deterrent power of such quality and magnitude that it affords optimum capabilities to inhibit aggression across the entire conflict spectrum. *See also* Deterrence, Finite Deterrence, and Minimum Deterrence

M-DAY — The day on which mobilization is to begin. *See also* D-Day

MILITARY ASSISTANCE — Aid extended from a country to the armed forces of another country, including goods and services furnished as grant aid or military sales. *See also* Foreign Military Sales and Grant Aid

MILITARY ASSISTANCE SALES — *See* Foreign Military Sales

MILITARY STRATEGY — The art and science of employing military power under all circumstances to attain national security objectives by applying force or the threat of force.

MINIMUM DETERRENCE — Deterrent power predicated on the belief that countries possessing even a few nuclear weapons are automatically guaranteed immunity from rational attack, since the penalty for aggression presumably would be intolerable. *See also* Deterrence, Finite Deterrence, and Maximum Deterrence

MOBILIZATION — The act of preparing for war or other emergencies by assembling and organizing raw materials; focusing industrial efforts on national security objectives; marshalling and readying Reserve and National Guard units and individuals for active military service; and/or activating and readying new military organizations filled with personnel inducted from civilian life. *See also* Mobilization Base

MOBILIZATION BASE — The total manpower, materiel, and service resources which a country can make available to satisfy foreseeable military and civilian wartime requirements, together with the plans and programs needed to put those assets to effective use. *See also* Mobilization

MUTUAL AND BALANCED FORCE REDUCTION — A form of arms control in which opposing powers concurrently reduce the capabilities of their over-all military establishments or selected elements thereof. Personnel strengths and numbers or types of weapons are the most common considerations.

MUTUAL DETERRENCE — A stable situation in which two or more countries or coalitions of countries are inhibited from attacking each other because the casualties and/or damage resulting from retaliation would be unacceptable. *See also* Deterrence

NATIONAL COMMAND AUTHORITIES — The top national security decision-makers of a country. In the United States, those decision-makers are the President, the Secretary of Defense, and their duly deputized alternates or successors.

NATIONAL INTERESTS — A highly generalized concept of elements that constitute a state's compelling needs, including self-preservation, independence, national integrity, military security, and economic well-being.

NATIONAL OBJECTIVES — The fundamental aims, goals, or purposes of a nation toward which policies are directed and energies are applied. These may be short-, mid-, or long-range in nature.

NATIONAL POLICIES — Broad courses of action or statements of guidance adopted by a government in pursuit of national objectives.

NATIONAL POWER — The sum total of any nation's capabilities or potential derived from available political, economic, military, geographic, social, scientific, and technological resources. Leadership and national will are the unifying factors.

NATIONAL SECURITY — The protection of a nation from all types of external aggression, espionage, hostile reconnaissance, sabotage, subversion, annoyance, and other inimical influences. *See also* National Security Interests, National Security Objectives, and National Security Policies

NATIONAL SECURITY INTERESTS — Those national interests primarily concerned with preserving a state from harm. *See also* National Interests and National Security

NATIONAL SECURITY OBJECTIVES — Those national objectives primarily concerned with shielding national interests from threats, both foreign and domestic. *See also* National Objectives and National Security

NATIONAL SECURITY POLICIES — Those national policies which provide guidance primarily for attaining national security objectives. *See also* National Policies and National Security

NATIONAL STRATEGY — The art and science of employing national power under all circumstances, during peace and war, to attain national objectives. *See also* Grand Strategy

NATIONAL WILL — The temper and morale of the people, as they influence a nation's ability to satisfy national security interests and/or attain national security objectives.

Nth COUNTRY — A nonnuclear country that could develop or acquire nuclear capabilities if it so desired. Used in context with nuclear proliferation.

NUCLEAR BLACKMAIL — An attempt to extract political, economic, territorial, or other concessions from a country or coalition of countries by threatening nuclear war.

NUCLEAR CLUB — A slang term referring to countries that have developed their own nuclear capability.

NUCLEAR DELIVERY SYSTEM — A nuclear weapon, together with its means of propulsion (aircraft, artillery, missile) and associated equipment. *See also* Nuclear Weapon

NUCLEAR-FREE ZONE — A geographic area where nuclear weapons are prohibited by international agreement.

NUCLEAR NONPROLIFERATION — Arms control measures designed to prevent the acquisition of nuclear weapons and delivery means by nations that do not have a nuclear capability. *See also* Nuclear Proliferation

NUCLEAR PROLIFERATION — The process by which one country after another comes into possession of nuclear delivery systems or attains the right to determine the use of nuclear weapons possessed by another power. *See also* Nuclear Nonproliferation

NUCLEAR STABILITY — *See* Stability

NUCLEAR WAR — Conflict in which one or more strategic or tactical nuclear weapons are detonated for exemplary, symbolic, or combative purposes.

NUCLEAR WEAPON — A bomb, artillery shell, missile warhead, or other deliverable ordnance item (as opposed to an experimental device) that explodes as a result of energy released by reactions from the fission, fusion, or both of atomic nuclei. The term excludes delivery means whenever such equipment is separable from the explosive projectile. *See also* Nuclear Delivery System

NUCLEAR YIELD — The energy released by the detonation of a nuclear weapon, measured in equivalent kilotons or megatons of TNT. *See also* Nuclear Weapon

OBJECT — *See* National Objectives and National Security Objectives

OBJECTIVE — *See* National Objectives and National Security Objectives

OFFENSE — Positive measures taken by a country or coalition of countries to exercise, retain, or seize the initiative by attacking the foe politically, militarily, economically, socially, psychologically, and/or technologically. *See also* Defense

OVERKILL — Destructive capabilities in excess of those which logically should be adequate to destroy specified targets and/or attain specific security objectives.

PARITY — A condition in which opposing forces possess capabilities of certain kinds that are approximately equal in over-all effectiveness. *See also* Sufficiency and Superiority

PASSIVE DEFENSE — All measures, other than the application of armed force, taken to minimize the effects of hostile action. These include the use of cover, concealment, dispersion, protective construction, mobility, and subterfuge. *See also* Active Defense and Civil Defense

PEACE — A condition characterized by the absence of hostile activities and/or intent in the relations between two or more sovereign states. *See also* War

PEOPLE'S WAR — A term used primarily by Communist China and its disciples to connote revolutionary war. *See also* Revolutionary War and War of National Liberation

PERIPHERAL WAR — *See* Limited War

PIECEMEALING — *See* Graduated Response

PLANS — *See* Strategic Plans

POINT DEFENSE — The protection of particular positions, as opposed to geographic expanses. Cities and military installations are representative points in the strategic context. Point defenses often are combined with area defense. *See also* Area Defense

POLICY — *See* National Policies and National Security Policies

POLITICAL WARFARE — The offensive or defensive use of diplomacy, negotiations, and other tools of international relations to achieve national security objectives by augmenting friendly capabilities and diminishing or neutralizing enemy capabilities and potential.

POSTURE — The combined strategic intentions, capabilities, and vulnerabilities of a country or coalition of countries, including the strength, disposition, and readiness of its armed forces.

POWER — *See* National Power

PREEMPTIVE WAR — A war initiated on the basis of incontrovertible evidence that an enemy attack is imminent. *See also* Preventive War

275

PREVENTIVE WAR — A war initiated in the belief that armed conflict, while not imminent, is inevitable, and that to delay would involve greater risk. *See also* Preemptive War

PRINCIPLE — A governing law of national conduct; an opinion, attitude, or belief that exercises a directing influence on the life style of a nation.

PRINCIPLES OF WAR — A collection of abstract considerations that have been distilled from historical experience and which, applied to specific circumstances with acumen, assist strategists in selecting suitable courses of action.

PRODUCTION BASE — The total industrial capacity that a country can make available to satisfy foreseeable military and civilian wartime requirements, together with the plans and programs needed to put those assets to effective use.

PROLIFERATION — *See* Nuclear Proliferation and Nuclear Nonproliferation

PROPAGANDA — Any form of communication designed to influence the opinions, emotions, attitudes, or behavior of any group, thereby supporting the sponsor's national security objectives. *See also* Black Propaganda, Gray Propaganda, White Propaganda, and Psychological Warfare

PROXY WAR — A form of limited war in which great powers avoid a direct military confrontation by furthering their national security interests and objectives through conflict between representatives or associates. *See also* Limited War

PSYCHOLOGICAL WARFARE — The planned use of propaganda and related tools to influence enemy thought patterns in ways that further national security objectives. *See also* Propaganda

PURPOSE — *See* National Objectives and National Security Objectives

PYRRHIC VICTORY — The attainment of national security objectives despite enemy intervention, but at costs so high in proportion to gains that national interests suffer. *See also* Defeat and Victory

REGIONAL WAR — War of any intensity, conducted by any means, that is confined to a geographically restricted theater. Regional conflicts are a means of limiting war if one or more belligerents deliberately avoid expanding the arena. *See also* Limited War

REQUIREMENT — An established need that justifies the timely allocation of national resources to attain prescribed national security objectives.

RESERVE — *See* Strategic Reserve

REVOLUTIONARY WAR — Efforts to seize political power by illegitimate and coercive means, destroying existing systems of government and social structures in the process. *See also* Counterinsurgency, Guerrilla Warfare, Insurgency, People's War, and War of National Liberation

RISK — The danger of disadvantage, defeat, or destruction that results from a gap between ends and means.

SANCTIONS — An economic warfare tool, usually adopted by several states acting in concert, to compel a country or coalition of countries to cease undesirable practices or otherwise bow to the wielder's will. *See also* Economic Warfare

SANCTUARY — A nation or area contiguous to or near a combat zone which by tacit agreement between belligerents is exempt from armed attack, and therefore is used with impunity by a country or coalition of countries for staging military forces, logistics, and/or other purposes.

SEA CONTROL — The employment of naval forces, supplemented by land and aerospace forces as appropriate, to destroy enemy naval forces, suppress enemy oceangoing commerce, protect vital shipping lanes, and establish local superiority in areas of naval operations. *See also* Sea Superiority and Sea Supremacy

SEA SUPERIORITY — Dominance on the high seas to a degree that permits friendly land, aerospace, and naval forces to operate at specific times and places on, over, or adjacent to the high seas without prohibitive interference by enemy naval elements. *See also* Sea Control and Sea Supremacy

SEA SUPREMACY — That degree of sea superiority that permits friendly land, aerospace, and naval forces to operate at will on, over, or adjacent to the high seas without effective interference by enemy naval elements. *See also* Sea Control and Sea Superiority

SECOND STRIKE — The first counteroffensive move of a war. When applied to general war, the term implies the ability to survive a surprise first strike and retaliate effectively. *See also* First Strike and First Use

SECURITY — *See* National Security

SEQUENTIAL STRATEGY — A series of discrete, interrelated steps that are carefully planned and appraised in terms of anticipated results. If any stage is materially altered for any reason, subsequent plans and actions usually must be reshaped. *See also* Cumulative Strategy

SHOW OF FORCE — The purposeful exhibition of armed might before an enemy or potential enemy, usually in a crisis situation, to reinforce deterrent demands. *See also* Symbolic Attack

SIGNAL — *See* Strategic Signal

SOFT TARGET — A target not protected against blast, heat, and/or radiation produced by nuclear explosions. *See also* Hard Target and Target

SPASM WAR — A brief, cataclysmic conflict in which all available destructive power is employed with scant regard for the consequences. If super powers are involved, spasmic combat is a form of general war. *See also* General War

SPECIFIED COMMAND — A top-echelon U.S. combatant organization with regional or functional responsibilities, which normally is composed of forces from one military service. It has a broad, continuing mission and is established by the President, through the Secretary of Defense, with the advice and assistance of the Joint Chiefs of Staff. *See also* Unified Command

SPECTRUM OF WAR — *See* Conflict Spectrum

STABILITY — A state of strategic equilibrium or stalemate that encourages restraint and prudence by opponents. Stability is a prime goal of deterrence. *See also* Deterrence

STRATEGIC AIR WAR — Aerospace operations directed against the enemy's war-making capacity. Typical targets include industry, stockpiles of raw materials and finished products, power systems, transportation and communication centers, and strategic weapons systems.

STRATEGIC AREA — *See* Core Area

STRATEGIC ARMS LIMITATION TALKS — Negotiations between the United States and the Soviet Union to curtail the expansion of, and if possible reduce, strategic offensive and defensive weapons systems of both countries in an equitable fashion. *See also* Arms Control, Arms Limitation, and Strategic Weapons System

STRATEGIC BARGAINING — Diplomacy, often accompanied by armed actions, in search of compromise solutions to strategic problems.

STRATEGIC CENTER OF GRAVITY — The point of decision. It may be tangible, like a geographic feature, or intangible, like national morale.

STRATEGIC DEFENSE — The strategy and forces designed primarily to protect a nation, its outposts and/or allies from the hazards of general war. It features defense against missiles, both land- and sea-launched, and long-range bombers. *See also* Strategic Offense

STRATEGIC INTELLIGENCE — Evaluated, integrated, interpreted information required for the development of national security objectives, policies, strategies, and plans. *See also* Information and Intelligence

STRATEGIC MOBILITY — The ability to shift personnel, equipment, and supplies effectively and expeditiously between theaters of operation.

STRATEGIC OFFENSE — The strategy and forces designed primarily to destroy the enemy's war-making capacity during general war or to so degrade it that the opposition collapses. *See also* Strategic Defense and Strategic Retaliatory (Concepts and Forces)

STRATEGIC PLANS — *Short-Range Plans* cover a period two years into the future. *Mid-Range Plans* cover a period from 3–10 years in the future. *Long-Range Plans* cover a period from 11–20 years in the future.

STRATEGIC RESERVE — Uncommitted forces of a country or coalition of countries which are intended to support national security interests and objectives, as required.

STRATEGIC RETALIATORY (CONCEPTS AND FORCES) — Second-strike strategies and forces designed primarily to destroy the enemy's war-making capacity during general war or to so degrade it that the opposition collapses. *See also* Strategic Defense and Strategic Offense

STRATEGIC SIGNAL — An act, attitude, or communication that conveys threats or promises intended to influence enemy decisions.

STRATEGIC WARNING — Notification that enemy offensive operations of any kind may be imminent. The alert may be received minutes, hours, days, or longer before hostilities commence. *See also* Tactical Warning

STRATEGIC WEAPONS SYSTEM — An offensive or defensive projectile, its means of delivery, and ancillary equipment designed primarily for general-war purposes. *See also* Mass Destruction (War, Weapons), Nuclear Delivery System, and Nuclear Weapon

STRATEGY — *See* Cumulative Strategy, Grand Strategy, Military Strategy, National Strategy, and Sequential Strategy

SUBVERSION — Action designed to undermine the strength of a regime by insidious means. *See also* Countersubversion

SUFFICIENCY — Capabilities adequate to attain national security objectives without waste. It demands quantitative and/or qualitative superiority under some circumstances; parity suffices under less demanding conditions; and inferiority sometimes is acceptable. *See also* Parity and Superiority

SUPERIORITY — A condition wherein one country or coalition of countries possesses markedly greater capabilities of certain kinds than the opposition. *See also* Parity and Sufficiency

SURVEILLANCE — Periodic or continuous verification procedures, accomplished from a distance (as by reconnaissance satellite), to determine compliance with arms-control agreements. *See also* Inspection and Verification

SURVIVABILITY — The ability of armed forces and civilian communities to withstand attack and still function effectively. It is derived mainly from active and passive defenses. *See also* Active Defense, Civil Defense, and Passive Defense

SYMBOLIC ATTACK — A specialized form of exemplary attack that deliberately avoids casualties or damage, but nevertheless communicates a message to the enemy. A display of nuclear fire power near a great city, but just outside the radius of destruction, would serve symbolic purposes. *See also* Exemplary Attack and Show of Force

SYSTEMS ANALYSIS — An interdisciplinary technique used by strategic planners. It isolates and examines relevant facts, logical propositions, and assumptions in ways that highlight alternatives, so that decision-makers can apply judgment sagaciously, and relationships between ends and means can be optimized.

TACTICS — The detailed methods used to carry out strategic designs. Military tactics involve the employment of units in combat, including the arrangement and maneuvering of units in relation to each other and/or to the enemy. *See also* Grand Strategy, Military Strategy, and National Strategy

TACTICAL WARNING — Notification that enemy offensive operations of any kind are in progress. The alert may be received at any time from the moment the attack is launched until its effect is felt. *See also* Strategic Warning

TALIONIC ATTACK — A "tit-for-tat" exchange. The punishment inflicted by defenders corresponds in kind and degree to the injuries they received, as "an eye for an eye."

TARGET — A specific entity, either animate or inanimate, to be damaged, destroyed, seized, or controlled by operations on political, military, economic, or psychological planes. *See also* Hard Target, Soft Target, and Target Acquisition

TARGET ACQUISITION — The detection, identification, characteristics, and location of a target, determined in such detail that it can be attacked dexterously. *See also* Target

TECHNOLOGICAL WARFARE — The offensive and defensive use of research and development, particularly that related to military matters, to attain national security objectives by augmenting friendly capabilities and diminishing or neutralizing enemy capabilities and potential.

THREAT — The capabilities, intentions, and actions of actual or potential enemies to prevent or interfere with the successful fulfillment of national security interests and/or objectives.

THRESHOLD — An intangible and adjustable line between levels and types of conflict, such as the separation between nuclear and nonnuclear warfare. *See also* Firebreak, High Threshold, and Low Threshold

TOTAL WAR — Conflict in which the political, military, economic, and psychological resources of at least one belligerent are fully engaged, and the survival of one or more belligerents is at stake. Revolutionary war is invariably a form of total war. A spasm nuclear war, terminated before all resources could be employed, technically would not qualify. *See also* General War, Revolutionary War, Spasm War

TRIAD — The tripartite U.S. strategic retaliatory force, which comprises manned bombers, intercontinental ballistic missiles, and ballistic-missile submarines.

TRIPWIRE — A largely symbolic force positioned on an ally's soil to advertise the owner's commitment to a particular country or coalition of countries. Attacks against the token contingent would trigger a massive response.

TYPE I DETERRENCE — Deterrent power that inhibits direct attacks against the wielder's homeland. *See also* Deterrence

TYPE II DETERRENCE — Deterrent power that inhibits serious infractions, short of attacks against the wielder's homeland, such as aggression against friends or allies. *See also* Deterrence

TYPE III DETERRENCE — Deterrent power that inhibits aggressive adventurism by making limited provocations appear unprofitable. *See also* Deterrence

UNCONVENTIONAL (FORCES, WAR, WEAPONS) — The three interrelated fields of guerrilla warfare, evasion and escape, and subversion conducted within enemy or enemy-controlled territory by predominantly indigenous personnel, who may be supported and/or directed by outsiders. *See also* Conventional (Forces, War, Weapons)

UNIFIED COMMAND — A top-echelon U.S. combatant organization with regional or functional responsibilities, which normally is composed of forces from two or more military services. It has a broad, continuing mission and is established by the President, through the Secretary of Defense, with the advice and assistance of the Joint Chiefs of Staff. When authorized by the JCS, commanders of unified commands established by the President may form one or more subordinate unified command within their jurisdictions. *See also* Specified Command

UNLIMITED WAR — *See* Total War

VERIFICATION — Inspection and/or surveillance measures to determine compliance with arms-control agreements. *See also* Inspection and Surveillance

VICTORY — The attainment of national security objectives despite enemy intervention, without suffering political, military, economic, social, or psychological damage to national interests. *See also* Defeat and Pyrrhic Victory

281

VIOLENCE — The infliction of pain for punishment, coercive, bargaining, or signalling purposes. Actions need have no direct relationship to national security objectives. *See also* Force

VITAL — Connotes the involvement of national survival, including assets that make survival meaningful.

VULNERABILITY — The susceptibility of a nation to any action by any means that would diminish its capabilities and/or will to ensure national security.

WAR — A condition characterized by hostile activities and/or intent in the relations between two or more sovereign states. *See also* Accidental War, Catalytic War, Central War, Coalition War, Cold War, Conflict Spectrum, Controlled War, Controlled Counterforce War, Conventional War, Economic Warfare, General War, Guerrilla Warfare, Just War, Limited War, Limited Strategic War, Mass-Destruction War, Nuclear War, People's War, Political Warfare, Preemptive War, Preventive War, Proxy War, Psychological Warfare, Regional War, Revolutionary War, Spasm War, Strategic Air War, Technological Warfare, Total War, Unconventional War, and War of National Liberation

WAR-FIGHTING — Actions to prosecute, rather than prevent, conflicts. *See also* Deterrence

WAR OF NATIONAL LIBERATION — A term used primarily by the Soviet Union and its disciples to connote revolutionary war. *See also* People's War and Revolutionary War

WHITE PROPAGANDA — Information, ideas, doctrines, and/or special appeals whose source is acknowledged by the sponsor. *See also* Black Propaganda, Gray Propaganda, and Propaganda

WILL — *See* National Will

YIELD — *See* Nuclear Yield

II Specialized Abbreviations

AAA	Antiaircraft Artillery
AABNCP	Advanced Airborne Command Post
ABM	Antiballistic Missile
ACDA	Arms Control and Disarmament Agency
AEC	Atomic Energy Commission
AFB	Air Force Base
ALCOM	Alaskan Command
ANMCC	Alternate National Military Command Center
ARVN	Army of Vietnam
ASW	Antisubmarine Warfare
AWACS	Airborne Warning and Control System
BMEWS	Ballistic Missile Early Warning System
BNSP	Basic National Security Policy
CD	Civil Defense
CENTO	Central Treaty Organization
CF	Counterforce
CHICOM	Chinese Communist
CI	Counterintelligence
CIA	Central Intelligence Agency
CINCAL	Commander-in-Chief, Alaska Command
CINCCONAD	Commander-in-Chief, Continental Air Defense Command
CINCEUR	Commander-in-Chief, Europe
CINCLANT	Commander-in-Chief, Atlantic Command
CINCNORAD	Commander-in-Chief, North American Air Defense Command
CINCPAC	Commander-in-Chief, Pacific Command
CINCSAC	Commander-in-Chief, Strategic Air Command
CINCSO	Commander-in-Chief, Southern Command
COMUSMACV	Commander, United States Military Assistance Command, Vietnam
COMZ	Communications Zone
CONAD	Continental Air Defense Command

CONUS	Continental United States
CORDS	Civil Operations and Revolutionary Development Support
CV	Countervalue
DCA	Defense Communications Agency
DEW Line	Distant Early Warning Line
DMZ	Demilitarized Zone
DOD	Department of Defense
DPRC	Defense Program Review Committee
DSA	Defense Supply Agency
DSTP	Director, Strategic Target Planning
EUCOM	European Command
FIDP	Foreign Internal Defense Policy
FOBS	Fractional Orbit Bombardment System
FYDP	Five-Year Defense Program
GCD	General and Complete Disarmament
ICBM	Intercontinental Ballistic Missile
IRBM	Intermediate-Range Ballistic Missile
JCS	Joint Chiefs of Staff
JSTPS	Joint Strategic Target Planning Staff
KT	Kiloton
LANTCOM	Atlantic Command
LOC	Lines of Communication
MAC	Military Airlift Command
MAP	Military Assistance Program
MAR	Multi-Function Array Radar
MBFR	Mutual and Balanced Force Reduction
MBT	Main Battle Tank
MIRV	Multiple Independently Targeted Reentry Vehicle
MLF	Multilateral Force
MRBM	Medium-Range Ballistic Missile
MSC	Military Sealift Command
MSR	Missile Site Radar; Main Supply Route
MT	Megaton
NATO	North Atlantic Treaty Organization
NCA	National Command Authorities
NEACP	National Emergency Airborne Command Post
NMCC	National Military Command Center
NMCS	National Military Command System
NORAD	North American Air Defense Command
NPT	Non-Proliferation Treaty
NSA	National Security Agency
NSC	National Security Council
Nuke	Nuclear Weapon
OEP	Office of Emergency Preparedness
OSD	Office of the Secretary of Defense

OTH	Over-the-Horizon Radar
PACOM	Pacific Command
PAR	Perimeter Acquisition Radar
PLA	People's Liberation Army (Red China)
POL	Petrol, Oil, and Lubricants
PPBS	Planning-Programming-Budgeting System
Psywar	Psychological Warfare
R & D	Research and Development
REDCOM	Readiness Command
RO/RO	Roll-on/Roll-off
SAC	Strategic Air Command
SACEUR	Supreme Allied Commander, Europe
SACLANT	Supreme Allied Commander, Atlantic
SALT	Strategic Arms Limitation Talks
SAM	Surface-to-Air Missile
SDF	Strategic Defensive Forces
SEATO	Southeast Asia Treaty Organization
SECDEF	Secretary of Defense
SHAPE	Supreme Headquarters, Allied Powers Europe
SIOP	Single Integrated Operational Plan
SLBM	Submarine-Launched Ballistic Missile; Sea-Launched Ballistic Missile
SLCM	Submarine-Launched Cruise Missile; Sea-Launched Cruise Missile
SOF	Strategic Offensive Forces
SOUTHCOM	Southern Command
SPADATS	Space Detection and Tracking System
UW	Unconventional Warfare
WWMCCS	Worldwide Military Command and Control System

Notes on Sources

THE EVOLUTION OF STRATEGIC THOUGHT

1. Crane Brinton, Gordon A. Craig, and Felix Gilbert, "Jomini," in *Makers of Modern Strategy: Military Thought From Machiavelli to Hitler.* Edited by Edward Mead Earle. (Princeton, N.J.: Princeton University Press, 1943), pp. 79, 85.

2. Louis Hacker, Introduction to *The Influence of Sea Power Upon History, 1660–1783,* by Alfred Thayer Mahan. American Century Series. (New York: Hill and Wang, 1957), p. v.

3. Karl von Clausewitz, *On War.* Translated by O. J. Matthijs Jolles. (Washington, D.C.: Infantry Journal Press, 1950), pp. 164, 210.

PART I. THE FRAMEWORK OF GRAND STRATEGY

Chapter 1

1. B. H. Liddell Hart, *Strategy,* 2d ed. (New York: Praeger, 1967), p. 351.

2. Clausewitz, *On War,* pp. 465–6.

3. *Global Defense; U.S. Military Commitments Abroad.* (Washington, D.C.: Congressional Quarterly Service, 1969), p. iv.

4. André Beaufre, *An Introduction to Strategy.* (New York: Praeger, 1965), pp. 26–9. The points made by Beaufre have been amplified by this author.

5. Based on Charles F. Bunnell, Jr., *Ends and Means—The Military Component.* (Washington, D.C.: The National War College Strategic Research Group, 1972), pp. 12–16. The author of this text has added some thoughts of his own to the considerations addressed by Bunnell.

Chapter 2

1. Sherman Kent, *Strategic Intelligence for American World Policy.* (Princeton, N.J.: Princeton University Press, 1966), p. 164.

2. *Ibid.,* p. xxiv.

3. *Ibid.,* p. xxii.

4. Washington Platt, *Strategic Intelligence Production.* (New York: Praeger, 1957), pp. 50, 53–4.

Chapter 3

1. Clausewitz, *On War,* p. 117.

2. Liddell Hart, *Strategy,* p. 339.

3. Sun Tzu, *The Art of War.* Translated by Samuel B. Griffith. Foreword by B. H. Liddell Hart. (New York: Oxford University Press, 1963), p. 77.

4. J. C. Wylie, *Military Strategy: A General Theory of Power Control.* (New Brunswick, N.J.: Rutgers University Press, 1967), pp. 23–9.

5. *Ibid.,* p. 25.

6. Beaufre, *An Introduction to Strategy,* p. 134.

7. *Ibid.,* pp. 134–5.

8. Wylie, *Military Strategy,* pp. 65–75.

9. Robert Thompson, *No Exit From Vietnam.* (New York: David McCay Co., Inc., 1969), p. 125.

10. Clausewitz, *On War,* p. 118.

Chapter 4

1. Background data on the Principles of War were drawn primarily from the following sources:
   a. *Field Manual 100–5,* "Operations of Army Forces in the Field." (Washington, D.C.: Headquarters, Department of the Army, September 1968), pp. 5–1 and 5–2.
   b. Nathan F. Twining, *Neither Liberty Nor Safety.* (New York: Holt, Rinehart and Winston, 1966), pp. 198–225.
   c. Charles A. Willoughby, *Maneuver in War.* (Harrisburg, Pa.: The Military Service Publishing Company, 1939), pp. 25–44.

2. Napoleon Bonaparte, *Memoirs.* Vol. II. (London: H. Colburn and Co., 1823–24), p. 2.

3. Liddell Hart, *Strategy,* p. 347.

4. Curtis E. LeMay, *America is in Danger.* (New York: Funk & Wagnalls, 1968), p. 302.

5. Wylie, *Military Strategy,* p. 83.

6. *Ibid.,* p. 85.

PART II. THE STRATEGIC ENVIRONMENT

Chapter 5

1. *On Deterrence,* an unpublished study, author unidentified, (Philadelphia: Foreign Policy Institute, University of Pennsylvania, 1969), p. 19. Forwarded to Secretary of Defense Laird by William R. Kintner.

2. Herman Kahn, *On Thermonuclear War.* 2d. ed. (New York: The Free Press, 1969), pp. 10–11.

3. *Ibid.,* pp. 22–3.

4. Max Lerner, *The Age of Overkill.* (New York: Simon and Schuster, 1962), p. 27.

5. Y. Harkabi, *Nuclear War and Nuclear Peace.* (Jerusalem: Ma'arachot, Publishing House of the Israel Defense Forces, 1966), pp. 29–30.

6. Kahn, *On Thermonuclear War,* p. 130.

7. Stefan T. Possony and J. E. Pournelle, *The Strategy of Technology.* (Cambridge, Mass.: Dunellen, 1970), pp. 179–80.

8. LeMay, *America is in Danger,* pp. 66–8.

9. Kahn, *On Thermonuclear War,* p. 163.

10. Thomas C. Schelling, *Arms and Influence.* (New Haven: Yale University Press, 1966), pp. 204–5.

11. *Ibid.,* pp. 215–20.

12. *Ibid.,* p. 211.

Chapter 6

1. Bernard Brodie, *Strategy in the Missile Age.* (Princeton, N.J.: Princeton University Press, 1965), p. 311.

2. Robert McClintock, *The Meaning of Limited War.* (Boston: Houghton Mifflin Co., 1967), p. 205.

3. V. D. Sokolovsky, *Military Strategy: Soviet Doctrine and Concepts.* (New York: Praeger, 1963), p. 189.

4. Thornton Read, in *Limited Strategic War.* Edited by Klaus Knorr and Thornton Read. (New York: Praeger, 1962), pp. 76–7.

5. Alain C. Enthoven, Chapter 6 in *Problems of National Strategy*. Edited by Henry A. Kissinger. (New York: Praeger, 1965), p. 124.

6. Bernard Brodie, *Escalation and the Nuclear Option*. (Princeton, N.J.: Princeton University Press, 1966), p. 109–10.

7. Nathan F. Twining, *Neither Liberty Nor Safety*. (New York: Holt, Rinehart and Winston, 1966), p. 245.

8. U.S. Congress. Senate. Committee on Armed Services, *Air War Against North Vietnam, Hearings,* before the Committee on Armed Services, Senate, 90th Cong., 1st sess., Part 5, (Washington, D.C.: U.S. Government Printing Office, 1967), pp. 476–8.

9. *Ibid.,* p. 481.

10. Robert Endicott Osgood, *Limited War: The Challenge to American Strategy*. (Chicago: The University of Chicago Press, 1957), pp. 244–5.

11. Herman Kahn, *On Escalation: Metaphors and Scenarios*. (New York: Praeger, 1965), pp. 4–8.

12. Henry A. Kissinger, *The Necessity for Choice: Prospects of American Foreign Policy*. (New York: Doubleday and Co., Inc., 1962), pp. 61–2.

Chapter 7

1. Chalmers Johnson, *Revolution and the Social System*. (Stanford University: The Hoover Institution on War, Revolution, and Peace, 1964), pp. 27–30.

2. Robert Thompson, *Revolutionary War in World Strategy, 1945–1969*. (New York: Taplinger Publishing Co., 1970), p. 2.

3. David Galula, *Counterinsurgency Warfare: Theory and Practice*. (New York: Praeger, 1964), pp. 6–7.

4. William J. Buchanan, *A Primer on Revolutionary War*. (Washington, D.C.: The National War College, 20 March 1969), pp. 8–29. The sections on The Prerequisites for Revolution and Phases of Revolutionary War also drew from this document.

5. Thompson, *Revolutionary War in World Strategy*, pp. 6–9.

6. Mao Tse-tung, *On the Protracted War*. (Peking: Foreign Languages Press, 1954), pp. 43–59. *See also* Robert C. Suggs and Brenda M. Wolak, "Phases of Development" in *Strategies of Revolutionary Warfare*. Edited by Jerry M. Tinker. (New Delhi: S. Chand and Co.), pp. 43–9.

Chapter 8

1. Robert S. Byfield, *The Fifth Weapon*. (New York: The Bookmailer, 1954), pp. 9–10, 19, 22.

2. *Ibid.*, pp. 22–37.

3. Paul M. A. Linebarger, *Psychological Warfare*. 2d ed. (New York: Duell, Sloan and Pearce, 1954), pp. 40–1.

4. Robert T. Holt and Robert W. van de Velde, *Strategic Psychological Operations*. (Chicago: Chicago University Press, 1960), p. 33.

5. Byfield, *The Fifth Weapon*, pp. 37–51.

6. Holt and van de Velde, *Strategic Psychological Operations*, pp. 35–6, 38.

7. *Ibid.*, pp. 38–41.

8. Linebarger, *Psychological Warfare*, p. 43.

9. Yuan-li Wu, *Economic Warfare*. (New York: Prentice-Hall, Inc., 1952), pp. 14–15.

10. *Ibid.*, p. 11.

11. Thomas W. M. Smith, *The Strategic Implications of International Monetary Reform*. (Washington, D.C.: The National War College Strategic Research Group, 1972), pp. 3–4, 13–14.

12. Richard A. Bowen, *Strategic Implications of Multinational Enterprise: An Overlooked Opportunity for Application of the Indirect Approach*. (Washington, D.C.: The National War College Strategic Research Group, 1972), pp. 1–2, 17–18, 21.

13. Wu, *Economic Warfare*, p. 14.

PART III. CONTEMPORARY U.S. SCHOOLS OF THOUGHT

Chapter 9

1. William R. Kintner and Robert L. Pfaltzgraff, Jr., *Soviet Military Trends: Implications for U.S. Security*. (Washington, D.C.: American Enterprise Institute, 1971), pp. 9–12.

2. *Ibid.*, p. 10.

3. For an excellent analysis of Soviet military policy under the Brezhnev-Kosygin regime *see* Thomas W. Wolfe, *Soviet Power and Europe, 1945–1970*. (Baltimore: Johns Hopkins Press, 1970), pp. 427–58.

4. *The Military Balance, 1972–73.* (London: The International Institute for Strategic Studies, 1971), pp. 3, 6–8.

5. This table was compiled from multiple sources, most notably *The Military Balance, 1972–73,* pp. 65–7; Elliot L. Richardson, *Statement Before the Senate Armed Services Committee on the FY 1974 Defense Budget and FY 1974–1978 Program,* 28 March 1973, pp. 31–3, 53–4, 119; and Thomas H. Moorer, *Statement Before the Defense Appropriations Subcommittee of the Senate Committee on Appropriations on United States Military Posture for FY 1974,* 27 March 1973, p. 61.

6. Henry A. Kissinger, *White House Press Conference.* (Moscow: Office of the White House Press Secretary, 27 May 1972), p. 5.

7. Richardson, *Statement on the FY 1974 Defense Budget,* pp. 34–5; and Moorer, *United States Military Posture for FY 1974,* pp. 32–6, 42.

8. Moorer, *United States Military Posture for FY 1974,* pp. 51–8. For background, *see* Malcolm Mackintosh, "The Evolution of the Warsaw Pact," *Adelphi Papers,* No. 58. (London: The International Institute for Strategic Studies, June 1969).

9. William Proxmire, "The Soviet Fleet Is No Match for the U.S. Fleet— Reply to Admiral Zumwalt's Letter of June 2, 1972." *Congressional Record,* 12 June 1972, pp. S9186–7, S9194.

10. Richardson, *Statement on the FY 1974 Defense Budget,* p. 36; and Moorer, *United States Military Posture for FY 1974,* pp. 37–44. *See also* Raymond V. B. Blackburn, *Jane's Fighting Ships,* 1972–73. (London: Sampson, Low, Marston and Co., Ltd., 1972), particularly the foreword.

11. Proxmire, "The Soviet Fleet Is No Match for the U.S. Fleet," pp. S9179–95.

12. Richardson, *Statement on the FY 1974 Defense Budget,* pp. 37–8; and Moorer, *United States Military Posture for FY 1974,* pp. 25–7.

13. Arthur Huck, *The Security of China.* (New York: Columbia University Press, 1970), pp. 47–61.

14. Ralph L. Powell, "Maoist Military Doctrine," *Asian Survey,* April, 1968, pp. 240–3.

15. William F. Scott, "The Contrast in Chinese and Soviet Military Doctrines," *Air University Review,* January-February 1968, pp. 57–63.

16. Lin Piao, "Long Live the Victory of People's War," *Peking Review,* No. 36, 3 September 1965, pp. 9–30.

17. Charles H. Murphy, "China: An Emerging Military Superpower," *Air Force Magazine,* July, 1972, pp. 52–7.

18. Moorer, *United States Military Posture for FY 1974,* p. 26.

19. Huck, *The Security of China,* pp. 62–78.

20. Samuel B. Griffith, II, *The Chinese People's Liberation Army.* (New York: McGraw-Hill, 1967), pp. 5–6, 262–4.

Chapter 10

1. Richard M. Nixon, *State of the Union, Address of the President of the United States Delivered Before a Joint Session of the Senate and the House of Representatives,* 91st Cong., 2d sess., House of Representatives Document No. 91–226. (Washington, D.C.: U.S. Government Printing Office, 22 January 1970), p. 2.

2. Richard M. Nixon, *U.S. Foreign Policy for the 1970's: A New Strategy for Peace.* (Washington, D.C.: U.S. Government Printing Office, 18 February 1970), p. 155.

3. Melvin R. Laird, *Statement Before the House Armed Services Committee on the FY 1972–1976 Defense Program and the 1972 Defense Budget,* 9 March 1971, p. 12.

4. Nixon, *U.S. Foreign Policy for the 1970's,* 18 February 1970, pp. 4, 18, 27, 127, 134, 142.

5. Earle G. Wheeler, "US Military Strategy," *Ordnance,* September, 1969, pp. 147–9.

6. *Ibid.,* pp. 148–9. The present author has amplified the material taken from Wheeler.

7. Richard M. Nixon, *U.S. Foreign Policy for the 1970's: Building for Peace.* (Washington, D.C.: U.S. Government Printing Office, 25 February 1971), pp. 5–6.

8. Laird, *Statement on the FY 1972 Defense Budget,* p. 15.

9. *Ibid.,* pp. 16–17.

10. *Ibid.,* p. 19.

11. Samuel P. Huntington, "After Containment: The Functions of the Military Establishment." *The Annals of the American Academy of Political and Social Science,* March 1973, pp. 1–16.

Chapter 11

1. Kahn, *On Thermonuclear War,* pp. 126–7.

2. *The Nature of General War.* (Croton-on-Hudson, N.Y.: Hudson Institute, Inc., HI–1537–BN, 5 November 1971), Chart 11, p. 5. Unpublished memoranda produced for the convenience of seminar participants.

3. Herman Kahn, *Thinking About the Unthinkable.* (New York: Horizon Press, 1962), p. 129.

4. Kissinger, *The Necessity for Choice,* pp. 53–8.

5. Thomas C. Schelling, *The Strategy of Conflict.* (Cambridge, Mass: Harvard University Press, 1960), pp. 187–203.

6. Harkabi, *Nuclear War and Nuclear Peace,* p. 36.

7. Kahn, *On Thermonuclear War,* pp. 291–5.

8. Bertrand Russell, *Common Sense and Nuclear Warfare.* (New York: Simon and Schuster, 1959), pp. 30–1.

9. LeMay, *America is in Danger,* p. 50.

10. Brodie, *Strategy in the Missile Age,* pp. 275–6.

11. Arthur Waskow, "The Theory and Practice of Deterrence." Chapter 3 in *Problems of National Strategy.* Edited by Henry A. Kissinger. (New York: Praeger, 1965), p. 66.

12. Kahn, *On Thermonuclear War,* pp. viii–x, 13–36; and *The Nature of General War,* Hudson Institute, p. 3.

13. Bernard Brodie, *Escalation and the Nuclear Option,* p. 65.

14. Harry S. Truman, *Memoirs,* Vol. II, *Years of Trial and Hope.* (New York: Garden City, 1956), p. 312.

15. Robert M. Hutchins, *The New York Times,* 9 June 1946. p. 6.

16. Albert Wohlstetter, "The Delicate Balance of Terror," Chapter 2 in *Problems of National Strategy.* Edited by Henry A. Kissinger. (New York: Praeger, 1965), pp. 35–58.

17. John Foster Dulles, "The Evolution of Foreign Policy." A speech made before the Council on Foreign Relations, New York City, January 12, 1954. *Department of State Bulletin,* January 25, 1954, pp. 107–9.

18. U.S. Congress, Senate. *Statements by John Foster Dulles and Admiral Arthur W. Radford Before the Senate Committee on Foreign Relations,* 19 March and 14 April 1954, respectively, pp. 4, 5, 29, 30, and 50.

19. Robert S. McNamara, "Address at the Commencement Exercises, University of Michigan, June 16, 1962." *Department of State Bulletin,* July 9, 1962, p. 67.

20. U.S. Congress, House. *Subcommittee of the Committee on Appropriations, Department of Defense Appropriations for 1965, Hearings.* 88th Cong. 1st sess. Part 4. (Washington, D.C.: U.S. Government Printing Office, 1965), pp. 25–8.

21. Robert S. McNamara, *Statement Before the House Armed Services Committee on the FY 1968–72 Defense Program and 1968 Budget.* (Washington, D.C.: U.S. Government Printing Office, 1968), pp. 38–9.

22. U.S. Congress. Senate. *Message from the President of the United States Transmitting the ABM Treaty and Interim Agreement and Associated Protocol.* 92d Cong. 2d sess. Executive L. (Washington, D.C.: U.S. Government Printing Office, 1972), pp. viii, 2.

23. Nixon, *U.S. Foreign Policy for the 1970's,* 18 February 1970, p. 122.

Chapter 12

1. Robert S. McNamara, *Statement before the Senate Armed Services Committee on the FY 1969–73 Defense Program and 1969 Defense Budget,* 22 January 1968, p. 43.

2. Thomas H. Moorer, *Statement Before the Senate Armed Services Committee on United States Military Posture for FY 1973,* 15 February 1972, p. 8.

3. *Ibid.,* pp. 11, 15–17.

4. *Ibid.,* p. 10.

5. *Ibid.,* pp. 7, 11.

6. U.S. Congress. House. *Supplementary Hearings Before the House Armed Services Committee,* June 1972, "Defense Procurement Authorization Relating to SALT Agreements." (Washington, D.C.: U.S. Government Printing Office, 1972), pp. 12098, 48.

7. *Public Law 92–436,* "Fy 73 Armed Forces Appropriations Authorization Act," 26 September 1972.

8. ASW expenditures for Fiscal Years 1969–1972 were extracted from Five-Year Defense Programs (FYDP) published by the Department of Defense for those years.

9. Kahn, On *Thermonuclear War,* p. 19.

10. McNamara, *Statement on 1969 Defense Budget,* pp. 41–61. Discusses the rationale for U.S. deterrent strategy and retaliatory concepts during the period 1961–1967.

11. *Ibid.,* p. 50.

12. *Ibid.,* p. 51.

13. Robert S. McNamara, *The Essence of Security.* (New York: Harper and Row, 1968), p. 57.

14. George McGovern, "Toward a More Secure America: an Alternative National Defense Posture." *The Congressional Record,* in Extension of Remarks, 19 January 1972, p. E149.

15. U.S. Congress. Senate. *Message from the President of the United States Transmitting the ABM Treaty and Interim Agreement and Associated Protocol,* p. 13.

16. Mark D. Mariska, "The Single Integrated Operational Plan." *Military Review,* March 1972, pp. 38–9. Sequence of paragraphs reversed from original.

17. "The Worldwide Military Command and Control System." *DOD Instruction 5100.30,* 2 December 1971, p. 2.

18. Thomas S. Power, *Design for Survival.* (New York: Coward-McCann, Inc., 1965), pp. 155–6.

19. Joel Larus, *Nuclear Weapons Safety and the Common Defense.* (Ohio: Ohio State University Press, 1967), pp. 66–8, 76–7.

20. Nixon, *U.S. Foreign Policy for the 1970's: The Emerging Structure of Peace.* (Washington, D.C.: U.S. Government Printing Office, 9 February 1972), p. 156.

Chapter 13

1. Possony and Pournelle, *The Strategy of Technology,* pp. 115–6.

2. Donald G. Brennan, in Extension of Remarks by John G. Schmitz. *Congressional Record,* 13 September 1971, p. E9439.

3. Possony and Pournelle, *The Strategy of Technology,* pp. 116–21.

4. McNamara, *Statement on the 1969 Defense Budget,* p. 53.

5. *Ibid.,* pp. 53, 63.

6. Nixon, *U.S. Foreign Policy for the 1970's,* 18 February 1970, pp. 124–6.

7. U.S. Congress. Senate. *Message from the President Transmitting the ABM Treaty and Interim Agreement and Associated Protocol,* pp. 1–4.

8. Seth J. McKee, *Statement before the Armed Services Investigating Subcommittee of the House Armed Services Committee in Hearings on Cuban Plane Incident at New Orleans.* (Washington, D.C.: U.S. Government Printing Office, 1972), pp. 34–5.

9. *Ibid.;* and *Hearings before the Senate Armed Services Committee on FY 73 Authorization for Military Procurement, Research and Development, Construction Authorization for the Safeguard ABM, and Active Duty and Selected*

Reserve Strengths, Part 6 of 6 Parts, "Bomber Defense, Tactical Air Power, and F–14." (Washington, D.C.: U.S. Government Printing Office, 1972), p. 3386.

10. Richardson, *Statement on the FY 1974 Defense Budget,* p. 63.

11. McNamara, *The Essence of Security,* pp. 63–4.

12. *Ibid,* pp. 164–6.

13. U.S. Congress. House. *Hearings Before Subcommittees of the House Appropriations Committee on Safeguard Antiballistic Missile System,* (Washington, D.C.: U.S. Government Printing Office, 1969), p. 39.

14. Nixon, *Foreign Policy for the 1970's,* 18 February 1970, pp. 125–6.

15. *Ibid.,* p. 126.

16. Laird, *Annual Defense Department Report, FY 1973,* pp. 76–7; and Moorer, *United States Military Posture for FY 1973,* p. 18.

17. Moorer, *United States Military Posture for FY 1974,* p. 22; and U.S. Congress. Senate. *Message from the President Transmitting the ABM Treaty and Interim Agreement and Associated Protocol,* pp. 1–2, 9.

18. Arthur M. Schlesinger, Jr., *A Thousand Days.* (Boston: Houghton Mifflin Co., 1965), p. 748.

19. Donald Smith, "So *That's* Whatever Happened to Civil Defense." *Washington Star,* 10 January 1971, p. 14.

20. Based on a chart in *Highlights of the U.S. Civil Defense Program,* Department of Defense, June 1963.

Chapter 14

1. Maxwell D. Taylor, *The Uncertain Trumpet.* (New York: Harper and Brothers, 1959), pp. 5–7.

2. *Ibid.,* pp. 65–6.

3. *Ibid.,* p. 128.

4. Keith Borman, Steven Hecht, Roger Fonseca, and Gregory Millikan, *Perspectives on Contemporary American Military Strategy* (Los Angeles: A report by the Political Research Organization of Occidental College, May 1971), pp. I–19.

5. Twining, *Neither Liberty nor Safety,* pp. 118–9.

6. *Department of State Bulletin* (Washington, D.C.: U.S. Government Printing Office, 25 January 1954), p. 108.

7. Twining, *Neither Liberty nor Safety,* p. 119.

8. Taylor, *The Uncertain Trumpet,* pp. 146–7.

9. McNamara, *The Essence of Security,* pp. 69, 78–9.

10. *Ibid.,* p. 79.

11. *Ibid.,* pp. 83–4.

12. *Ibid.,* p. 80.

13. LeMay, *America is in Danger,* p. 25.

14. Nixon, *U.S. Foreign Policy for the 1970's, 9 February 1972,* pp. 4–5. Sequence of paragraphs reversed from the original.

15. *Ibid.,* p. 6–8.

Chapter 15

1. Jack C. Plano and Roy Olton, *The In-ter-na-tion-al Re-la-tions Dic-tion-ary.* (Holt, Rinehart and Winston, Inc., 1969), p. 274.

2. A. F. K. Organski, *World Politics.* 2d ed. (New York: Alfred A. Knopf, 1968), p. 424.

3. Advantages and disadvantages of collective security draw heavily on a lecture entitled "A Critical Evaluation of U.S. Strategy" delivered by Admiral Arleigh Burke, U.S. Navy (Retired), at the National War College, 20 December 1970.

4. *Public Papers of the Presidents of the United States: Harry S. Truman, 1947.* (Washington, D.C.: U.S. Government Printing Office, 1963), pp. 178–9.

5. *Global Defense; U.S. Military Commitments Abroad.* (Washington, D.C.: Congressional Quarterly Service, 1969), pp. 37–44.

6. William P. Rogers, "The Fiscal 1972 Budget Request for Development Assistance and Security Assistance." *Department of State Bulletin,* 27 September 1971, pp. 336–8.

7. *Global Defense; U.S. Military Commitments Abroad,* p. 2.

8. Richard M. Nixon, "Address at the Air Force Academy Commencement Exercises in Colorado Springs, Colorado, June 4, 1969;" *Public Papers of the Presidents of the United States: Richard Nixon, 1969* (Washington, D.C.: U.S. Government Printing Office, 1971), pp. 433–4.

9. Nixon, *U.S. Foreign Policy for the 1970's,* 25 February 1971, pp. 12–14.

10. *Ibid.,* pp. 15–16.

Chapter 16

1. Capabilities were deduced from Moorer, *U.S. Military Posture for FY*

1974; Richardson, *Annual Defense Department Report for FY 1974,* pp. 36–49; and a variety of other sources.

2.   Thomas W. Wolfe, *Soviet Power and Europe, 1945–1970.* (Baltimore: Johns Hopkins Press, 1970), p. 456.

3.   Nixon, *U.S. Foreign Policy for the 1970's,* 9 February 1972, pp. 42–3.

4.   Wolfe, *Soviet Power and Europe,* p. 197.

5.   *Ibid.,* pp. 197–9, 203, 209, 211, 456–8.

6.   Alain C. Enthoven and K. Wayne Smith, *How Much is Enough?: Shaping the Defense Program, 1961–1969.* (New York: Harper and Row, 1971), p. 127.

7.   Carl H. Amme, Jr., "National Strategies Within the Alliance: West Germany." *NATO's Fifteen Nations,* August-September 1972, p. 82.

8.   U.S. Congress. Senate. *Hearings Before the Senate Armed Services Committee on FY 1973 Authorization for Military Procurement,* Part 2 of 6 Parts. (Washington, D.C.: U.S. Government Printing Office, 1972), p. 530.

9.   France has not undertaken any agreement to realign herself militarily with NATO. The use of French forces and territory in times of crises would be subject to a political decision. NATO therefore does not plan on French participation. U.S. Congress. Senate. *Hearings on FY 1973 Authorization for Military Procurement.* Part 2, p. 523. For implications of de Gaulle's decision to evict NATO forces from France, *see* Gordon A. Moon, II, "Uncertain Future," *Army,* March 1967, and "Invasion in Reverse," *Army,* February 1967.

10.   U.S. Congress. House. *Hearings Before a Subcommittee of the House Appropriations Committee on Military Construction Appropriations for 1973.* (Washington, D.C.: U.S. Government Printing Office, 1972), Part 4, p. 20; and *NATO Facts and Figures.* (Brussels: NATO Information Service, October 1971), p. 92.

11.   Enthoven and Smith, *How Much is Enough?* p. 125.

12.   U.S. Congress. Senate. *Hearings on FY 1973 Authorization for Military Procurement,* Part 2, p. 1123.

13.   *Ibid.,* p. 1069.

14.   *Ibid.,* pp. 642, 1195; and U.S. Congress. House. *Hearings Before the Special Subcommittee on North Atlantic Treaty Organization Commitments of the House Armed Services Committee.* (Washington, D.C.: U.S. Government Printing Office, 1972), p. 13344.

15.   U.S. Congress. Senate. *Hearings on FY 1973 Authorization for Military Procurement,* Part 2, pp. 1194–5.

16. Laird, *Annual Defense Department Report for FY 1971*, pp. 99–100.

17. John Newhouse, with Melvin Croan, Edward R. Fried, and Timothy W. Stanley, *U.S. Troops in Europe: Issues, Costs, and Choices.* (Washington, D.C.: The Brookings Institution, 1971), p. 108; and Edward T. Lampson, *The United States and NATO.* (Washington, D.C.: Congressional Research Service, 21 July 1972), p. 112.

18. U.S. Congress. House. House Armed Services Committee, "The American Commitment to NATO." *Report of the Special Subcommittee on North Atlantic Treaty Organization Commitments.* (Washington, D.C.: U.S. Government Printing Office, 17 August 1972), p. 14964.

19. U.S. Congress. House. *Hearings on North Atlantic Treaty Organization Commitments,* p. 12976.

20. Nixon, *U.S. Foreign Policy for the 1970's,* 25 February 1971, p. 33.

Chapter 17

1. Edwin O. Reischauer, *Beyond Vietnam: The United States and Asia.* (New York: Vantage Press, 1968), pp. 54–6.

2. *Ibid.,* p. 96.

3. Nixon, *U.S. Foreign Policy for the 1970's,* 25 February 1971, pp. 92, 94.

4. Nixon, *U.S. Foreign Policy for the 1970's,* 18 February 1970, pp. 56, 129.

5. Dean Acheson, *Present at the Creation.* (New York: Signet, 1970), pp. 465–6.

6. Douglas MacArthur, *Duty, Honor, Country: A Pictorial Autobiography.* (New York: McGraw-Hill Book Co., 1965), p. 195.

7. Nixon, *U.S. Foreign Policy for the 1970's,* 25 February 1971, pp. 95–6.

8. Nixon, *U.S. Foreign Policy for the 1970's,* 9 February 1972, pp. 36–7.

9. Nixon, *U.S. Foreign Policy for the 1970's,* 25 February 1971, p. 110.

Chapter 18

1. Nixon, *U.S. Foreign Policy for the 1970's,* 25 February 1971, pp. 122, 129–30.

2. *ARAMCO Handbook: Oil and the Middle East.* (Dhahran, Saudi Arabia: Arabian American Oil Company, 1 July 1968), pp. 78, 86.

3. Nixon, *U.S. Foreign Policy for the 1970's,* 25 February 1971, pp. 123–4.

4. *Ibid.,* pp. 124–5.

5. *Global Defense: U.S. Military Commitments Abroad,* pp. 23, 25.

6. *Ibid.,* pp. 21, 24–5.

7. Hanson Baldwin, *Strategy for Tomorrow.* (New York: Harper and Row, 1970), pp. 168–70.

8. *Ibid.,* p. 202.

9. Nixon, *U.S. Foreign Policy for the 1970's,* 25 February 1971, p. 126.

10. *Ibid.,* p. 131.

11. Earle G. Wheeler, Speech to Forum Club, Richmond, Virginia, 20 May 1968.

Chapter 19

1. Galula, *Counterinsurgency Warfare,* pp. 64–9. The courses outlined by Galula have been amplified by the author of this text.

2. Robert Thompson, *Defeating Communist Insurgency.* (New York: Praeger, 1966), pp. 50–8.

3. Galula, *Counterinsurgency Warfare,* pp. 70–1.

4. *Ibid.,* pp. 74–9.

5. Thompson, *Defeating Communist Insurgency,* p. 58.

6. Galula, *Counterinsurgency Warfare,* pp. 80–1.

7. Elliot L. Richardson, "The Foreign Policy of the Nixon Administration: Its Aims and Strategy." *Department of State Bulletin,* 22 September 1969. (Washington, D.C.: U.S. Government Printing Office, 1969), p. 258.

8. Robert W. Komer, "Pacification: A Look Back." *Army,* June 1970, p. 29.

9. *Ibid.,* p. 28.

10. Thompson, *No Exit From Vietnam,* pp. 77, 176–8.

11. Harry E. Ruhsam, "The Revolutionary War Dilemma." The National War College Strategic Research Group. Unpublished monograph.

PART IV. SPECIAL CONSIDERATIONS

Chapter 20

1. Alfred Thayer Mahan, *The Influence of Sea Power Upon History, 1660–1783.* American Century Series. (New York: Hill and Wang, 1957), pp. 25–70.

2. Halford J. Mackinder, "The Geographical Pivot of History." *Geographical Journal,* Vol XXIII, 1904, pp. 421–44.

3. Alexander P. de Seversky, *Air Power: Key to Survival.* (New York: Simon and Schuster, 1950), pp. 107–11.

4. *Department of the Army Pamphlet No. 39–3: The Effects of Nuclear Weapons,* Rev. ed., (Washington, D.C.: U.S. Government Printing Office, February 1964), pp. 436–88.

5. Hans J. Morgenthau, *Politics Among Nations: the Struggle for Power and Peace.* 4th ed. (New York: Alfred A. Knopf, 1967), pp. 110–14.

Chapter 21

1. James V. Forrestal, *The Forrestal Diaries.* Edited by Walter Millis with the collaboration of E. S. Duffield. (New York: The Viking Press, 1951), pp. 389, 393, 395–6, 462, 476–7.

2. *Department of Defense Directive No. 5100.1, Functions of the Department of Defense and its Major Components,* 31 December 1958, pp. 6–13; and *JCS Pub. 2, Unified Action Armed Forces* (UNAAF), (Washington, D.C.: U.S. Government Printing Office, November 1959), with changes, pp. 16–28.

3. Forrestal, *Forrestal Diaries,* pp. 391, 462, 476–7.

4. *JCS Pub 2,* pp. 17–19.

5. *Ibid.,* pp. 20–3.

6. *Ibid.,* pp. 25–8.

7. *Ibid.,* pp. 20–4.

8. Sign displayed in the National Headquarters of the U.S. Selective Service System in Washington, D.C.

9. *JCS Pub. 2,* pp. 8, 16.

10. David Kahn, *The Code Breakers.* (New York: The Macmillan Co., 1967), pp. 561–613.

11. Klaus Knorr, *Military Power and Potential.* (Lexington, Mass.: D.C. Heath and Co., 1970), pp. 22–3.

Chapter 22

1. Nixon, *U.S. Foreign Policy for the 1970's,* 18 February 1970, pp. 142–3.

2. Twining, *Neither Liberty nor Safety,* pp. 136–9.

3. U.S. Congress. Senate. *Hearings Before the Senate Foreign Relations*

Committee on the Nuclear Test Ban Treaty. (Washington, D.C.: U.S. Government Printing Office, 1963), p. 272.

4. *Ibid.,* p. 275.

5. U.S. Arms Control and Disarmament Agency, *Arms Control and Disarmament Agreements: 1959–1972.* (Washington, D.C.: Arms Control and Disarmament Agency, 1 June 1972), pp. 64–76.

6. U.S. Arms Control and Disarmament Agency, *9th Annual Report to Congress.* (Washington, D.C.: U.S. Arms Control and Disarmament Agency, 20 January 1970), p. 19.

7. Alastair Buchan, "The Multilateral Force: An Historical Perspective." *Adelphi Papers No. 13.* (London: The Institute for Strategic Studies, October 1964), pp. 3–14.

8. *Arms Control and Disarmament Agreements,* pp. 37–63.

9. Nixon, *U.S. Foreign Policy for the 1970's,* 18 February 1970, pp. 144–5.

10. John M. Collins, *The Impact of SALT I on U.S. Nuclear Deterrence: A Military Assessment.* (Washington, D.C.: Congressional Research Service, the Library of Congress, 26 July 1972), pp. 1, 4, 7. This study includes verbatim texts of the ABM treaty, the interim agreement with respect to the limitation of strategic offensive arms, the associated protocol, agreed interpretations, and unilateral statements.

11. *Ibid.,* 4, 7–8, 40–3.

12. *Ibid.,* 5, 8–14, 44–6.

13. *Ibid.,* 6, 47–54.

14. Henry A. Kissinger, "Nixon, Kissinger Brief Hill Members on SALT." *The Washington Post,* 16 June 1972, p. A–19.

15. Collins, *The Impact of SALT I,* pp. 14–15.

16. ACDA, *Arms Control and Disarmament Agreements,* pp. 98–107.

17. ACDA, *9th Annual Report to Congress,* p. 25.

18. Nixon, *U.S. Foreign Policy for the 1970's,* 25 February 1971, pp. 195–6.

Chapter 23

1. U.S. Arms Control and Disarmament Agency, *World Military Expenditures.* (Washington, D.C.: U.S. Government Printing Office, July 1971), p. 9.

2. Oskar Morgenstern, *The Question of National Defense.* (New York: Random House, 1959), pp. 193–6.

3. James M. Roherty, *Decisions of Robert S. McNamara.* (Coral Gables, Fla.: University of Miami Press, 1970), pp. 71–2.

4. *Ibid.,* pp. 72–3.

5. McNamara, *The Essence of Security,* p. 88.

6. Morgenthau, *Politics Among Nations,* pp. 139–40.

7. Morgenstern, *The Question of National Defense,* p. 204.

8. Enthoven and Smith, *How Much is Enough?,* pp. 13–14.

9. Taylor, *The Uncertain Trumpet,* p. 70.

10. Dwight D. Eisenhower, "The Eisenhower Tax Program." *U.S. News and World Report,* 29 May 1953, p. 98.

11. Enthoven and Smith, *How Much is Enough?,* p. 15.

12. McNamara, *The Essence of Security,* pp. 90–1. The two paragraphs have been transposed in this text.

13. Enthoven and Smith, *How Much is Enough?,* p. 325.

14. McNamara, *Statement Before the Senate Armed Services Committee on the FY 1969–73 Defense Program and 1969 Defense Budget,* p. 214.

15. Nixon, *U.S. Foreign Policy for the 1970's,* 25 February 1971, p. 228.

16. Nixon, "Address at the Air Force Academy, June 4, 1969," p. 436.

Chapter 24

1. Herman Kahn and Anthony J. Wiener, *The Year 2000.* (New York: The Macmillan Co., 1967), p. 67.

2. *Ibid.,* pp. 67–8.

3. Laird, *Statement on the FY 1972 Defense Budget,* p. 37.

4. *The Soviet Military Technological Challenge.* Special Report Series: No. 6. (Washington, D.C.: The Center for Strategic Studies, Georgetown University, 1967), p. 96.

5. Klaus Knorr and Oskar Morgenstern, *Science and Defense: Some Critical Thoughts on Military Research and Development.* (Princeton, N.J.: Princeton University Press, 1965), pp. 19–27.

6. Laird, *Statement on the FY 1972 Defense Budget,* p. 37.

7. John S. Foster, Jr., "Russia vs. U.S.—Coming Crisis in Arms." *Newsweek,* 30 November 1970, p. 24.

8. *The Soviet Military Technological Challenge,* Georgetown University, pp. 89–90.

Chapter 25

1. Morgenthau, *Politics Among Nations,* pp. 122, 127–8.

2. Organski, *World Politics,* p. 87.

3. *Ibid.,* pp. 87–91.

4. Clausewitz, *On War,* p. 126.

5. Ralph L. Giddings, Jr., "Power, Strategy, and Will." *Air University Review,* January-February 1971, p. 25.

6. Robert W. Tucker, *Just War and the Vatican Council II: A Critique.* (New York: The Council on Religion and International Affairs, 1966), pp. 8–9.

7. *Ibid.,* pp. 7–8.

8. Michael Howard, *Studies in War and Peace.* (New York: The Viking Press, 1971), p. 248.

9. Morgenthau, *Politics Among Nations,* pp. 232–3.

10. *Ibid.,* p. 234.

11. Niccolo Machiavelli, *The Prince and Selected Discourses.* Translated by Daniel Donno. (New York: Bantam Books, 1966), p. 62.

12. Howard, *Studies in War and Peace,* p. 239.

PART V. THE ROAD TO STRATEGIC SUPERIORITY

Chapter 26

1. Edward M. Collins, *War, Politics and Power.* (Chicago: Henry Regnery Co., 1962), p. 57.

Chapter 27

1. Gene M. Lyons and Louis Morton, *Schools for Strategy: Education and Research in National Security Affairs.* (New York: Praeger, 1965), pp. 7–10.

Chapter 28

1. Robert Leider and Charles F. Bunnell, Jr., *War By Other Means: Extending the Concept of Force.* (Washington, D.C.: The National War College Strategic Research Group, 22 September 1972), pp. 1–17.

2. Robert Leider, *The Environmental Issue in International Relations.* (Washington, D.C.: The National War College Strategic Research Group, 15 February 1972), pp. 5, 7, 17. Sequence of paragraphs transposed from the original.

3. Beaufre, *An Introduction to Strategy,* pp. 44–6.

PART VI. APPLIED STRATEGY

Chapter 29

1. Multiple sources were used to identify national security interests, objectives, policies, and strategies analyzed in this case study. The following two are representative:

a. *United States-Vietnam Relations, 1945–1967,* U.S. Department of Defense (Washington, D.C.: U.S. Government Printing Office, 1971), Book 7 of 12, Part V, Justification of the War.

> Vol. I: A—The Truman Administration
> B—The Eisenhower Administration
> C—The Kennedy Administration
> Vol. II: D—The Johnson Administration

b. *Selected Statements on Vietnam by DOD and Other Administration Officials,* prepared by the U.S. Air Force (SAFAA) as Executive Agent for the Department of Defense, semiannual.

2. Thompson, *No Exit From Vietnam,* p. 92.

3. Nixon, *U.S. Foreign Policy for the 1970's,* 25 February 1971, pp. 12–13.

4. *Public Papers of the Presidents of the United States: Richard M. Nixon, 1970.* (Washington, D.C.: U.S. Government Printing Office, 1971), p. 410.

5. Robert Shaplen, *Time Out of Hand.* (New York: Harper Colophon Books, 1970), p. 446.

6. Neil Sheehan and others, *The Pentagon Papers,* as published by *The New York Times.* (New York: Quadrangle Books, 1971), p. 28.

7. Thompson, *No Exit From Vietnam,* p. 115.

8. Sheehan, *The Pentagon Papers,* p. 286.

9. Earle G. Wheeler, "Vietnam Testing Ground for Freedom vs Communism." *Speech to the Commonwealth Club, San Francisco,* 7 May 1965.

10. Sheehan, *The Pentagon Papers,* p. 283.

11. Arthur J. Goldberg, "Initiative for Peace." *Department of State Bulletin,* 10 October 1966, p. 518.

12. Thompson, *No Exit From Vietnam,* p. 120.

13. Shaplen, *Time Out of Hand,* pp. 451–2.

14. Thompson, *No Exit From Vietnam,* p. 107.

15. Nixon, *U.S. Foreign Policy for the 1970's,* 25 February 1971, pp. 12, 14.

16. Clausewitz, *On War,* p. 18.

17. Thompson, *No Exit From Vietnam,* p. 161.

18. Shaplen, *Time Out of Hand,* p. 386.

19. Thompson, *No Exit From Vietnam,* p. 149.

20. Patrick J. Honey, *Communism in North Vietnam.* (Cambridge, Mass.: The M.I.T. Press, 1963), p. 168.

21. Douglas Pike, *Viet Cong.* (Cambridge, Mass.: The M.I.T. Press, 1967), pp. 367–8.

22. *Ibid.,* p. 371.

23. "North Vietnam's *Blitzkrieg*—An Interim Assessment." *Conflict Studies.* Edited by Brian Crozier. (London: The Institute for the Study of Conflict, Ltd., October, 1972); *see* especially pp. 1–3, 9, 12–17.

24. Henry A. Kissinger, *White House Press Conference.* (Washington, D.C.: News Release, Bureau of Public Affairs, Department of State Office of Media Services, 11:35 A.M. 26 October 1972), pp. 2–3.

25. "DRV Government Issues Statement on Vietnam Negotiations." Hanoi Vietnam News Agency International Service in English, 0811 GMT 26 October 1972, p. K–4.

26. *Ibid.*

27. Kissinger, *White House Press Conference,* 26 October 1972, pp. 1, 4.

28. Henry A. Kissinger, "Talks at Impasse, Kissinger Says." *The Washington Post,* 17 December 1972, pp. A–1, A–6.

29. For more complete discussion, *see* Maxwell D. Taylor, "The Lessons of Vietnam." *U.S. News and World Report,* 27 November 1972, pp. 22–6; and Edward Vallentiny, "Communist Lessons Learned." *Air University Review,* November-December 1972, pp. 72–6.

30. Personal correspondence from Lieutenant General Richard G. Stilwell, then Deputy Chief of Staff for Military Operations, U.S. Army, to the author, 20 March 1972.

31. Hugh Sidney, "The Most Important No. 2 Man in History." *Life,* 11 February 1972, p. 48.

Suggested Reading

THE EVOLUTION OF STRATEGIC THOUGHT

The Conduct of War, 1789–1961, by J. F. C. Fuller. New Brunswick: Rutgers University Press, 1961.
Major General Fuller, one of Britain's greatest military historians, reviews the impact of the French, Industrial, and Russian revolutions on the modern strategic environment.

The Generalship of Alexander the Great, by J. F. C. Fuller. New York: Minerva Press, 1968. *See* especially Chapters 4–6, 10.
A strategic analysis of campaigns conducted by the "great grandfather" of all Western grand strategists. Alexander's masterful concepts, unprecedented in his time, have rarely been excelled in the past 2,300 years.

Makers of Modern Strategy; Military Thought from Machiavelli to Hitler. Edited by Edward M. Earle. Princeton: Princeton University Press, 1943.
This excellent symposium reviews the evolution of strategic thought during the last four centuries. Some twenty authors interpret contributions made by outstanding strategists.

The Theory and Practice of War; Essays Presented to B. H. Liddell Hart. Edited by Michael Howard. London: Cassell, 1965.
In this collection of essays, leading authorities, whose work has been influenced and inspired by Liddell Hart, trace the development of strategic and tactical theory in the West.

PART I. THE FRAMEWORK OF GRAND STRATEGY

The Art of War, by Sun Tzu. Translated by Samuel B. Griffith. With an introduction by the translator and a foreword by B. H. Liddell Hart. New York: Oxford University Press, 1963.
This military classic formulates clearly a rational basis for modern strategic thought. Influential for centuries in the Orient, it has only recently begun to make its mark in the West.

The Command of the Air, by Giulio Douhet. Translated by Sheila Fischer. Rome: "Rivista Aeronautica" E., 1958.
Originally published in 1921, this book laid the foundation for concepts of strategic air power, and hugely influences the aerospace school of strategic thought.

The Influence of Sea Power Upon History, 1660–1783, by Alfred Thayer Mahan. New York: Hill and Wang, 1957.
Originally copyrighted in 1890 by Captain Mahan, this book established the modern maritime school of strategic thought. It brought about a basic change in the concepts of all major naval powers.

An Introduction to Strategy: with Particular Reference to Problems of Defense, Politics, Economics, and Diplomacy in the Nuclear Age, by André Beaufre. Translated by R. H. Barry. With a preface by B. H. Liddell Hart. New York: Praeger, 1965.
The Director of the Institut Français d'Etudes Strategiques constructs a modern "algebra of war" that incorporates classic military strategy as well as nuclear and indirect strategies, examines them as abstract concepts of attack, surprise, and deception, and shows how and when they can be used most effectively.

Military Strategy: A General Theory of Power Control, by J. C. Wylie. New Brunswick: Rutgers University Press, 1967.
Admiral Wylie reviews sequential and cumulative approaches, continental, maritime, air, and revolutionary schools of thought, then seeks a general theory that might make use of them all.

Politics Among Nations, 4th ed., by Hans Morgenthau. New York: Alfred A. Knopf, 1967.
A comprehensive coverage of international relations and national power which addresses strategic complexities. Dr. Morgenthau is Professor of Political Science and Modern History at the University of Chicago.

On War, by Karl von Clausewitz. Translated by O. J. Matthijs Jolles. Washington, D.C.: Combat Forces Press, 1953.
This classic text, which underlies the continental school of strategic thought, has exerted enormous influences on strategic theories and concepts for more than 100 years. *See* especially Book III, "Of Strategy in General."

Peace and War: A Theory of International Relations, by Raymond Aron. Translated by Richard Howard and Annette Baker Fox. New York: Doubleday and Co., 1966.
This scholarly, philosophical work on strategic interactions identifies constants and variables and points out the pitfalls of general theories. The author is France's foremost political scientist.

Strategy, 2d ed., by B. H. Liddell Hart. New York: Praeger, 1967.
A modern classic that outlines and discusses strategic fundamentals in an

historical matrix, while delineating Liddell Hart's views regarding the indirect approach.

Strategic Intelligence for American World Policy, by Sherman Kent. Princeton, N. J.: Princeton University Press, 1966.
The most thorough treatment of strategic intelligence in print today, emphasizing the relationships between threat assessments and strategy formulation.

World Politics, 2d ed., by A. F. K. Organski. New York: Alfred A. Knopf, 1968.
In this interdisciplinary study of international relations, Dr. Organski, Professor of Political Science at the University of Michigan, places major emphasis on the concept of national power and its determinants.

PART II. THE STRATEGIC ENVIRONMENT

Arms and Influence, by Thomas C. Schelling. New Haven: Yale University Press, 1966.
A review of ways and means in which force or the threat of force can be used as bargaining power, the so-called "diplomacy of violence."

Controlling Small Wars: A Strategy for the 1970's, by Lincoln P. Bloomfield and Amelia C. Leiss. New York: Alfred A. Knopf, 1969.
More than fifty of the small wars that have taken place since World War II are used to develop the patterns such wars follow. The authors, who are political scientists connected with the Arms Control Project at the Massachusetts Institute of Technology, suggest a new method for controlling strategy, and use five representative cases to illustrate their analysis. Dr. Bloomfield is the director of the Arms Control Project.

Counterinsurgency Warfare: Theory and Practice, by David Galula. New York: Praeger, 1964.
An authoritative review of revolutionary war by a former French Army officer who prepared this treatise under the auspices of the Center for International Affairs at Harvard University.

Economic Warfare, by Yuan-li Wu. New York: Prentice-Hall, Inc., 1952.
The most illuminating volume on all aspects of economic warfare, by a distinguished professor who formerly was Assistant Secretary of Defense for International Security Affairs.

Limited War and American Defense Policy: Building and Using Military Power in a World of War, 2d ed., by Seymour J. Deitchman. Cambridge: M. I. T. Press, 1969.
The Director of the Overseas Defense Research Agency, Office of the Director of Defense Research and Engineering, Department of Defense, discusses the problems of limited war from the standpoint of defense planning.

Nuclear War and Nuclear Peace, by Y. Harkabi. Translated by Yigal

Shenkman. Jerusalem: Israel Program for Scientific Translations, 1966. Brigadier General Yehoshafat Harkabi was director of Strategic Research in the Israeli Ministry of Defence in 1966. In this work he explores the fundamentals of nuclear strategy, discusses the effects of nuclear weapons within the framework of the international system, and analyzes a variety of problems, including the proliferation of nuclear weapons, the limitations of war, surprise, and deterrence.

On Thermonuclear War: Three Lectures and Several Suggestions, 2d ed., by Herman Kahn. New York: Free Press, 1969.
A sweeping survey of general-war problems and potential solutions by the Director of the Hudson Institute. The book was first published in 1960 but, with the addition of a new preface, is just as relevant today as when it was written.

Revolutionary War in World Strategy, 1945–1969, by Robert Thompson. New York: Taplinger Publishing Co., 1970.
A renowned authority in this field dissects the workings of Soviet and Chinese Communist revolutionary movements since World War II.

Selected Works of Mao Tse-Tung. 4 vols. London: Lawrence and Wishart, Ltd., 1954–56.
A collection of writings by Mao Tse-Tung, including those that generated the revolutionary school of strategic thought. These works have profoundly influenced nearly every significant contributor to insurgent theories and concepts since the 1930s.

Strategic Psychological Operations, by Robert T. Holt and Robert W. van de Velde. Chicago: Chicago University Press, 1960.
The first half of this book, which outlines principles, policies, and considerations, is particularly pertinent for students of cold-war strategies.

Strategy in the Missile Age, by Bernard Brodie. Princeton, N. J.: Princeton University Press, 1965.
A sweeping review of contemporary strategic problems. Dr. Brodie, one of the original faculty members at the National War College and now Professor of Political Science at the University of California (Los Angeles), covers many sides of controversial issues related to general and limited war.

PART III. CONTEMPORARY U.S. SCHOOLS OF THOUGHT

1. External Threats to U.S. Security

The Military Balance. Published annually. London: The International Institute for Strategic Studies.
A quantitative evaluation of the military power and defense expenditures of Western, communist, and major non-aligned countries. This authoritative

series stresses the strategic balance between the United States and the Soviet Union and between NATO and the Warsaw Pact.

Military Strategy, 3d ed., by V. D. Sokolovsky. Washington, D.C.: Foreign Technology Division, U.S. Air Force Systems Command, 1968.
Sokolovsky, a Marshal of the Soviet Union and member of the Central Committee of the Soviet Communist Party, was an internationally renowned strategic theoretician. The original version of this work, published in 1962, gave Western analysts a sweeping view of Soviet strategic thought related to general nuclear war and regional war in Europe. This update contains many significant changes.

The Nuclear Revolution in Soviet Military Affairs. Translated and edited, with introduction and commentary, by William R. Kintner and Harriet Fast Scott. Norman: University of Oklahoma Press, 1968.
This is a collection of significant Soviet writings on military doctrine and strategy that have been published since October 1964. The writings emphasize nuclear weapons and the impact the nuclear era has had on military affairs. Dr. Kintner is Director of the Foreign Policy Research Institute and a Professor of Political Science at the University of Pennsylvania.

The Security of China; Chinese Approaches to Problems of War and Strategy, by Arthur Huck. New York: Columbia University Press for the Institute for Strategic Studies, London, 1970.
The author examines China's outlook on foreign relations, strategy, and military policy. Arthur Huck teaches Chinese Politics at the University of Melbourne, Australia.

Soviet Military Policy; A Historical Analysis, by Raymond L. Garthoff. New York: Praeger, 1966.
The author offers a comprehensive study of how the communist world views and uses military instruments in limited war and in the political arena. In 1966 Dr. Garthoff was Special Assistant for the Soviet Bloc Politico-Military Affairs, Department of State, and Lecturer at the School of Advanced International Studies, The Johns Hopkins University.

Soviet Power and Europe, 1945–1970, by Thomas W. Wolfe. Baltimore: Johns Hopkins Press, 1970.
Dr. Wolfe, a senior staff member of Rand and a faculty member of the Sino-Soviet Institute of George Washington University, presents a perceptive analysis of Soviet military doctrine, policy, and strategic concepts. The coverage ranges beyond Europe to address general-war matters.

Statements Before the Congress on the Defense Budget, Defense Programs, and/or Defense Posture, by the Secretary of Defense, the Chairman of the Joint Chiefs of Staff, and chiefs of military services. Published annually. Washington, D.C.: Department of Defense.
These annual reports to the Congress, by the top civilian and military leaders

311

in our defense establishments are the most authoritative unclassified versions of contemporary U.S. military strategy and force posture.

The Strategic Survey. Published annually. London: The International Institute for Strategic Studies.
A panorama of developments in strategic policy, relationships, and thought of the previous year in every major country and key area of the world. The text summarizes conflicts around the globe during the period covered, and concludes with a chronology.

2. The U.S. Response

America and the World, From the Truman Doctrine to Vietnam, by Robert E. Osgood and others. Baltimore: Johns Hopkins Press, 1970.
A series of essays that provide a comprehensive reappraisal of American foreign policy during the Cold War, assess domestic and international pressures, and analyze the key policy issues that will face the United States in the near future. Robert E. Osgood, Director of the Washington Center of Foreign Policy Research, and Professor of American Foreign Policy in the School of Advanced International Studies, served on the staff of the National Security Council.

America is in Danger, by Curtis E. LeMay. New York: Funk and Wagnalls, 1968.
One of America's most outspoken military professionals challenges U.S. strategies for general and limited wars.

American Defense Policy. 2d ed. U.S. Air Force Academy, Dept. of Political Science. Edited by Mark E. Smith and Claude J. Johns. With a foreword by Richard F. Rosser. Baltimore: Johns Hopkins Press, 1968.
A source book of information on the machinery and strategy of American defense policy. In 1968 Mark E. Smith was Associate Professor of Political Science, and Claude J. Johns was Tenure Associate Professor of Political Science at the U.S. Air Force Academy.

The Balance of Power in the Asian-Pacific Area, c. 1980, by Robert E. Osgood and William C. Johnstone. Washington, D.C.: The Washington Center of Foreign Policy Research, School of Advanced International Studies, The Johns Hopkins University, 1968.
A perceptive analysis of interactions among the great powers in Asia, their relationships with lesser states and crucial zones of potential conflict, together with alternative U.S. strategies.

The Future of Deterrence in U.S. Strategy. Edited by Bernard Brodie. Los Angeles: University of California, Security Studies Project, 1968.
Six experts try to predict the usefulness of deterrence in terms of present alliances; Russian and Chinese capabilities and behavior; the international set; the posture emphasis and military capabilities of the U.S.; and the influ-

ence of scientific and technological breakthroughs. Dr. Brodie is the director of the Security Studies Center, University of California, Los Angeles.

Global Defense; US Military Commitments Abroad. Washington, D.C.: Congressional Quarterly Service, 1969.
Summarizes and interprets U.S. collective security arrangements, discusses military assistance programs, and outlines significant trends.

National Defense and National Priorities: A Report of the Council on Trends and Perspectives. Washington, D.C.: Chamber of Commerce of the United States of America, Economic Analysis and Study Group, 1972.
An appraisal of national defense and foreign relations as they influence U.S. national policy.

NATO: The Transatlantic Bargain, by Harlan B. Cleveland. New York: Harper & Row, 1970.
The author, U.S. ambassador to NATO from 1965 to 1969, reviews the crises that have faced NATO; considers the development of NATO's strategy; and looks ahead to the prospects for the 1970s. Ambassador Cleveland argues for a strong conventional military force in Europe that can respond to a limited attack without using nuclear weapons.

No Exit From Vietnam, by Robert Thompson. New York: McKay, 1969.
A shrewd appraisal of North Vietnamese objectives, policy, and strategy and U.S. countermeasures, highlighting the fundamental differences between revolutionary and conventional wars. By a British authority who was summoned to the United States as personal advisor to President Nixon when the President was beginning to formulate his strategy for Vietnam.

Problems of National Strategy, edited by Henry A. Kissinger. New York: Praeger, 1965.
An anthology prepared by such authorities as Wohlstetter, Waskow, Kahn, Schelling, Brodie, and Teller. The 1965 date in no way invalidates the value of this book.

Soviet-American Rivalry in the Middle East, edited by J. C. Hurewitz. New York: Praeger, 1969.
Outlines the scope of our confrontation with the U.S.S.R. in the Middle East and assesses alternative strategies open to both sides.

Statements Before the Congress on the Defense Budget, Defense Programs, and/or Defense Posture, by the Secretary of Defense, the Chairman of the Joint Chiefs of Staff, and chiefs of military services. Published annually. Washington, D.C.: Department of Defense.
See note to same heading in Part III, 1. External Threats to U.S. Security above.

Strategic Power and National Security, by J. I. Coffey. Pittsburgh: University of Pittsburgh Press, 1971.

A synthesis of considerations across a broad range of national security issues affected by strategic power: war-fighting, deterrence, collective security, and arms control. Dr. Coffey, Professor of Public and International Affairs at the University of Pittsburgh, has served with the Department of Defense, the White House Staff, and the Policy Planning Council of the Department of State.

Strategy for Tomorrow, by Hanson W. Baldwin. New York: Harper & Row, 1970.
Mr. Baldwin, military historian and former *New York Times* correspondent, surveys U.S. defense needs for the 1970s and 1980s. This treatise, written under the auspices of the Center for Strategic and International Studies, Georgetown University, touches on global and regional strategies across the board.

Survival and the Bomb; Methods of Civil Defense. Edited by Eugene P. Wigner. Bloomington: Indiana University Press, 1969.
A compilation of articles that examine political and emotional attitudes on civil defense; consider the physical, economic, and psychological factors involved in protection against the hazards of nuclear war; and discuss the effect of civil defense on the likelihood of war. Dr. Wigner, a former winner of the Nobel Prize for Physics, is Thomas D. Jones Professor of Mathematical Physics at Princeton University.

"Toward a More Secure America: An Alternative National Defense Posture, " by George McGovern. Washington, D.C.: Congressional Record, 19 January 1972, pp. E147–E162.
A strategic appraisal of U.S. defense posture by the Democratic candidate for President of the United States in 1972. A survey that challenges basic objectives, policies, assumptions, and concepts.

The Uncertain Trumpet, by Maxwell D. Taylor. New York: Harper and Brothers, 1959.
This slim volume, written when General Taylor was Army Chief of Staff, enunciates the original arguments for the concept of flexible response, which reoriented U.S. defense strategy after President Kennedy took office.

U.S. Foreign Policy for the 1970's, by Richard M. Nixon. Published annually beginning 1970. Washington, D.C.: U.S. Government Printing Office.
These annual reports to the Congress by President Nixon are the most authoritative and complete unclassified versions of contemporary U.S. national security policy. They form the basis of U.S. grand strategy.

U.S. Troops in Europe: Issues, Costs, and Choices, by John Newhouse, with Melvin Croan, Edward R. Fried, and Timothy W. Stanley. Washington, D.C.: The Brookings Institution, 1971.
Comprehensive coverage of strategic considerations underlying U.S. military commitments to NATO, as they impact on force requirements.

314

Why ABM? Policy Issues in the Missile Defense Controversy. Edited by Johan J. Holst and William Schneider, Jr. New York: Pergamon, 1969.
An anthology of conflicting views on the utility of defenses against ballistic-missile attack. Provides an appreciation of considerations entertained by strategists during negotiations that preceded the SALT I treaty to limit ABM sites in the United States and Soviet Union.

PART IV. SPECIAL CONSIDERATIONS

Arms Control and Disarmament Agreements, 1959–1972. Washington, D.C.: U.S. Arms Control and Disarmament Agency, 1 June 1972.
Verbatim texts of arms control agreements concluded by the United States since 1959, together with lists of participating parties and dates of signature and ratification.

Christian Ethics and the Dilemmas of Foreign Policy, by Kenneth W. Thompson. Durham, N.C.: published for the Lilly Endowment Research Program in Christianity and Politics by the Duke University Press, 1959.
This careful analysis presents the views of prominent Western thinkers concerning the conflicts met in relating the moral tenets of Christianity to armaments, colonialism, and diplomacy. Mr. Thompson, a former member of the faculties of the University of Chicago and Northwestern University, is Vice-President of the Rockefeller Foundation.

The Diplomatic Persuaders; New Role of the Mass Media in International Relations. Edited by John Lee. New York: Wiley, 1968.
Sixteen specialists from various countries explore the use of mass media as an arm of diplomacy and the resulting new breed of diplomatic specialists— career press and information officers. In 1968 Mr. Lee was Associate Professor of Journalism at the University of Arizona.

The Economics of Defense Spending: A Look at the Realities. Washington, D.C.: Department of Defense (Comptroller), July 1972.
An exposition of "myths" and "realities" regarding U.S. defense budget issues and trends, as seen from the Pentagon.

Ethics and Deterrence; A Nuclear Balance Without Hostage Cities? by Arthur L. Burns. London: The International Institute for Strategic Studies, 1970.
The author concludes that deterrent and war-fighting strategies which deliberately sought to spare noncombatants would be less evil than counter-city or mixed-target strategies. Dr. Burns is Professor of Political Science at the Australian National University, Canberra.

Geography and Politics in a World Divided, by Saul B. Cohen. New York: Random House, 1963.
An excellent exposé of geopolitical and geostrategic concepts related to major power cores and spheres of contact/influence.

315

How Much is Enough? Shaping the Defense Program, 1961-1969, by Alain C. Enthoven and K. Wayne Smith. New York: Harper and Row, 1971.
A provocative and controversial analysis of the U.S. approach to grand strategy, interrelating interests, objectives, policies, force requirements, and resource allocation. Provides penetrating insights into economic and fiscal constraints.

Military Power and Potential, by Klaus E. Knorr. Lexington, Mass.: Heath, 1970.
In studying the components and conditions of military power and the environment in which such power is exerted, Dr. Knorr focuses on a state's potential for international military power. The author is Professor of International Affairs, Woodrow Wilson School, Princeton University.

Military Technology and the European Balance (Adelphi Paper Number Eighty-Nine), by Trevor Cliffe. London: The International Institute for Strategic Studies, August 1972.
A concise review of technological and economic developments as they influence NATO and Warsaw Pact strategies. Its numerous tables that compare the characteristics, costs, and other features of weapons systems are especially valuable.

The Prince and Selected Discourses, by Niccolo Machiavelli. Translated by Daniel Donno. New York: Bantam Books, 1966.
A classic on the interplay between strategy and ethics by the most renowned figure of all time in that field.

Setting National Priorities: The 1973 Budget, by Charles L. Schultze, Edward R. Fried, Alice M. Rivlin, and Nancy H. Teeters. Washington, D.C.: The Brookings Institution, 1972.
Chapters 2 to 5 relate foreign policy to national security. The authors identify key decisions that shaped the U.S. 1973 defense budget, and project the consequences for the rest of this decade. Alternative defense policies and budgets are developed and analyzed in a broad strategic context.

The Soviet Union and Arms Control: A Superpower Dilemma, by Roman Kolkowicz, Matthew P. Gallagher, and Benjamin S. Lambeth, with Walter C. Clemens, Jr. and Peter W. Colm. Baltimore: Johns Hopkins Press, 1970.
The authors discuss Soviet attitudes toward arms control and consider the realities on which U.S.—Soviet negotiations must be based. Dr. Kolkowicz is a Senior Research Associate at the Institute for Defense Analyses.

The Strategy of Technology; Winning the Decisive War, by Stefan T. Possony and J. E. Pournelle. Cambridge, Mass.: University Press of Cambridge, 1970.
The authors compare U.S. and Soviet technological strategies and investigate special problems, including technological breakthroughs, technological races, strategic and tactical nuclear weapons, surprise attack, and arms control. Dr. Possony is a Senior Fellow at the Hoover Institution on War, Revolution,

316

and Peace; and Mr. Pournelle is former Managing Director of the Pepperdine Research Institute at Pepperdine College, Los Angeles.

Unified Action Armed Forces (JCS Pub. 2), with changes. Washington, D.C.: The Joint Chiefs of Staff, November 1959.
The basic document that sets forth principles, doctrines, and functions that govern the activities and performance of U.S. armed forces in joint and combined capacities. It also provides elemental planning guidance to the military services.

PART V. THE ROAD TO STRATEGIC SUPERIORITY

Schools for Strategists: Education and Research in National Security Affairs, by Gene M. Lyons and Louis Morton. New York: Praeger, 1965.
A review of national security activities in academia, contract agencies, and free-lance "think tanks" at the height of such endeavors.

MISCELLANEOUS

Dictionary of United States Military Terms for Joint Usage (JCS Pub. 1), with changes. Washington, D.C.: The Joint Chiefs of Staff, 3 January 1972.
U.S. official military terminology, with NATO, SEATO, CENTO glossaries included.

The In-ter-na-tion-al Re-la-tions Dic-tion-ary, by Jack C. Plano and Roy Olton. New York: Holt, Rinehart and Winston, Inc., 1969.
A glossary of commonly used terms related to grand strategy.

Strategic Terminology, by Urs Schwarz and Laszlo Hadik. New York: Praeger, 1966.
A trilingual (English, German, and French) glossary, the first of its kind to be published. Each definition is accompanied by a short discussion.

Authorized military abbreviations are contained in:
a. Army Regulation 310–50, "Authorized Abbreviations and Brevity Codes."
b. Navy Bureau of Personnel Instructions 2340.1, "Standardized Abbreviations."
c. Air Force Manual 11–2, "Air Force Manual of Abbreviations."

Index

319

Emergency Airborne Command Post, 107; Advanced Airborne Command Post, 107n; for U.S. armed forces, 183, 184; unified, specified commands, 183, 278, 281
Commitments. *See* National security commitments
Communications. *See* Command and control
Communist China. *See* Peoples Republic of China
Communist threat. *See* Chinese Communist threat; Soviet threat
CONAD. *See* Continental Air Defense Command
Conflict spectrum: as a strategic constraint, 20; related to flexible response, 110, 116; defined, 265
Constraints. *See* Arms control; Defense budget; Ethical constraints; Geography; Legal constraints; National will; Technology
Containment: as U.S. policy, 4, 76, 78; applied to Vietnam, 239, 241, 243–4
Continental Air Defense Command: mentioned, 183
Continental strategy: as school of thought, 17–18; 168–9
Contingency operations: influence on force requirements, 114; defined, 265
Corbett, Julian: mentioned, 18
CORDS. *See* Civil Operations and Revolutionary Development Support
Core area: related to strategy, 171; in NATO Europe, 171; in U.S.S.R., 171, 173; related to geographic dispersion, 173; defined, 265
Cost effectiveness. *See* Defense budget
Counter city. *See* Countervalue
Counterforce: basic considerations, 17, 35; related to budgetary costs, 35; objectives, 36; discussed by LeMay, 37; combined with countervalue, 37; related to maximum deterrence, 84–5; as insurance, 86, 87; enhances war-fighting, 86; related to massive retaliation, 87; reviewed by Nixon, 89; options, 93–4; related to passive defense, 106; defined, 266
Counterforce as insurance. *See* Deterrence— Categories
Counterinsurgency: deemed passé, 80; problems identified, 157; geographic influences, 172; defined, 266

—Phase I measures: discussed, 157–9; expunging revolutionary causes, 158; direct action, 158; legal considerations, 158, 159; countersubversion, 158; indirect action, 159; objectives, 159; plans, 159; revolutionary infrastructure as key, 159; population as prime target, 159
—Phase II, III measures: discussed, 157, 160–1; priority operations, 157; objectives, 160–1; techniques, 161; need for local protection, 161; intelligence, 161
—U.S. concepts: influence of American character, 19–20, 162; discussed, 162–5; in 1950s, early 1960s, 162; policy problems, 162; criteria for involvement, 162–3; Foreign Internal Defense Policy, 162–3; related to Nixon Doctrine, 163; organization, 163; operational policies, 163–4; role of negotiations, 164; emphasis wanes, 164–5; goals in Southeast Asia, 240–3; policies in Southeast Asia, 243–7; strategic concepts in Southeast Asia, 247–50, 257–9
—*See also* Revolutionary war
Counterintelligence: importance of fragmentary data, 11; described, discussed, 12–13; communist strengths, 13; U.S. weaknesses, 13; related to Principle of Security, 27; defined, 266. *See also* Intelligence
Counterrevolutionary. *See* Counterinsurgency
Countervalue: basic considerations, 17, 35; objectives, 36; discussed by LeMay, 37; combined with counterforce, 37; related to minimum, finite deterrence, 84, 85–6; influence on U.S. strategic retaliatory forces, 94; related to civil defense, 107; defined, 266
Credibility: key to deterrence, 35; essential elements, 82; defined, 266
Crisis management: defined, 266
Critical terrain: related to strategy, 171; related to core areas, 171
Cumulative strategy: as basic strategic option, 15–16; related to revolutionary war, 18; defined, 266

Damage limitation: related to countervalue capabilities, 35; related to assured destruction, 88; related to counterforce capabilities, 93; defined, 266
Defeat: defined, 267

Vietnam, 244; sought independent South Vietnam, 250. *See also* McNamara, Robert S.

Kent, Sherman: on guidance for intelligence community, 10; on intentions, 10

Key terrain. *See* Critical terrain

Key West Conference: influence on roles, missions of U.S. armed forces, 178–9

Khrushchev, Nikita: Sino-Soviet split, 65; geographic miscalculation, 167; encourages wars of national liberation, 242

Kintner, William R.: on force in nuclear age, 32; on Soviet policy, 66

Kissinger, Henry A.: on utility of limited war, 46; 1971 conference in Red China, 71; places policy in perspective, 75; deterrence through uncertainty, 83; favors flexible response, 111, 116; explains foundations of SALT I, 192; Chairman of Defense Program Review Committee, 201; on official strategic thought, 226; as team member, 228; negotiates on Vietnam, 256–7; stresses national interests, 261

Knorr, Klaus: measuring military power, 184; on technological constraints, 207–8; relates technology to strategy, 208

Komer, Robert W.: on U.S. organization for counterinsurgency, 163; U.S. counterinsurgency policies in Vietnam, 163–4; Special Assistant for "Other War," 249

Korea. *See* Korean Peoples Republic; Republic of Korea

Korean Peoples Republic: *Pueblo, EC–121* incidents, 115; invades South Korea, 145; nuclear-free zone, 189

Laird, Melvin R.: deterrence as prime objective, 74; planning for 1970s, 78; differentiates U.S. strategies for Europe and Asia, 79; belief in flexible response, 113; overhauls Planning-Programming-Budgeting System, 201; relates technology to defense, 206

LANTCOM. *See* Atlantic Command

Larus, Joel: explains controls over U.S. Minuteman ICBMs, 99

Launch-on-warning: discussed, 90–1; defined, 271

Law. *See* Legal constraints

League of Nations: related to collective security, 118; related to ethical constraints, 215

Legal constraints: described, 20; laws of land warfare, 215; Hague Conventions, 215; Geneva Conventions, 215. *See also* Ethical constraints

Leider, Robert: relates environmental issues to strategy, 234

LeMay, Curtis E.: counterforce-countervalue combinations, 37; decries graduated response, 116; enjoys intellectual freedom, 229

Lemnitzer, Lyman L.: on collective security, 120

Lenin, V.I.: revolutionary theorist, xxiii, 4, 48; indirect approach, 16; contributed to Principles of War, 22; in 1917, 47; communist goals, 65; relates national will to strategy, 213; thumbnail sketch, 222

Leo the Wise: Byzantine strategist, xxi

Lerner, Max: irrationality and deterrence, 34

Liddell Hart, B. H.: influence between World Wars, xxiii; on political objects, military aims, 3; purpose of strategy, 15; indirect approach, 16; discounts Principles of War, 24; on stereotyped strategic thought, 223

Limited war: in ancient times, xx; related to Clausewitz's views, xxiv–xxv; described, 40; past and present, 40; forms of limitation, 40–5; objectives, 41; command and control, 41; arms limitations, 41–3; nuclear weapons, 41–3, 44, 132, 136; chemical and biological weapons, 43; target limitations, 43–4; use of proxies, 44; force limitations, 44; Soviet experience, 44; in NATO area, 45, 131–9; sanctuaries, 45, 172; war at sea, 45; escalation problems, 45–6; Soviet capabilities, 67–9, 130–1; effect of minimum deterrence, 84; effect of maximum deterrence, 85; related to massive retaliation, 112; influence of Nixon Doctrine, 127–8; ethical constraints, 216; related to Vietnam, 243–4, 245–6; defined, 271

Linebarger, Paul M. A.: U.S. psychological warfare, 56

Lines of communication: defined, 271. *See also* Geography; Strategic mobility

Lin Piao: revolutionary theorist, 48; concepts for peoples war, 71

LOCs. *See* Geography; Strategic mobility

Logistics: in ancient times, xx; defined, 271

Lyons, Gene M.: on funds for strategic thought, 227